# *best kept*
# Secrets
## of the South's
## Best Cooks

Oxmoor
House®

Library of Congress Control Number: 2004092996
ISBN: 0-8487-2814-9

Printed in the United States of America
Second Printing 2004

To order additional publications, call 1-800-765-6400.

For more books to enrich your life, visit **oxmoorhouse.com**

### Southern Living ®

Executive Editor: Susan Dosier
Senior Writer: Donna Florio
Foods Editors: Scott Jones, Andria Scott Hurst
Associate Foods Editors: Shirley Harrington,
    Kate Nicholson, Mary Allen Perry,
    Shannon Sliter Satterwhite, Joy E. Zacharia
Assistant Foods Editor: Vicki Poellnitz
Assistant Recipe Editor: John McMillan
Test Kitchens Director: Lyda H. Jones
Assistant Test Kitchens Director: James Schend
Test Kitchens Specialist/Food Styling:
    Vanessa A. McNeil
Test Kitchens Professionals: Rebecca Kracke Gordon,
    Pam Lolley, Alyssa Porubcan, Angela Sellers,
    Vie Warshaw
Senior Photographers: Ralph Anderson,
    Charles Walton IV
Photographers: Tina Cornett, William Dickey,
    Beth Dreiling, Laurey W. Glenn
Senior Photo Stylist: Buffy Hargett
Photo Stylist: Rose Nguyen
Assistant Photo Stylists: Lisa Powell, Cari South
Photo Services Director: Ann Nathews Griffin
Photo Services: Lisa Dawn Love
Editorial Assistant: Charlotte Liapis

..................................................

**Cover:** Quick Whipping Cream Biscuits (page 71) with Sunny Orange Marmalade (page 358).
Photography by William Dickey; styling by Buffy Hargett

### Oxmoor House, Inc.

Editor in Chief: Nancy Fitzpatrick Wyatt
Executive Editor: Susan Carlisle Payne
Art Director: Cynthia Rose Cooper
Copy Chief: Allison Long Lowery

### Best Kept Secrets of the South's Best Cooks

Editor: Rebecca Brennan
Assistant Editor: McCharen Pratt
Copy Editor: Diane Rose
Contributing Copy Editor: L. Amanda Owens
Senior Designer: Melissa Jones Clark
Editorial Assistants: Terri Laschober,
    Shannon Friedmann
Test Kitchens Director: Elizabeth Tyler Luckett
Test Kitchens Assistant Director: Julie Christopher
Test Kitchens Staff: Kristi Carter, Nicole Lee Faber,
    Kathleen Royal Phillips, Elise Weis,
    Kelley Self Wilton
Senior Photographer: Jim Bathie
Senior Photo Stylist: Kay E. Clarke
Director of Production: Phillip Lee
Production Manager: Theresa L. Beste
Production Assistant: Faye Porter Bonner
Publishing Systems Administrator: Rick Tucker

### Contributors:

Indexer: Mary Ann Laurens
Photo Stylists: Cindy Manning Barr,
    Mary Lyn H. Jenkins, Leslie Byars Simpson
Editorial Interns: Sheila Egts, Elizabeth Grezaffi

# contents

# welcome

We all know them—those cooks who seem to make every biscuit just a little lighter, every frosting a little fluffier, every meat a little more moist and tender. It's like they have some sort of secret to making food taste better. And you know what? They *do* have secrets! They've shared them with us, and we're happy to share them with you. It's the thing that sets this book apart from all the rest. Most recipes are accompanied with a Cook's Secret, the insider's tip on how to take each recipe from good to GREAT!

With over 350 recipes, we've included all the traditional Southern dishes you'd expect to find.

## Some of our favorites are...

- Old Southern Biscuits • Cream Cheese Pound Cake • Fresh Blackberry Pie
- Pralines • Mama's Fried Chicken • Crawfish Étouffée • Crunchy Fried Okra

We also added *some surprises, such as* ...

- Tiramisù Toffee Trifle Pie • Watermelon Sorbet • Mini Beef Wellingtons
- Chicken Enchiladas • Barbecue Eggplant • Mystery Pecan Pie

The recipes are arranged by food categories—appetizers and beverages; breads; desserts; main dishes; salads; sandwiches, soups, and condiments; and sides—so it's easy to find what you're looking for.

Dozens of how-to photographs reveal tried-and-true ways to achieve the ultimate recipe success.

## You'll see step-by-step how to make...

- Sister Schubert's Parker House Rolls • Lemon-Coconut Cake
- A picture-perfect piecrust • Classic Peanut Brittle

## You'll learn the easiest techniques for...

- Grilling baby back ribs • Perfecting giblet gravy • Mastering meringue

Many of the recipes in this book are contributed by the readers of *Southern Living*. Others come from the *Southern Living* Foods Staff, Southern chefs, and regional recipe contest winners. Each recipe has been tested in our Test Kitchens, so it's guaranteed to please. And now you can be even more assured of the success of each recipe because you have the insider's scoop that makes it a quintessential Southern classic.

We hope you'll enjoy reading these stories and secrets from fellow Southerners. And when you try the recipes in this new collection for family and friends, we think you'll enjoy being called one of the South's Best Cooks.

*the Editors*

# appetizers and beverages

# Top 10 Best Kept Appetizer Secrets

**1.** The most helpful tools for preparing appetizers for a crowd are sharp knives and large baking sheets.

**2.** If you don't have a chafing dish, a fondue pot or slow cooker set on low will do the job.

**3.** Plan your menu so that it contains hot and cold appetizers, as well as items that guests can easily serve themselves.

**4.** The secret to keeping appetizers fresh in the freezer is proper wrapping—be sure they're airtight to avoid freezer burn. Usually, you can let appetizers thaw overnight in the refrigerator (if they require refrigeration).

**5.** Avoid freezing appetizers that contain fresh vegetables, mayonnaise, or hard-cooked eggs.

**6.** When appetizers are going to be the entire meal, plan on 6 to 8 appetizer servings per guest. If a meal is to follow soon after the appetizers, plan on 2 to 4 appetizer servings per guest.

**7.** Use firm-textured raw fruits and vegetables as creative containers for dips. Try pineapple, cantaloupe, green pepper, or tomato. First, cut a narrow slice from the bottom so the container sits flat; then carve out the center, drain, and fill the cavity with dip.

**8.** For an instant appetizer, dress up a plain block of cream cheese with pepper jellies. For a sweeter taste, serve the cheese with gingersnaps instead of crackers.

**9.** For a quick, hearty appetizer, buy chicken fingers in the deli section of the grocery store, and pair them with a bowl of honey mustard or another dipping sauce.

**10.** Keep the following on hand so you'll be ready to serve snacks at a moment's notice: gourmet cheese and crackers, bottled salsa and chips, seasoned nuts.

Laura Morris makes having friends over for a get-together a cinch. Her secret? Easy dip recipes that take less than 20 minutes to prepare and are made ahead.

## Blue Cheese Dip

| | |
|---|---|
| 1 (8-ounce) package cream cheese, cubed | 2 tablespoons sour cream |
| 3 tablespoons dry white wine or buttermilk | 1 (4-ounce) package crumbled blue cheese |

• Process first 3 ingredients and half of blue cheese in a blender or food processor until smooth, stopping to scrape down sides. Stir in remaining blue cheese. Cover and chill 2 hours. Serve with apple or pear slices. Yield: 1½ cups.

*Laura Morris*
Bunnell, Florida

## Bacon-Cheese Dip

| | |
|---|---|
| ½ cup sour cream | 2 tablespoons diced onion |
| 1 (4-ounce) package crumbled blue cheese | ⅛ teaspoon hot sauce |
| 1 (3-ounce) package cream cheese, softened | 4 bacon slices, cooked and crumbled |

• Process first 5 ingredients in a blender or food processor until smooth, stopping to scrape down sides. Stir in half of bacon. Cover and chill 2 hours. Sprinkle with remaining bacon. Serve with crackers, raw vegetables, or potato chips. Yield: 1½ cups.

*Laura Morris*
Bunnell, Florida

*cook's secret...* Add a little milk to each of these dips to create two great salad dressings.

The Treviño family enjoys authentic *antojitos,* or appetizers. Mary Treviño, founder of El Mirador restaurant in San Antonio, has been serving appetizers, such as this one, and other Mexican fare for more than 35 years.

## Pico de Gallo

3  large tomatoes, chopped
½  cup chopped sweet onion
1  to 2 jalapeño peppers, seeded and
    minced

¼  cup chopped fresh cilantro
3  tablespoons lime juice
1  teaspoon salt
½  teaspoon freshly ground pepper

• Stir together all ingredients; serve with tortilla chips. Yield: 4 cups.

*Mary Treviño*
San Antonio, Texas

## Pumpkin Pie Dip

1  (8-ounce) package cream cheese,
    softened
2  cups powdered sugar
1  (15-ounce) can unsweetened pumpkin

1  teaspoon ground cinnamon
½  teaspoon ground ginger
Garnishes: ground cinnamon, cinnamon
    sticks

• Beat cream cheese and sugar at medium speed with an electric mixer until smooth. Add pumpkin, 1 teaspoon cinnamon, and ginger, beating well. Cover and chill 8 hours. Garnish, if desired. Serve with gingersnaps and apple or pear slices. Yield: 3 cups.

*Lisa Reid O'Rourke*
Baton Rouge, Louisiana

*cook's secret*... Canned pumpkin is the secret to this yummy dip. It has a firmer texture than fresh, which is why it works so well. If you prefer to use fresh, a 5-pound pumpkin yields about 4½ cups mashed cooked pumpkin, enough for two batches of dip.

It's no mystery that canned beans often get a bad rap. Will Mullins's recipe for Red Pepper Hummus, which substitutes navy beans for the classic chickpeas, and Test Kitchens Specialist Vanessa McNeil's White Bean Hummus, which uses canned great Northern beans, just might change your mind. Serve these spreads at your next dinner party. Imagine: Canned beans producing appetizers that are not only delicious, but also elegant. This can be our little secret.

# Red Pepper Hummus

| | | | |
|---|---|---|---|
| 1 | (15-ounce) can navy beans, rinsed and drained | ¼ | teaspoon ground cumin |
| 2 | garlic cloves | ¼ | teaspoon ground coriander |
| ½ | cup roasted red bell peppers | ¼ | teaspoon ground red pepper |
| ⅓ | cup tahini | 2 | tablespoons olive oil |
| ¼ | cup fresh lemon juice | 1 | tablespoon chopped fresh cilantro |
| ¾ | teaspoon salt | | Garnishes: lettuce, toasted sesame seeds, chopped green onions |

• Process first 9 ingredients in a food processor or blender until smooth, stopping to scrape down sides. With processor running, pour oil through food chute in a slow, steady stream; process until smooth. Stir in cilantro; chill 1 hour. Garnish, if desired. Serve with tortilla or pita chips. Yield: 2 cups.

*Will Mullins*
Baton Rouge, Louisiana

*cook's secret*... Big on convenience? Use roasted red bell peppers from a jar. Big on fresh flavor? Roast your own red bell peppers. Just chop the peppers, and spread in a single layer in a roasting pan. Drizzle peppers with 1 to 2 tablespoons olive oil, and sprinkle with salt and black pepper. Roast at 450° for 6 to 8 minutes, stirring once.

# White Bean Hummus

2   garlic cloves
1   teaspoon fresh rosemary leaves
2   (15.5-ounce) cans great Northern beans,
      rinsed and drained
3   tablespoons lemon juice

3   tablespoons tahini
¾   teaspoon salt
¼   teaspoon ground red pepper
¼   cup olive oil
    Garnish: paprika

• Pulse garlic and rosemary in a food processor 3 or 4 times or until minced.
• Add beans and next 4 ingredients; process until mixture is smooth, stopping to scrape down sides.
• With processor running, pour oil through food chute in a slow, steady stream; process until smooth. Cover and chill 1 hour. Garnish, if desired. Serve with crackers, sliced cucumber, pimiento-stuffed olives, and pitted kalamata olives. Yield: 3 cups.

*Vanessa McNeil*
Test Kitchens Specialist

*cook's secret...* Wash your sprig of fresh rosemary, and press it between paper towels to dry before stripping the leaves from the sprig. It's easier to wash on the stem.

Chef and restaurateur Frank Stitt, owner of Highlands Bar and Grill, Bottega, and Chez Fonfon restaurants in Birmingham, Alabama, finds pleasure in cooking simple meals for his friends. He prefers easy menus prepared from the very finest ingredients. "You don't have to have a ton of different things for it to be a wonderful meal," he says. His Tapenade—a chunky paste of olives, capers, and garlic—offers a casual and delicious start to a meal.

## Tapenade

1   (6-ounce) jar pitted kalamata olives
      (about 1½ cups)
1   tablespoon drained capers
1   tablespoon sherry vinegar*
1   teaspoon lemon juice

1   small garlic clove
¼   teaspoon freshly ground pepper
1   teaspoon rum (optional)
3   tablespoons extra-virgin olive oil

• Pulse first 6 ingredients and, if desired, rum in a blender or food processor 3 or 4 times. Gradually add olive oil, and pulse 3 or 4 times or until mixture forms a coarse paste, stopping to scrape down sides. Serve with fresh raw vegetables and toasted French baguette slices. Yield: 1 cup.

*White wine vinegar may be substituted for sherry vinegar.

*Chef Frank Stitt*
Birmingham, Alabama

cook's secret... The secret to a tasty tapenade is to use full-flavored olives. You can't go wrong with high-quality kalamatas.

# Guacamole

*For added pizzazz, stir in a few drops of hot sauce*
*and 4 slices of crumbled cooked bacon.*

| | |
|---|---|
| 3 ripe avocados | 1 tablespoon lemon or lime juice |
| ½ cup chopped tomato | 1 teaspoon salt |
| ¼ cup finely chopped onion | Freshly ground pepper (optional) |
| 1 jalapeño pepper, chopped | |

• Cut avocados in half, and remove seed from each avocado (photo 1). Scoop out avocado pulp into a large bowl (photo 2). Mash until avocado is desired consistency.
• Add chopped tomato and next 4 ingredients to bowl; stir until mixture is blended. Top with pepper, if desired (photo 3). Serve with tortilla chips. Yield: 2½ cups.

**Preparing Guacamole**

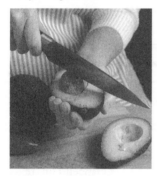  

**1.** Hold avocado in palm of hand; stab the seed with a sharp knife. Gently twist knife, and remove seed.

**2.** Scoop out buttery soft pulp with a spoon.

**3.** A few grinds from a pepper mill add the finishing touch.

*cook's secret*... Guacamole turns brown when exposed to air for very long, so it's best served within an hour of making. Store guacamole in the refrigerator with plastic wrap pressed directly on the surface to help prevent browning. If, despite your efforts, browning occurs, don't panic; just scrape off the browned part before serving.

Former Houston Oilers quarterback Dante "Dan" Pastorini escaped the hustle and bustle of Houston for the picturesque town of Chappell Hill, Texas, where he jumped at the opportunity to join the Chappell Hill Volunteer Fire Department. When they're not fighting fires, Dan and the other volunteers enjoy cooking together, both for recreation and to raise money for the fire department. Here's Dan's recipe for an appetizer with Southwestern flair.

*regional favorite*

## Texas Caviar

- 2 medium tomatoes, seeded and chopped
- 1 medium-size red bell pepper, chopped
- 1 bunch green onions, chopped
- 2 garlic cloves, minced
- 1 (15.8-ounce) can black-eyed peas, rinsed and drained
- 1 (15.5-ounce) can white hominy, rinsed and drained
- 1 (8-ounce) jar medium picante sauce
- ½ cup chopped fresh cilantro
- 3 tablespoons lime juice
- ½ teaspoon salt

• Stir together all ingredients in a large bowl. Cover and chill, stirring occasionally, 8 hours. Serve with tortilla chips. Yield: 6 cups.

*Dan Pastorini*
*Chappell Hill, Texas*

*cook's secret...* Rinsing the juices from canned peas and hominy removes cloudiness and the "canned" taste from this chunky dip.

Grace Vick clipped this recipe from our pages more than 20 years ago. When she wrote to tell us that it's still one of her favorites, we decided to try it again. And although we still like the original Pickled Black-Eyed Peas, we know that you'll also savor former Test Kitchens Professional Jan Moon's fabulous updated version of the classic, Marinated Black-Eyed Peas, which appears below the main recipe.

## Pickled Black-Eyed Peas

| | |
|---|---|
| 2 (15.8-ounce) cans black-eyed peas, rinsed and drained | 1 small onion, diced |
| ⅔ cup vegetable oil | 1 garlic clove, minced |
| ⅓ cup white wine vinegar | ½ teaspoon salt |
| | ⅛ teaspoon pepper |

• Stir together all ingredients; cover and chill mixture at least 2 hours. Serve with tortilla chips. Yield: 5 cups.

*Mrs. Ted M. Robertson*
Canton, Texas

**Marinated Black-Eyed Peas:** Substitute olive oil for vegetable oil and ½ red onion for onion; increase pepper to ½ teaspoon. Add 1 (15.25-ounce) can sweet whole kernel corn, drained; 1 jalapeño pepper, minced; and ½ red bell pepper, chopped. Cover and chill 4 hours. Yield: 5½ cups.

*Jan Moon*
Former Test Kitchens Professional

*cook's secret...* Serve dip with bite-size chips to eliminate the possibility of "double dipping."

# Spicy Crab-and-Ginger Salsa
## with Sesame Won Tons

3 tablespoons rice wine vinegar

2 tablespoons vegetable oil

1 tablespoon lime juice

1 to 2 teaspoons Asian chili garlic sauce or
    paste

1 teaspoon sesame oil

½ teaspoon salt

12 ounces lump crabmeat, drained and
    coarsely chopped

1 cucumber, peeled, seeded, and diced

2 green onions, sliced

2 tablespoons chopped pickled ginger

Peanut oil

24 won tons

2 tablespoons sesame seeds, toasted

- Whisk together rice wine vinegar and next 5 ingredients. Stir in crabmeat and next 3 ingredients. Cover and chill until ready to serve.
- Pour peanut oil to a depth of ½ inch into a large skillet. Fry won tons, in batches, in hot oil over medium-high heat 30 seconds on each side or until golden. Drain on paper towels; sprinkle with sesame seeds. Serve won tons with salsa. Yield: 8 appetizer servings.

**NOTE:** *Chili garlic sauce or paste may be found in the Asian section of the supermarket or in gourmet stores.*

*Edwina Gadsby*
Great Falls, Montana

*cook's secret...* Edwina Gadsby adds zip to her favorite salsa with a secret ingredient: crab. "The ginger and lime seem to enhance the crab for delicious results," she says.

When Sue Thompson talks about the Taste Fair, it's hard not to get excited. The event, which is usually held the Friday before Thanksgiving, originally started over 15 years ago as a small church fund-raiser. Today, it includes more than one thousand visitors. The Ladies Ministry of Woodlawn United Pentecostal Church in Columbia, Mississippi, begins planning this affair a year in advance. "We enjoy the fellowship with everyone, and it's known for miles around," says Sue. For guests who want to remember the food for years to come, an annual cookbook is available later in the year. Here, Sue shares a favorite appetizer.

## Rosemary Cheese with Fig Preserves

1   (8-ounce) package cream cheese, softened
1   (3-ounce) log goat cheese, softened
1   tablespoon chopped fresh rosemary
2   teaspoons honey

1   teaspoon coarsely ground pepper
¾   cup fig preserves
    Garnish: fresh rosemary sprigs

• Process first 5 ingredients in a food processor until smooth, stopping to scrape down sides.
• Spoon cheese mixture into a lightly greased 1½-cup mold lined with plastic wrap. Cover and chill at least 2 hours.
• Invert chilled cheese mixture onto a serving dish; discard plastic wrap. Spoon fig preserves over cheese. Garnish, if desired. Serve with crackers, toasted French bread slices, or bagel chips. Yield: 2 cups.

*cook's secret...* If you don't have fresh rosemary, use an equal amount of dried. Rosemary is the only herb that doesn't follow the standard substitution recommendation of 3 parts fresh to 1 part dried.

Growing up in El Paso, Lucinda Hutson was exposed to food and culture with a decidedly "border" flair. "We ate in a style very similar to that of North Mexico—grilled meats and wild game and chili con queso made with true *queso blanco,* a wonderful Mexican-style white cheese. In other words, real Tex-Mex," says Lucinda. Today, her kitchen comes alive with the smells, flavors, and spirit of the Southwestern and Mexican cultures that she holds so dear. "Don't be surprised to find garlic and chile peppers in many of my recipes," says Lucinda. "After all, they are as inherent to the Southwest as sunshine."

## Basil-Cheese Torta

1 (8-ounce) package cream cheese,
   softened
1 (4-ounce) package crumbled feta cheese
2 tablespoons butter or margarine,
   softened
Lucinda's Garden Pesto

2 (6-ounce) packages provolone cheese
   slices
Roasted Red Pepper Salsa, divided
¼ cup chopped pine nuts, toasted
Garnishes: chopped fresh basil, fresh basil
   sprigs, pine nuts

• Process first 3 ingredients in a blender or food processor until smooth, stopping to scrape down sides. Stir in Lucinda's Garden Pesto, blending well.
• Line an 8- x 4-inch loafpan with plastic wrap, allowing 1 inch to hang over on each side.
• Arrange one-third of provolone cheese slices on bottom and up sides of pan. Layer evenly with half of pesto mixture, ⅓ cup Roasted Red Pepper Salsa, 2 tablespoons pine nuts, and half of remaining cheese slices. Repeat layers, ending with cheese slices, gently pressing each layer. Fold cheese slices toward center. Cover and chill 8 hours.
• Invert torta onto a serving platter. Top with ⅓ cup salsa; garnish, if desired. Serve with remaining salsa and toasted French baguette slices. Yield: 12 servings.

## Lucinda's Garden Pesto:

| | |
|---|---|
| 3 cups fresh basil leaves | 2 to 3 tablespoons shredded Romano cheese |
| 4 to 6 garlic cloves | |
| ½ cup pine nuts, walnuts, or pecans | ⅔ cup olive oil |
| ¾ cup shredded Parmesan cheese | |

• Process basil and garlic in a food processor until chopped. Add pine nuts and cheeses, and process until blended, stopping to scrape down sides. With processor running, pour oil through food chute in a slow, steady stream; process until smooth. Chill up to 5 days, if desired. Yield: 1 cup.

## Roasted Red Pepper Salsa:

| | |
|---|---|
| 4 red bell peppers | 2 to 3 garlic cloves, minced |
| 1 tablespoon olive oil | ½ teaspoon salt |
| ½ cup dried tomatoes* | ½ teaspoon fresh rosemary, finely chopped |
| 3 tablespoons chopped fresh basil | ¼ teaspoon ground red pepper |
| 1 tablespoon balsamic vinegar | |

• Bake bell peppers on an aluminum foil–lined baking sheet at 500° for 12 minutes or until peppers look blistered, turning once.
• Place peppers in a zip-top freezer bag; seal and let stand 10 minutes to loosen skins. Peel peppers; remove and discard seeds. Coarsely chop peppers. Drizzle with 1 tablespoon olive oil; set aside.
• Pour boiling water to cover over dried tomatoes. Let stand 3 minutes; drain and coarsely chop.
• Stir together bell pepper, tomato, basil, and remaining ingredients. Cover and chill salsa up to 2 days, if desired. Yield: 2 cups.

*⅓ cup dried tomatoes in oil may be substituted for dried tomatoes. Drain tomatoes well, pressing between layers of paper towels.

*Lucinda Hutson*
Austin, Texas
Adapted from *The Herb Garden Cookbook:*
*The Complete Gardening and Gourmet Guide* (Lone Star Books)

*cook's secret...* Try to keep things simple, relying on bold flavors and garnishes to make dishes festive, colorful, and fun.

Robin Jean Davis and Scott Segal treat guests at their annual Christmas party to a menu that includes several of their family's special recipes. This appetizer, which features curry powder in a delicious twist on cream-cheese spread, is a crowd pleaser.

*special occasion*

# Curry-Almond Cheese Spread

2  (8-ounce) packages cream cheese, softened
1  (9-ounce) jar mango chutney
1  cup slivered almonds, toasted
1  tablespoon curry powder

½  teaspoon dry mustard
Toasted slivered almonds
Garnishes: thinly sliced Granny Smith apple, fresh parsley sprigs, fresh cranberries

• Process first 5 ingredients in a food processor until smooth, stopping to scrape down sides. Cover and chill 1 hour.
• Shape mixture into a ball. Chill until ready to serve. Sprinkle with almonds. Garnish, if desired. Serve with assorted crackers. Yield: 3 cups.

*Robin Jean Davis and Scott Segal*
Charleston, West Virginia

*cook's secret...* To make your own curry powder, combine ¼ cup ground coriander, 2 tablespoons ground cumin, 2 tablespoons ground turmeric, and 1 tablespoon ground ginger. Store your new curry blend in an airtight container.

# Daisy's Fig-Cranberry Chutney

1 cup walnuts, chopped
3 (8-ounce) packages dried figs*
2 (6-ounce) packages sweetened dried
   cranberries
1 cup dried currants*
1 cup bourbon, divided
1 cup orange juice, divided
1 cup firmly packed dark brown sugar
1 cup cider vinegar
1 navel orange, unpeeled and finely
   chopped

1 large onion, diced
2 tablespoons mustard seeds
2 tablespoons grated fresh ginger
2 teaspoons ground cinnamon
1 teaspoon freshly ground nutmeg
½ teaspoon salt
½ teaspoon ground cloves
⅛ teaspoon ground red pepper

• Bake walnuts in a shallow pan at 350°, stirring occasionally, 5 to 10 minutes or until toasted.

• Stir together figs, cranberries, currants, ½ cup bourbon, and ½ cup orange juice in a Dutch oven; let stand 20 minutes.

• Add brown sugar, remaining ½ cup bourbon, remaining ½ cup orange juice, and next 10 ingredients to fig mixture; cook over medium heat 30 minutes. Stir in toasted walnuts. Cool slightly. Serve over cream cheese with assorted crackers. Yield: about 10 cups.

*4 cups quartered fresh figs may be substituted for dried figs, and 1 cup fresh currants may be substituted for dried currants.

*Louise Reynolds*
Demopolis, Alabama

*cook's secret*... A fig's tender flesh surrounds a center of tiny edible seeds, which give the fruit a poppy seed–like crunch. It's said that figs are sweeter when their stems are "popped" off by hand rather than cut off with a knife—something to consider if you use fresh figs for this flavorful holiday chutney.

L isa Reid O'Rourke gives Mrs. Wilmuth Page credit for inspiring her to cook. "Mrs. Page did things the Southern way. She was afraid nobody would do things that way anymore, so she taught my mother, Eleanor Reid, who then passed on the knowledge to me," Lisa says.

Lisa shares her philosophy for stress-free entertaining: Cook as much as you can in advance. Follow her two do-ahead recipes, and you *and* your guests will enjoy the party.

*make-ahead*

## Pecan Sticks

| | |
|---|---|
| 1 cup butter or margarine, softened | 1 teaspoon ground cinnamon |
| 1 cup sugar | 1 teaspoon ground nutmeg |
| 1 large egg, separated | 1 teaspoon vanilla extract |
| 2 cups all-purpose flour | 1¼ cups chopped pecans |

• Beat butter and sugar at medium speed with an electric mixer until creamy; add egg yolk, flour, and next 3 ingredients, beating well. Press mixture evenly into a lightly greased 15- x 10-inch jellyroll pan.
• Beat egg white until soft peaks form; spread over dough in pan. Sprinkle with chopped pecans, gently pressing into dough.
• Bake at 325° for 25 minutes. Cut into 2- x 1-inch sticks while warm. Cool on wire racks. Store in an airtight container up to 2 weeks, or freeze up to 3 months. Yield: about 5 dozen.

*Lisa Reid O'Rourke*
Baton Rouge, Louisiana

*cook's secret*... Lisa starts cooking a couple of weeks before the occasion so she'll have as few things as possible to do close to the party.

# Creole Roasted Pecans

| 3 | cups pecan halves | 1 | tablespoon Worcestershire sauce |
|---|---|---|---|
| ¼ | cup butter, melted | 1 | teaspoon Creole seasoning |

- Stir together first 3 ingredients in a 15- x 10-inch jellyroll pan.
- Bake at 250° for 45 minutes, stirring every 15 minutes. Drain on paper towels. Sprinkle with seasoning. Store in airtight container 1 week, or freeze up to 2 months. Yield: 3 cups.

*Lisa Reid O'Rourke*
*Baton Rouge, Louisiana*

*cook's secret...* Any nut will work in this spicy favorite, but pecans keep the recipe true to its seasoning roots.

*kid–friendly*
# Popcorn Mix

| ¼ | cup chopped pecans | 1½ | cups popped popcorn |
|---|---|---|---|
| ½ | cup toasted oat O-shaped cereal | ¾ | cup crisp rice cereal squares |
| ⅓ | cup dry-roasted peanuts | | |

- Layer all ingredients in a 1-quart jar; tightly seal. Yield: 1 gift jar.

**Crazy Mixed-Up Popcorn:** Sprinkle 1 jar of Popcorn Mix in a lightly greased roasting pan. Bring ¼ cup firmly packed brown sugar, 2 tablespoons butter or margarine, and 1 tablespoon light corn syrup to a boil in a 3-quart saucepan over medium heat, stirring constantly. Boil, without stirring, 5 minutes or until a candy thermometer registers 250° (hard ball stage). Remove from heat; stir in ¼ teaspoon vanilla extract and ⅛ teaspoon baking soda. Pour over popcorn mixture, stirring to coat. Bake at 250° for 1 hour, stirring every 20 minutes. Cool in pan on a wire rack; break apart. Store in an airtight container. Yield: 4 cups.

*cook's secret...* You can substitute different cereals and nuts in this recipe, but think about their order as you layer them in the jar. Add each in an order that makes the layers look pretty.

Think smoking only works for meats? Then think again. This trio of unusual appetizers really takes to the technique, which makes for take-it-easy cooking. Smoke from the wood chips seals in the natural juices.

# Easy Smoked Cheddar

Hickory wood chips
2 (16-ounce) blocks Cheddar cheese

Vegetable cooking spray
Cheesecloth

- Soak wood chips in water at least 30 minutes.
- Prepare charcoal fire in smoker; let burn 15 to 20 minutes.
- Place 1 cheese block on top of the other; coat with cooking spray. Place lengthwise in center of a 24-inch piece of cheesecloth. Tightly wrap cheesecloth around stacked cheese. Place wrapped cheese crosswise in center of another 24-inch piece of cheesecloth; tightly wrap.
- Drain chips, and place on coals. Place water pan in smoker; add water to depth of fill line. Place wrapped cheese, seam side down, on upper food rack; cover with smoker lid.
- Cook cheese 2 hours. Yield: 2 (16-ounce) blocks.

*Gerry N. Brown*
Conyers, Georgia

*cook's secret...* Two blocks of cheese stacked together meld into one large chunk of cheese over the smoldering wood chips. Wrapping the blocks in cheesecloth fashions a rustic, textured look.

*kid-friendly*

# Smoked Nachos

1 (9-ounce) package tortilla chips
3 cups (12 ounces) shredded
    Cheddar-Jack-American cheese blend

½ cup sliced fresh or canned jalapeño
    peppers

• Spread chips in a lightly greased aluminum foil–lined 13- x 9-inch pan; sprinkle with cheese and jalapeños. Place pan on food rack, and grill, covered with grill lid, over low heat (under 300°) 15 to 20 minutes. Yield: 6 to 8 servings.

*Lynn and George O'Connor*
*Little Rock, Arkansas*

## cook's secret... You don't have to use a smoker to get wood-smoked flavor—your grill with a lid will give the same results.

# Smoky Pecans

*You'll eat these like popcorn, but save some for other uses.*

Hickory wood chips
2 pounds pecan halves

½ cup butter or margarine, melted
1 teaspoon salt

• Soak wood chips in water at least 30 minutes.
• Prepare charcoal fire in smoker; let burn 15 to 20 minutes.
• Drain chips, and place on coals. Place water pan in smoker; add water to depth of fill line.
• Stir together pecans, butter, and salt in a 24- x 12-inch pan. Place on upper food rack; cover with smoker lid.
• Cook 1 hour or until golden, stirring once after 30 minutes. Yield: 2 pounds.
**NOTE:** *Use a baking pan that fits your grill if the 24- x 12-inch pan is too large.*

*Richard Powell*
*Enid, Oklahoma*

## cook's secret... Sprinkle a few pecan halves over green salads, or add chopped pecans to breading for catfish or pork chops.

The secret's in the seasoning of these crunchy breadsticks that are great as appetizers or served with homemade soup. Baking guru Sister Schubert makes large batches of the spicy blend to keep on hand. She uses it in the dough and sprinkled on top of these versatile breadsticks.

## Breadsticks

| | |
|---|---|
| 1 teaspoon active dry yeast | 1 teaspoon minced garlic |
| ½ cup warm water (100° to 110°) | ½ teaspoon salt |
| 1 cup all-purpose flour | ½ teaspoon sugar |
| ¼ cup grated Parmesan cheese | 1 tablespoon olive oil |
| 1 teaspoon Sister's Spicy Seasoning Salt | Additional Sister's Spicy Seasoning Salt |

• Line a large baking sheet with parchment paper or wax paper. Set aside.
• Combine yeast and warm water in a 1-cup liquid measuring cup; let stand 5 minutes.
• Combine flour and next 5 ingredients in a large bowl. Add yeast mixture, stirring until well blended. Turn dough out onto a well-floured surface, and knead lightly 4 or 5 times.
• Roll dough into a 14- x 8-inch rectangle; cut lengthwise into 8 equal strips, using a sharp knife. Place strips on prepared baking sheet, and brush with olive oil. Sprinkle strips lightly with desired amount of Sister's Spicy Seasoning Salt. Bake at 300° for 45 minutes or until breadsticks are lightly browned. Remove breadsticks from baking sheets, and let cool on wire racks. Yield: 8 breadsticks.

*Sister Schubert*
Troy, Alabama
From *Sister Schubert's Secret Bread Recipes* (Oxmoor House)

*cook's secret*... There's a good reason for always preheating the oven when baking bread. During the first 10 to 15 minutes of baking, heat causes the dough to expand quickly, form the crust, and give shape to the loaf. If the oven is not preheated, the dough may overrise before the crust is formed. This will result in a misshapen loaf.

## Sister's Spicy Seasoning Salt:

| | | | | |
|---|---|---|---|---|
| 1 | cup kosher salt | 1½ | teaspoons onion powder |
| 2 | tablespoons dried parsley flakes | 1½ | teaspoons ground oregano |
| 2½ | teaspoons paprika | 1½ | teaspoons ground red pepper |
| 2 | teaspoons dry mustard | ½ | teaspoon ground thyme |
| 1½ | teaspoons garlic powder | | |

• Combine all ingredients. Store in airtight container at room temperature. Yield: 1¼ cups.

*Sister Schubert*
Troy, Alabama
From *Sister Schubert's Secret Bread Recipes* (Oxmoor House)

*cook's secret...* "My seasoning salt recipe yields enough for you to use again and again. It keeps indefinitely in an airtight container," says Sister.

# Parmesan Twists

| | | | | |
|---|---|---|---|---|
| ½ | cup butter or margarine, softened | 2 | teaspoons dried Italian seasoning |
| 1 | cup shredded Parmesan cheese | 1 | egg yolk |
| 1 | (8-ounce) container sour cream | 1 | tablespoon water |
| 2 | cups all-purpose flour | 2 | tablespoons sesame seeds |

• Beat butter at medium speed with an electric mixer until fluffy. Add cheese and sour cream, beating until blended.
• Combine flour and Italian seasoning. Gradually add to butter mixture; beat at low speed until blended. Cover and chill 30 minutes.
• Turn dough out onto a lightly floured surface; knead 3 or 4 times. Divide dough in half. Roll half of dough into a 12- x 6-inch rectangle. Cut into 6- x ½-inch strips. Stir together egg yolk and 1 tablespoon water; brush over breadsticks. Sprinkle with 1 tablespoon sesame seeds. Twist strips, and place on lightly greased baking sheets. Repeat with remaining dough, egg wash, and sesame seeds. Bake at 350° for 15 minutes or until golden. Freeze up to 3 months, if desired. Yield: 4 dozen.

*Elizabeth A. Crawley*
New Orleans, Louisiana

*cook's secret...* If you don't have Italian seasoning, substitute half basil and half oregano.

Cheese straws, those icons of the Southern table, are known for their melt-in-your-mouth texture. These recipes call for a food processor, but if you don't have one, you can use a heavy-duty mixer. Our Test Kitchens staff discovered that both recipes can be either shaped with a cookie press or rolled and cut as desired.

*special occasion*

## Easy-as-Pie Cheese Straws

1  (11-ounce) package piecrust mix
1  (5-ounce) jar sharp process cheese spread
¼  teaspoon ground red pepper

• Process piecrust mix and remaining ingredients in a food processor 30 seconds or until mixture forms a ball, stopping to scrape down sides.
• Use a cookie press fitted with a bar-shaped disk to shape dough into 2½-inch straws, following manufacturer's instructions. Or divide dough in half, and form each portion into a 7-inch log; wrap in plastic wrap, and chill 1 hour. Cut into ¼-inch slices. Place cheese straws on lightly greased baking sheets.
• Bake at 375° for 8 to 10 minutes or until lightly browned. Transfer to wire racks to cool. Yield: 5 dozen.

**NOTE:** *For testing purposes only, we used Betty Crocker piecrust mix.*

*cook's secret*... For treating pop-in guests, cheese straws are a hostess's best-kept secret. Bake them ahead, and freeze up to 1 month. Before serving, crisp them in a 200° oven for 10 to 15 minutes.

# Italian Cheese Straws

1 (8-ounce) package shredded mozzarella
    cheese
½ cup butter, softened
1½ cups all-purpose flour

1 teaspoon dried Italian seasoning
½ teaspoon salt
¼ teaspoon ground white pepper

• Pulse cheese and butter 3 or 4 times in a food processor until combined. Add flour and remaining ingredients; process 20 seconds or until mixture forms a ball and leaves sides of bowl.

• Use a cookie press fitted with a bar-shaped disk to shape dough into 2½-inch straws, following manufacturer's instructions. Or divide dough into fourths, and roll each portion into a ¼-inch-thick rectangle on floured wax paper. Cut into 2- x ½-inch strips with a knife or pastry wheel. Place on ungreased baking sheets.

• Bake at 375° for 8 to 10 minutes or until lightly browned. Transfer to wire racks to cool. Yield: 5 dozen.

*cook's secret...* Use a fluted pastry wheel to cut this dough into strips with pretty rippled edges.

## Secrets to Cheese Straw Success

• Soften butter at room temperature 2 hours before using.

• Spoon the flour into a dry measuring cup, and level with the edge of a knife for an accurate measurement.

• For flaky cheese straws, don't overmix the dough.

• Roll dough between sheets of parchment paper or wax paper for easy cleanup.

• Preportion dough, and keep the remainder chilled until ready to use. If dough gets soft, refrigerate 10 to 15 minutes.

• Shiny baking sheets produce golden-brown cheese straws. Food placed on dark baking sheets cooks faster and sometimes overbrowns.

• Set your timer for 1 to 2 minutes less than the recommended baking time, as oven temperatures vary.

• Place baked cheese straws between sheets of wax paper, and store them in tightly sealed tins and containers.

In one of my "Life At" columns in the magazine, I asked readers to send their favorite shrimp cocktail sauce recipes. I got a lot of tasty renditions, but a call from my friend Virginia Spencer was one of my most enjoyable responses. She said that her husband, Bill, made the best cocktail sauce that I would ever taste. I politely said to have Bill send it and let our Test Kitchens decide. Guess what? The pros thought that, of all the recipes we received, those from Bill, Jim Goodrich, and Belle Fields rated tops. So boil some shrimp, and try these favorites.

*John Floyd*
Editor in Chief, *Southern Living*

*editor's choice*

## Grandpa Jim's Shrimp Sauce

| | | | |
|---|---|---|---|
| ½ | cup chili sauce | 1½ | teaspoons Worcestershire sauce |
| ⅓ | cup prepared horseradish | ½ | to 1 teaspoon hot sauce |
| ⅓ | cup ketchup | ¼ | teaspoon salt |
| 2 | tablespoons lemon juice | ¼ | teaspoon pepper |

• Stir together all ingredients until blended. Cover and chill until ready to serve. Yield: 1⅓ cups.

*Jim Goodrich*
Enid, Oklahoma

*cook's secret*... To turn this sauce into a salad dressing, stir together equal parts Grandpa Jim's Shrimp Sauce and mayonnaise. Serve over salad greens tossed with shrimp, sliced onion, diced celery, and diced hard-cooked eggs, if desired.

# Shrimp Cocktail Sauce

½ cup mayonnaise
½ cup ketchup
½ cup chili sauce
2⅓ tablespoons lemon juice

1 tablespoon lime juice
2 teaspoons prepared horseradish
½ to 1 teaspoon hot sauce

• Stir together all ingredients until blended. Cover and chill until ready to serve. Yield: 1¾ cups.

*William M. Spencer III*
Birmingham, Alabama

*cook's secret*... Mayonnaise is the surprise ingredient that distinguishes this sauce from similar sauces. Use a low-fat version if you prefer, since it's hard to tell the difference in this spicy recipe.

# Shrimp Sauce

6 tablespoons prepared horseradish

6 tablespoons ketchup

• Stir together horseradish and ketchup. Cover and chill until ready to serve. Yield: ¾ cup.

*Belle S. Fields*
Columbia, South Carolina

*cook's secret*... Simplicity is the key here. Just remember, it's equal parts horseradish to ketchup. Use freshly made horseradish, since the piquant flavor is so predominant.

The fragrance of rosemary leaves is described as a combination of pine and nutmeg, while its flavor is somewhat peppery, warm, spicy, and resinous. Explore the wonders of rosemary with this shrimp appetizer from Lucinda Hutson.

## Garlic-and-Rosemary Shrimp

*Serve this dish either as an appetizer or as a main dish served over pasta.*

| | | | |
|---|---|---|---|
| 1 | pound unpeeled, medium-size fresh shrimp | 1 | tablespoon lemon juice |
| 2 | tablespoons butter or margarine | 3 | dried red chile peppers |
| ¼ | cup extra-virgin olive oil | 3 | bay leaves |
| 1 | large garlic bulb | 1 | teaspoon salt |
| ½ | cup dry white wine | 1 | teaspoon dried oregano |
| 2 | tablespoons chopped fresh rosemary | ½ | teaspoon dried crushed red pepper |
| 2 | tablespoons white wine vinegar | | Garnishes: lemon slices, red chile peppers, fresh rosemary sprigs |

• Peel shrimp, leaving tails on; devein, if desired, and set aside.
• Melt butter with oil in a skillet over medium-high heat. Cut garlic bulb in half crosswise; separate and peel cloves. Add to butter mixture; sauté 2 minutes.
• Stir in wine and next 8 ingredients; cook, stirring constantly, 1 minute or until thoroughly heated.
• Add shrimp; cook 5 to 6 minutes or just until shrimp turn pink. Remove bay leaves. Garnish, if desired. Yield: 4 appetizer servings or 2 main-dish servings.

*Lucinda Hutson*
Austin, Texas
Adapted from *The Herb Garden Cookbook:*
*The Complete Gardening and Gourmet Guide*
(Lone Star Books)

*cook's secret...* Use the woody stems of rosemary as skewers for kabobs; or toss large, leafy stems onto hot coals to add flavor to grilled food.

Use an indoor smoking pan to smoke small food items, such as shrimp, on your stove-top. Some smoke may escape during cooking, so be sure to open a window.

## Stove-Top Smoked Shrimp

*These are great peel-and-eat appetizers. They also give shrimp cocktail and shrimp salad a terrific flavor boost.*

| | | | |
|---|---|---|---|
| 1 | cup finely ground hickory wood chips | ½ | teaspoon salt |
| 3 | pounds unpeeled, large fresh shrimp | ¼ | teaspoon freshly ground pepper |
| 3 | tablespoons olive oil | | |

• Place wood chips into center of stove-top smoking pan. Insert drip pan and food rack.
• Toss shrimp with remaining ingredients. Arrange shrimp on food rack; cover with smoker lid.
• Cook shrimp over medium heat 10 minutes or just until shrimp turn pink.
Yield: 3 pounds.

*cook's secret...* Soak your favorite wood chips in water at least 30 minutes before using. Wet wood smokes slowly; dry wood flames and quickly burns.

Peggy Dean and Gene St. Martin aren't formally trained cooks. However, Southern foods—especially those of Louisiana—have been a part of their lives since childhood. Peggy Dean grew up in Shreveport's Washington-Youree Hotel—where her father was manager—and spent many hours observing the hotel's chef.

Gene, a retired physician, is a born-and-raised Cajun from Houma and a true oyster aficionado. A favorite recipe is Oysters Pierre, which Gene named after himself. "When I was at Tulane Medical School, my buddies and I gave each other nicknames. They dubbed me 'Pierre' because of the notoriously wild Cajun stories I loved to tell. Cajuns love to weave tall tales, and I was not an exception," Gene says.

But the St. Martins' skills in the kitchen are no exaggeration. Try their oyster recipes, and see for yourself.

*editor's choice*

## Oysters Pierre

*Serve with crackers for a tasty treat.*

| | | | |
|---|---|---|---|
| 6 | green onions, thinly sliced | ½ | teaspoon salt |
| 2 | garlic cloves, minced | ½ | teaspoon pepper |
| ⅓ | cup vegetable oil | 2 | pints fresh oysters, undrained |
| 2 | tablespoons lemon juice | | |

• Stir together first 6 ingredients in a medium bowl; cover and chill 2 hours. Stir in oysters and liquid just before serving. Yield: 6 to 8 servings.

*Peggy Dean and Gene St. Martin*
Shreveport, Louisiana

*cook's secret...* If you'd rather not eat oysters raw due to health concerns, broil them in their own juices in a pan until their edges curl. Cover and chill them; then use the broiled oysters and juices in this recipe as if they were raw.

# Fried Bacon-Wrapped Oysters

1 cup all-purpose flour
1 teaspoon salt
1 teaspoon pepper
2 pints fresh oysters (about 46), rinsed
    and drained

23 bacon slices, cut in half
Peanut oil

• Combine first 3 ingredients in a shallow dish. Dredge oysters in flour mixture. Wrap each oyster with a bacon piece, and secure with a wooden pick. Pour peanut oil to a depth of 1 inch into a deep cast-iron skillet or Dutch oven; heat to 350°.
• Fry oysters, in batches, 2½ to 3 minutes or until bacon is cooked. Drain on paper towels. Serve immediately. Yield: 23 appetizer servings or 6 to 8 main-dish servings.

*Peggy Dean and Gene St. Martin*
Shreveport, Louisiana

*cook's secret*... Peanut oil is one of the best oils for frying because you can cook it at a high temperature without it smoking. The higher the temperature of your frying oil, the less oil the food will absorb.

... Live oysters can be covered with a damp towel and refrigerated up to 3 days; however, the sooner they're used, the better they'll taste. Refrigerate shucked oysters, covered in their liquor, up to 2 days; or freeze up to 3 months.

# Topless Oysters

*Offer guests three sauces to spoon over these oysters.*

| | | | |
|---|---|---|---|
| 2½ | cups water | 1½ | teaspoons lite soy sauce |
| 2 | fresh kumquats | 1 | shallot, minced |
| ¼ | cup fresh lime juice | 2 | dozen fresh oysters (in the shell) |
| 1 | teaspoon grated fresh ginger | | Fresh Tomato Salsa |
| ¼ | cup rice vinegar | | Lemon wedges |

• Bring 2½ cups water to a boil in a small saucepan. Reduce heat, and add kumquats; simmer 1 minute or until tender. Drain; let cool. Remove seeds, and cut kumquats into thin slices.

• Combine kumquats, lime juice, and ginger, tossing gently to coat. Set aside.

• Stir together vinegar, soy sauce, and shallot.

• Scrub oyster shells; open, discarding tops. Arrange shell bottoms (containing oysters) over crushed ice on a serving platter. Serve with kumquat sauce, vinegar sauce, Fresh Tomato Salsa, and lemon wedges. Yield: 4 to 6 servings.

## Fresh Tomato Salsa:

| | | | |
|---|---|---|---|
| 3 | plum tomatoes, peeled, seeded, and diced | 1 | to 2 teaspoons minced jalapeño pepper |
| 2 | tablespoons chopped fresh cilantro | 1 | teaspoon fresh lime juice |
| 1 | tablespoon minced onion | ⅛ | teaspoon salt |

• Combine all ingredients in a small bowl. Yield: 1½ cups.

*Caroline Stuart*
New York, New York

*cook's secret*... Live oysters are best eaten as fresh as possible. Throw away any that do not have tightly closed shells or that don't snap shut when tapped.

# Dressed Mini Oyster Po'boys

1¼ cups self-rising cornmeal

2 tablespoons Creole seasoning

2 (8-ounce) containers fresh Select oysters, drained

Peanut or vegetable oil

1 cup mayonnaise, divided

2 tablespoons white vinegar

2 tablespoons Dijon mustard

1 (10-ounce) package shredded cabbage

2 tablespoons ketchup

1 tablespoon prepared horseradish

1 teaspoon Creole seasoning

¾ teaspoon paprika

12 French bread rolls, split and toasted

Garnish: lemon wedges

• Combine cornmeal and 2 tablespoons Creole seasoning. Dredge oysters in cornmeal mixture.

• Pour oil to a depth of 1 inch into a Dutch oven; heat to 375°. Fry oysters, in 3 batches, 3 to 4 minutes or until golden. Drain oysters on paper towels.

• Stir together ½ cup mayonnaise, vinegar, and mustard. Stir in cabbage; set slaw aside.

• Stir together remaining ½ cup mayonnaise, ketchup, and next 3 ingredients in a small bowl.

• Spread cut sides of French bread rolls with ketchup mixture; place oysters and slaw evenly on bottom half of each roll. Cover with tops. Serve po'boys immediately. Garnish, if desired. Yield: 4 to 6 servings.

*Vanessa McNeil*
Test Kitchens Specialist

*cook's secret*... To save time, purchase premade coleslaw to spoon on these sassy sandwiches.

Sharing her talents launched a new career for Debbi Covington. "I prepared the food for the 70th birthday party of one of our church members, and the next thing I knew, I was in the catering business," she explains. Now, her company, Catering by Debbi Covington, regularly turns out fabulous appetizers that transform any gathering into a festive event. To make preparation easier, she chops, bags, and measures ingredients the day before a party.

## Crab Imperial

| | | | |
|---|---|---|---|
| 1 | tablespoon butter or margarine | ½ | teaspoon prepared mustard |
| 1 | (2-ounce) jar diced pimiento, drained | ⅛ | teaspoon ground red pepper |
| 2 | small celery ribs, chopped | ⅛ | teaspoon hot sauce |
| ½ | small green bell pepper, chopped | 3 | tablespoons mayonnaise |
| 1 | tablespoon chopped fresh parsley | 1 | large egg |
| 1 | teaspoon Old Bay seasoning | 1 | pound fresh lump crabmeat, drained |

• Melt butter in a large skillet over medium-high heat. Add pimiento, celery, and bell pepper; saute 3½ minutes or until tender. Remove from heat; stir in parsley and next 4 ingredients.
• Stir together mayonnaise and egg in a bowl until blended; stir in pimiento mixture. Fold in crabmeat. Spoon into a lightly greased 1-quart baking dish.
• Bake at 375° for 15 minutes. Serve with assorted crackers. Yield: 4 to 6 servings.

*Debbi Covington*
Beaufort, South Carolina

*cook's secret...* Carefully pick through the crab to remove bits of shell, if you like, but try to leave the pricey lump meat as whole as possible. Otherwise, there's no need to pay extra for lump crabmeat.

# Ham-and-Asparagus Cheesecake

| | | | |
|---|---|---|---|
| 1 | sleeve round buttery crackers, crushed | 2 | cups (8 ounces) shredded Swiss cheese |
| 6 | tablespoons butter or margarine, melted | 1¼ | cups diced cooked ham |
| 1 | (8-ounce) package cream cheese, softened | 2 | (10½-ounce) cans asparagus cuts, drained and chopped* |
| 3 | large eggs | 4 | green onions, minced |
| 1 | (8-ounce) container sour cream | | Garnishes: chopped green onions, cooked asparagus tips |
| ¼ | cup all-purpose flour | | |
| ¼ | teaspoon pepper | | |

• Stir together cracker crumbs and melted butter, and press crumb mixture into bottom of a 9-inch springform pan.

• Bake crumb mixture at 350° for 10 minutes; cool on a wire rack. Reduce oven temperature to 300°.

• Beat cream cheese at medium speed with an electric mixer 2 to 3 minutes or until light and fluffy.

• Add eggs, 1 at a time, beating well after each addition. Add sour cream, flour, and pepper, beating until blended. Stir in Swiss cheese.

• Pour one-third of cheese mixture into prepared pan; sprinkle evenly with ham.

• Pour half of remaining cheese mixture evenly over ham; sprinkle with asparagus and onions. Top evenly with remaining cheese mixture.

• Bake at 300° for 1 hour or until center of cake is set. Turn off oven, and let cake stand in oven 1 hour with door partially open. Cover and chill, if desired. Garnish, if desired. Yield: 1 (9-inch) cheesecake, about 24 appetizer servings.

*1 pound fresh asparagus, trimmed and cut into 1-inch pieces, may be substituted for canned asparagus.*

**NOTE:** *For testing purposes only, we used Keebler Town House crackers.*

*Debbi Covington*
Beaufort, South Carolina

*cook's secret...* Use a flat-bottom glass to tamp the crust into the pan and smooth it evenly.

Figs are a fleeting treasure: They must be picked during peak ripeness, and once they're harvested, they don't last long. Since these gems are so perishable, they're rarely available for more than a few days at farmers markets. The best way to get your fill is to grow your own—or make friends with someone who does.

## Baked Fig Bites

*This regional twist on a classic Italian appetizer*
*uses country ham instead of prosciutto.*

| | |
|---|---|
| 14 small fresh figs, stemmed and halved | ¼ pound thinly sliced country ham, cut in |
| 10 ounces Gorgonzola cheese, crumbled* | half lengthwise |
| 1 teaspoon finely chopped fresh rosemary | Garnish: fresh rosemary sprigs |
| ½ teaspoon pepper | |

• Top each fig half evenly with Gorgonzola cheese, and sprinkle evenly with rosemary and pepper. Wrap ham around each fig, securing with a wooden pick; place bites, seam side down, on an aluminum foil–lined baking sheet.

• Bake at 350° for 10 minutes or until cheese melts. Garnish, if desired. Yield: 28 bites.

*\*10 ounces crumbled blue cheese may be substituted for crumbled Gorgonzola cheese.*

*Miles Eustis*
Arden, North Carolina

*cook's secret...* When not eaten out of hand, figs most often show up in sweet treats. However, we've found them to be an ideal match for thin slices of salty country ham and Gorgonzola cheese.

# Artichoke-Stuffed Mushrooms

| | |
|---|---|
| 1½ pounds large fresh mushrooms | 3 green onions, chopped |
| ¼ cup chopped onion | ½ cup grated Parmesan cheese |
| 2 garlic cloves, chopped | ½ cup mayonnaise |
| 1 tablespoon olive oil | ¼ teaspoon salt |
| ¼ cup dry white wine | ¼ teaspoon pepper |
| ¼ cup soft breadcrumbs | |
| 1 (14-ounce) can artichoke hearts, drained and chopped | |

• Rinse and pat mushrooms dry. Remove stems, and chop; reserve mushroom caps.
• Sauté mushroom stems, onion, and garlic in hot oil in a large skillet over medium heat 5 minutes or until onion is tender.
• Add wine, and cook 2 minutes or until liquid evaporates. Stir in breadcrumbs. Remove from heat, and let cool.
• Combine onion mixture, artichoke hearts, and remaining ingredients. Spoon 1 teaspoonful into each mushroom cap. Place on a lightly greased rack in a roasting pan.
• Bake at 350° for 12 to 15 minutes or until golden. Yield: 25 to 30 appetizer servings.

*Robin Jean Davis and Scott Segal*
Charleston, West Virginia

*cook's secret...* Never wash mushrooms ahead of time. They're like sponges: They will absorb the water and lose texture.

*make-ahead*

# Asparagus Rollups

*Freeze unbaked rollups up to 1 month in an airtight container.*
*Thaw in refrigerator, and bake as directed.*

24  fresh asparagus spears
1  (8-ounce) package cream cheese,
      softened
1  (4-ounce) package crumbled blue cheese
2  tablespoons mayonnaise
1  tablespoon chopped fresh chives

12  bread slices
12  thinly sliced deli ham slices
¼  cup butter or margarine, melted
   Paprika
   Garnishes: green onion curl, red bell pepper

• Snap off tough ends of asparagus. Arrange asparagus in a steamer basket over boiling water. Cover and steam 4 to 6 minutes or until crisp-tender. Remove from steamer, and cool on paper towels.
• Stir together cream cheese and next 3 ingredients.
• Remove crusts from bread; reserve crusts for another use. Flatten bread slices with a rolling pin. Spread 2 tablespoons cream cheese mixture on 1 side of each slice; top each with 1 ham slice.
• Place 2 asparagus spears, tips pointed toward opposite ends, on 1 end of each bread slice; roll up, and place, seam side down, on a greased baking sheet. Brush with butter; sprinkle with paprika.
• Bake at 400° for 12 minutes or until golden. Serve immediately. Garnish, if desired. Yield: 12 appetizer servings.

*Robin Jean Davis and Scott Segal*
Charleston, West Virginia

*cook's secret*... Use a serrated knife to trim the crusts from the bread. Stack 2 or 3 slices to trim at the same time to speed up the process. Grind the crusts in a food processor, and freeze up to 1 month to use as fresh breadcrumbs.

In the home of Mabel and Santo Formica, cooking is both a pleasure and a passion. "You can learn a lot about our Sicilian heritage when you sit down for a meal with us," says Santo. He and Mabel pride themselves on their authentic yet easy recipes.

*make–ahead*

## Olives Scaciati

*Double this recipe for a dramatic presentation that easily feeds a large group.*

| | | | | |
|---|---|---|---|---|
| 2 | pounds large unpitted green olives | | 2 | tablespoons dried oregano |
| 2 | cups ½-inch celery pieces with leaves | | 1 | teaspoon black pepper |
| ¾ | cup extra-virgin olive oil | | ¾ | teaspoon dried crushed red pepper |
| ¼ | cup red wine vinegar | | 6 | garlic cloves, coarsely chopped |

• Wash olives, and drain. Gently pound each olive with a wooden mallet to open. (Don't mash, and don't remove pit.) Place olives and celery in a large bowl.

• Whisk together olive oil and next 5 ingredients until blended; pour over olive mixture, tossing to coat. Cover and chill 8 hours. Refrigerate up to 1 month. Serve at room temperature. Yield: 6 cups.

*Mabel and Santo Formica*
Sherwood, Arkansas

*cook's secret*... This marinated olive recipe provides the perfect opportunity to use extra-virgin olive oil. This oil is pressed without the use of heat or chemicals and is considered the finest available.

Purchased piecrusts offer great shortcuts. Several forms of commercial piecrusts—piecrust mixes, frozen ready-to-bake pastry shells, and refrigerated piecrusts—are available. We prefer the flavor, texture, appearance, and convenience of refrigerated piecrusts because they are closest to homemade. You'll discover that for yourself when you make these easy miniature quiches.

## Spinach Quiches

| | | | |
|---|---|---|---|
| 1 | (15-ounce) package refrigerated piecrusts | 1 | tablespoon Worcestershire sauce |
| 2 | tablespoons butter or margarine | 1 | teaspoon salt |
| 1 | small onion, chopped | ½ | teaspoon pepper |
| 2 | green onions, chopped | 3 | large eggs |
| ¼ | cup chopped fresh parsley | ¼ | cup milk |
| 1 | (10-ounce) package frozen chopped spinach, thawed and well drained | 1 | cup (4 ounces) shredded Swiss cheese |

• Unfold each piecrust, and slice each crust into 24 equal wedges. Shape into balls, and press into lightly greased miniature muffin pans.
• Melt butter in a large skillet over medium heat. Add onions and parsley; sauté until onions are tender. Add spinach; cook 2 minutes. Stir in Worcestershire sauce, salt, and pepper. Remove from heat.
• Whisk together eggs and milk until blended; stir in cheese. Add egg mixture to spinach mixture; spoon evenly into prepared pans.
• Bake at 350° for 30 to 35 minutes. Remove immediately from pans, and cool on wire racks. Yield: 4 dozen.

*Lisa Reid O'Rourke*
Baton Rouge, Louisiana

*cook's secret...* For a big party, make these little quiches ahead and freeze up to 2 months. Thaw frozen quiches in refrigerator; bake at 300° for 10 minutes or until thoroughly heated.

ouise and Pete Reynold's home, perched in a bend of a river, offers the perfect vantage for viewing the light-bedecked boats in the Christmas on the River parade in Demopolis, Alabama. Louise marks the event with a buffet of what she calls "basic good food." Here's one of her favorite appetizers.

*time-saver*

# Pesto-Cheese Pastry Wrap

| | |
|---|---|
| 1 (8-ounce) can refrigerated crescent rolls | ½ cup Louise's Basil Pesto* |
| 1 (3-ounce) log goat cheese, cut into pieces | |

• Unroll crescent rolls on a lightly greased baking sheet, and separate into 2 squares; press perforations to seal. Top each square evenly with goat cheese and Louise's Basil Pesto, leaving a 1-inch border around all the edges. Gather corners over mixture, pinching to seal.
• Bake at 375° for 10 to 15 minutes or until golden brown. Cut each square into 6 servings. Serve warm or at room temperature. Yield: 12 appetizer servings.
*\*Refrigerated commercial pesto may be substituted for Louise's Basil Pesto.*

## Louise's Basil Pesto:

| | |
|---|---|
| 2 to 4 garlic cloves | ½ cup fresh parsley leaves |
| 2 cups fresh basil leaves | ½ cup olive oil |
| 1 cup pecans | ¼ cup shredded Romano cheese |
| 1 cup shredded Parmesan cheese | ½ teaspoon salt |

• Process all ingredients in a blender or food processor until mixture is smooth, stopping to scrape down sides. Yield: 2 cups.

*Louise Reynolds*
*Demopolis, Alabama*

*cook's secret...* Use the remaining pesto to toss with hot cooked pasta. Or spoon leftover pesto into ice cube trays, and freeze just until firm. Pop out the frozen cubes, and freeze in a zip-top freezer bag for up to 3 months.

Tapas, a buzzword for appetizers, comes from a Spanish word that means "to cover." It's believed that the first tapa was a slice of ham served on top of a sherry glass, allegedly to keep out dust and other nuisances. And from that time, different types of tapas have emerged.

A great variety of tapas—small portions of food offered on little saucers—are served in lively eateries and bustling taverns throughout Spain.

Vanessa McNeil, Test Kitchens Specialist, thought it would be exciting to concoct some versions sporting a Southern flair. Enjoy Vanessa's creations that feature favorite flavors.

## Peppered Pork with Pecan Biscuits

| | | | |
|---|---|---|---|
| 1 | teaspoon pepper | 1 | cup buttermilk |
| ½ | teaspoon salt | ½ | cup finely chopped pecans |
| 1 | pound pork tenderloin | ¼ | cup butter or margarine, melted |
| 1 | (¼-ounce) envelope rapid-rise yeast | 2 | tablespoons pesto |
| 1 | tablespoon sugar | 16 | pecan halves |
| ¾ | cup warm water (100° to 110°) | | Coarse-grained Dijon mustard |
| 4 | cups all-purpose baking mix* | | |

• Combine pepper and salt, and rub evenly over tenderloin. Place on a lightly greased rack inside a roasting pan.
• Bake at 450° for 20 to 25 minutes or until a meat thermometer inserted into thickest portion registers 160°. Let stand 10 minutes; thinly slice.
• Combine yeast, sugar, and ¾ cup warm water in a large bowl; let mixture stand 5 minutes.
• Add baking mix and next 4 ingredients to bowl, stirring until dry ingredients are moistened. Turn dough out onto a lightly floured surface.
• Pat or roll dough to 1-inch thickness; cut with a 2-inch round cutter. Place biscuits on a lightly greased baking sheet; place a pecan half in center of each biscuit.
• Bake at 425° for 20 to 25 minutes or until lightly browned. Split biscuits; serve pork in biscuits with mustard. Yield: 6 to 8 servings.

*For testing purposes only, we used Bisquick All-Purpose Baking Mix.

*Vanessa McNeil*
Test Kitchens Specialist

# Black-Eyed Pea Cakes

*Using canned black-eyed peas and packaged hush puppy*
*mix makes this recipe a snap to prepare.*

1   small onion, chopped
1   tablespoon olive oil
2   (15.8-ounce) cans black-eyed peas,
      rinsed, drained, and divided
1   (8-ounce) container chive-and-onion
      cream cheese, softened
1   large egg

½   teaspoon salt
1   teaspoon hot sauce
1   (8-ounce) package hush puppy mix with
      onion
Olive oil
Toppings: sour cream and green tomato
      relish

• Sauté onion in 1 tablespoon hot oil in a large skillet over medium-high heat until tender.
• Process onion, 1 can of peas, and next 4 ingredients in a blender or food processor until mixture is smooth, stopping to scrape down sides. Stir in hush puppy mix, and gently fold in remaining can of peas.
• Shape mixture by 2 tablespoonfuls into 3-inch patties, and place on a wax paper–lined baking sheet. Cover and chill 1 hour.
• Cook patties, in batches, in 3 tablespoons hot oil, adding oil as needed, in a large skillet over medium heat for 1½ minutes on each side or until patties are golden brown. Drain patties on paper towels, and keep warm. Serve with desired toppings. Yield: 30 appetizer servings.

*Vanessa McNeil*
Test Kitchens Specialist

*cook's secret...* If you can't find chive-and-onion cream cheese, mince
1 green onion and stir it into an 8-ounce container of regular cream cheese.

P am Binkowski first tasted this appetizer at a New Year's Eve party. "I changed things around until it became what it is," says Pam. Pam occasionally serves her version, which was a Runner Up in the 2001 *Southern Living* Holiday Recipe Contest, as a light meal for herself and her husband.

*contest winner*

## Spinach Crostini

| | | | |
|---|---|---|---|
| 1 | (10-ounce) package frozen chopped spinach, thawed and drained | ¼ | cup mayonnaise |
| 2 | plum tomatoes, diced | ¼ | cup sour cream |
| 1 | small onion, diced | ¼ | teaspoon pepper |
| 1 | garlic clove, minced | 1 | (16-ounce) French bread loaf, cut into ½-inch slices |
| ½ | cup crumbled feta cheese | | |

• Combine first 8 ingredients; spread on 1 side of each bread slice, and place on a baking sheet.
• Bake at 350° for 18 minutes or until golden. Yield: 8 appetizer servings.

*Pam Binkowski*
Cullman, Alabama

*cook's secret...* To drain frozen spinach, place it in a colander and press it with paper towels to absorb excess moisture.

I find cooking to be one-third chemistry, one-third surgery, and one-third presentation," says Dr. Samuel Oliver, Jr. "If guests are relaxed and hungry, they will think anything is good when it's presented well. We eat with our eyes first." He suggests serving Sauvignon Blanc or Chardonnay with this appetizer.

*make-ahead*

# Spinach and Artichokes in Puff Pastry

| | | | |
|---|---|---|---|
| 1 | (10-ounce) package frozen chopped spinach, thawed | 1 | teaspoon onion powder |
| 1 | (14-ounce) can artichoke hearts, drained and chopped | 1 | teaspoon garlic powder |
| ½ | cup mayonnaise | ½ | teaspoon pepper |
| ½ | cup grated Parmesan cheese | ¼ | teaspoon salt |
| | | 1½ | (17.3-ounce) packages frozen puff pastry |

• Drain spinach well, pressing between layers of paper towels.
• Stir together spinach, artichoke hearts, and next 6 ingredients.
• Thaw puff pastry at room temperature 30 minutes. Unfold 1 sheet pastry, and place on a lightly floured surface or heavy-duty plastic wrap. Spread one-third of spinach mixture (about 1 cup) evenly over pastry sheet, leaving a ½-inch border. Roll up pastry, jellyroll fashion, pressing to seal seam; wrap in heavy-duty plastic wrap. Repeat procedure twice with remaining pastry and spinach mixture. Freeze 30 minutes; cut into ½-inch-thick slices. Place on ungreased baking sheets.
• Bake at 400° for 15 minutes or until golden brown. Yield: 4 dozen.

*Dr. Samuel Oliver, Jr.*
*Charleston, West Virginia*

*cook's secret...* The rolls may be frozen up to 3 months before slicing and baking.

Every year, Terri Kurlan holds a Christmas party for one hundred folks. "I always try to come up with something different," she says. "These are great because you can make them ahead. I made five hundred last year, and within an hour they were all gone!" Her recipe was a Grand Prize Winner in the 2001 *Southern Living* Holiday Recipe Contest.

*contest winner*

## Mini Prime Ribs and Yorkshire Puddings

| | |
|---|---|
| 3 large eggs, lightly beaten | 1 teaspoon salt |
| 1 cup all-purpose flour | 1 teaspoon pepper |
| 1 cup milk | Horseradish sauce or prepared horseradish* |
| 1 (4- to 6-pound) bone-in prime rib roast | Garnish: sliced green onions |

- Stir together eggs, flour, and milk; cover and chill batter 8 hours.
- Sprinkle roast with salt and pepper. Place roast on an aluminum foil–lined rack in a roasting pan.
- Bake at 500° for 30 minutes. Reduce temperature to 350°, and bake 30 more minutes. Increase temperature to 450°; bake 35 more minutes or to desired degree of doneness. Remove roast, and let stand 15 minutes before thinly slicing, reserving about ½ cup drippings in pan.
- Spoon drippings into miniature muffin pans, filling one-fourth full.
- Bake at 450° for 2 minutes or until thoroughly heated.
- Stir chilled batter; spoon into miniature muffin pans, filling half full.
- Bake at 450° for 9 minutes or until puffy and golden. Remove from oven, and make a well in center of pudding. Arrange prime rib slices in centers; top with horseradish sauce or horseradish. Garnish, if desired. Serve warm. Yield: 64 puddings.

*½ cup sour cream, 1 tablespoon prepared horseradish, 2 tablespoons lemon juice, and ¼ teaspoon salt combined may be substituted for horseradish sauce. Yield: about ⅔ cup sauce.*

*Terri Kurlan*
*McKinney, Texas*

*cook's secret...* Freeze Yorkshire Puddings, if desired. Let thaw at room temperature 30 minutes; reheat at 400° for 5 to 7 minutes. Assemble as directed.

**P**art of the kick in these meatballs comes from a jalapeño pepper, which can yield hot to very hot heat. The recipe calls for one small pepper, but there are really no rules on how your taste buds react to peppers. Taste carefully, experiment with the amount of heat you like, and enjoy.

## Spicy Meatballs

| | | | |
|---|---|---|---|
| 2 | small onions, finely chopped and divided | 1 | pound ground beef |
| 2 | tablespoons olive oil | 1 | small jalapeño pepper, seeded and finely chopped |
| 1 | (10¾-ounce) can tomato puree | 1 | large egg, lightly beaten |
| 1 | cup water | ½ | cup cracker meal |
| ¼ | cup red wine vinegar | ½ | cup ketchup |
| 2 | to 3 tablespoons prepared mustard | 1 | teaspoon salt |
| 1 | tablespoon Worcestershire sauce | 1 | teaspoon pepper |
| 1 | teaspoon brown sugar | ½ | teaspoon hot sauce |
| ½ | teaspoon salt | | Garnish: fresh chopped sage |
| ½ | teaspoon chili powder | | |
| ¼ | teaspoon garlic powder | | |

• Sauté 1 chopped onion in hot oil in a large skillet over medium-high heat 5 minutes or until tender.

• Add tomato puree and next 8 ingredients. Bring to a boil; reduce heat, and simmer, stirring occasionally, 1 hour.

• Combine ground beef, remaining 1 onion, jalapeño pepper, and next 5 ingredients. Shape into 40 (½-inch) balls. Place on a lightly greased rack in a roasting pan.

• Bake at 350° for 25 minutes or until no longer pink; add to sauce in skillet, stirring gently to coat. Stir in hot sauce just before serving. Garnish, if desired. Yield: 10 to 12 servings.

*Robin Jean Davis and Scott Segal*
Charleston, West Virginia

*cook's secret...* Cooked or uncooked meatballs may be frozen up to 1 month. Reheat frozen cooked meatballs in a 350° oven 10 to 12 minutes or until thoroughly heated. Bake frozen uncooked meatballs in a 350° oven 25 to 30 minutes. Freeze sauce separately; thaw sauce in refrigerator, and cook until thoroughly heated.

Glogg, a hot spiced wine popular in Sweden, is steeped with mixed dried fruit and almonds for three days before serving. The result is fabulous! Louise Mayer serves her version of this traditional recipe to take the chill off winter nights.

*regional favorite*

# Glogg

| | |
|---|---|
| 4 cups sweet red wine | ⅓ cup raisins |
| 2 cups dry red wine | 1 tablespoon whole cloves |
| ½ cup sugar | 2 (3-inch) cinnamon sticks |
| ¾ pound mixed dried fruit | 1 cup apricot brandy |
| ¾ cup chopped almonds | |

- Stir together first 3 ingredients in Dutch oven.
- Place mixed dried fruit, almonds, and next 3 ingredients on a 6-inch square of cheesecloth; tie with string. Add to Dutch oven.
- Bring spiced wine mixture to a boil over medium heat; reduce heat, and simmer 15 minutes. Cover mixture, and let stand 3 days.
- Remove and discard spice bag; stir in apricot brandy. Cook over medium heat until thoroughly heated. (Do not boil.) Yield: 6 cups.

**NOTE:** *For testing purposes only, we used Burgundy for sweet red wine and Cabernet for dry red wine.*

*Louise Mayer*
*Richmond, Virginia*

*cook's secret*... We recommend not boiling Glogg once you add the brandy because boiling will dissipate most of the alcohol.

# Coffee Nog

3 (½-gallon) containers vanilla ice cream, softened

3 cups brandy

2 cups coffee liqueur

½ teaspoon ground nutmeg

½ teaspoon ground cinnamon

• Place ice cream in a large punch bowl, stirring until smooth. Add brandy and coffee liqueur, stirring until smooth; sprinkle with nutmeg and cinnamon. Yield: 1½ gallons.

**NOTE:** *For testing purposes only, we used Kahlúa for coffee liqueur.*

*Peggy Monroe*
Birmingham, Alabama

*cook's secret...* This cold, potent beverage is so rich it can be served as a dessert.

# Low-Fat Cappuccino Cooler

1½ cups brewed coffee, chilled

1½ cups low-fat chocolate ice cream

¼ cup chocolate syrup

Reduced-fat frozen whipped topping, thawed (optional)

• Process first 3 ingredients in a blender until smooth. Serve immediately over crushed ice. Top with whipped topping, if desired. Yield: 3 cups.

*Dottie B. Miller*
Jonesborough, Tennessee

*cook's secret...* Use coffee- or mocha-flavored ice cream in place of whipped topping for a bigger coffee kick.

# Chocolate Iced Coffee

| | |
|---|---|
| 3½ cups water | ¾ teaspoon ground cinnamon |
| 1 cup ground coffee | 2 cups half-and-half |
| 2 tablespoons sugar | ⅓ cup chocolate syrup |

• Bring 3½ cups water and coffee to a boil in a saucepan; remove from heat, and let stand 10 minutes. Pour mixture through a fine wire-mesh strainer into a bowl, discarding coffee grounds. Stir 2 tablespoons sugar and ¾ teaspoon cinnamon into coffee until sugar dissolves; let cool. Stir in half-and-half and syrup; chill 2 hours. Serve over ice. Yield: 2 quarts.

*Sandi Pichon*
Slidell, Louisiana

*cook's secret...* To keep this beverage from diluting, freeze cubes of half-and-half and leftover coffee to use in place of ice.

# The Peabody Peppermint Patti

*This grown-up version of hot chocolate is a specialty of the house at The Peabody in Memphis.*

| | |
|---|---|
| 4 (1-ounce) envelopes hot chocolate mix | ¼ cup peppermint schnapps |
| 4 cups boiling water | Sweetened whipped cream (optional) |

• Empty all envelopes of hot chocolate mix into a large pitcher. Add 4 cups boiling water to pitcher, stirring until hot chocolate mix dissolves. Stir in peppermint schnapps.
• Pour mixture into 4 mugs, and top each serving with sweetened whipped cream, if desired. Yield: 4½ cups.

*The Peabody*
Memphis, Tennessee

*cook's secret...* Peppermint sticks make clever stirrers for this hot-and-spicy sipper.

We received this recipe from Jannet Ewing, a missionary in Honduras. Because her kitchen utensils are limited, Jannet sent the following instructions: "Put the frozen contents in a baggie, wrap in a dishcloth, and smash with a clean kitchen river rock." While we chose to use an electric mixer for blending the drink, we think Jannet would approve of the results.

## Café Latte Slush

½ to ¾ cup sugar
2 cups strong brewed coffee or espresso

2 cups milk or half-and-half, divided*
Garnish: chocolate syrup

• Combine sugar and hot coffee in a large mixing bowl, stirring until sugar dissolves; stir in 1 cup milk. Cover and freeze 8 hours.
• Let thaw slightly in refrigerator; add remaining 1 cup milk. Beat at medium speed with an electric mixer until smooth. Garnish, if desired. Serve immediately. Yield: 7 cups.
*Fat-free milk or fat-free half-and-half may be substituted for regular milk or half-and-half.

*Jannet Ewing*
La Ceiba, Honduras

*cook's secret*... Anytime you have leftover coffee, freeze it to whip up this recipe at a moment's notice.

My Aunt Kat has a secret family recipe that I'm divulging now—please don't tell her. The family has served it proudly every Christmas since she was a little girl. Her mother, my grandmother Lillie, made it in generous amounts for everyone who would drop in during the holidays. As a younger woman, though, Grandmother Lillie believed that eggnog was a sinful potion.

Aunt Kat loves to tell the story of the first Christmas Grandmother Lillie spent with her husband's family. Lillie came from a long line of Baptist ministers who preached against the evils of alcohol. She was shocked when her father-in-law pulled a jug of bourbon from the mahogany sideboard in the dining room. When he poured the whiskey into the cut-glass punch bowl of eggnog, Lillie fainted with fear. When she came to, she was lovingly presented a small cup of the very same eggnog. Aunt Kat laughs and says, "After that, Mother never did serve eggnog without the bourbon."

Our Foods staff liked this wonderfully rich cup of Christmas cheer so much that we gave it our highest rating. I hope you will give Aunt Kat's eggnog a try—she would be so proud.

*Jan Moon*
Former Test Kitchens Professional

# Aunt Kat's Creamy Eggnog

| | |
|---|---|
| 1 quart milk | ¾ cup to 1½ cups bourbon* |
| 12 eggs | 1 tablespoon vanilla extract |
| ¼ teaspoon salt | ½ teaspoon ground nutmeg, divided |
| 1½ cups sugar | 1 quart whipping cream |

• Heat milk in a large saucepan over medium heat. (Do not boil.)

• Beat eggs and salt at medium speed with an electric mixer until thick and pale; gradually add sugar, beating well. Gradually stir about one-fourth of hot milk into egg mixture; add to remaining hot milk, stirring constantly.

• Cook over medium-low heat, stirring constantly, 25 to 30 minutes or until milk mixture thickens and reaches 160°.

• Stir in bourbon, vanilla, and ¼ teaspoon nutmeg. Remove from heat, and cool. Cover and chill up to 2 days.

• Beat whipping cream at medium speed with an electric mixer until soft peaks form. Fold whipped cream into milk mixture. Sprinkle with remaining ¼ teaspoon nutmeg before serving. Yield: 3 quarts.

*1½ to 2 cups milk may be substituted for bourbon.

*cook's secret...* Remember to keep eggnog cool when it's in a punch bowl; even after cooking, eggs and milk remain perishable.

*Lyda Jones*
Test Kitchens Director

*kid-friendly*

# Creamy Nog Punch

1 gallon vanilla ice cream
½ gallon commercially made eggnog
1 teaspoon ground nutmeg

½ teaspoon ground cinnamon
1 (16-ounce) container frozen whipped
   topping, thawed

• Scoop ice cream into a punch bowl. Pour eggnog over ice cream, and sprinkle with nutmeg and cinnamon; stir in whipped topping. Serve immediately. Stir, as needed. Yield: 1½ gallons.

*Paula Kay Wilson*
*Texarkana, Texas*

*cook's secret...* Make ice cubes from eggnog to help keep this punch icy cold as the ice cream melts. Use plain eggnog rather than the spiked variety for the cubes, as alcohol would prevent a solid freeze.

*kid-friendly*

# Raspberry Sorbet Punch

1 (64-ounce) bottle cranberry-raspberry
   juice drink
1 (2-liter) bottle raspberry ginger ale

1 (12-ounce) can frozen pink lemonade
   concentrate, thawed and undiluted
1 quart raspberry sorbet

• Combine first 3 ingredients in a large container, stirring well. Cover and chill 2 hours. Pour chilled mixture into a large punch bowl. Scoop sorbet into punch. Stir gently. Yield: 6½ quarts.

*cook's secret...* Freezing fruit juices in an ice ring for the punch keeps the ice ring from diluting the punch as it melts.

The tradition of serving punch at festive occasions is alive and well in the South. Boots Abercrombie offers a recipe that's perfect for any celebration. Her secret to a stunning presentation? She adds an exquisite ice ring of assorted fruits to the punch and circles the bowl with flowers.

# Champagne Punch

| | | | |
|---|---|---|---|
| 2 | cups cranberry juice cocktail | 1 | (375-milliliter) bottle Sauterne or dessert wine* |
| 1 | (12-ounce) can frozen orange juice concentrate, thawed | 2 | (750-milliliter) bottles Champagne, chilled |
| 1 | cup lemon juice | | Ice Ring |
| 1 | cup sugar | | |

- Combine first 4 ingredients, stirring well; chill at least 8 hours.
- Pour juice mixture into a chilled punch bowl. Gently stir in Sauterne and Champagne just before serving. Float Ice Ring, fruit side up, in punch. Yield: 20 servings.

*(375 ml) Bonny Doon Muscat Vin de Glacière or (375 ml) Quady Electra may be substituted.*

## Ice Ring:

| | | | |
|---|---|---|---|
| 1½ | to 2 cups orange juice | 10 | to 12 orange slices, seeded |
| ½ | cup cranberry juice | 8 | to 10 whole strawberries |
| 6 | to 8 seedless red grape clusters | | Fresh mint sprigs |

- Combine juices. Line bottom of 6-cup ring mold with grape clusters and half of orange slices, using grapes to stand orange slices vertically. Pour a thin layer of juices into mold; freeze until firm, about 2 hours. Arrange remaining orange slices, strawberries, and mint sprigs around grapes. Pour remaining juices almost to top of mold. Freeze 8 hours.
- Unmold by dipping bottom half of mold in several inches of warm water 5 to 10 seconds to loosen, repeating as necessary to release ring. (Do not immerse entire mold in water.) Invert ring onto plate.

*Boots Abercrombie*
*Hoover, Alabama*

*cook's secret...* To speed up making the ice ring, try this trick: Combine juices. Fill bottom of 6-cup ring mold with 2 cups crushed ice. Lay grape clusters over ice. Arrange orange slices, strawberries, and fresh mint sprigs around grapes. Pour juices around fruit almost to top of mold. Freeze 8 hours or until firm.

New Orleans's famed Commander's Palace, consistently named one of the best restaurants in the world, is an ideal spot for a late morning brunch. This recipe for Bloody Marys is adapted from *Commander's Kitchen* by Ti Adelaide Martin and Jamie Shannon.

## Bloody Marys

| | |
|---|---|
| 4 cups vegetable or tomato juice | 8 teaspoons Worcestershire sauce |
| 1½ cups chilled vodka | 14 drops hot sauce |
| 8 teaspoons prepared horseradish | Garnishes: pickled okra, cherry peppers |

• Whisk together first 5 ingredients in a large pitcher until well blended. Place ice cubes in 8 old-fashioned glasses, filling two-thirds full. Pour mixture evenly into glasses. Garnish, if desired. Yield: 8 servings.

**NOTE:** *For testing purposes only, we used Crystal Hot Sauce.*

*Ti Adelaide Martin and Jamie Shannon*
New Orleans, Louisiana
Adapted from *Commander's Kitchen* (Broadway Books)

*cook's secret*... Bartenders at Commander's Palace skewer the garnish on a stick of sugarcane, but a wooden skewer works, too.

# Watermelon Daiquiri

4 cups peeled, seeded, and cubed watermelon

1 (6-ounce) can frozen limeade concentrate
½ cup light rum

- Place watermelon cubes in a zip-top plastic bag; seal bag, and freeze cubes 8 hours.
- Process half each of watermelon, limeade, and rum in a blender until smooth, stopping to scrape down sides. Repeat procedure with remaining watermelon, limeade, and rum. Serve immediately. Yield: 5 cups.

*Baxter Cooper*
Demopolis, Alabama

# Strawberry Slush

7 cups water
2 cups sugar
4 regular-size tea bags
1 (12-ounce) can frozen lemonade concentrate, undiluted

2 (10-ounce) packages frozen sliced strawberries, thawed
2 cups tequila
1 (2-liter) bottle lemon-lime soft drink, chilled (optional)

- Bring 7 cups water and sugar to a boil in a large saucepan, stirring constantly. Pour over tea bags, and steep until cool.
- Remove tea bags from liquid, squeezing gently.
- Stir together tea, lemonade concentrate, strawberries, and tequila in a large bowl; cover and freeze 8 hours, stirring occasionally. Serve straight from freezer (mixture will not freeze firm), or stir in lemon-lime soft drink, if desired. Yield: 3 quarts.

*Andrea S. Lerbs*
League City, Texas

*cook's secret...* Cut fruit garnishes are a natural with these drinks. When adding a fruit garnish to a beverage, select a fruit already in the drink or one that will complement it. Cut the fruit into thin slices. Then just slice the fruit from 1 edge of the slice to the center, and slip it over the rim of the glass. Or you can skewer fruit onto wooden picks to make edible stirrers that your guests can enjoy.

The mojito was a favorite drink of Ernest Hemingway. It's something of a cross between a mint julep and a limeade, excepting all that rum, of course. Light, cool, and refreshing, a mojito is the perfect summertime drink.

Nearly every swank hotel and restaurant in Florida touts a mojito on their list of specialty cocktails. Ordering one elsewhere in the South may be dicey, but then, such is the penalty of being hip to new fads. Better still, impress your friends by making your own at home.

After sampling almost every mojito in South Florida, I found my favorite at The Ritz-Carlton, Key Biscayne. The hotel has kindly shared its one-serving recipe with us.

*Morgan Murphy*
Travel Editor

*editor's choice*

## A Ritzy Mojito

| | |
|---|---|
| 10 mint leaves | Ice |
| 2 tablespoons sugar | Splash of club soda |
| Juice from ½ lime | Garnish: mint sprig |
| 1½ ounces rum | |

- Mix mint leaves, sugar, and lime juice in a small mortar bowl; crush mint.
- Add rum, and stir. Pour into a glass with ice.
- Add a splash of club soda, and garnish with a mint sprig, if desired.

*The Ritz-Carlton*
Key Biscayne, Florida

*cook's secret...* Crushing the mint releases maximum flavor from the potent herb.

$C$hef Marvin Woods of Hollywood Prime in Hollywood, Florida, suggests letting guests man the blender for this festive beverage.

*chef recipe*

## Citrus Batida

2  cups orange juice
2  cups Ruby Red grapefruit juice
1  cup rum

⅔  cup fresh lemon juice
¾  cup superfine sugar

• Process all ingredients in a blender until frothy. Serve over ice. Yield: 5 cups.

*Chef Marvin Woods*
Hollywood, Florida

*cook's secret*... When having a party, premeasure ingredients into one-batch containers, and chill. When you're ready for another round, all you have to do is pour a batch into the blender, and push the button.

## Swamp Breeze

1  (6-ounce) can frozen limeade juice
     concentrate
1  cup spiced rum
¾  cup dark rum

⅓  cup orange liqueur
Crushed ice
2  to 3 fresh mint sprigs
Garnish: fresh mint sprigs

• Process first 4 ingredients in a blender until smooth. Add ice to 5-cup level; process until smooth. Add mint, and process until smooth. Garnish, if desired. Yield: 5 cups.

*Lynn and George O'Connor*
Little Rock, Arkansas

*cook's secret*... Crushed ice blends quicker and easier into blender beverages than ice cubes.

The Kentucky Derby is celebrated on the first Saturday in May, with visitors from around the world gathering at the racetrack and all over Louisville. As "My Old Kentucky Home" plays before the race, julep cups are raised high. To Kentuckians, a mint julep is more than a drink; it's a cupful of tradition.

The classic version is served in silver julep cups. The ingredients remain constant, but opinions about the proper way to make them are as varied as the colors of jockeys' silks. Many crush the mint and sugar together (referred to as muddling), while others insist that the mint should be smelled and not tasted.

Always chill julep cups or glass tumblers before filling with crushed ice to prevent the ice from melting too quickly. Julian P. Van Winkle III, president of Old Rip Van Winkle Distillery in Frankfort, Kentucky, prefers his ice in small chunks. "Wrap ice cubes in a thick towel or cloth bag, and hammer away until you have small chunks," says Julian.

Before tasting, insert a cocktail straw or coffee stirrer near the mint sprig. Inhale a deep breath, and slowly sip until someone says, "May I fix you another mint julep?"

*Cynthia Ann Briscoe*
Associate Foods Editor

# Classic Mint Julep

| | |
|---|---|
| 3 fresh mint leaves | 1 (4-inch) cocktail straw or coffee stirrer |
| 1 tablespoon Mint Simple Syrup | 1 fresh mint sprig |
| Crushed ice | Powdered sugar (optional) |
| 1½ to 2 tablespoons (1 ounce) bourbon | |

• Place mint leaves and Mint Simple Syrup in a chilled julep cup. Gently press leaves against cup with back of spoon to release flavors. Pack cup tightly with crushed ice; pour bourbon over ice. Insert straw, place mint sprig directly next to straw, and serve immediately. Sprinkle with powdered sugar, if desired. Yield: 1 (8-ounce) julep.

## Mint Simple Syrup:

| | |
|---|---|
| 1 cup sugar | 10 to 12 fresh mint sprigs |
| 1 cup water | |

• Bring sugar and water to a boil in a medium saucepan. Boil, stirring often, 5 minutes or until sugar dissolves. Remove from heat; add mint, and let cool completely. Pour into a glass jar; cover and chill 24 hours. Remove and discard mint. Yield: 2 cups.

**NOTE:** *For testing purposes only, we used Woodford Reserve Distiller's Select Bourbon.*

*cook's secret*... This drink is best made individually "to taste," using only the freshest ingredients.

••• Leftover simple syrup keeps refrigerated about 1 week and perfectly sweetens iced tea.

Kyle Tabler of The Red Lounge in Louisville adds a martini twist to the standard mint julep, combining the expected Kentucky bourbon with unexpected vanilla vodka and crème de menthe.

# Mint Julep Martini

¼ cup bourbon

¼ cup orange liqueur

1 teaspoon vanilla vodka*

1 teaspoon clear crème de menthe

6 ice cubes

Garnishes: fresh mint sprig, orange rind curl

• Combine first 5 ingredients in a martini shaker. Cover with lid, and shake until thoroughly chilled. Remove lid, and strain into a chilled martini glass. Garnish, if desired. Serve immediately. Yield: 1 serving.

*½ teaspoon vanilla extract may be substituted.

**NOTE:** *For testing purposes only, we used Smirnoff Vanilla Twist for vanilla vodka and Grand Marnier for orange liqueur.*

*Kyle Tabler*
*Louisville, Kentucky*

*cook's secret*... This recipe makes 1 serving, but you can easily double or triple it. Make the desired number of servings, and store them in a pitcher in the refrigerator. No need to strain the drink over ice if it's already chilled.

# Tea Juleps

1 (0.24-ounce) package sugar-free iced
  tea mix

¼ cup peppermint schnapps
¼ cup bourbon

• Prepare tea according to package directions; stir in schnapps and bourbon. Cover and chill 2 hours. Serve over ice. Yield: 2 quarts

**NOTE:** *For testing purposes only, we used Crystal Light iced tea mix.*

*Maugie Pastor*
Aaah! T'Frere's House and Garçonniere
Lafayette, Louisiana

*cook's secret...* Avoid diluting drinks served with ice by freezing a carbonated beverage, tonic, or soda water into cubes instead of using regular ice cubes. Or you can freeze a portion of the recipe itself. This option makes colorful cubes.

# Garden Sangría

*Lucinda Hutson's unique take on the Latin wine cooler
sangría makes a refreshing treat.*

1 gallon dry white wine
2 cups brandy
1 cup orange liqueur
4 oranges, sliced
1 bunch fresh mint leaves

1 (1-liter) bottle club soda, chilled*
1 quart whole strawberries
2 lemons, thinly sliced
2 limes, thinly sliced
Garnishes: lemon and lime wedges

• Combine first 5 ingredients in a large container; cover and chill 8 hours.
• Add club soda and next 3 ingredients just before serving; serve sangría over ice, if desired. Garnish, if desired. Yield: 1½ gallons.

*Ginger ale may be substituted for club soda.*

*Lucinda Hutson*
Austin, Texas
Adapted from *The Herb Garden Cookbook:
The Complete Gardening and Gourmet Guide* (Lone Star Books)

*cook's secret...* If you aren't serving a crowd, halve this recipe. Sangría starts to lose its fizz once you add the club soda, so leftovers don't store well.

# breads

# Top 10 Best Kept Bread Secrets

**1.** For easy storage and measuring, empty a bag of flour into an airtight plastic storage container. To measure, just lightly spoon the flour into a dry-ingredient measuring cup, and level it off with the flat side of a knife, letting the excess fall back into the container.

**2.** To let yeast rise in a warm spot (about 85°), place an 8- or 9-inch square dish of hot tap water on the lower oven rack. Place the bowl of yeast dough, covered with a clean kitchen towel, on the oven rack above it to rise until doubled. Close the oven door to keep the interior temperature close to 85°. Remember to remove the dough before preheating the oven!

**3.** Choose shiny pans to bake bread. They reflect heat best and produce baked goods with nicely browned and tender crusts.

**4.** Stir muffin batter just until the dry ingredients are moistened. Overstirring will cause muffins to peak and have tunnels and a coarse texture.

**5.** For easy cleanup, use paper baking cups to line muffin pans. Spray the insides of the paper cups with vegetable cooking spray, and you'll be able to easily peel the cups off the muffins.

**6.** Bake on the center rack of the oven unless the recipe directs otherwise. Baking on the lowest or highest rack could mean burned bread bottoms or tops.

**7.** A rule of thumb is to bake quick breads until a wooden pick inserted in the center comes out clean. The length of time varies depending on the size and type of bread.

**8.** Remove breads and rolls from the pans immediately, and cool on wire racks, unless otherwise directed. If breads or rolls are left in the pan, steam condensation can cause soggy crusts.

**9.** It's easier to slice bread with a serrated-edge knife than a straight edge. Use a gentle sawing motion.

**10.** Bread will get stale faster in the refrigerator than at room temperature. If you want to keep bread for up to 3 days, cover it with airtight wrap, and store it at room temperature. For storage up to 1 month, freeze it in an airtight wrap.

My favorite childhood memory in the kitchen involves a rolling pin. A very special lady cooked for my family, and she taught me everything! My favorite part of helping her in the afternoons was rolling out the biscuits for supper and the dumplings for chicken and dumplings. I can still picture her with flour on her hands instructing me with the rolling pin, "Don't push too hard!" Being the youngest child and the only girl, I was, of course, spoiled rotten, especially by her. She made me my own "big biscuit" when we had biscuits (which was whenever we didn't have cornbread). I always knew she'd thought of me each time I devoured one of my special biscuits.

*Lyda Jones*
Test Kitchens Director

## Baking Powder Biscuits

| | | | |
|---|---|---|---|
| 2 | cups all-purpose flour | ⅓ | cup shortening |
| 1 | tablespoon baking powder | ¾ | cup milk |
| ½ | teaspoon salt | | |

• Combine first 3 ingredients; cut in shortening with a pastry blender or fork until mixture is crumbly. Add milk, stirring just until dry ingredients are moistened.
• Turn dough out onto a floured surface, and knead lightly 3 or 4 times.
• Roll dough to ½-inch thickness; cut with a 2½-inch round cutter. Place on a lightly greased baking sheet. Bake at 425° for 15 minutes or until golden. Yield: 1 dozen.

*cook's secret*... Dip your biscuit cutter into flour; this keeps the dough from sticking.

# Quick Whipping Cream Biscuits

*These biscuits can be on the table in 25 minutes.*

½   cup butter or margarine

2   cups self-rising flour

¾   to 1 cup whipping cream

¼   cup butter or margarine, melted

• Cut ½ cup butter into flour with a pastry blender or fork until crumbly. Add whipping cream, stirring just until dry ingredients are moistened.

• Turn dough out onto a lightly floured surface, and knead lightly 3 or 4 times.

• Roll or pat dough to ¾-inch thickness. Cut with a 2-inch round cutter; place biscuits on a lightly greased baking sheet.

• Bake at 400° for 13 to 15 minutes. Brush hot biscuits with ¼ cup melted butter. Yield: 1 dozen.

*cook's secret...* Our Foods staff preferred the whipping cream version, but if you like a slightly tangy biscuit, here's the secret: Substitute ¾ cup buttermilk mixed with 1 tablespoon sugar for the cream. Either way, they'll fly off the plate.

*Joy Zacharia*
Associate Foods Editor

### Secrets to Successful Biscuits

• Do not substitute all-purpose flour for self-rising in biscuit recipes because the biscuits won't rise correctly.

• Stir dough just until dry ingredients are moistened. Overstirring makes biscuits tough.

• If you're intimidated by rolling pins, simply pat the biscuit dough onto a floured surface to about ¾-inch thickness before cutting.

At the biennial Stars Over Mississippi concert, a fund-raiser for the Mary Kirkpatrick Haskell Scholarship Foundation, Amory's 7,000 residents roll out the red carpet for their special guests. Before it's over, film, television, and music stars attend everything from a catfish fry to an elegant dinner for more than eight hundred. What's more, everything is prepared by local volunteers.

One of the unusual aspects of the weekend is that many of the stars stay with local families. Some even become close friends. Such is the case with Amory resident Wanda Wright and Emmy- and Golden Globe–winning performer Debbie Allen. Over a heaping plate of Wanda's light-as-air Old Southern Biscuits, the two women formed a lasting bond.

## Old Southern Biscuits

| | |
|---|---|
| ¼ cup shortening | 1 cup buttermilk |
| 2 cups self-rising flour | Melted butter (optional) |

• Cut shortening into flour with a pastry blender or fork until crumbly. Add buttermilk, stirring just until dry ingredients are moistened.
• Pat dough to ½-inch thickness on a lightly floured surface; cut with a 2-inch round cutter. Place on a lightly greased baking sheet.
• Bake at 425° for 14 minutes or until golden. Brush hot biscuits with melted butter, if desired. Yield: 1 dozen.

*Wanda D. Wright*
Amory, Mississippi

*cook's secret...* If you like biscuits with crusty sides, place them 1-inch apart on a shiny baking sheet. For soft sides, arrange them close together in a shallow baking dish or pan.

Charlotte Bryant, a frequent recipe contributor to *Southern Living*, works as a caregiver. "I get some of my best recipes from my patients," she says.

# Cheesy Onion Biscuits

| | | | |
|---|---|---|---|
| 2 | cups all-purpose flour | ⅓ | cup butter or margarine |
| 3 | tablespoons instant nonfat dry milk powder | ½ | cup grated Parmesan cheese |
| | | 2 | tablespoons finely chopped green onions |
| 4 | teaspoons baking powder | ¾ | cup water |
| ¾ | teaspoon salt | | |

- Combine first 4 ingredients in a large bowl; cut in butter with a pastry blender or fork until mixture is crumbly.
- Stir in Parmesan cheese and green onions. Add ¾ cup water, stirring mixture with a fork just until dry ingredients are moistened.
- Turn dough out onto a lightly floured surface, and knead lightly 5 or 6 times.
- Roll dough to ½-inch thickness; cut with a 3-inch round cutter. Place on a lightly greased baking sheet.
- Bake at 400° for 15 minutes or until lightly browned. Yield: 8 biscuits.

*Charlotte Bryant*
Greensburg, Kentucky

*cook's secret...* Keep bread warm at the table by placing aluminum foil between the bread basket and basket liner.

Florida native Caroline Stuart comes from a long line of cooks. After moving to New York, she became friends with the late James Beard, considered by many to be the father of American cooking. "He knew I was from the South because he could hear the 'grits' in my voice," remembers Caroline. "I began developing recipes for his cookbooks and became his assistant full-time." Although Caroline and her husband reside north of the Mason-Dixon line, she continues to embrace all things Southern. "I've raised my family on grits and greens, biscuits and gravy, fried chicken and barbecue," she says. Caroline's tender Sweet Potato Biscuits are sublime covered with butter.

## Sweet Potato Biscuits

1  (¼-ounce) envelope active dry yeast
¼  cup warm water (100° to 110°)
1  (15-ounce) can sweet potatoes in syrup, drained and mashed
½  cup butter or margarine, softened

½  cup sugar
1  teaspoon salt
2½  cups all-purpose flour
1  teaspoon baking powder
Melted butter

• Combine yeast and ¼ cup warm water in a glass measuring cup; let stand 5 minutes.
• Stir together sweet potatoes and butter, blending well. Stir in sugar and salt; add yeast mixture, stirring until smooth. Combine flour and baking powder; gradually stir into potato mixture until well blended. Lightly knead until dough holds together. Shape dough into a ball; place in a buttered mixing bowl. Brush top with melted butter. Cover and let rise in a warm place (85°), free from drafts, 2½ hours or until doubled in bulk.
• Punch down dough, and turn out onto a floured surface. Roll dough to ½-inch thickness; cut with a 2-inch round cutter. Place on greased baking sheets.
• Cover and let rise in a warm place, free from drafts, 2 hours or until doubled in bulk.
• Bake at 400° for 12 minutes or until golden. Yield: 34 biscuits.

*Caroline Stuart*
New York, New York

*cook's secret*... The 4½-hour total rising time is correct. Sweet potatoes add density to the dough, and you'll need that extra time for the biscuits to rise.

These luscious scones, which take just 25 minutes to prepare, received our Test Kitchens' top rating, ranking them among the best scones we've ever tried.

# Classic Cream Scones

| | | | |
|---|---|---|---|
| 2 | cups all-purpose flour | 1 | large egg |
| 2 | teaspoons baking powder | 1½ | teaspoons vanilla extract |
| ⅛ | teaspoon salt | 1 | egg white |
| ¼ | cup sugar | 1 | teaspoon water |
| ⅓ | cup butter or margarine, cubed | | Sugar |
| ½ | cup whipping cream | | |

• Combine first 4 ingredients. Cut in butter with a pastry blender or fork until mixture is crumbly.

• Whisk together cream, egg, and vanilla; add to flour mixture, stirring just until dry ingredients are moistened.

• Turn dough out onto a lightly floured surface.

• Pat dough to ½-inch thickness; cut with a 2½-inch round cutter. Place on lightly greased baking sheets.

• Whisk together egg white and 1 teaspoon water; brush mixture over tops of scones. Sprinkle scones with additional sugar.

• Bake at 425° for 13 to 15 minutes or until lightly browned. Yield: 1 dozen.

*cook's secret...* Keep a light hand when working with scone dough. Overworking the dough makes scones tough.

When you live at the lake, every day seems like a vacation. For Rosalie and Leslie "Nick" Nicholson, home is the perfect place to enjoy time with their kids and grandkids. Before the fun begins, they fuel the hungry crew with their favorite Peach Streusel Muffins.

# Peach Streusel Muffins

| | | | |
|---|---|---|---|
| ¼ | cup butter or margarine, softened | 1 | teaspoon vanilla extract |
| ⅓ | cup sugar | 1½ | cups chopped fresh or frozen peeled |
| 1 | large egg | | peaches |
| 2⅓ | cups all-purpose flour | ¼ | cup sugar |
| 1 | tablespoon baking powder | 3 | tablespoons all-purpose flour |
| ½ | teaspoon salt | ¼ | teaspoon ground cinnamon |
| ¾ | cup milk | 2½ | tablespoons chilled butter or margarine |

• Beat ¼ cup butter at medium speed with an electric mixer until creamy; gradually add ⅓ cup sugar, beating until light and fluffy. Add egg, beating mixture until blended.

• Combine 2⅓ cups flour, baking powder, and salt. Add flour mixture to butter mixture alternately with milk, stirring well after each addition. Stir in vanilla, and fold in chopped peaches.

• Spoon muffin batter into a greased or paper-lined muffin pan, filling two-thirds full.

• Combine ¼ cup sugar, 3 tablespoons flour, and cinnamon; cut in 2½ tablespoons butter with a pastry blender or fork until mixture resembles crumbs. Sprinkle evenly over muffin batter.

• Bake at 375° for 20 minutes or until golden. Remove from pan, and cool on a wire rack. Yield: 1 dozen.

*Rosalie and Leslie "Nick" Nicholson*
Jasper, Alabama

*cook's secret*... Frozen peaches allow you to make these muffins year-round. If you use frozen peaches, thaw them and drain any liquid before chopping.

Teresa Stokes is a busy mom who homeschools her three boys and chauffeurs them to soccer, basketball, art, and Boy Scouts. Yet she always manages to serve a great meal to her family. Her Cheddar-Nut Bread is ready to eat in just 25 minutes.

## Cheddar-Nut Bread

| | | | |
|---|---|---|---|
| 3¾ | cups all-purpose baking mix | 1 | large egg |
| 1½ | cups (6 ounces) shredded Cheddar cheese | 1 | (12-ounce) can evaporated milk |
| | | ½ | cup chopped pecans, toasted |

• Combine baking mix and cheese in a large bowl; make a well in center of mixture. Stir together egg and milk; add to dry ingredients, stirring just until moistened. Stir in toasted pecans, and spoon into greased muffin pans, filling two-thirds full.
• Bake at 375° for 12 to 15 minutes or until lightly browned. Yield: 21 muffins.

*Teresa Stokes*
Birmingham, Alabama

*cook's secret...* Use sharp Cheddar for the best flavor in cheese breads. Full-fat cheese melts better than lower fat versions.

Old-fashioned "pone bread," or hot-water bread, is a Southern tradition, but since it usually has to be fried in batches, the cook stays busy at the stove. David Newell, who grew up along the Natchez Trace Parkway in Mississippi, shares his secret for a method that has 12 patties ready and piping hot all at the same time. He drops the cornmeal batter onto a jellyroll pan and pops it into the oven.

David suggests making large patties for adults and smaller ones for children. "You always need to have one of these in hand when you sit down to a bowl of greens or butterbeans," says David.

Here, we share the traditional fried version, the baked version, and flavor variations.

## Hot-Water Cornbread

| | | | |
|---|---|---|---|
| 2 | cups white cornmeal | 1 | tablespoon vegetable oil |
| ¼ | teaspoon baking powder | 1 | to 2 cups boiling water |
| 1¼ | teaspoons salt | | Vegetable oil |
| 1 | teaspoon sugar | | Softened butter |
| ¼ | cup half-and-half | | |

• Combine first 4 ingredients in a bowl; stir in half-and-half and 1 tablespoon oil. Gradually add boiling water, stirring until batter is the consistency of grits.
• Pour oil to a depth of ½ inch into a large cast-iron skillet; place over medium-high heat. Scoop batter into a ¼-cup measure; drop into hot oil, and fry in batches 3 minutes on each side or until golden. Drain on paper towels. Serve with softened butter. Yield: 1 dozen.
**NOTE:** *The amount of boiling water needed varies depending on the type of cornmeal used. Stone-ground (coarsely ground) cornmeal requires more liquid.*

**Baked Hot-Water Cornbread:** Omit skillet procedure. Pour ⅓ cup vegetable oil into a 15- x 10-inch jellyroll pan, spreading to edges. Drop batter as directed onto pan. Bake at 475° for 12 to 15 minutes. Turn and bake 5 more minutes or until golden brown.

**Country Ham Hot-Water Cornbread:** After adding boiling water, stir in 1 to 2 cups finely chopped cooked country ham.

**Bacon-Cheddar Hot-Water Cornbread:** After adding boiling water, stir in 8 slices cooked and crumbled bacon, 1 cup shredded sharp Cheddar cheese, and 4 minced green onions.

**Southwestern Hot-Water Cornbread:** After adding boiling water, stir in 1 jalapeño pepper, seeded and minced; 1 cup shredded Mexican cheese blend; 1 cup frozen whole kernel corn, thawed; and ¼ cup minced fresh cilantro.

*David Newell*
Trussville, Alabama

*cook's secret...* David says his mom knew the trick for baking rather than frying Hot-Water Cornbread. "You don't want thin cornmeal batter; the batter should hold its shape when dropped onto the baking sheet," he confirms.

## Ironclad Rules

The most treasured pieces of cast-iron cookware are those seasoned windfalls we're fortunate enough to inherit from a much-loved relative or friend. With proper care, they will last for years longer. Even that rare flea market find, splattered with rust, can be scoured with a steel-wool soap pad and seasoned again.

If you've never purchased a new piece of cast-iron cookware, you might be surprised by its gray color. During the seasoning process, oil is absorbed into the pores of the iron, creating a slick, black surface that only improves with age.

- To season new cast iron, scrub with steel-wool soap pads; then wash with dish soap and hot water. Dry thoroughly. Spread a layer of vegetable shortening on the inside, including the underside of the lid. Bake at 250° for 15 minutes. Remove from oven, and wipe out shortening with a paper towel. Bake for 2 more hours. Remove from oven, and cool to room temperature. Repeat 2 or 3 times.
- Once your cast iron is seasoned, never use soap to clean it and never put it in a dishwasher.
- Clean with a plastic scrubber or stiff brush under hot running water. Dry immediately, and rub with a thin coating of vegetable oil.
- If your skillet loses its seasoning, you can repeat the seasoning procedure—or just fry something in it.

*Mary Allen Perry*
Associate Foods Editor

According to Brenda Cason-Brown, the name for this recipe comes from the old levee camps in Greenville, Mississippi, where the cakes were a popular dish with the workers.

# Levee Camp Griddle Cakes

*Serve these as appetizers at an evening meal along with slices of country ham or pork sausage.*

| | |
|---|---|
| 1 cup white cornmeal | 1 cup buttermilk |
| 1 cup all-purpose flour | ½ cup sour cream |
| 1 teaspoon baking soda | 1 large egg, lightly beaten |
| ½ teaspoon salt | Honey or maple syrup |
| ½ teaspoon baking powder | |

• Combine cornmeal and next 4 ingredients in a large bowl.
• Combine buttermilk, sour cream, and egg; add to dry ingredients, stirring just until moistened.
• Pour about 3 tablespoons batter for each cake onto a hot, lightly greased griddle. Cook pancakes 3 minutes or until tops are covered with bubbles and edges look cooked; turn and cook 2 minutes. (Cakes should be golden brown.) Serve with honey or maple syrup. Yield: 12 pancakes.

*Brenda Cason-Brown*
Shreveport, Louisiana

*cook's secret*... Equal amounts of cornmeal and flour are the key to a perfect texture in these corncakes. The meal lends the familiar crunch while the flour keeps them light and tender.

Clay Nordan, Managing Editor of *Southern Living,* shares his late uncle Pat Wyatt's secret for these light-as-a-feather gems. "Uncle Pat had a real gift for cooking for crowds, so he would multiply this recipe for what my mom called a 'log rolling,' where he would make more than a hundred of these at a time," says Clay.

## Uncle Pat's Hush Puppies

*Pile a platter high with these crispy, melt-in-your-mouth morsels, and watch them disappear.*

| | | | |
|---|---|---|---|
| 1½ | cups cornmeal | 1 | tablespoon sugar |
| ½ | cup all-purpose flour | ½ | medium onion, chopped |
| 1 | tablespoon baking powder | 1 | cup buttermilk |
| ⅛ | teaspoon baking soda | 1 | large egg |
| 1 | teaspoon salt | | Vegetable oil |

- Combine first 7 ingredients in a bowl; make a well in center of mixture.
- Whisk together buttermilk and egg; add to dry ingredients, stirring just until moistened.
- Pour oil to a depth of 3 inches into a Dutch oven; heat to 350°.
- Drop batter by rounded teaspoonfuls into hot oil. Fry in batches 1 to 2 minutes on each side or until golden. Drain on paper towels; serve immediately. Yield: 3 dozen.

*cook's secret...* The oil for frying hush puppies should be about 3 inches deep and heated until very hot, about 350° to 375°. Fry only a few at a time so that the oil doesn't cool down; you want them to be crisp and golden.

On most weekends from Memorial Day to Labor Day, you'll find Lynn and George O'Connor out on Lake Ouachita in their houseboat. A no-fuss menu allows them time to enjoy company and to be the perfect hosts. This easy bread recipe goes well with almost any casual menu.

## Mustard Bread

½ cup butter or margarine, softened
3 tablespoons horseradish mustard
4 green onions, chopped
1 to 2 tablespoons poppy seeds

1 (16-ounce) French or Italian bread loaf
6 bacon slices, cooked and crumbled
2 (6-ounce) packages Swiss cheese slices

- Stir together first 4 ingredients until well blended.
- Slice bread in half lengthwise; spread butter mixture evenly on cut side of bottom half. Sprinkle with bacon; top with cheese. Replace top bread half; wrap in aluminum foil.
- Bake at 350° for 30 to 35 minutes or until bread is thoroughly heated. Yield: 6 to 8 servings.

*Lynn and George O'Connor*
Little Rock, Arkansas

*cook's secret...* Wrapping this loaf tightly in aluminum foil lets you bake it long enough for the cheesy filling to melt nicely without overbrowning the crust. Let it bake unattended while you prepare the rest of the meal indoors or outside on the grill.

For twenty-seven years, Brother Boniface, a German-born monk, was the cook for Mepkin Abbey, a Trappist monastery near Charleston, South Carolina. He explains that his twenty-seven brothers performed physical labor and required hearty meals. "They needed to have good bread, not the stuff you buy from the store," explains Brother Boniface.

Try his spicy pumpkin bread for breakfast, alongside soup for lunch, or as an unexpected addition to your favorite entrée.

## Brother Boniface's Pumpkin Bread

| | |
|---|---|
| 4 cups all-purpose flour | ½ teaspoon ground cloves |
| 3 cups sugar | ¼ teaspoon ground ginger |
| 2 teaspoons baking soda | 4 large eggs |
| 1½ teaspoons salt | 1 cup vegetable oil |
| 1 teaspoon baking powder | 1 (15-ounce) can pumpkin |
| 1 teaspoon ground cinnamon | ⅔ cup water |
| 1 teaspoon ground nutmeg | 1 cup chopped pecans |
| ½ teaspoon ground allspice | |

• Beat first 14 ingredients at medium speed with an electric mixer just until dry ingredients are moistened. Fold in pecans. Spoon evenly into 2 greased and floured 9- x 5-inch loafpans.

• Bake at 350° for 1 hour or until a wooden pick inserted in center comes out clean.

• Cool in pans on wire racks 10 minutes; remove from pans, and cool completely on wire racks. Yield: 2 loaves.

*Brother Boniface*
From *Baking with Brother Boniface*
(Independent Publishers Group, 1997)

*cook's secret...* Using a mixer for most bread recipes yields a tough product, but a mixer is recommended for this one. This bread batter is much like a cake batter, and the higher sugar content is key to keeping the end product moist and tender.

In France they call French toast *pain perdu,* or "lost bread," because it's made from stale bread. This recipe comes from Commander's Palace restaurant in New Orleans.

*chef recipe*

# Pain Perdu

| | | | |
|---|---|---|---|
| 2 | (16-ounce) French bread loaves | 4 | teaspoons vanilla extract |
| 8 | large eggs | 1½ | cups Champagne |
| 4 | cups whipping cream | 2 | cups cane syrup |
| 1 | cup granulated sugar | 4 | cups raspberries and blueberries |
| ½ | to 1 tablespoon ground cinnamon | 4 | tablespoons cream cheese (optional) |
| 1½ | teaspoons ground nutmeg | | Garnish: powdered sugar |

• Cut bread into 24 (¾-inch-thick) diagonal slices.

• Whisk together eggs and next 5 ingredients until well blended.

• Place bread slices in a 13- x 9-inch baking dish; pour egg mixture evenly over slices. Let stand 30 minutes or until liquid is absorbed.

• Remove bread slices from egg mixture, letting excess drip off. Cook bread slices, in batches, in a lightly greased nonstick skillet or on a griddle over medium-high heat 2 minutes on each side or until golden.

• Place bread slices on baking sheets; keep warm in a 200° oven.

• Cook Champagne in a large saucepan over high heat until reduced by half. Gradually stir in syrup; cook over low heat until blended and warm.

• Arrange bread slices on serving plates; top with raspberries and blueberries and, if desired, cream cheese. Drizzle evenly with syrup mixture. Garnish, if desired. Yield: 8 to 12 servings.

*Chef Tory McPhail*
Commander's Palace
New Orleans, Louisiana

*cook's secret...* Whipping cream rather than the usual choice of milk makes this the richest, creamiest French toast you've ever tasted. Using French bread and allowing it only a quick soak instead of an overnight one lends more texture than usual.

There's something so delicious about waking up to French toast right out of the skillet. W. N. Cottrell II makes it even better by serving thick slices of French bread stuffed with a luscious mixture of orange marmalade, cream cheese, and—for that Southern touch—chopped pecans. Grill until golden, and let the goodness melt in your mouth.

## Stuffed French Toast

*Serve with your favorite syrup.*

½ (8-ounce) package cream cheese, softened

¼ cup chopped dates

¼ cup chopped pecans, toasted

4 teaspoons orange marmalade

2 French bread loaves, cut diagonally into 8 (1-inch-thick) slices

4 large eggs

1 cup milk

1 teaspoon ground cinnamon

3 tablespoons butter or margarine

2 tablespoons powdered sugar

- Stir together first 4 ingredients.
- Cut a horizontal pocket in top crust of each bread slice. Spoon about 2 teaspoons cream cheese mixture into each pocket.
- Whisk together eggs, milk, and cinnamon; dip stuffed bread slices into mixture, coating all sides.
- Melt butter in a large nonstick skillet over medium-high heat. Cook bread slices, in batches, 2 minutes on each side or until golden. Sprinkle with powdered sugar. Yield: 8 servings.

*W. N. Cottrell II*
New Orleans, Louisiana

*cook's secret*... Purchase unsliced bread so that you can cut slices thick enough to hold the cream cheese filling.

Robyn Arnold used to fight the mall crowds on Christmas Eve just to buy cinnamon rolls for the next morning—until she developed her own fabulous recipe. Now, she says, "My family loves waking up to the smell of home-baked cinnamon rolls with just the right amount of fuss and very little cleanup."

## Mama's Mini-Cinnis

*This recipe doubles easily for a crowd.*

| | |
|---|---|
| 2 (8-ounce) cans refrigerated crescent rolls | 1 teaspoon ground cinnamon |
| 6 tablespoons butter or margarine, softened | ⅔ cup powdered sugar |
| ⅓ cup firmly packed brown sugar | 1 tablespoon milk or half-and-half |
| ¼ cup chopped pecans | ¼ teaspoon almond or vanilla extract |
| 1 tablespoon granulated sugar | ⅛ teaspoon salt |

• Unroll crescent rolls, and separate each dough portion along center perforation to form 4 rectangles; press diagonal perforations to seal.
• Stir together butter and next 4 ingredients; spread evenly over 1 side of each rectangle. Roll up, jellyroll fashion, starting at long end. Gently cut each log into 6 (1-inch-thick) slices, using a serrated knife. Place rolls ¼ inch apart in 2 (8-inch) greased cakepans.
• Bake at 375° for 15 to 18 minutes or until golden. Cool 5 to 10 minutes.
• Stir together powdered sugar and remaining ingredients. Drizzle over warm rolls. Yield: 2 dozen.

*Robyn Arnold*
Houston, Texas

*cook's secret*... To make slicing easier, place unbaked rolls on a baking sheet, and freeze for 10 minutes to firm up the dough.

# Pecan Crescent Twists

| | |
|---|---|
| **2** (8-ounce) cans refrigerated crescent rolls | **1** teaspoon ground cinnamon |
| **6** tablespoons butter or margarine, melted and divided | **⅛** teaspoon ground nutmeg |
| **½** cup chopped pecans | **½** cup powdered sugar |
| **¼** cup granulated sugar | **2** tablespoons maple syrup or milk |

• Unroll crescent rolls, and separate each can into 4 rectangles, pressing perforations to seal. Brush evenly with 4 tablespoons melted butter.

• Stir together pecans and next 3 ingredients; sprinkle 1 tablespoon mixture on each rectangle, pressing in gently.

• Roll up, starting at a long side, and twist. Cut 6 shallow (½-inch-long) diagonal slits in each roll.

• Shape rolls into rings, pressing ends together; place on a lightly greased baking sheet. Brush rings with remaining 2 tablespoons butter. Bake at 375° for 12 minutes or until golden.

• Stir together powdered sugar and maple syrup until glaze is smooth; drizzle over warm twists. Yield: 8 servings.

*Nancy Matthews*
Grayson, Georgia

*cook's secret...* Work quickly to shape these twists, and use dough directly out of the refrigerator. The dough is easier to work with while cold.

Jennifer Dale asked us to transform her family's favorite dense, buttery sour cream breakfast treat into one loaded with flavor, not fat and calories.

# Sour Cream Coffee Cake

Vegetable cooking spray
1 cup coarsely chopped pecans, toasted
1 cup firmly packed light brown sugar
1 tablespoon ground cinnamon
3 cups all-purpose flour
1½ teaspoons baking soda
1½ teaspoons baking powder
¾ teaspoon salt
¼ cup butter, softened

1 (8-ounce) package fat-free cream cheese, softened
1½ cups granulated sugar
1 large egg
½ cup egg substitute
2 teaspoons vanilla extract
1 (16-ounce) container fat-free sour cream
1 cup powdered sugar
1 tablespoon orange juice

- Coat a 12-cup nonstick Bundt pan with cooking spray.
- Combine pecans, brown sugar, and cinnamon; set aside.
- Combine flour, baking soda, baking powder, and salt.
- Beat butter, cream cheese, and granulated sugar at medium speed with an electric mixer until creamy. Add egg, and beat until blended. Add egg substitute and vanilla, beating until blended. Add flour mixture to butter mixture alternately with sour cream, beginning and ending with flour mixture. Beat on high 1 minute.
- Pour one-third of batter into prepared pan. Sprinkle batter with half of pecan mixture. Repeat layers, ending with batter.
- Bake at 350° for 50 minutes or until a long wooden pick inserted in center comes out clean. Cool in pan on a wire rack 10 minutes. Run a knife around edges to loosen sides. Gently turn cake out onto wire rack. Cool 1 hour. Transfer to a serving plate.
- Whisk together powdered sugar and orange juice. Drizzle over cake. Yield: 16 servings.

*Jennifer Dale*
Clarksville, Tennessee

*cook's secret*... For this recipe, fat-free sour cream and cream cheese provide moisture and a creamy tang. A splash of orange juice adds fresh flavor and fragrance.

Louise Reynolds serves this coffee cake at the annual buffet her family hosts in Demopolis, Alabama, to celebrate the Christmas on the River festivities.

## Betsy's Almond Torte Coffee Cake

½   cup butter, melted
1½  cups sugar
2   large eggs
1½  cups all-purpose flour

⅛   teaspoon salt
2   teaspoons almond extract
¼   cup sliced almonds

• Beat butter and sugar at medium speed with an electric mixer until smooth. Add eggs, 1 at a time, beating until blended after each addition. Add flour, salt, and almond extract, beating at low speed until smooth.

• Line a 9-inch cast-iron skillet with aluminum foil, leaving excess hanging over sides. Pour batter into aluminum foil–lined skillet; sprinkle with almonds.

• Bake at 350° for 30 to 40 minutes or until lightly browned. Let cool 5 to 10 minutes. Lift foil sides, removing cake from skillet. Cool completely, and wrap tightly in foil to store. Yield: 10 servings.

*Louise Reynolds*
Demopolis, Alabama

*cook's secret*... If you use regular aluminum foil (instead of the new nonstick kind), don't peel it off when the cake is warm because it sticks. You may wrap the cake in the foil, put it in a zip-top freezer bag, and freeze up to 1 month.

# Homemade Butter Rolls

2 (¼-ounce) envelopes active dry yeast
1 cup sugar, divided
2 cups warm water (100° to 110°)
1 cup butter or margarine, melted

6 large eggs, lightly beaten
1½ teaspoons salt
8½ to 9½ cups all-purpose flour

• Stir together yeast, 2 tablespoons sugar, and 2 cups warm water in a 4-cup glass measuring cup; let stand 5 minutes.
• Stir together yeast mixture, remaining sugar, and butter in a large bowl; stir in eggs and salt. Gradually stir in enough flour to make a soft dough. Cover and chill 8 hours.
• Divide dough into fourths. Turn each portion out onto a lightly floured surface, and roll into a 12-inch circle. Cut each circle into 12 wedges. Roll up each wedge, starting at wide end; place on greased baking sheets. (Rolls may be frozen at this point.)
• Cover and let rise in a warm place (85°), free from drafts, 2 hours or until doubled in bulk.
• Bake at 400° for 10 minutes or until golden. Yield: 4 dozen.

*Joyce Metevia*
Baton Rouge, Louisiana

*cook's secret...* You can freeze these rolls before their final rise, and pull out from the freezer exactly how many you want to bake for dinner. Once shaped, place on a greased baking sheet and freeze until frozen. Once frozen, transfer to a zip-top freezer bag and freeze up to 1 month. About 2½ hours before you want to serve them, place frozen rolls on greased baking sheets. Cover and let rise in a warm place (85°), free from drafts, 2 hours or until doubled in bulk. Bake as directed.

# Sour Cream Dinner Rolls

1  (8-ounce) container sour cream
½  cup butter or margarine
½  cup sugar
1¼  teaspoons salt
2  (¼-ounce) envelopes active dry yeast

½  cup warm water (100° to 110°)
2  large eggs
4  cups all-purpose flour
2  tablespoons butter or margarine, melted

• Cook sour cream and next 3 ingredients in a saucepan over medium-low heat, stirring occasionally, 5 minutes or until butter melts. Cool to 100° to 110°.
• Combine yeast and ½ cup warm water in a 1-cup liquid measuring cup; let stand 5 minutes.
• Stir together yeast mixture, sour cream mixture, eggs, and flour in a large bowl until well blended; cover and chill 8 hours or overnight.
• Divide dough into fourths, and shape each portion into a ball. Roll each to ¼-inch thickness on a floured surface. (Dough will be slightly sticky.) Let dough rest 5 minutes. Cut dough into rounds with a 2½- to 3-inch round cutter.
• Brush rounds evenly with 2 tablespoons melted butter. Make a crease across each round with a knife, and fold in half; gently press edges to seal. Place rolls in a 15- x 10-inch jellyroll pan with sides of rolls touching.
• Cover and let rise in a warm place (85°), free from drafts, 45 minutes or until doubled in bulk.
• Bake at 375° for 12 to 15 minutes. Yield: 3½ dozen.

*cook's secret...* These wonderfully delicate rolls require no kneading. The dough gets its first rise overnight in the refrigerator, which replaces the traditional kneading.

The first time I ever made my Parker House Rolls was for Thanksgiving dinner with my family and friends. I was nervous about the whole idea of making yeast rolls because the technique was new to me. But the rolls came out of the oven golden, light, and with an aroma that called everyone to the table before I could ring the dinner bell.

Grandmother Wood gave me the original recipe, which came from a cook in her mother's family. I don't know the cook's name, but I think she'd be pleased to know that so many people are enjoying her rolls after all these years.

*Sister Schubert*
Troy, Alabama

## Sister Schubert's Parker House Rolls

*Today, Sister Schubert's homemade rolls are shipped to stores in 28 states.*
*The secret to the light-as-a-feather texture of these rolls: Don't knead the dough!*

| | |
|---|---|
| 1 (¼-ounce) envelope active dry yeast | ½ cup shortening, melted |
| 1½ cups warm water (100° to 110°) | 2 large eggs, lightly beaten |
| 5 cups sifted all-purpose flour, divided | ½ cup butter, melted |
| ½ cup sugar | 1¼ cups all-purpose flour, divided |
| 1½ teaspoons salt | |

• Combine yeast and warm water in a 2-cup liquid measuring cup; let stand 5 minutes.
• Combine 4 cups sifted flour, ½ cup sugar, and salt in a large bowl. Stir in yeast mixture and shortening. Add eggs and remaining 1 cup sifted flour; stir vigorously until well blended. (Dough will be soft and sticky.) Brush or lightly rub dough with some of the melted butter.
• Cover loosely; let rise in a warm place (85°), free from drafts, 1½ hours or until doubled in bulk.
• Grease 4 (8-inch) round cakepans; set aside.
• Sift ¾ cup flour in a thick layer evenly over work surface; turn dough out onto floured surface. (Dough will be soft.) Sift ½ cup flour evenly over dough. Roll dough to ½-inch thickness (photo 1); brush off excess flour.
• Cut out dough using a floured 2-inch round cutter (photo 2). Gently stretch each round into an oval about 2½ inches long. Dip 1 side of oval into melted butter. Fold oval in half, buttered side facing out (photo 3). (Floured side will form the famous Parker House pocket.)

- For each pan, place the folds of 10 rolls against side of prepared pan, pressing center fronts of rolls together gently to seal. Place 5 rolls in inner circle, and 1 roll in center for a total of 16 rolls per pan.
- Cover loosely, and let rise in a warm place, free from drafts, 1 hour or until doubled in bulk.
- Preheat oven to 400°. Bake rolls, uncovered, for 12 to 15 minutes or until lightly browned. Yield: 64 rolls.

*Sister Schubert*
Troy, Alabama
From *Sister Schubert's Secret Bread Recipes* (Oxmoor House)

## Preparing Parker House Rolls

**1.** Before rolling the dough, sift ¾ cup flour evenly in a thick layer over the work surface. Turn dough out onto work surface, and sift ½ cup flour evenly over dough. Roll dough to ½-inch thickness.

**2.** Cut the dough into rounds using a floured 2-inch round cutter, cutting the rounds as close together as possible. Lightly press the remnants together, and reroll to ½-inch thickness; cut the dough into rounds.

**3.** Gently stretch each round into a 2½-inch long oval. Dip one side of each oval in melted butter; fold in half, buttered side out, and place in greased pan.

*cook's secret...* Most bags of flour are presifted and don't require sifting, but Sister always sifts for her recipes. For her Parker House Rolls, sift the flour into a large bowl before measuring out the amount the recipe requires.

# Sausage Rolls

*This variation of Parker House Rolls contains a savory*
*surprise—smoked cocktail sausages.*

64   smoked cocktail sausages        1   recipe Parker House Rolls dough (page 92)

• Place sausages in a single layer in a shallow pan. Bake at 350° for 20 minutes. Drain well
on paper towels.
• To assemble, fold the buttered cut-out dough for Parker House Rolls around the
cooked sausages before placing rolls in the prepared pans. Continue preparing rolls as
directed in Parker House Rolls recipe. Yield: 64 rolls.

*Sister Schubert*
Troy, Alabama
From *Sister Schubert's Secret Bread Recipes* (Oxmoor House)

*cook's secret*... Bake the sausages before inserting them in the rolls to
keep the sausages from making the rolls greasy.


# Cheese Buns

1   (¼-ounce) envelope active dry yeast        ¼   cup shortening
2   cups all-purpose flour, divided            2   tablespoons sugar
1   (5-ounce) jar sharp process cheese spread  ½   teaspoon salt
½   cup water                                  1   large egg, beaten

• Combine yeast and 1 cup flour in a large mixing bowl; set aside. Combine cheese
spread and next 4 ingredients in a small saucepan; heat to 100° to 110°, stirring constantly.
• Add cheese mixture and egg to yeast mixture; beat 30 seconds at low speed with an
electric mixer, scraping sides of bowl. Beat 3 minutes at high speed. Stir in remaining
1 cup flour.
• Turn dough out onto a lightly floured surface, and knead 1 to 2 minutes. Shape dough
into 12 balls. Place in well-greased muffin pans.
• Cover and let rise in a warm place (85°), free from drafts, 1½ hours or until doubled in
bulk. Bake at 350° for 15 to 18 minutes. Yield: 1 dozen.

*cook's secret*... To turn these into **Cheesy Onion Buns,** add 2
tablespoons of minced onion with the egg.

Having fifty guests for dinner is a breeze for Judy Johnson and her close circle of friends who host engagement parties for their children. Each party reflects the personality of the honoree, while these women shower guests with food and fun. This roll recipe is Judy's contribution. It makes a generous 3½ dozen per batch.

## Potato Yeast Rolls

| | | | |
|---|---|---|---|
| 1 | (¼-ounce) envelope active dry yeast | ⅓ | cup vegetable oil |
| ½ | cup warm water (100° to 110°) | 2 | large eggs |
| 1 | cup mashed potatoes | 2 | teaspoons salt |
| ½ | cup sugar | 6¼ | to 6½ cups all-purpose flour |
| 1 | cup warm milk (100° to 110°) | | Melted butter |

• Stir together yeast and ½ cup warm water in a 1-cup liquid measuring cup; let stand 5 minutes.

• Beat yeast mixture, potatoes, and next 5 ingredients at low speed with an electric mixer until blended. Gradually stir in enough flour to make a medium-stiff dough. Place in a well-greased bowl, turning to grease top. Cover and chill 8 hours.

• Punch dough down; turn out onto a well-floured surface, and knead lightly 4 or 5 times. Roll to ¼-inch thickness; cut with a 2-inch round cutter. Brush rolls with melted butter; make a crease across center of each circle with a knife, and fold in half. Gently press edges to seal. Place in 2 greased 13- x 9-inch pans.

• Cover and let rise in a warm place (85°), free from drafts, 1½ hours or until doubled in bulk.

• Bake at 400° for 8 minutes or until lightly browned. Yield: 3½ dozen.

*Judy Johnson*
Knoxville, Tennessee

*cook's secret*... The high temperature and short cooking time on these rolls brown them quickly, which keeps the interior tender and moist.

Test Kitchens Director Lyda Jones recommends your oven for the perfect draft-free environment for letting dough rise. Place the dough on the middle rack and a pan of hot water on the bottom rack. Close the oven door, and allow the dough to rise until doubled.

# Honey-Oat Crescent Rolls

| | | | |
|---|---|---|---|
| 1¾ | cups water | 1½ | teaspoons salt |
| ½ | cup honey | 3 | (¼-ounce) envelopes active dry yeast |
| ½ | cup vegetable oil | 2 | large eggs |
| 1⅔ | to 2 cups bread flour, divided | 2½ | cups whole wheat flour |
| 1 | cup uncooked regular oats | 1 | egg white |
| ½ | cup unprocessed oat bran | 1 | tablespoon water |

• Combine first 3 ingredients in a saucepan; heat to 120° to 130°.

• Combine 1⅔ cups bread flour, oats, and next 3 ingredients in a large mixing bowl. Gradually add honey mixture and eggs, beating at low speed with an electric mixer until blended. Beat at medium speed 3 more minutes. Gradually stir in wheat flour and enough remaining bread flour to form a soft dough.

• Turn dough out on a well-floured surface (photo 1). Knead until smooth and elastic, about 10 minutes (photo 2). Place in a well-greased bowl, turning to grease top.

• Cover and let rise in a warm place (85°), free from drafts, 1 hour or until doubled in bulk.

• Punch dough down; let rest 15 minutes. Divide dough into fourths; roll each portion into a 10-inch circle on a lightly floured surface. Cut each circle into 12 wedges; roll up wedges, beginning at wide ends (photo 3). Pinch the point of the dough to seal. Place rolls, point side down, on greased baking sheets.

• Cover and let rise 20 minutes or until doubled in bulk.

• Combine egg white and 1 tablespoon water; brush rolls with mixture.

• Bake at 375° for 10 to 12 minutes or until lightly browned. Yield: 4 dozen.

## Kneading and Shaping Honey-Oat Crescent Rolls

 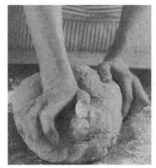 

**1.** Flour the work surface well before kneading the dough. Turn dough out onto floured surface, shaping dough into a ball.

**2.** To knead dough, press the heel of your hand into the dough and push it away from you. Then fold the dough in half, give it a quarter turn, and repeat the process until smooth and elastic. Let dough rise; then divide into fourths.

**3.** Roll each fourth of dough into a 10-inch circle, and cut into 12 wedges. To form the crescents, roll up each wedge, beginning at the wide end, and seal the point.

*cook's secret*... While the dough rises, cover it with plastic wrap coated with cooking spray to prevent the dough from sticking and tearing. The temperature of the honey-oil mixture reads higher than temperatures in other roll recipes because the yeast is being added directly to the flour mixture.

My mom, Mattie H. Scott, bakes some of the best bread in the world. With countless dozens of hot, tender yeast rolls, she spreads love to family, friends, and church members. Most weekends find her wearing a light dusting of flour and experimenting with yeast breads. Anyone who comes to her door when she's baking is greeted with, "Taste this, and tell me what you think."

She bakes a lot by sight and feel, guided by such instructions as "not too much flour" and "knead until it feels right." Here's her basic roll recipe and a sweet variation.

*Andria Scott Hurst*
Foods Editor

## Easy Yeast Rolls

| | | |
|---|---|---|
| 2 | (¼-ounce) envelopes active dry yeast | |
| ½ | cup warm milk (100° to 110°) | |
| 1 | cup milk | |
| ½ | cup sugar | |
| ½ | cup shortening, melted | |

| | |
|---|---|
| 2 | large eggs, beaten |
| 1 | teaspoon salt |
| 5½ | cups all-purpose flour |
| ½ | cup butter, melted and divided |

• Combine yeast and ½ cup warm milk in a 2-cup liquid measuring cup; let stand 5 minutes.

• Combine yeast mixture, 1 cup milk, sugar, and next 3 ingredients in a large bowl. Gradually add 1 cup flour, stirring until smooth. Gradually stir in enough remaining flour to make a soft dough. Place in a well-greased bowl, turning to grease top.

• Cover and let rise in a warm place (85°), free from drafts, 1 hour or until doubled in bulk.

• Turn dough out onto a floured surface; knead 5 or 6 times. Divide dough in half. Roll each dough portion on a lightly floured surface to ¼-inch thickness. Cut with a 2-inch round cutter. Brush rounds evenly with ¼ cup melted butter, and fold in half. Place rolls in 3 lightly greased 9-inch round cakepans.

• Cover and let rise in a warm place, free from drafts, 1 hour or until doubled in bulk.

• Bake at 375° for 15 to 18 minutes or until golden. Brush with remaining ¼ cup melted butter. Yield: 3 dozen.

*Mattie H. Scott*
Birmingham, Alabama

# Citrus-Pecan Rolls

2 cups granulated sugar
½ cup grated orange rind
¼ cup grated lime rind
1 recipe Easy Yeast Rolls dough
    (opposite page)
½ cup butter, melted

1½ cups finely chopped toasted pecans
2½ cups powdered sugar
2 tablespoons grated orange rind
¼ cup fresh orange juice
2 tablespoons lime juice

• Combine 2 cups granulated sugar, ½ cup grated orange rind, and ¼ cup grated lime rind; set aside.

• Prepare 1 recipe Easy Yeast Roll dough, letting dough rise once for 1 hour. Turn dough out onto a lightly floured surface; knead 5 or 6 times. Divide dough in half. Roll each dough portion on a lightly floured surface into an 18- x 24-inch rectangle.

• Brush each dough rectangle with ¼ cup melted butter. Spread half of granulated sugar mixture evenly over 1 dough rectangle; sprinkle with half of pecans. Cut dough rectangle in half crosswise, forming 2 (18- x 12-inch) rectangles; roll up each, jellyroll fashion, starting at long ends. Repeat procedure with second dough rectangle.

• Cut each dough log into 15 slices (about 1¼-inch each). Place slices in 5 lightly greased 8-inch round cakepans (12 rolls per cakepan).

• Let rise, uncovered, in a warm place 1 hour or until doubled in bulk.

• Bake at 375° for 15 to 18 minutes or until lightly browned. Cool slightly in pans.

• Stir together powdered sugar and remaining ingredients until blended. Drizzle powdered sugar mixture evenly over warm rolls, and serve immediately. Yield: about 5 dozen.

*Mattie H. Scott*
Birmingham, Alabama

*cook's secret...* If you think the dry yeast in your pantry might be too old to be active, you can proof it as a test before sacrificing any bread ingredients. Dissolve it in a little warm water (100° to 110°) with a pinch of sugar. Set it aside in a warm place for 5 to 10 minutes. If the mixture starts to bubble and swell, it's alive and ready to use. If the mixture lies dormant, toss it out, and buy fresh yeast. You should store yeast in a cool, dry place; it also can be refrigerated or frozen. Make sure the yeast is at room temperature before dissolving it, and always discard any dry yeast when the expiration date on its package has passed.

Carol Barclay's roll recipe was such a hit in our Test Kitchens that we experimented to create two variations. See if you don't agree that the recipes for Cinnamon Rolls and Herb Rolls (opposite page) are winners, too!

# Oatmeal Dinner Rolls

| | | | |
|---|---|---|---|
| 2 | cups water | 1 | tablespoon granulated sugar |
| 1 | cup quick-cooking oats | 4 | cups all-purpose flour |
| 3 | tablespoons butter or margarine | 1½ | teaspoons salt |
| 2 | (¼-ounce) envelopes active dry yeast | ⅓ | cup firmly packed brown sugar |
| ½ | cup warm water (100° to 110°) | | |

• Bring 2 cups water to a boil in a medium saucepan; stir in oats and butter. Boil, stirring constantly, 1 minute. Remove from heat; let cool to 110°.

• Combine yeast, ½ cup warm water, and 1 tablespoon granulated sugar in a 2-cup measuring cup; let stand 5 minutes.

• Beat oat mixture, yeast mixture, flour, salt, and brown sugar at medium speed with an electric mixer until smooth.

• Turn dough out onto a lightly floured surface; knead until smooth and elastic (about 5 minutes). Place in a well-greased bowl, turning to grease top.

• Cover and let rise in a warm place (85°), free from drafts, 1 hour or until dough is doubled in bulk.

• Punch dough down, and divide in half; shape each portion into 16 (1½-inch) balls. Place evenly in 2 lightly greased 9- x 1¾-inch round cakepans.

• Cover and let rise in a warm place (85°), free from drafts, 30 minutes or until doubled in bulk.

• Bake at 375° for 15 minutes or until golden brown. Yield: 32 rolls.

**NOTE:** *Reserve 1 portion of dough for Cinnamon Rolls recipe (opposite page), if desired.*

*Carol Barclay*
*Portland, Texas*

*cook's secret*... These rolls may be chilled overnight after the second rising; let stand at room temperature 30 minutes before baking as directed. Or freeze rolls for up to 1 month after the second rising; thaw overnight in refrigerator, and let stand at room temperature 30 minutes before baking as directed.

# Cinnamon Rolls

½   Oatmeal Dinner Rolls dough     1   to 2 teaspoons ground cinnamon
     (opposite page)      ¼   cup chopped pecans
3   tablespoons butter or margarine, melted     ½   cup powdered sugar
⅓   cup firmly packed brown sugar      2   teaspoons milk

• Roll dough on a lightly floured surface into a 16- x 12-inch rectangle; brush with butter.

• Combine brown sugar and cinnamon; sprinkle over butter, and top with pecans.

• Roll up, jellyroll fashion, starting at long end; cut into ¾-inch-thick slices. Arrange in 2 lightly greased 13- x 9-inch pans.

• Cover and let rise in a warm place (85°), free from drafts, 30 minutes or until doubled in bulk.

• Bake at 375° for 25 minutes or until golden brown. Whisk together powdered sugar and milk; drizzle over warm rolls. Yield: 28 rolls.

**Herb Rolls:** Substitute ½ teaspoon each of freeze-dried chives, dried basil, and dried rosemary for brown sugar and cinnamon, or use 1 teaspoon each of fresh herbs. Add 3 to 4 tablespoons grated Parmesan cheese, if desired. Omit glaze.

## Knead-to-Know Secrets

• Make sure yeast is not out of date. (Package is stamped with an expiration date.)

• Dissolve yeast in warm water (100° to 110°).

• Measure all ingredients carefully, including salt. Salt plays a definite role in developing the dough's flavor and helps control the rising rate of the dough.

• When kneading the dough, flatten and fold it toward you, and use the heels of your hands to push the dough away from you in a rolling motion.

• Rotate dough a quarter turn; repeat the folding, pushing, and turning steps.

• Use a little more flour if dough feels too sticky, always working the flour into the dough.

• Don't let dough continue to rise beyond the time called for in the recipe.

• Avoid letting the temperature become too high during the dough-rising period; it will kill the yeast. If the temperature is too low, the dough will take longer to rise.

This top-rated roll recipe is from *A Skillet Full of Traditional Southern Lodge Cast Iron Recipes and Memories,* a community cookbook benefiting the Historic Preservation Society of South Pittsburg, Tennessee. The town is home to both the National Cornbread Festival and the Lodge Manufacturing Company, makers of cast-iron cookware. These delicious rolls are ready for the oven in 10 minutes.

# Spoon Rolls

| 1 | (¼-ounce) envelope active dry yeast | ¾ | cup butter or margarine, melted |
| 2 | cups warm water (100° to 110°) | ¼ | cup sugar |
| 4 | cups self-rising flour | 1 | large egg, lightly beaten |

- Combine yeast and 2 cups warm water in a large bowl, and let mixture stand 5 minutes.
- Stir in flour and remaining ingredients until blended. Spoon into well-greased cast-iron muffin pans, filling two-thirds full, or into well-greased cast-iron drop biscuit pans, filling half full.
- Bake at 400° for 20 minutes or until rolls are golden brown. Yield: 14 rolls.

**NOTE:** *Unused batter may be stored in an airtight container in the refrigerator for up to 1 week.*

*Sarah Kirkwood Lodge and Billie Cline Hill*
South Pittsburg, Tennessee
*From A Skillet Full of Traditional Southern*
*Lodge Cast Iron Recipes and Memories*

*cook's secret*... These can be baked in any well-greased muffin pan, but as with cornbread, cast iron creates a wonderfully crisp crust. If you're a fan of crusty muffin tops, try baking these rolls in a drop biscuit pan.

# Potato-Caramelized Onion Buns

*Serve meaty cheeseburgers or grilled fish inside these delicious buns.*

| | |
|---|---|
| 3 (¼-ounce) envelopes active dry yeast | 7 cups plus 1 tablespoon all-purpose flour |
| 2 cups warm water (100° to 110°) | 1 tablespoon salt |
| 1 cup refrigerated or frozen mashed potatoes, thawed and warmed | Caramelized Onions |
| 2 tablespoons sugar | 1 egg, lightly beaten |
| 2 tablespoons butter, melted | 1½ teaspoons poppy seeds (optional) |

• Preheat oven to 200°. Stir together yeast and 2 cups warm water in a large mixing bowl of a heavy-duty electric stand mixer until dissolved. Let stand 5 minutes.

• Add potatoes, sugar, and butter to yeast mixture; beat at medium speed, using dough hook attachment, until blended. Add 7 cups flour and salt; beat at low speed 2 minutes. Add Caramelized Onions, and beat at medium speed 5 minutes. (Dough will be very sticky.) Sprinkle dough with remaining 1 tablespoon flour, and remove from bowl.

• Shape into a ball, and place in a lightly greased bowl, turning to grease top. Turn off oven.

• Cover bowl with plastic wrap, and let rise in oven 30 minutes or until doubled in bulk.

• Remove from oven. Remove and discard plastic wrap. Punch dough down, and turn out onto a lightly floured surface. Divide into 21 portions. With floured hands, shape each portion into a ball. Place no more than 8 balls on each parchment paper–lined baking sheet. Cover with plastic wrap, and let rise again in a warm place (85°), free from drafts, for 15 to 20 minutes or until doubled in bulk. Brush with egg and sprinkle with poppy seeds, if desired.

• Bake buns at 350° for 15 to 18 minutes or until golden brown. Remove from pans, and cool on wire racks. Yield: 21 buns.

## Caramelized Onions:

| | |
|---|---|
| ¼ cup butter | ½ teaspoon salt |
| 2 large sweet onions, chopped | |

• Melt butter in a large skillet over medium heat; add onions and salt. Sauté 20 minutes or until caramel-colored. Cool.

*Virginia Ann Towne*
Lansing, Michigan

*cook's secret...* Brushing these buns with a beaten egg before baking makes them bake up extra golden. The parchment paper lining keeps the egg from baking into a hard-to-remove crust on the baking sheet.

# Dried Cherry–Walnut Sweet Rolls

1 (25-ounce) package frozen roll dough, thawed according to package directions*
½ cup chopped walnuts
¼ cup butter, melted
½ (6-ounce) package dried cherries, chopped

3 tablespoons granulated sugar
¾ teaspoon pumpkin pie spice
2 cups powdered sugar
3 tablespoons hot water

- Preheat oven to 200°.
- Place dough balls in 2 greased 9-inch round cakepans. Turn off oven. Cover dough balls with plastic wrap; let rise in oven 25 to 30 minutes or until doubled in bulk. Remove from oven. Remove and discard plastic wrap.
- Stir together walnuts and next 4 ingredients, and sprinkle mixture evenly over dough in pans.
- Bake at 350° for 12 to 15 minutes or until golden brown. Cool.
- Stir together powdered sugar and 3 tablespoons hot water. Drizzle evenly over rolls. Yield: about 2 dozen.

**Pecan–Golden Raisin Sweet Rolls:** Omit walnuts, cherries, granulated sugar, and pumpkin pie spice. Replace with 1½ cups chopped pecans, ½ cup golden raisins, ½ cup firmly packed dark brown sugar, and ¾ teaspoon apple pie spice, stirring together with melted butter. Proceed as directed.

**Apricot–Orange Sweet Rolls:** Omit walnuts, cherries, 1 tablespoon granulated sugar, and pumpkin pie spice. Replace with 1 (6-ounce) package dried apricots, chopped, and 1 tablespoon grated orange rind, stirring together with melted butter. Proceed as directed. For glaze, omit hot water, and replace with 3 tablespoons fresh orange juice, stirring together with powdered sugar. Proceed as directed.

*For testing purposes only, we used Rich's Enriched Homestyle Roll Dough.

# cook's secret...

This heavenly sweet roll recipe starts with frozen bread dough, so it's super easy to make, and the taste is nothing less than awesome.

## Double-Duty Rolls

A package of Rich's Enriched Homestyle Roll Dough provides instructions for shaping all sorts of clever rolls, from cloverleaf to Parker House, but what they don't tell you is that the dough also makes terrific little sandwich buns. Instead of buying expensive cocktail buns at local bakeries, you can make them yourself for a fraction of the cost. Divide the frozen balls of dough from 1 (25-ounce) package between 2 greased baking sheets, leaving ample space for rising between each roll. Follow the package directions for thawing and baking, and you'll end up with 2 dozen beautiful little buns.

In the Test Kitchens, we all have our favorite ways of serving them, whether we're splurging for a formal affair with beef tenderloin and horseradish sauce or grilling baby hamburgers for a backyard full of wild and crazy kids. For a taste of New Orleans, former staffer Laura Martin makes miniature po'boys and tucks them alongside bowls of steaming hot gumbo. Vanessa McNeil stuffs them with Texas barbecue. Filled with deli meats and cheeses or homemade chicken salad, they're perfect for boxed lunches.

*Mary Allen Perry*
Associate Foods Editor

# Sister's Sticky Buns

| | |
|---|---|
| 1 cup water | 4½ cups all-purpose flour |
| ½ cup granulated sugar, divided | 1 teaspoon salt |
| ½ cup butter | 1 cup butter, melted and divided |
| 1 (¼-ounce) envelope active dry yeast | 1½ cups firmly packed brown sugar, divided |
| ½ cup warm water (100° to 110°) | ½ cup light corn syrup |
| 1 teaspoon granulated sugar | 1½ cups coarsely chopped pecans |
| 1 large egg, lightly beaten | 1 tablespoon ground cinnamon |

• Combine 1 cup water, ¼ cup granulated sugar, and ½ cup butter in a saucepan; heat until butter melts, stirring occasionally. Cool to 100° to 110°.

• Combine yeast, warm water, and 1 teaspoon granulated sugar in a 1-cup liquid measuring cup; let stand 5 minutes. Combine butter mixture and yeast mixture. Add egg, and stir well.

• Combine yeast mixture, 2 cups flour, and salt in a large bowl. Add remaining 2½ cups flour, ½ cup at a time, stirring vigorously until dough is no longer sticky and pulls away from sides of bowl. Brush or lightly rub dough with some of the melted butter.

• Cover loosely, and let rise in a warm place (85°), free from drafts, 1 hour or until doubled in bulk.

• Combine ½ cup melted butter, 1 cup brown sugar, corn syrup, and pecans; sprinkle mixture evenly in bottom of a well-greased 13- x 9-inch pan. Set pan aside. Combine remaining ½ cup brown sugar, remaining ¼ cup granulated sugar, and cinnamon in a small bowl; set aside.

• Punch dough down; turn out onto a well-floured surface, and roll dough into an 18- x 15-inch rectangle. Brush dough generously with some of the remaining melted butter; sprinkle evenly with cinnamon mixture. Roll up, jellyroll fashion, starting at long end. Cut roll into 12 (1½-inch) slices. Place slices, cut side down, in prepared pan. Brush slices with remaining melted butter. Cover loosely, and let rise in a warm place, free from drafts, 1 hour or until tops of rolls rise just above top of pan.

• Bake rolls at 350°, uncovered, for 18 to 22 minutes or until golden. Cool in pan on a wire rack 8 minutes. Invert pan onto wax paper; let rolls stand, covered with pan, 1 minute. Remove pan, scraping any remaining pecan mixture from pan onto rolls. Serve warm. Yield: 1 dozen.

*Sister Schubert*
Troy, Alabama
From *Sister Schubert's Secret Bread Recipes* (Oxmoor House)

*cook's secret*... Preheat the oven toward the end of the final rise. Then the oven will be ready when the buns are.

# Braided Egg Bread

*This slightly sweet bread is also known as challah (pronounced KHAH-lah).*

| | | | |
|---|---|---|---|
| 1½ | cups fat-free milk | 1 | egg yolk |
| 2 | (¼-ounce) envelopes active dry yeast | ½ | cup honey |
| 5½ | cups all-purpose flour | | All-purpose flour |
| 1 | teaspoon salt | 1 | egg, lightly beaten |
| ¼ | cup shortening | 1 | teaspoon sesame seeds (optional) |
| ½ | cup egg substitute | | |

- Preheat oven to 200°.
- Microwave 1½ cups milk at HIGH in a microwave-safe glass bowl 2 to 3 minutes or until heated. Stir in yeast; let stand 5 minutes.
- Combine 5½ cups flour and salt in a large bowl; stir in yeast mixture. Add shortening and next 3 ingredients. Beat at low speed with an electric mixer 1 to 2 minutes. Beat at medium speed 5 more minutes.
- Sprinkle dough with additional flour, and remove from bowl. (Dough will be very sticky.) Place dough in a lightly greased bowl, turning to grease top. Turn off oven.
- Cover bowl with plastic wrap, and let rise in oven 30 minutes or until doubled in bulk. Remove from oven. Remove and discard plastic wrap.
- Punch dough down, and divide in half. Divide each half into 3 equal portions. Roll each portion into a 14-inch-long rope; pinch 3 ropes together at 1 end to seal, and braid. Repeat with remaining dough portions, and place braids on a parchment paper–lined baking sheet.
- Cover braids with plastic wrap, and let rise in a warm place (85°), free from drafts, 25 to 30 minutes or until doubled in bulk. Brush evenly with beaten egg, and sprinkle with sesame seeds, if desired.
- Bake at 350° for 25 minutes or until golden and a wooden pick inserted into center comes out clean. Yield: 2 loaves.

*Penny Abrams*
Sarasota, Florida

*cook's secret...* This sweet bread makes delicious French toast if you have leftovers.

M aking sourdough bread takes a while due to the long rising times, but you can be doing other things while it rises. I remove the starter from the refrigerator in the morning and allow it to warm up and work all day. That evening, I make the dough and leave it to rise overnight. The next morning, I prepare the loaves, leaving them to rise during the day. Then I bake the loaves for dinner.

*Sister Schubert*
Troy, Alabama

## Mama's Sourdough Bread

| | |
|---|---|
| 1½ cups warm water (100° to 110°) | 6 cups all-purpose flour |
| 1 cup Sourdough Starter | 1 teaspoon salt |
| ½ cup shortening, melted | 3 tablespoons butter, melted |

• Combine first 3 ingredients in a large bowl.
• Combine flour and salt in a large bowl. Add 2 cups flour mixture to starter mixture, stirring until well blended. Add remaining flour mixture to starter mixture, 1 cup at a time, stirring vigorously until dough holds together. (Dough will be very stiff.) Place dough in a well-greased bowl, turning to grease top.
• Cover loosely, and let rise in a warm place (85°), free from drafts, 6 hours or until doubled in bulk.
• Grease 2 (9- x 5-inch) loafpans; set aside.
• Punch dough down; turn dough out onto a lightly floured surface, and knead until smooth and elastic (5 to 8 minutes). Divide dough in half. Roll 1 portion of dough into a 14- x 9-inch rectangle. Roll up dough, starting at short side, pressing firmly to eliminate air pockets; pinch ends to seal. Place dough, seam side down, in a prepared pan. Repeat procedure with remaining portion of dough.
• Brush loaves with melted butter. Cover loosely, and let rise in a warm place, free from drafts, 6 hours or until dough rises above tops of pans.
• Bake loaves at 350° for 35 to 45 minutes or until golden and loaves sound hollow when tapped. Remove bread from pans immediately; cool completely on wire racks. Yield: 2 loaves.

## Sourdough Starter:

|   |   |   |   |
|---|---|---|---|
| 2 | (¼-ounce) envelopes active dry yeast | ⅔ | cup sugar |
| 1½ | cups warm water (100° to 110°), divided | 3 | tablespoons instant potato flakes |

• Combine yeast and ½ cup warm water in a 1-cup liquid measuring cup; let stand 5 minutes.

• Combine yeast mixture, remaining 1 cup warm water, sugar, and potato flakes in a large bowl, stirring until well blended.

• Cover loosely, and let stand in a warm place (85°), free from drafts, 8 hours. (Starter is ready to use at this point.) Refrigerate starter after 8 hours.

## Feed Sourdough Starter every 3 days with:

|   |   |   |   |
|---|---|---|---|
| 1 | cup warm water (100° to 110°) | 3 | tablespoons instant potato flakes |
| ⅔ | cup sugar |   |   |

• After feeding starter, cover loosely, and let stand in a warm place (85°), free from drafts, 8 hours. Refrigerate starter after 8 hours.

*cook's secret...* The temperature of the water is critical in making Sourdough Starter. Use a candy thermometer to be sure that the water isn't too hot. If you prefer a strong sourdough flavor, allow the dough to rise longer.

*Sister Schubert*
Troy, Alabama
From *Sister Schubert's Secret Bread Recipes* (Oxmoor House)

### Sourdough Secrets

• Store sourdough starter in glass or crockery containers because metal may adversely affect sourdough flavor.

• Don't store sourdough starter in an airtight container. Starter is alive and growing, and it requires oxygen.

• Allow sourdough starter to come to room temperature before using it.

• Don't rush the rising time for sourdough bread. It takes several hours for the natural fermentation of the potato water, sugar, flour, and yeast to occur.

• Replenish, or feed, sourdough starter every 3 days.

• Discard starter that has changed color or has developed mold.

Warm beignets are a sweet Southern Louisiana treat, and no trip to New Orleans is complete without one. *Beignet* is French for *fritter,* and in the Crescent City, these concoctions come light and yeasty.

This is an easy dough to work with, and it can be made a day ahead and stored in the refrigerator. Maintain the oil temperature at 375°, and gently lower (don't drop) beignets into the oil using a spatula. No special equipment is necessary; a Dutch oven or deep frying pan is all you need.

## French Market Beignets

| | | | |
|---|---|---|---|
| 1 | (¼-ounce) envelope active dry yeast | 1 | large egg, lightly beaten |
| 1 | cup warm water (100° to 110°) | 4 | to 4½ cups all-purpose flour |
| ¾ | cup evaporated milk | | Vegetable oil |
| ¼ | cup granulated sugar | | Sifted powdered sugar |
| 1 | teaspoon salt | | |

• Combine yeast and warm water in a 2-cup liquid measuring cup; let stand 5 minutes.
• Combine yeast mixture, evaporated milk, and next 3 ingredients. Gradually stir in enough flour to make a soft dough. Cover and chill 8 hours or overnight.
• Punch dough down; turn dough out onto a well-floured surface, and knead 5 or 6 times. Roll dough into a 15- x 12½-inch rectangle; cut into 2½-inch squares.
• Pour oil to depth of 3 to 4 inches into a Dutch oven; heat to 375°. Fry 3 or 4 beignets at a time, 1 minute on each side or until golden. Drain; sprinkle with powdered sugar. Yield: 2½ dozen.

*cook's secret...* No room-temperature rising time is needed for this recipe. The dough rises overnight and puffs again as soon as the dough squares meet the hot oil.

A cross between cake and bread, this ring-shaped sweet treat has been around since colonial times. Though we don't know who Sally Lunn was, some sources contend that she was a woman who sold bread in England. Other historians say that the name may have come from the French words *soleil* (sun) and *lune* (moon) because the bread has a top as golden as the sun and a bottom as pale as the moon. The secret to this recipe is an easy-to-make yeast batter. You don't have to knead the dough.

## Sally Lunn Bread

| | | | | |
|---|---|---|---|---|
| 2 | (¼-ounce) envelopes active dry yeast | | 1 | teaspoon salt |
| ½ | cup warm water (100° to 110°) | | 2 | large eggs |
| 1½ | cups milk | | 5 | cups all-purpose flour |
| ¾ | cup sugar | | | Blackberry Butter (optional) |
| ½ | cup butter or margarine | | | |

- Combine yeast and ½ cup warm water in a 1-cup measuring cup; let stand 5 minutes.
- Heat milk and next 3 ingredients in a saucepan over medium heat, stirring until butter melts. Cool to 100° to 110°.
- Beat yeast mixture, milk mixture, and eggs at medium speed with an electric mixer until blended. Gradually add flour, beating at lowest speed until blended. (Mixture will be a very sticky, soft dough.) Cover and let rise in a warm place (85°), free from drafts, 1 hour or until doubled in bulk. Stir dough down; cover and let rise in a warm place, free from drafts, 30 minutes or until doubled in bulk.
- Stir dough down, and spoon into a well-greased 10-inch Bundt pan or tube pan. Cover and let rise in a warm place, free from drafts, 20 to 30 minutes or until doubled in bulk.
- Bake at 350° for 35 to 40 minutes or until golden brown and a long wooden pick inserted into center comes out clean. Remove from pan immediately. Serve bread with Blackberry Butter, honey, molasses, or jelly, if desired. Yield: 12 to 16 servings.

**Blackberry Butter:** Stir 2 to 3 tablespoons seedless blackberry jam into ½ cup softened butter.

*cook's secret*... There are a multitude of ways to eat this bread besides slathered with butter and hot from the oven. Try it in a luscious tomato sandwich, for French toast, or as the base for croutons.

One of the tastiest foods unique to the Lone Star State—with its strong food traditions, from barbecue to heavenly Tex-Mex cooking—has managed to go relatively unnoticed: the alluring *pan dulce,* or sweet bread, of the Rio Grande Valley.

Unlike traditional pastries, pan dulce gets most of its sweetness from fruit-based fillings and various pastes and glazes; the bread itself is only slightly sweet. Here, we offer two examples.

## Anillos

*These airy, jelly-filled breads are similar to baked doughnuts.*

| | | | |
|---|---|---|---|
| 1 | (¼-ounce) envelope active dry yeast | 6 | tablespoons shortening |
| 1 | cup warm water (100° to 110°) | ¼ | teaspoon salt |
| ½ | cup granulated sugar, divided | ¾ | cup strawberry preserves |
| 5 | cups bread flour | 1 | cup powdered sugar |
| 2 | large eggs | ⅓ | cup water |

• Stir together yeast, 1 cup warm water, and 2 tablespoons granulated sugar in a 2-cup liquid measuring cup; let stand 5 minutes.
• Stir together remaining 6 tablespoons granulated sugar, flour, and next 3 ingredients in bowl of a heavy-duty electric stand mixer. Add yeast mixture, and beat at medium speed with mixer, using dough hook attachment, 6 minutes.
• Divide dough into 12 equal portions; shape each portion into a ball, and place on 2 lightly greased baking sheets (6 balls per baking sheet). Flatten to 4-inch-wide circles with hand; press thumb in center of each circle to make an indentation (about the size of a quarter). Spoon 1 tablespoon preserves into each indentation.
• Cover and let stand in a warm place (85°), free from drafts, 20 minutes. (Dough will not double in bulk.)
• Bake at 375° for 13 to 15 minutes or until golden brown. Cool on baking sheets on wire racks. Stir together powdered sugar and ⅓ cup water; drizzle evenly over breads. Yield: 1 dozen.

*cook's secret*... If you don't have a heavy-duty electric stand mixer, you can mix the dough for the recipes on these two pages by hand. (We don't recommend using a hand mixer.)

# Semitas

*These small, sweet loaves have a texture similar to that of Kaiser rolls.*

| | | | |
|---|---|---|---|
| 1 | (¼-ounce) envelope active dry yeast | 1 | (2.3-ounce) jar anise seeds (½ cup) |
| 1 | cup warm water (100° to 110°) | 6 | tablespoons shortening |
| ½ | cup sugar, divided | 2 | large eggs |
| 5 | cups bread flour | ¼ | teaspoon salt |

• Stir together yeast, 1 cup warm water, and 2 tablespoons sugar in a 2-cup liquid measuring cup; let stand 5 minutes.

• Stir together remaining 6 tablespoons sugar, flour, and remaining 4 ingredients in bowl of a heavy-duty electric stand mixer. Add yeast mixture, and beat at medium speed with mixer, using dough hook attachment, 6 minutes.

• Divide dough into 12 equal portions. Shape each portion into a round loaf, and place on 3 lightly greased baking sheets (4 loaves per baking sheet).

• Cover and let rise in a warm place (85°), free from drafts, 2 to 3 hours or until doubled in bulk.

• Bake at 425° for 8 to 10 minutes or until golden brown. Cool on baking sheets on wire racks. Yield: 1 dozen.

*cook's secret...* These recipes call for bread flour, which contains more hard wheat than all-purpose and cake flours. Bread flour increases a dough's elasticity and ability to rise.

## Baking Basics

• Make sure your ingredients are at room temperature. Bring out eggs and milk about 15 minutes before starting.

• Select good heavy pans and baking sheets for long-term use. Choose shiny pans, which reflect heat best and produce tender, nicely browned baked goods.

• Place the pan in the center of the oven to be sure your bread bakes evenly. If you are baking more than 1 batch in the same oven, leave space around each pan so that heat can circulate freely.

desserts

# Top 10 Best Kept Dessert Secrets

**1.** For baked goods, use butter or margarine containing more than 70% fat. Soft butter spreads and reduced-fat or tub margarines contain water and do not work well in baked goods.

**2.** Fat-free half-and-half performs the same as its heavier cousin. Cook with it, and discover that there's no difference in taste or texture in any recipe.

**3.** Store bags of chocolate morsels in a cool, dry place. If stored at too warm a temperature, they will appear ashy gray. We don't recommend freezing them because chocolate that's exposed to too much humidity may develop a slightly grainy texture. These visual and textural changes will not affect your recipes.

**4.** Toss raisins in a little flour before adding them to batter to keep them evenly distributed through the mix. If your recipe calls for chopped raisins, tuck them in the freezer for a while so that they won't be so sticky and hard to work with.

**5.** To add flavor to piecrusts for sweet pies, add a pinch of cinnamon, nutmeg, grated orange or lemon peel, or diced nuts (about ¼ cup nuts for a single crust). If you're using a refrigerated piecrust, open it on a flat surface. Sprinkle the flavor addition evenly over the crust, and blend it into the dough using a rolling pin.

**6.** You can successfully freeze cake layers up to 1 month. Bake the layers, cool completely, and store them in a zip-top freezer bag or airtight container. Thaw completely, uncovered; then frost or decorate as desired.

**7.** Make a quick, disposable piping bag from a zip-top freezer bag. Just snip a small hole in a corner of the bag, and place the tip in the bag so that it pokes out of the hole. Add frosting, seal the bag, and decorate. If you simply want a plain drizzle, skip the metal tip, snip a tiny hole in a corner of the bag, and drizzle directly from the bag.

**8.** When making a chocolate cake, dust cakepans with cocoa powder instead of all-purpose flour.

**9.** Cakes and soft cookies stay moist if you place a piece of cut apple in the airtight container.

**10.** Store desserts that contain fruit or have a cream base in the refrigerator, both before serving if you make them ahead and afterward if you have leftovers.

"Where There's Coke, There's Hospitality." Coca-Cola came up with that slogan in 1948, but reader Anne Kracke knows that the sentiment holds just as true today whenever she serves her fabulous Coca-Cola Cake. This Southern-to-the-core dessert has been a tradition in her family ever since she began making it for each of her four children's birthdays.

Although her kids are now grown, she continues to offer this cake at dinner parties, church gatherings, and summer picnics. We love this cake because it's simple to prepare, easy to slice, and convenient to freeze. We guarantee you'll enjoy it—but don't count on leftovers.

## Coca-Cola Cake

*Don't make the frosting ahead; you need to pour it over the cake shortly after baking.*

| | |
|---|---|
| 1 cup Coca-Cola | ¼ cup cocoa |
| ½ cup buttermilk | 1 teaspoon baking soda |
| 1 cup butter or margarine, softened | 1½ cups miniature marshmallows |
| 1¾ cups sugar | Coca-Cola Frosting |
| 2 large eggs, lightly beaten | Garnish: ¾ cup chopped pecans, |
| 2 teaspoons vanilla extract | toasted |
| 2 cups all-purpose flour | |

• Combine Coca-Cola and buttermilk; set aside.
• Beat butter at low speed with an electric mixer until creamy. Gradually add sugar; beat until blended. Add eggs and vanilla; beat at low speed until blended.
• Combine flour, cocoa, and soda. Add to butter mixture alternately with cola mixture, beginning and ending with flour mixture. Beat at low speed just until blended.
• Stir in marshmallows. Pour batter into a greased and floured 13- x 9-inch pan.
• Bake at 350° for 30 to 35 minutes. Remove from oven; cool 10 minutes. Pour Coca-Cola Frosting over warm cake. Garnish, if desired. Yield: 12 servings.

## Coca-Cola Frosting:

½ cup butter or margarine
⅓ cup Coca-Cola
3 tablespoons cocoa

1 (16-ounce) package powdered sugar
1 tablespoon vanilla extract

• Cook first 3 ingredients in a large, heavy saucepan over medium heat, stirring constantly, just until butter melts. Remove from heat; whisk in sugar and vanilla. Yield: 2¼ cups.

*Anne Kracke*
*Birmingham, Alabama*

*cook's secret*... This recipe is a favorite because of its adaptability. As Anne indicates, "Over the years, I've modified the recipe to suit our tastes. I like dark chocolate, so I add more cocoa. And I place the nuts on only half of the icing to please all the family."

# Mississippi Mud Cake

2 cups sugar
1 cup butter, melted
½ cup unsweetened cocoa
4 large eggs, lightly beaten
1 teaspoon vanilla extract

⅛ teaspoon salt
1½ cups all-purpose flour
1½ cups coarsely chopped pecans, toasted
1 (10.5-ounce) bag miniature marshmallows
Chocolate Frosting

• Whisk together first 6 ingredients in a large bowl. Stir in flour and chopped pecans. Pour batter into a greased and floured 15- x 10-inch jellyroll pan.
• Bake at 350° for 20 to 25 minutes or until a wooden pick inserted in center comes out clean. Remove from oven; top warm cake evenly with marshmallows. Return to oven; bake 5 minutes. Drizzle Chocolate Frosting over warm cake. Cool completely. Yield: 15 servings.
**NOTE:** *2 (19.5-ounce) packages brownie mix, prepared according to package directions, may be substituted for first 7 ingredients. Stir in chopped pecans. Bake at 350° for 30 minutes. Proceed with marshmallows and frosting as directed.*

## Chocolate Frosting:

1 (16-ounce) package powdered sugar
½ cup milk

⅓ cup unsweetened cocoa
¼ cup butter, softened

• Beat all ingredients at medium speed with an electric mixer until smooth. Yield: 2 cups.

This Southern delight is noted for being baked in a cast-iron skillet. Our Test Kitchens' skillet got a workout as we tested recipes in search of the all-time best. The cake that wowed us came from *My Mother's Southern Desserts* by James and Martha Pearl Villas. The gooey pineapple and cherries coated with a buttery brown sugar glaze were scrumptious. But it was the cake base that tasted like no other: light and tender. The pineapple juice helped add volume and flavor; egg whites folded into the batter lightened it.

*regional favorite*

# Skillet Pineapple Upside-Down Cake

*Use a cast-iron skillet that measures 9 inches across the bottom to be sure that the cake doesn't overflow. We used light brown sugar for our cake, but you can use whichever type you have on hand.*

¼ cup butter
⅔ cup firmly packed light or dark brown sugar
1 (20-ounce) can pineapple slices, undrained
9 maraschino cherries
2 large eggs, separated

¾ cup granulated sugar
¾ cup all-purpose flour
⅛ teaspoon salt
½ teaspoon baking powder
Whipped cream or vanilla ice cream (optional)

• Melt butter in a 9-inch cast-iron skillet. Spread brown sugar evenly over bottom of skillet. Drain pineapple, reserving ¼ cup juice; set juice aside. Arrange pineapple slices in a single layer over brown sugar mixture, and place a cherry in center of each pineapple ring; set skillet aside.
• Beat egg yolks at medium speed with an electric mixer until thick and lemon-colored; gradually add granulated sugar, beating well.
• Heat reserved pineapple juice in a small saucepan over low heat. Gradually add juice mixture to yolk mixture, beating until blended.
• Combine all-purpose flour, salt, and baking powder; add dry ingredients to the yolk mixture, beating at low speed with electric mixer until blended.

• Beat egg whites until stiff peaks form; fold egg whites into batter. Spoon batter evenly over pineapple slices.

• Bake at 325° for 45 to 50 minutes. Cool cake in skillet 30 minutes; invert cake onto a serving plate. Serve warm or cold with whipped cream or ice cream, if desired. Yield: 8 to 10 servings.

*James and Martha Pearl Villas*
Adapted from *My Mother's Southern Desserts*
(William Morrow and Company, Inc., 1998)

**Express Pineapple Upside-Down Cake:** Follow original recipe directions for first 4 ingredients. Substitute 1 (9-ounce) package golden yellow cake mix for next 5 ingredients. Prepare cake mix according to package directions, substituting ½ cup pineapple juice for ½ cup water. Spoon batter over prepared pineapple slices as directed. Bake at 350° for 20 to 25 minutes or until a wooden pick inserted in center comes out clean.
**NOTE:** *For testing purposes only, we used Jiffy Golden Yellow Cake Mix.*

*cook's secret...* When inverting the cake, make sure that the plate is larger than the skillet to catch additional fruit juices. If you're short on time, check out our express version, which uses a cake mix.

I've always loved a good piece of pound cake. There's just something about its buttery vanilla simplicity, its grassroots goodness. I must admit, however, that this humble dessert takes on a splashy new character when paired with the dynamic strawberry—as in this Cream Cheese Pound Cake with Strawberries and Cream. A luscious Strawberry Syrup is the secret to this recipe's special taste.

*Susan Dosier*
Executive Editor

## Cream Cheese Pound Cake with Strawberries and Cream

*If you don't have cake flour, substitute 1 cup minus 2 tablespoons sifted all-purpose flour for each cup of cake flour.*

| | |
|---|---|
| 1 (16-ounce) container fresh strawberries, sliced | 3 cups sifted cake flour |
| 2 tablespoons sugar | ⅛ teaspoon salt |
| 1 cup butter, softened | 1½ teaspoons vanilla extract |
| 1 (8-ounce) package cream cheese, softened | 1 cup whipping cream |
| 2½ cups sugar | 3 tablespoons sugar |
| 6 large eggs | Strawberry Syrup |
| | Garnish: whole fresh strawberries |

• Sprinkle sliced strawberries with 2 tablespoons sugar; cover and chill until ready to serve.

• Beat butter and cream cheese at medium speed with an electric mixer until creamy; gradually add 2½ cups sugar, beating well. Add eggs, 1 at a time, beating until combined. Stir in flour by hand just until moistened. Stir in salt and vanilla. Pour batter into a greased and floured 10-inch tube pan.

• Bake at 300° for 1 hour and 50 minutes or until a long wooden pick inserted in center comes out clean. Cool in pan on a wire rack 10 to 15 minutes; remove from pan, and let cool completely on wire rack. Cut into slices.

• Beat whipping cream and 3 tablespoons sugar at high speed with an electric mixer until stiff peaks form. Serve with cake; top with strawberry mixture, and drizzle with Strawberry Syrup. Garnish, if desired. Yield: 1 (10-inch) cake.

## Strawberry Syrup:

1   pint (2 cups) fresh strawberries*          ¼   teaspoon lemon juice
2   cups sugar

● Process strawberries in a food processor until smooth. Pour strawberry puree through a wire-mesh strainer into a saucepan, discarding seeds.
● Stir in sugar and juice; cook over low heat, stirring until sugar dissolves. Bring to a boil over medium-high heat; reduce heat, and simmer 5 minutes. Remove from heat; cool. Yield: 2¼ cups.
*2 cups frozen strawberries, thawed, may be substituted.

*cook's secret*... We got great results for this recipe using a hand mixer, and then stirring in the flour by hand. High-powered stand mixers can overbeat some pound cakes, giving them a rough texture.

### Secrets to Successful Pound Cakes

● To measure flour, spoon it into a dry measuring cup and level with a knife. (Don't scoop the measuring cup into the flour or pack the flour.)
● Soften the butter to room temperature (don't melt it) before adding it to the mixture. Remove the butter from the refrigerator about 2 hours before you plan to use it. If you're in a hurry, cut it into cubes to speed the process.
● Grease the sides and bottom of the pan with solid vegetable shortening; sprinkle it well with flour to cover the inside surfaces. Shake out excess flour.
● Place the pan in the center of the preheated oven, and bake as directed. (A temperature that is too low will cause the cake to fall.)
● Keep the oven door closed until minimum baking time has elapsed. Test the cake for doneness with a cake tester or long wooden pick. Insert it in the center of the cake; it should come out with no batter or crumbs clinging to it.
● Cool the cake in the pan on a wire rack 10 to 15 minutes. Removing it too soon may cause the cake to fall apart.
● Store the cake in an airtight container up to 3 days. You may also wrap it with plastic wrap and aluminum foil, and refrigerate up to 1 week or freeze up to 2 months. Thaw the cake without unwrapping for best results.

When our Test Kitchens staff stumbled onto an extremely simple method of making a pound cake, we doubted it would work twice. A procedure that broke all the rules—not adding the eggs one at a time, not alternating the milk and flour, not beating the butter and sugar until fluffy—surely would be doomed to fail.

But we gave the method another whirl. Two additional tests also produced beautiful cakes: tall, crusty on top, with a fine, velvety texture and buttery flavor. They were every bit as wonderful as their traditionally made counterparts. Here, we share both the two-step and traditional methods.

## Two-Step Pound Cake

*This cake requires a heavy-duty stand mixer with a 4-quart bowl and a paddle attachment.*

| | |
|---|---|
| 4 cups all-purpose flour | ¾ cup milk |
| 3 cups sugar | 6 eggs |
| 1 pound butter, softened | 2 teaspoons vanilla extract |

• Place all ingredients in order listed in a 4-quart bowl. Beat at low speed with a heavy-duty electric mixer 1 minute, stopping to scrape down sides. Beat at medium speed 2 minutes. Pour into a greased and floured 10-inch tube pan.

• Bake at 325° for 1 hour and 30 minutes or until a long wooden pick inserted in center comes out clean. Cool in pan on a wire rack 10 minutes; remove from pan, and let cool completely on wire rack. Yield: 1 (10-inch) cake.

**Traditional Method:** Beat butter at medium speed with an electric mixer 2 minutes or until creamy; gradually add sugar, beating until light and fluffy. Add eggs, 1 at a time, beating after each addition.

• Add flour to butter mixture alternately with milk, beginning and ending with flour. Beat at low speed just until blended after each addition. Stir in vanilla. Pour batter into a greased and floured 10-inch tube pan. Bake as directed in two-step method.

*cook's secret...* When greasing a cake pan, nothing works as well as shortening, and it doesn't have to be a messy process. Slip your fingers into a small plastic bag, dip fingers into shortening, wipe the bag over the pan, and toss the bag.

oth Vie Warshaw of our Test Kitchens staff and Joy Zacharia, Associate Foods Editor, say their favorite *Southern Living* dessert recipe to use at home is Chocolate Pound Cake, submitted by Editor in Chief John Floyd's late mother, Louise Floyd, for the November 1994 issue. As Joy explains, "It's easy to make, and the results are a moist, chocolaty, perfect–every–time cake."

*editor's choice*

# Chocolate Pound Cake

| | |
|---|---|
| 1 cup butter or margarine, softened | ¼ cup cocoa |
| 1 cup shortening | ½ teaspoon baking powder |
| 3 cups sugar | ½ teaspoon salt |
| 5 large eggs | 1 cup milk |
| 3 cups all-purpose flour | 1 tablespoon vanilla extract |

• Beat butter and shortening at medium speed with an electric mixer about 2 minutes or until creamy. Gradually add sugar, beating at medium speed 5 to 7 minutes. Add eggs, 1 at a time, beating just until yellow disappears.

• Combine flour and next 3 ingredients; add to butter mixture alternately with milk, beginning and ending with flour mixture. Mix at low speed just until blended after each addition. Stir in vanilla. Pour batter into a greased and floured 10-inch tube pan.

• Bake at 325° for 1 hour and 30 minutes or until a long wooden pick inserted in center comes out clean. Cool in pan on a wire rack 10 to 15 minutes; remove from pan, and let cool completely on wire rack. Yield: 1 (10-inch) cake.

*Louise Floyd*
Potters Station, Alabama

*cook's secret*... Traditional pound cakes have no leavening other than eggs, but this version adds a smidgen of baking powder for extra oomph.

A homemade pound cake is a dessert that says Southern hospitality. The texture ensures that it travels well and freezes nicely, making it just right for giving. This recipe from *Southern Living* Editor in Chief John Floyd's wife, Pam, always gets rave reviews.

*special occasion*

# Buttered Rum Pound Cake with Bananas Foster Sauce

| | |
|---|---|
| 1 cup butter, softened | 1 teaspoon vanilla extract |
| 2½ cups sugar | 1 teaspoon lemon extract |
| 6 large eggs, separated | ½ cup sugar |
| 3 cups all-purpose flour | Buttered Rum Glaze |
| ¼ teaspoon baking soda | Bananas Foster Sauce |
| 1 (8-ounce) container sour cream | Vanilla ice cream |

• Beat butter at medium speed with a heavy-duty electric stand mixer until creamy. Add 2½ cups sugar, beating 4 to 5 minutes or until fluffy. Add egg yolks, 1 at a time, beating just until yellow disappears.

• Combine flour and baking soda; add to butter mixture alternately with sour cream, beginning and ending with flour mixture. Stir in extracts.

• Beat egg whites until foamy; gradually add ½ cup sugar, 1 tablespoon at a time, beating until stiff peaks form. Fold into batter. Pour batter into a greased and floured 10-inch tube pan.

• Bake at 325° for 1 hour and 30 minutes or until a long wooden pick inserted in center comes out clean. Cool in pan 10 to 15 minutes; remove from pan, and place on a serving plate. While warm, prick cake surface at 1-inch intervals with a wooden pick; pour warm Buttered Rum Glaze over cake. Let stand 4 hours or overnight before serving. Serve with Bananas Foster Sauce and vanilla ice cream. Yield: 1 (10-inch) cake.

**Lemon Pound Cake:** Add 2 tablespoons grated lemon rind to batter. Proceed with cake recipe as directed. Omit Buttered Rum Glaze and Bananas Foster Sauce.

## Buttered Rum Glaze:

- 6 tablespoons butter, cut into pieces
- 3 tablespoons light rum
- ¾ cup sugar
- 1½ tablespoons water
- ½ cup chopped pecans, toasted

• Stir together first 4 ingredients in a heavy, 1-quart saucepan; cook over medium heat, stirring frequently until mixture comes to a boil. Remove from heat, and stir in pecans. Yield: 1¼ cups.

## Bananas Foster Sauce:

- ¼ cup butter or margarine, cut into pieces
- ½ cup firmly packed brown sugar
- ⅓ cup banana liqueur
- ¼ teaspoon ground cinnamon
- 4 bananas, peeled and sliced
- ⅓ cup light rum

• Stir together first 4 ingredients in a large skillet; cook over medium heat, stirring constantly, until mixture begins to bubble. Add bananas, and cook 2 to 3 minutes or until thoroughly heated. Remove from heat.
• Heat rum in a small saucepan over medium heat. (Do not boil.) Quickly pour rum over banana mixture, and immediately ignite with a long match just above the liquid mixture to light the fumes (not the liquid itself). Let flames die down; serve immediately with Buttered Rum Pound Cake. Yield: 12 servings.

*Pam Floyd*
Birmingham, Alabama

*cook's secret...* Whipping the egg whites with a little sugar before folding them into the cake batter stabilizes the whites and encourages a stately cake that travels well and freezes nicely.

One of my family's favorite ways to savor strawberries is in short-cake. My Midwestern husband grew up eating it made with those tender cake cups you buy at the grocery store. But when he came South, I introduced him to a secret shortcut that calls for frozen biscuits topped with butter, cinnamon, and sugar. He adopted the recipe as his own, quickly mastering the art of whipping cream with precisely the right amount of sugar and then layering it with juicy sugared berries.

For a fancier rendition, try our Party-Perfect Strawberry Shortcakes. This recipe uses sour cream for flavor and enough egg to lend a cakelike (rather than biscuit-style) texture, even though we still knead the dough.

*Susan Dosier*
Executive Editor

*editor's choice*

## Party-Perfect Strawberry Shortcakes

| | |
|---|---|
| 1 (16-ounce) container fresh strawberries, sliced | 1 teaspoon vanilla extract |
| ½ cup sugar, divided | 1 cup whipping cream |
| 2½ cups all-purpose flour | 2 tablespoons sugar |
| 4 teaspoons baking powder | 2 tablespoons strawberry jam |
| ¾ cup butter or margarine, cut into pieces | ¼ teaspoon chopped fresh mint |
| 2 large eggs | Garnishes: fresh mint leaves, strawberry halves |
| 1 cup sour cream | |

- Combine sliced strawberries and ¼ cup sugar. Cover strawberry mixture, and set aside.
- Combine all-purpose flour, baking powder, and remaining ¼ cup sugar; cut in butter with a fork or pastry blender until mixture is crumbly.
- Whisk together eggs, sour cream, and vanilla until blended; add to flour mixture, stirring just until dry ingredients are moistened.
- Turn dough out onto a lightly floured surface, and knead 6 times. Pat dough into an 8-inch square; cut into 16 (2-inch) squares. Place dough squares on a lightly greased baking sheet.
- Bake at 425° for 9 to 11 minutes or until golden.

• Beat whipping cream at medium speed with an electric mixer until foamy. Gradually add 2 tablespoons sugar, beating mixture at high speed until stiff peaks form.

• Remove shortcakes from oven, and split in half horizontally. Combine strawberry jam and chopped mint; spread cut sides of bottom shortcake halves evenly with jam mixture, and top evenly with half of strawberry mixture. Cover mixture evenly with whipped cream; top with remaining strawberry mixture and remaining shortcake halves. Garnish, if desired. Serve immediately. Yield: 16 servings.

**Round Shortcakes:** Pat dough to a ½-inch thickness, and cut with a 3-inch round cutter. Place dough on a lightly greased baking sheet, and proceed with recipe as directed. Yield: 12 servings.

**Shortcut Shortcakes:** Combine 1 (16-ounce) container of strawberries, sliced, and ¼ cup sugar; cover and set aside. Brush 9 large frozen biscuits with 3 tablespoons melted butter. Combine 3 tablespoons sugar and 1 teaspoon ground cinnamon; sprinkle over biscuits. Bake according to package directions. Serve immediately with strawberry mixture and whipped cream. Yield: 9 servings.

*cook's secret...* The small shortcakes in the main recipe are sized to serve on a cake stand. To keep them moist and delicious, we spread strawberry jam onto the bottom cut sides of each shortcake before adding the strawberries and whipped cream. For a cool twist, we've stirred a secret ingredient into the jam: chopped mint!

# Lemon-Coconut Cake

3 large eggs
1 (8-ounce) container sour cream
¾ cup vegetable oil
¾ cup cream of coconut
¾ teaspoon coconut flavoring
½ teaspoon lemon extract

1 (18.25-ounce) package white cake mix
   with pudding
Lemon-Coconut Filling
Fluffy Lemon Frosting
1½ cups to 2 cups sweetened flaked coconut
Garnish: lemon wedges

• Beat eggs at high speed with an electric mixer 2 minutes. Add sour cream and next 4 ingredients, and beat well. Add cake mix; beat at low speed until blended. Beat at high speed 2 minutes. Pour batter into 3 greased and floured 9-inch round cakepans.
• Bake at 325° for 20 to 25 minutes or until a wooden pick inserted in center comes out clean. Cool in pans on wire racks 10 minutes; remove from pans, and let cool completely on wire racks.
• Spread Lemon-Coconut Filling between layers. Spread Fluffy Lemon Frosting on top and sides of cake. Gently press coconut into frosting. Garnish, if desired. Yield: 1 (9-inch) cake.

## Lemon-Coconut Filling:

1 cup sugar
3 tablespoons cornstarch
⅛ teaspoon salt
1 tablespoon grated lemon rind
⅔ cup fresh lemon juice

⅓ cup water
5 egg yolks
½ cup butter or margarine
½ cup sweetened flaked coconut

• Stir together first 3 ingredients in a heavy saucepan. Stir in rind, juice, and water. Bring to a boil over medium heat; boil, stirring constantly, 1 minute. Beat egg yolks until thick and pale; gradually stir half of hot mixture into yolks; add yolk mixture to remaining hot mixture, stirring constantly. Cook, stirring constantly, 1 minute. Remove from heat; add butter and coconut, stirring until butter melts. Cool completely. Yield: 2½ cups.

## Fluffy Lemon Frosting:

1 cup granulated sugar
⅓ cup water
2 tablespoons light corn syrup
2 egg whites

¼ cup powdered sugar
1 teaspoon grated lemon rind
¼ teaspoon lemon extract

• Stir together first 3 ingredients in a heavy saucepan over medium heat, and cook, stirring constantly, until clear. Cook, without stirring, until a candy thermometer registers 232° (thread stage).

• Beat egg whites at medium speed with an electric mixer until soft peaks form; continue to beat, quickly adding syrup mixture. Add powdered sugar, lemon rind, and lemon extract, beating until stiff peaks form and frosting is spreading consistency. Yield: about 3 cups.

## Secrets to Lemon-Coconut Cake Success

### Preparing the Pans

**1.** For this cake, our Test Kitchens staff prefers the old way of greasing and flouring cakepans: Use about 1 teaspoon shortening per pan, rubbed over bottom and up sides. Place 1 to 2 table-spoons all-purpose flour in each pan; tap and tilt pan until greased bottom and sides are coated. Turn pan over and tap out excess flour.

### Making the Fluffy Lemon Frosting

**2.** A hot mixture of sugar, water, and corn syrup is beaten into egg whites. It's often called a "seven-minute frosting," because that's about how long it takes to make. Pour hot sugar mixture into the egg whites at a quick, steady pace, with mixer on medium speed. For the fluffiest frosting, beat as much air as possible into the egg whites before the hot mixture cooks them.

### Filling, Frosting, and Garnishing

**3.** To protect the cake stand from smears of frosting, cut an 8-inch circle from the center of a 12-inch square of wax paper, and discard the circle. Place the wax paper square on the cake stand; center the bottom cake layer on the stand so that the wax paper square is surrounding it.

**4.** For ease in frosting, hold cake layers in place with wooden skewers; remove them when through frosting. This trick works great for layer cakes with thick fillings, such as this one.

**5.** Frost the cake's sides first, starting from the bottom layer and working up over the top edge. Spread frosting over the top to finish. The frosting sets quickly, so be sure to work quickly.

**6.** To decorate the cake sides with coconut, cup your hand, fill with coconut, and press against the frosting; sprinkle over the top. When you've finished, pull opposite corners of wax paper and tear it away from under the cake.

cakes 129

Wish you had the time and talent to make great cakes like your mother or grandmother made? Then take some advice from Nashville food writer Anne Byrn, aka The Cake Mix Doctor. In her book *The Cake Mix Doctor,* she offers updated versions of some favorite Southern cakes that have graced family dinners and covered-dish suppers for a generation.

"I wrote a story for *The Tennessean* in Nashville in June 1998, sharing cake mix recipes my family had doctored," Anne explains. "The reaction was so strong, I asked readers to send in their own favorites. I got five hundred recipes within one week and quickly realized this should be a book."

*The Cake Mix Doctor* was a runaway success. Anne soon had a Web site, www.cakemixdoctor.com, and a second book. She most recently turned to savory foods with *The Dinner Doctor* (Workman Publishing Company, Inc.). Of course, the book includes her signature cakes as well.

Her efforts have helped other time-pressed cooks produce delicious desserts. Anne says, "*The Cake Mix Doctor* has made baking accessible to an awful lot of people who haven't had any luck with it before."

We especially love the luscious caramel frosting for her Tennessee Jam Cake. It's easier and quicker than others we've tried.

# Tennessee Jam Cake

| | |
|---|---|
| 1 (18.25-ounce) package spice cake mix | 3 large eggs |
| 1 cup buttermilk | ¼ teaspoon ground cinnamon |
| ⅓ cup sweetened applesauce | ½ cup blackberry jam |
| ⅓ cup vegetable oil | Quick Caramel Frosting |

- Beat first 6 ingredients at low speed with an electric mixer for 1 minute. Scrape down sides, and beat at medium speed 2 more minutes until well blended, stopping to scrape down sides, if needed. Pour batter evenly into 2 greased and floured 9-inch round cakepans.
- Bake at 350° for 26 to 28 minutes or until cakes are light brown and spring back when lightly pressed with your finger.
- Cool in pans on wire racks 10 minutes; remove from pans, and let cool completely on wire racks.
- Place 1 layer on a serving platter. Spread with blackberry jam, leaving a ½-inch border. Spread a smooth, thin layer of warm Quick Caramel Frosting over jam. Top with remaining cake layer. Spread top and sides of cake with remaining frosting, working quickly before the frosting hardens. Let cake stand 10 minutes. Yield: 1 (9-inch) cake.

NOTE: *For testing purposes only, we used Knott's Berry Farm Blackberry Jam.*

## Quick Caramel Frosting:

| | |
|---|---|
| ½ cup butter or margarine | ¼ cup milk |
| ½ cup firmly packed light brown sugar | 2 cups powdered sugar, sifted |
| ½ cup firmly packed dark brown sugar | 1 teaspoon vanilla extract |

- Bring first 3 ingredients to boil in a 3½-quart saucepan over medium heat, whisking constantly, about 2 minutes.
- Stir in milk, and bring to a boil; remove from heat. Add powdered sugar and vanilla, stirring with a wooden spoon until smooth. Use immediately. Yield: 3 cups.

*Anne Byrn*
Nashville, Tennessee
Adapted from *The Cake Mix Doctor*
(Workman Publishing Company, Inc.)

*cook's secret...* If caramel frosting becomes too firm to spread while frosting the cake, place it over low heat for 1 minute, stirring constantly, to thin it back down to a spreading consistency.

# Triple-Decker Strawberry Cake

*We doubled the frosting called for in Anne's original recipe to add*
*extra richness to this cake. The cake keeps best in the refrigerator.*

| | |
|---|---|
| 1 (18.25-ounce) package white cake mix | ½ cup finely chopped fresh strawberries |
| 1 (3-ounce) package strawberry gelatin | 1 cup vegetable oil |
| 4 large eggs | ½ cup milk |
| ½ cup sugar | Strawberry Buttercream Frosting |
| ¼ cup all-purpose flour | Garnish: whole strawberries |

• Beat cake mix and next 7 ingredients at low speed with an electric mixer 1 minute. Scrape down sides, and beat at medium speed 2 more minutes, stopping to scrape down sides, if needed. (Strawberries should be well blended into batter.) Pour batter into 3 greased and floured 9-inch cakepans.

• Bake at 350° for 23 minutes or until cakes spring back when lightly pressed with your finger. Cool in pans on wire racks 10 minutes; remove from pans, and let cool completely on wire racks. Spread Strawberry Buttercream Frosting between layers and on top and sides of cake. Store in refrigerator. Garnish, if desired. Yield: 1 (3-layer) cake.

**NOTE:** *For testing purposes only, we used Duncan Hines Moist Deluxe Classic White Cake Mix without pudding.*

## Strawberry Buttercream Frosting:

| | |
|---|---|
| 1 cup butter, softened | 1 cup finely chopped fresh strawberries |
| 2 (16-ounce) packages powdered sugar, sifted | |

• Beat butter at medium speed with an electric mixer 20 seconds or until fluffy. Add powdered sugar and chopped strawberries, beating at low speed until creamy. (Add more sugar if frosting is too thin, or add strawberries if too thick.) Yield: 2½ cups.

*Anne Byrn*
Nashville, Tennessee
Adapted from *The Cake Mix Doctor*
(Workman Publishing Company, Inc.)

*cook's secret*... This is a great cake to make ahead. There are tricks that will help you cover and chill the cake without disturbing the frosting: Place finished cake in the refrigerator, uncovered, and chill for 30 minutes or until the frosting sets. Cover gently with wax paper, and store in the refrigerator for up to 1 week. To freeze, wrap chilled cake with aluminum foil, and freeze up to 6 months. Thaw cake overnight in the refrigerator.

# Ultimate Chocolate Cake with Rich Chocolate Buttercream

| | |
|---|---|
| 4 (1-ounce) unsweetened chocolate baking squares | ¾ teaspoon salt |
| ½ cup shortening | ½ teaspoon baking powder |
| 2 cups sugar | ¾ cup buttermilk |
| 2 large eggs | ¾ cup water |
| 2 cups sifted cake flour | 1 teaspoon vanilla extract |
| 1 teaspoon baking soda | Rich Chocolate Buttercream |

• Place chocolate in top of a double boiler; bring water to a boil. Reduce heat to low; cook until chocolate melts, stirring often. Remove from heat.

• Beat shortening at medium speed with an electric mixer until creamy; gradually add sugar, beating well. Add eggs, 1 at a time, beating after each addition. Add chocolate, mixing well.

• Combine flour and next 3 ingredients; add to chocolate mixture alternately with buttermilk, beginning and ending with flour mixture. Mix at low speed after each addition until blended. Add ¾ cup water, mixing well. Stir in vanilla. Pour batter into 2 greased and floured 9-inch round cakepans.

• Bake at 350° for 30 to 35 minutes or until a wooden pick inserted in center comes out clean. Cool in pans on wire racks 10 minutes; remove from pans, and cool completely on wire racks. Frost with Rich Chocolate Buttercream. Yield: 1 (9-inch) cake.

## Rich Chocolate Buttercream:

| | |
|---|---|
| 2 (1-ounce) unsweetened chocolate baking squares | 4 cups sifted powdered sugar |
| 2 (1-ounce) semisweet chocolate baking squares | ¼ cup cocoa |
| | ¼ cup milk |
| 1 cup butter or margarine, softened | 2 teaspoons vanilla extract |

• Place chocolate in top of a double boiler; bring water to a boil. Reduce heat to low; cook until chocolate melts, stirring often. Remove from heat.

• Beat butter at medium speed with an electric mixer until creamy. Add chocolate, powdered sugar, and remaining ingredients; beat until spreading consistency. Yield: 3¾ cups.

*cook's secret...* For cupcakes, spoon batter into paper-lined muffin pans, filling each cup half full. Bake at 350° for 15 to 18 minutes. Remove from pans, and cool on wire racks. Frost as desired. Yield: 3 dozen.

ila Bryning took a Grand Prize for Gracious Southern Desserts in the 2001 *Southern Living* Holiday Recipe Contest with her Praline-Pumpkin Torte. She admits that she gets rave reviews for this cake that she adapted from her sister's recipe. "I've taken this cake all over—to church gatherings and family reunions," she says, "and I've given the recipe to everyone."

The entries in the desserts category for the 2001 recipe contest were so good that Editor in Chief John Floyd suggested selecting two Grand Prize winners. Betty Skinner's recipe for Orange Date-Nut Cake (page 137) was also chosen as a Grand Prize Winner.

*contest winner*

## Praline-Pumpkin Torte

*A crunchy pralinelike topping bakes into each layer of the cake.*
*Stack the layers with the praline side up. It's almost a shame to cover*
*the praline crust with frosting, but you'll be glad you did.*

| | |
|---|---|
| ¾ cup firmly packed brown sugar | ¼ teaspoon vanilla extract |
| ⅓ cup butter or margarine | 2 cups all-purpose flour |
| 3 tablespoons whipping cream | 2 teaspoons baking powder |
| ¾ cup chopped pecans | 2 teaspoons pumpkin pie spice |
| 4 large eggs | 1 teaspoon baking soda |
| 1⅔ cups granulated sugar | 1 teaspoon salt |
| 1 cup vegetable oil | Whipped Cream Topping |
| 1 (15-ounce) can pumpkin | Chopped pecans |

• Cook first 3 ingredients in a saucepan over low heat, stirring until brown sugar dissolves. Pour into 2 greased 9-inch round cakepans; sprinkle evenly with ¾ cup pecans. Cool.

• Beat eggs, granulated sugar, and oil at medium speed with an electric mixer. Add pumpkin and vanilla; beat well.

• Combine flour and next 4 ingredients; add to pumpkin mixture, beating until blended. Spoon batter evenly into prepared cakepans.

• Bake at 350° for 30 to 35 minutes or until a wooden pick inserted in center comes out clean. Cool in pans on wire racks 5 minutes; remove from pans, and let cool completely on wire racks.

• Place 1 cake layer on a serving plate, praline side up; spread evenly with half of Whipped Cream Topping. Top with remaining layer, praline side up, and spread remaining Whipped Cream Topping over top of cake. Sprinkle cake with chopped pecans. Store in refrigerator. Yield: 1 (9-inch) cake.

## Whipped Cream Topping:

1¾ cups whipping cream
¼ cup powdered sugar

¼ teaspoon vanilla extract

• Beat whipping cream until soft peaks form. Add sugar and vanilla, beating until blended. Yield: 3½ cups.

*Mila Bryning*
Alexandria, Virginia

*cook's secret...* If you don't have pumpkin pie spice, use 1 teaspoon ground cinnamon, ½ teaspoon ground ginger, ¼ teaspoon ground allspice, and ¼ teaspoon ground nutmeg instead.

# Black Cake (A Kwanzaa Fruitcake)

*For Sharon and Darrell Green, Black Cake is the star at their
Kwanzaa celebration. They rely on close friend Margarite Reed's recipe
for one of the best fruitcakes you'll ever taste.*

| | | | |
|---|---|---|---|
| 1¾ | cups currants | ⅛ | teaspoon ground nutmeg |
| 1½ | cups raisins | ½ | pound butter |
| 1½ | cups pitted prunes | ½ | pound dark brown sugar |
| 1 | (8-ounce) package candied cherries | 2 | cups all-purpose flour |
| ½ | (7-ounce) package dried mixed fruit | 1½ | teaspoons baking powder |
| 2 | cups dark rum | ¼ | cup burnt sugar syrup |
| 6 | large eggs | 2 | cups tawny port wine |
| ⅛ | teaspoon ground cinnamon | | Whipped cream (optional) |

• Combine first 6 ingredients in a large bowl; cover and chill 8 hours or up to 1 week.

• Remove fruit mixture from refrigerator, and process, in batches, in a food processor
until smooth, stopping to scrape down sides; set aside.

• Whisk together eggs, cinnamon, and nutmeg until foamy.

• Beat butter and dark brown sugar at medium speed with an electric mixer until creamy.
Add egg mixture, beating until blended. Add fruit puree; blend well.

• Combine flour and baking powder; stir into fruit mixture. Stir in burnt sugar syrup.
Spoon batter evenly into a greased and floured 10-inch springform pan.

• Bake at 300° for 1 hour and 40 minutes or until a wooden pick inserted in center
comes out clean. Cool in pan on a wire rack 1 hour; remove from pan, and let cool
completely on wire rack.

• Pour 1 cup port wine evenly over top of cake; let stand 10 minutes. Pour remaining
1 cup wine over cake. Wrap cake with cheesecloth, and place in a covered container.
Let stand 2 to 3 days. (Do not refrigerate.) Serve with whipped cream, if desired.
Yield: 1 (10-inch) fruitcake.

**NOTE:** *Burnt sugar syrup is available by mail order from Eve Sales Corporation. Contact them
at evesalesny@aol.com, or call (718) 589-6800.*

*Margarite Reed*
Atlanta, Georgia

*cook's secret...* Black Cake is easy to make. The key is soaking the
fruit. The longer you soak it, the better the flavor and texture of the cake. Some in my family start
soaking the fruit several months ahead.

*Sharon Green*
Atlanta, Georgia

B etty Skinner's recipe was a Grand Prize Winner in the 2001 *Southern Living* Holiday Recipe Contest. "I've had this recipe for more than 50 years," Betty says. "It's such a rich cake that you don't need but a small slice."

*contest winner*

# Orange Date-Nut Cake

| | |
|---|---|
| 1 cup butter or margarine, softened | 1 (8-ounce) package chopped sugared |
| 4 cups sugar, divided |   dates |
| 4 large eggs | 1 cup chopped pecans, toasted |
| 4 cups all-purpose flour | 4 teaspoons grated orange rind, divided |
| 1 teaspoon baking soda | 1 cup orange juice |
| 1½ cups buttermilk | |

• Beat butter at medium speed with an electric mixer until fluffy. Gradually add 2 cups sugar, beating well. Add eggs, 1 at a time, beating until blended after each addition.

• Combine flour and baking soda; add to butter mixture alternately with buttermilk, beginning and ending with flour mixture. Beat at low speed until blended after each addition. Stir in dates, pecans, and 2 teaspoons orange rind. Pour batter into a greased and floured 10-inch tube pan.

• Bake at 350° for 1 hour and 10 minutes or until a long wooden pick inserted in center comes out clean.

• Bring orange juice, remaining 2 cups sugar, and remaining 2 teaspoons rind to a boil in a saucepan; cook, stirring constantly, 1 minute.

• Gently run a knife around edge of cake; prick cake surface with a wooden pick. Drizzle glaze over warm cake. Let cool in pan on a wire rack. Yield: 10 servings.

*Betty W. Skinner*
*Blacksburg, Virginia*

*cook's secret...* If you can't find chopped dates, substitute an equal weight of whole pitted dates. Cut into small pieces using kitchen shears and toss them lightly in sugar before stirring into the batter.

This recipe from Marie Rizzio was a 2001 *Southern Living* Holiday Recipe Contest Runner Up. Marie claims that she hasn't found a single person who doesn't like this dessert. "And who won't fight over the last bite on the plate." she adds.

*contest winner*

## Festive Piña Colada Cheesecake

| | |
|---|---|
| 6 tablespoons unsalted butter, melted | 1 cup cream of coconut |
| 1¾ cups graham cracker crumbs | 1 cup sour cream |
| ¾ cup chopped pecans, toasted | ⅓ cup light rum |
| 1 tablespoon sugar | 4 teaspoons coconut extract |
| 3 (8-ounce) packages cream cheese, softened | 1 (8-ounce) can crushed pineapple, drained |
| ½ cup sugar | Glaze |
| 5 large eggs | Garnishes: whipped cream and toasted coconut |

• Stir together first 4 ingredients, and press into bottom and 1½ inches up sides of a lightly greased 10-inch springform pan.

• Beat cream cheese and ½ cup sugar at medium speed with an electric mixer 3 minutes or until fluffy. Add eggs, 1 at a time, beating well after each addition. Add cream of coconut and next 4 ingredients, beating until blended. Pour mixture into crust.

• Bake at 325° for 1 hour and 15 minutes or until center is almost set. Remove from oven, and cool in pan on a wire rack. Spread Glaze over top of cheesecake. Cover and chill at least 8 hours. Release sides of pan. Garnish, if desired. Yield: 1 (10-inch) cheesecake.

### Glaze:

| | |
|---|---|
| 1 tablespoon cornstarch | ¼ cup sugar |
| 1 tablespoon water | 2 tablespoons lemon juice |
| 1 (8-ounce) can crushed pineapple | |

• Stir together cornstarch and 1 tablespoon water until smooth. Combine cornstarch mixture, crushed pineapple, ¼ cup sugar, and lemon juice in a saucepan over medium heat; cook, stirring constantly, 5 minutes or until mixture is thickened and bubbly. Remove from heat; let cool completely. Yield: 1 cup.

*Marie Rizzio*
Traverse City, Michigan

# Chocolate Chunk Cheesecake

| | | | |
|---|---|---|---|
| 2 | cups cream-filled chocolate sandwich cookie crumbs (about 20 cookies) | 2 | teaspoons vanilla extract |
| 2 | tablespoons butter or margarine, melted | 1¾ | cups semisweet chocolate chunks, divided |
| 4 | (8-ounce) packages cream cheese, softened | 1½ | cups coarsely crushed cream-filled chocolate sandwich cookies (about 14 cookies) |
| 1½ | cups sugar | ⅓ | cup whipping cream |
| 4 | large eggs | | |

• Stir together 2 cups cookie crumbs and butter; press mixture into bottom and ½ inch up sides of a 9-inch springform pan.

• Beat cream cheese and sugar at medium speed with an electric mixer until blended. Add eggs, 1 at a time, beating just until blended after each addition. Stir in vanilla, 1 cup chocolate chunks, and coarsely crushed cookies. Pour into crust.

• Bake at 325° for 55 minutes or until center is almost set. Turn off oven; let cheesecake stand in oven, with oven door partially open, 20 minutes.

• Remove cheesecake from oven; cool in pan on a wire rack 30 minutes. Cover and chill at least 8 hours. Release sides of pan.

• Microwave remaining ¾ cups chocolate chunks and whipping cream in a glass bowl at HIGH 1 minute; stir until chocolate melts. Chill 30 minutes. Pour over cheesecake. Yield: 12 to 14 servings.

*cook's secret...* Smooth the crust into the springform pan using a flat-bottomed and straight-sided glass. A glass of this shape will even the bottom and sides of the crust nicely without leaving thicker portions like those often found around the edges of cheesecake.

M any of our readers refer to mincemeat as a traditional favorite, but for others it's an acquired taste. This tangy preserve of fruits, nuts, and spices mellowed in liquor works well in both sweet and savory dishes.

Marilyn Rush declares that her Mincemeat Cheesecake has "more personality than other cakes and pies." We agreed wholeheartedly.

## Mincemeat Cheesecake

| | | | |
|---|---|---|---|
| 2 | cups graham cracker crumbs | 1 | cup sugar |
| ⅓ | cup butter or margarine, melted | 4 | large eggs |
| ¼ | cup sugar | 1 | tablespoon grated orange rind |
| ½ | cup cinnamon-covered raisins (optional) | 1 | tablespoon fresh orange juice |
| 3 | (8-ounce) packages cream cheese, softened | 1 | (8-ounce) container sour cream |
| | | 1 | cup prepared mincemeat |

• Stir together first 3 ingredients and, if desired, raisins. Press mixture into bottom and 1½ inches up sides of a 9-inch springform pan.

• Beat cream cheese and 1 cup sugar at medium speed with an electric mixer until fluffy. Add eggs, 1 at a time, beating until blended after each addition. Add rind, juice, and sour cream, beating until blended. Spoon mixture into crust.

• Bake at 350° for 1 hour or until center is firm. Turn oven off; let cheesecake stand in oven, with oven door closed, 30 minutes. Remove to wire rack to cool completely.

• Spread mincemeat over cheesecake. Chill at least 8 hours. Yield: 12 to 14 servings.

*Marilyn Rush*
Sioux City, Iowa

*cook's secret*... You'll need to crumble about 28 graham cracker squares to yield 2 cups crumbs for this recipe. Or purchase a box of graham cracker crumbs, instead.

••• Most grocery stores carry two varieties of mincemeat, especially during the holiday season: ready-to-use mincemeat in the jar and the condensed boxed variety. Reconstitute the condensed variety with water, following directions on the back of the box. In most recipes, either type can be used. Store mincemeat unopened in your pantry for 1 year. Once opened, refrigerate for 3 to 4 days.

# Walnut Fudge Pie

3 large eggs, lightly beaten
½ cup firmly packed brown sugar
¼ cup all-purpose flour
¼ cup butter or margarine, melted
1 teaspoon vanilla extract
1 (12-ounce) package semisweet chocolate morsels, melted

1½ cups walnut halves or pecan pieces
½ (15-ounce) package refrigerated piecrusts
Coffee ice cream
Java Chocolate Sauce (optional)

• Stir together first 5 ingredients until blended; stir in melted chocolate morsels and nuts.
• Fit piecrust into a 9-inch pieplate according to package directions; fold edges under, and crimp. Spoon filling into crust.
• Bake at 375° for 30 minutes. Cool completely on a wire rack. Serve with coffee ice cream and, if desired, Java Chocolate Sauce. Yield: 8 servings.

## Java Chocolate Sauce:

1 (12-ounce) package semisweet chocolate morsels
½ cup whipping cream

1 tablespoon butter or margarine
¼ cup strong brewed coffee

• Heat chocolate morsels, cream, and butter in a heavy saucepan over low heat until chocolate and butter melt, stirring often. Cook, stirring constantly, 2 to 3 minutes or until smooth. Remove from heat; stir in coffee. Serve warm. Yield: 1¼ cups.

*cook's secret...* Chocolate can be melted in a heavy pan over low heat on the cook-top or in a microwave-safe container in the microwave. Be sure all utensils are very dry because even a little water will cause the chocolate to seize.

We had quite a few discussions around our tasting table trying to choose a grand pecan pie recipe. Each of us had a special way to serve it—warm or cold, with or without ice cream or whipped cream. Believe us when we say that we tasted a lot of pecan pies. Assistant Test Kitchens Director James Schend prepared every version. In the end we decided it all comes down to the type of pie you ate when growing up. Here are two of our favorites.

*regional favorite*

## Mom's Pecan Pie

| | | | |
|---|---|---|---|
| 1 | (15-ounce) package refrigerated piecrusts | 2 | tablespoons butter or margarine, melted |
| 3 | large eggs | 2 | teaspoons vanilla extract |
| 1 | cup sugar | ¼ | teaspoon salt |
| ¾ | cup light corn syrup | 1½ | cups pecan halves* |

• Unfold and stack 2 piecrusts; gently roll or press together. Fit into a 9-inch pieplate according to package directions; fold edges under, and crimp.
• Stir together eggs and next 5 ingredients; stir in pecans.
• Pour filling into crust. Bake at 350° for 55 minutes or until set. Serve warm or cold. Yield: 8 servings.

*Chopped pecans, a less expensive choice, may be substituted for the pecan halves.*

*Linda Schend*
Kenosha, Wisconsin

### Dressed-Up Crusts

Try these ideas when you're baking a pie for a special occasion.

• Cut pastry with cookie cutters for a quick-and-easy decoration for the top of a pie.
• Use a pizza cutter to make strips for a lattice design. Or use a one-piece lattice-style crust cutter.
• Braid pastry strips on a countertop. Then carefully arrange the pastry braids around the edge of the pie.
• Brush the piecrust with a lightly beaten egg before baking to add some color and shine.

# Mystery Pecan Pie

*Taste pecan pie and cheesecake together in this recipe,*
*and the only mystery will be where did it all go?*

| | |
|---|---|
| 1 (15-ounce) package refrigerated piecrusts | 2 teaspoons vanilla, divided |
| 1 (8-ounce) package cream cheese, softened | ¼ teaspoon salt |
| 4 large eggs, divided | 1 cup chopped pecans |
| ¾ cup sugar, divided | 1 cup light corn syrup |

- Unfold and stack 2 piecrusts; gently roll or press together. Fit into a 9-inch pieplate according to package directions; fold edges under, and crimp.
- Beat cream cheese, 1 egg, ½ cup sugar, 1 teaspoon vanilla, and salt at medium speed with an electric mixer until smooth. Pour into crust. Sprinkle with pecans.
- Stir together corn syrup, remaining eggs, remaining ¼ cup sugar, and remaining 1 teaspoon vanilla; pour mixture over pecans.
- Bake at 350° for 50 to 55 minutes or until set. Yield: 8 servings.

**NOTE:** *Be sure to store this pecan pie in the fridge since it has a cheesecake filling.*

*Gretchen Eickhorst*
St. Charles, Missouri

## Secrets to a Picture-Perfect Piecrust

Rolling 2 refrigerated crusts into a single crust is a trick we discovered in our Test Kitchens. Our method gives you an especially sturdy crust that doesn't allow the filling to seep through the bottom. Here's how to do it.

**1.** Unfold 1 piecrust, and press out fold lines.

**2.** Unfold second crust, and stack on top, turning so that fold lines do not match. Press edges to seal.

**3.** Roll crust into a 12-inch circle. Fit into a 9-inch pieplate. Trim dough to about ½ inch from edge of pieplate, fold under; flute or crimp as desired.

# Bourbon-Chocolate Pecan Pie

½ (15-ounce) package refrigerated piecrusts
4 large eggs
1 cup light corn syrup
6 tablespoons butter or margarine, melted
½ cup granulated sugar
¼ cup firmly packed light brown sugar

3 tablespoons bourbon
1 tablespoon all-purpose flour
1 tablespoon vanilla extract
1 cup coarsely chopped pecans
1 cup semisweet chocolate morsels

• Fit piecrust into a 9-inch pieplate according to package directions; fold edges under, and crimp. Whisk together eggs and next 7 ingredients until mixture is smooth; stir in chopped pecans and chocolate morsels. Pour into crust.
• Bake on lowest oven rack at 350° for 1 hour or until set. Yield: 8 servings.

*cook's secret*... Baking this pie on the lowest oven rack keeps the crust from becoming soggy.

# Fried Strawberry Pies

2 cups fresh strawberries, mashed
¾ cup granulated sugar
¼ cup cornstarch

1 (15-ounce) package refrigerated piecrusts
Vegetable oil
Powdered sugar

• Combine first 3 ingredients in a saucepan. Bring strawberry mixture to a boil over medium heat. Cook, stirring constantly, 1 minute or until thickened. Cool completely.
• Roll 1 piecrust to press out fold lines; cut into 9 circles with a 3-inch cutter. Roll circles to 3½-inch diameter; moisten edges with water. Spoon 2 teaspoons strawberry mixture in the center of a circle; fold over, pressing edges to seal. Repeat with remaining crust and strawberry mixture. Place pies in a single layer on a baking sheet, and freeze at least 1 hour.
• Pour oil to a depth of 1 inch into a large heavy skillet; heat to 350°. Fry pies, in batches, 1 minute on each side or until golden. Drain on paper towels; sprinkle with powdered sugar. Yield: 18 pies.

*Marjorie Henson*
Benton, Kentucky

*cook's secret*... Freezing Fried Strawberry Pies before frying them is the secret to keeping the crusts intact in the hot oil.

# Easy Strawberry Pie

*This simple, delicious dessert is reminiscent of a familiar*
*classic served at a well-known national restaurant chain.*

1 cup sugar
1 cup water
3 tablespoons cornstarch
¼ cup strawberry gelatin

4 cups fresh strawberries, halved
1 baked (9-inch) pastry shell
Sweetened whipped cream or frozen
    whipped topping (optional)

• Bring first 3 ingredients to a boil in a saucepan over medium heat, and cook, stirring constantly, 1 minute or until thickened. Stir in strawberry gelatin until dissolved. Remove from heat; chill 2 hours.

• Arrange strawberries in crust, and pour gelatin mixture over strawberries. Cover and chill 2 hours. Uncover and, if desired, serve pie with whipped cream. Yield: 8 servings.

*Thelma Clark*
Clarksville, Arkansas

*cook's secret...* For an especially pretty pie, take care how you arrange the berries in the pastry shell. They embed in a translucent ruby gelatin coating once you pour on the topping. Small strawberries look prettier than large ones, which can have hollow centers.

**K**ay Wilkerson recalls serving Strawberry-Mascarpone Tart for the first time to her supper club during the spring, when beautiful berries were available. She declares, "This recipe turned out perfectly and is the prettiest dessert I've ever made."

## Strawberry-Mascarpone Tart

*Plan ahead when preparing this recipe: The steps are easy,*
*but the components require chilling separately. Kay also*
*suggests using a good-quality balsamic vinegar.*

½  cup plus 2 tablespoons unsalted butter,
    softened
⅓  cup granulated sugar
2  tablespoons milk
1  egg yolk
1½  cups all-purpose flour

1  tablespoon powdered sugar
⅛  teaspoon salt
  Mascarpone Filling
  Marinated Strawberries
  Balsamic-Strawberry Syrup

• Beat butter at medium-high speed with an electric mixer until creamy; gradually add ⅓ cup granulated sugar, beating well. Add milk and egg yolk, beating until blended.

• Combine flour, powdered sugar, and salt. Add to butter mixture, beating at low speed just until a dough forms.

• Shape dough into a thick disk; wrap in plastic wrap, and chill 2 hours.

• Roll dough to ¼-inch thickness on a lightly floured surface. Carefully press dough into bottom and 2 inches up sides of a lightly greased 9-inch springform pan; trim off excess dough along edges. Freeze 10 minutes.

• Line dough with aluminum foil, and fill with pie weights or dried beans.

• Bake at 400° for 6 minutes. Remove pie weights and foil, and bake 6 to 10 more minutes or until firm. (Do not brown.) Cool on a wire rack. Gently run a knife around edge of pan, and release sides.

• Spread Mascarpone Filling in tart shell; arrange Marinated Strawberries over tart. Cut tart into slices, and drizzle with Balsamic-Strawberry Syrup. Serve immediately. Yield: 1 (9-inch) tart.

### Mascarpone Filling:

| | |
|---|---|
| 1 (16-ounce) package mascarpone cheese | 1 tablespoon vanilla extract |
| ⅓ cup sugar | ½ teaspoon grated orange rind |
| ¼ cup whipping cream | |

• Stir together all ingredients just until smooth. Yield: about 2½ cups.

### Marinated Strawberries with Balsamic-Strawberry Syrup:

| | |
|---|---|
| 3 pints fresh strawberries, sliced | 3 tablespoons sugar |
| ½ cup balsamic vinegar | |

• Toss together all ingredients until sugar dissolves. Cover strawberry mixture, and chill 2 hours, gently stirring occasionally.
• Pour strawberry mixture through a fine wire-mesh strainer into a saucepan, reserving strawberries for tart.
• Bring strawberry liquid to a boil over medium-high heat, and cook, stirring constantly, 2 minutes or until liquid is reduced to a syrup. Remove strawberry liquid from heat, and cool. Yield: ¼ cup.

*Kay Wilkerson*
Greenville, North Carolina

*cook's secret...* If you can't find mascarpone cheese, here's a simple substitute: Beat 2 (8-ounce) packages cream cheese, softened; ⅓ cup sour cream; and ¼ cup whipping cream until blended.

# Strawberry Tart

*A layer of pastry cream snuggles beneath a blanket of fresh berries in this classic French dessert from Frank Stitt, owner and chef at Highlands Bar and Grill, Bottega, and Chez Fonfon in Birmingham, Alabama.*

| | |
|---|---|
| 1½  cups all-purpose flour | 2  cups half-and-half |
| ⅓  cup sugar | 5  egg yolks |
| ½  teaspoon salt | 1  teaspoon rose water or orange-flower |
| ⅓  cup cold butter or margarine, cut into |     water (optional) |
|     pieces | 3  tablespoons butter or margarine |
| 2  tablespoons cold shortening | 1  teaspoon vanilla extract |
| 3  tablespoons cold water | 1  quart fresh strawberries, sliced |
| ½  cup sugar | Garnish: fresh mint sprig |
| ¼  cup cornstarch | |

• Pulse first 3 ingredients in a blender or food processor 3 or 4 times or until combined.
• Add ⅓ cup butter and shortening; pulse 5 or 6 times or until crumbly. With blender or processor running, gradually add 3 tablespoons cold water, and process until dough forms a ball and leaves sides of bowl, adding more water if necessary. Wrap dough in plastic wrap, and chill 1 hour.
• Roll dough to ⅛-inch thickness on a lightly floured surface. Press into bottom and up sides of a 9-inch tart pan. Line dough with parchment paper; fill with pie weights or dried beans.
• Bake at 425° for 15 minutes. Remove weights and parchment paper, and bake 3 more minutes.
• Combine ½ cup sugar and cornstarch in a medium saucepan.
• Whisk together half-and-half, egg yolks, and, if desired, rose water. Gradually whisk half-and-half mixture into sugar mixture in saucepan over medium heat. Bring to a boil, and cook, whisking constantly, 1 minute. Remove mixture from heat.
• Stir in 3 tablespoons butter and vanilla; cover and chill at least 4 hours. Spoon into crust; top with strawberry slices, and serve immediately. Garnish, if desired.
Yield: 1 (9-inch) tart.

*Chef Frank Stitt*
Birmingham, Alabama

*cook's secret*... Chilling the pastry before rolling it out relaxes the dough and makes it easier to handle.

# Fresh Blackberry Pie

1½  cups fresh blackberries
1¼  cups sugar, divided
 ½  (15-ounce) package refrigerated piecrusts
 3  tablespoons cornstarch
1¼  cups water

 ½  teaspoon vanilla extract
 1  (3-ounce) package raspberry gelatin
 4  drops blue liquid food coloring
Sweetened whipped cream (optional)

- Gently toss berries and ¼ cup sugar in a large bowl; cover and chill 8 hours. Drain.
- Fit piecrust into a 9-inch pieplate according to package directions; fold edges under, and crimp. Prick bottom and sides of piecrust with a fork. Bake at 450° for 7 to 9 minutes or until lightly browned.
- Stir together cornstarch and remaining 1 cup sugar in a small saucepan; slowly whisk in 1¼ cups water and vanilla. Cook over medium heat, whisking constantly, 7 to 8 minutes or until mixture thickens.
- Stir together raspberry gelatin and blue liquid food coloring in a small bowl; whisk into warm cornstarch mixture.
- Spoon blackberries into crust. Pour glaze evenly over berries, pressing down gently with a spoon to be sure all berries are coated. Chill 2½ hours. Serve with whipped cream, if desired. Yield: 8 servings.

*Karyn M. Dardar*
Montegut, Louisiana

*cook's secret...* Though this pie should be assembled and served the same day, you can get a head start by combining the berries and sugar and chilling them the night before.

For Mark and Nancy Miller Reichle, it wouldn't be Thanksgiving without pie. The couple—owners of Southmoreland on the Plaza, an inn in Kansas City, Missouri—gathers with family members before the holiday to prepare the twenty pies they'll enjoy as a fitting end to a day of feasting.

The family has been baking pies at Thanksgiving "forever." Mark explains, "We always did it at my mom's house in California, but for the past two years, we've gathered here." Here are five of their favorites.

## Cherry Pie

| | |
|---|---|
| 2 (14.5-ounce) cans pitted red tart cherries | 1 tablespoon butter |
| 1½ cups sugar | 1 teaspoon almond extract |
| ⅓ cup cornstarch | 1 (15-ounce) package refrigerated |
| 1 teaspoon ground cinnamon | piecrusts |

• Drain cherry juices into a saucepan; stir in next 3 ingredients, and bring to a boil over medium heat, stirring constantly; boil 1 minute or until thick and bubbly. Remove from heat, and stir in cherries, butter, and almond extract.
• Fit 1 piecrust into a 9-inch pieplate. Pour cherry mixture into crust.
• Roll remaining piecrust to press out lines, and cut into ½-inch strips. Arrange strips in a lattice design over filling; fold edges under, and crimp.
• Bake at 400° for 45 minutes or until golden, shielding pie with aluminum foil to prevent excessive browning, if necessary. Yield: 8 servings.

*Mark and Nancy Miller Reichle*
*Kansas City, Missouri*

*cook's secret...* Use a fluted pastry wheel to quickly zip decorative strips of dough for the crust.

# Southmoreland Harvest Pie

| | |
|---|---|
| 1 cup flour | ⅓ cup granulated sugar |
| ½ teaspoon salt | 2 tablespoons cornstarch |
| ¼ cup shortening | 1 teaspoon cinnamon |
| 2 tablespoons cold butter | 1 teaspoon grated orange rind |
| 3 tablespoons ice water | ⅛ teaspoon nutmeg |
| 5 Jonathan or Granny Smith apples, peeled and sliced | ½ cup butter, softened |
| 1¼ cups fresh cranberries | ½ cup granulated sugar |
| 3 tablespoons orange juice | ½ cup dark brown sugar |
| 1 teaspoon vanilla extract | 1 cup chopped walnuts |
| | ⅔ cup all-purpose flour |

• Combine 1 cup flour and salt; cut in shortening and 2 tablespoons cold butter with a fork or pastry blender until mixture is crumbly. Sprinkle water, 1 tablespoon at a time, evenly over surface; stir with a fork just until dry ingredients are moistened. Shape into a ball; chill 1 hour.

• Roll piecrust to ¼-inch thickness. Fit into a 9-inch pieplate. Trim excess pastry along edges. Fold edges under, and crimp.

• Combine apples and next 3 ingredients. Add ⅓ cup granulated sugar and next 4 ingredients, mixing well. Let stand 15 minutes. Spoon apple mixture into crust.

• Cream ½ cup butter, ½ cup granulated sugar, and ½ cup dark brown sugar at medium speed with an electric mixer until creamy. Stir in walnuts and flour; set aside.

• Bake pie at 375° for 30 minutes. Remove from oven, and crumble walnut topping over apple filling; bake 20 more minutes or until golden. Yield: 8 servings.

**NOTE:** *A refrigerated piecrust may be substituted for homemade crust.*

*Mark and Nancy Miller Reichle*
Kansas City, Missouri

*cook's secret*... It's easier to grate the rind before juicing the orange.

# Fancy Chocolate Pie

1 cup all-purpose flour
1 cup chopped pecans
½ cup butter, softened
1 cup whipping cream, divided
1 cup powdered sugar
1 (8-ounce) package cream cheese, softened
1 cup granulated sugar
¼ cup cornstarch

2 cups milk
3 egg yolks
2 (1-ounce) unsweetened chocolate baking squares
2 tablespoons butter
1 teaspoon vanilla extract
2 tablespoons granulated sugar
Garnish: grated chocolate, chopped pecans

• Stir together first 3 ingredients; press into bottom and up sides of a 10-inch deep-dish pieplate. Bake at 350° for 15 to 18 minutes or until lightly browned. Cool.
• Beat ¼ cup cream at medium speed with an electric mixer until foamy; gradually add powdered sugar, and beat until soft peaks form. Fold in cream cheese. Spread evenly over cooled crust.
• Combine granulated sugar and cornstarch in a saucepan; whisk in milk and egg yolks until blended. Add chocolate squares, and bring to a boil over medium heat, stirring constantly; boil 5 minutes or until thick. Remove from heat, and stir in butter and vanilla. Cool 15 to 20 minutes. Pour over cream cheese mixture. Place plastic wrap directly on surface; chill 2 hours or until set.
• Beat remaining ¾ cup cream at medium speed until foamy; add 2 tablespoons granulated sugar, and beat until soft peaks form. Remove plastic wrap, and spread whipped cream over chocolate filling. Garnish, if desired. Yield: 8 servings.

*Mark and Nancy Miller Reichle*
Kansas City, Missouri

# Luscious Lemon Pie

| | |
|---|---|
| 1 cup all-purpose flour | 3 tablespoons flour |
| 1 cup chopped pecans | ⅛ teaspoon salt |
| ½ cup butter, softened | 1½ cups water |
| 1 cup whipping cream, divided | 3 egg yolks, lightly beaten |
| 1 cup powdered sugar | 2 tablespoons butter |
| 1 (8-ounce) package cream cheese, softened | 2 teaspoons grated lemon rind |
| 1½ cups granulated sugar | ⅔ cup fresh lemon juice |
| 6 tablespoons cornstarch | 2 tablespoons granulated sugar |

• Stir together first 3 ingredients; press into bottom and up sides of a 10-inch deep-dish pieplate. Bake at 350° for 15 to 18 minutes or until lightly browned. Cool.

• Beat ¼ cup cream at medium speed with an electric mixer until foamy; gradually add powdered sugar, and beat until soft peaks form. Fold in cream cheese. Spread evenly over cooled crust.

• Combine 1½ cups granulated sugar and next 3 ingredients in a saucepan. Whisk in 1½ cups water until blended. Bring to a boil over medium heat, stirring constantly. Reduce heat, and cook 2 minutes, stirring constantly until thick.

• Remove from heat; gradually stir ¼ cup of hot mixture into egg yolks; add egg yolk mixture to remaining hot mixture. Cook over low heat, stirring constantly, 2 minutes. Remove from heat; stir in butter, lemon rind, and lemon juice. Cool. Spread over cream cheese mixture. Place plastic wrap directly on surface; chill 2 hours or until set.

• Beat remaining ¾ cup cream at medium speed until foamy; add 2 tablespoons granulated sugar, and beat until soft peaks form. Remove plastic wrap, and spread whipped cream over lemon filling. Yield: 8 servings.

*Mark and Nancy Miller Reichle*
Kansas City, Missouri

*cook's secret*... Both of these recipes can also be made in 2 (9-inch) pieplates, or doubled and put into a 13- x 9-inch pan.

# Sloan Family Upside-Down Apple Pie

| | |
|---|---|
| 3 tablespoons butter, softened and divided | ½ cup all-purpose flour |
| ¼ cup firmly packed dark brown sugar | 1 teaspoon ground cinnamon |
| ½ cup chopped pecans | ¼ teaspoon salt |
| 1 (15-ounce) package refrigerated piecrusts | 5 medium Granny Smith apples, peeled and sliced (about 6 cups) |
| 1¼ cups granulated sugar | |

• Combine 2 tablespoons butter, brown sugar, and pecans; spread in bottom of a
9-inch pieplate.
• Fit 1 piecrust over brown sugar mixture in pieplate according to package directions,
pressing down gently.
• Combine granulated sugar and next 3 ingredients in a large bowl; add apples, tossing to
coat. Spoon into crust; dot with remaining 1 tablespoon butter.
• Unfold and place remaining piecrust over apple filling; fold edges under, and crimp. Cut
slits in top for steam to escape.
• Place on an aluminum foil–lined baking sheet, and bake at 425° for 45 minutes or until
golden. Cool slightly on a wire rack. Invert warm pie onto a large plate to serve.
Yield: 8 servings.

*Mark and Nancy Miller Reichle*
Kansas City, Missouri

*cook's secret*... Don't worry if the warm pie oozes a little when you
invert it on the plate. The plate will catch the drips. You'll love the streusel-like "topping" on the
inverted crust.

# Sweet Potato Pie

½ (15-ounce) package refrigerated
    piecrusts
1 (14½-ounce) can mashed sweet potatoes
¾ cup evaporated milk
¾ cup firmly packed brown sugar

2 large eggs
1 tablespoon butter or margarine, melted
½ teaspoon salt
½ teaspoon ground ginger
½ teaspoon ground cinnamon

- Fit piecrust into a 9-inch pieplate according to package directions.
- Process remaining 8 ingredients in a blender until smooth, stopping once to scrape down sides. Pour mixture into crust.
- Bake at 400° for 10 minutes. Reduce heat to 350°, and bake 35 more minutes or until a knife inserted in center comes out clean, shielding edges of crust with aluminum foil after 15 minutes to prevent excessive browning. Cover and store in refrigerator. Yield: 8 servings.

*cook's secret...* To use fresh sweet potatoes for this pie instead of canned, substitute 2 large potatoes (1½ pounds) for the canned. Cut potatoes in half lengthwise; cook in boiling water to cover 30 to 45 minutes or until tender. Drain; cool and mash.

Jan Moon, formerly of our Test Kitchens, created cream pies with all the qualities of old-fashioned ones but without the fuss. The secret? You don't have to cook the filling (the traditional kind requires carefully cooked egg yolks). For these three dreamy, creamy pies, just spoon the filling into the cooled pastry shell.

## Coconut Cream Pie

1⅔ cups graham cracker crumbs
⅓ cup butter or margarine, melted
¼ cup sugar
1 (8-ounce) package cream cheese, softened
1 cup cream of coconut
1 (3.4-ounce) package cheesecake instant pudding mix
1 (7-ounce) package frozen sweetened flaked coconut, thawed
1 (8-ounce) container frozen whipped topping, thawed
1 cup whipping cream
Garnish: sweetened flaked coconut

• Stir together first 3 ingredients; press mixture evenly in bottom and up sides of a 9-inch pieplate.
• Bake at 350° for 8 minutes; remove to a wire rack, and cool completely.
• Beat cream cheese and cream of coconut at medium speed with an electric mixer until smooth. Add pudding mix, beating until blended.
• Stir in coconut; fold in whipped topping. Spread cream cheese mixture evenly into crust; cover and chill 2 hours or until set.
• Beat whipping cream with an electric mixer until soft peaks form, and spread evenly over top of pie. Garnish, if desired. Yield: 8 servings.
**NOTE:** *For testing purposes only, we used Jell-O Instant Pudding Cheesecake Flavor.*

*Jan Moon*
Former Test Kitchens Professional

*cook's secret...* Look for cream of coconut near the piña colada and margarita mixes.

# Orange Dream Pie

*Orange curd can be found in the jams and jellies area of the supermarket.*

1 (7.25-ounce) package butter cookies, crushed
¼ cup butter or margarine, melted
1 (8-ounce) package cream cheese, softened
⅓ cup powdered sugar
1 teaspoon vanilla extract
Orange liquid food coloring (optional)

1 (12-ounce) container frozen whipped topping, thawed and divided
1 (10-ounce) jar orange curd
2 teaspoons grated orange rind
2 tablespoons fresh orange juice
Garnishes: whipped topping, orange rind curls, almond bark curls

• Stir together cookie crumbs and butter; press evenly in bottom and up sides of a 9-inch pieplate.
• Bake at 350° for 8 minutes; remove to a wire rack, and cool completely.
• Beat cream cheese and powdered sugar at medium speed with an electric mixer until smooth. Stir in vanilla and, if desired, food coloring until blended; fold in 2 cups whipped topping. Spread cream cheese mixture evenly into crust.
• Stir together curd, rind, juice, and 2 tablespoons whipped topping. Spread evenly over cream cheese mixture; cover and chill 2 hours or until set. Garnish, if desired. Yield: 8 servings.

**NOTE:** *For testing purposes only, we used Pepperidge Farm Chessmen butter cookies and Dickinson's Orange Curd.*

*Jan Moon*
Former Test Kitchens Professional

*cook's secret*... Place the cookies in a zip-top plastic bag, and tap them on the counter with the dull edge of a meat mallet to crumble.

# Lemon-Blueberry Cream Pie

1⅔ cups graham cracker crumbs
⅓ cup butter or margarine, melted
¼ cup granulated sugar
1 (8-ounce) package cream cheese, softened
1 (14-ounce) can sweetened condensed milk
¼ cup powdered sugar

1 (3.4-ounce) package lemon instant pudding mix
2 teaspoons grated lemon rind
½ cup fresh lemon juice
1 pint fresh blueberries
2 tablespoons blueberry preserves
1 cup whipping cream
Garnishes: lemon slices, fresh blueberries

• Stir together first 3 ingredients; press evenly in bottom and up sides of a 9-inch pieplate.
• Bake at 350° for 8 minutes; remove to a wire rack, and cool completely.
• Beat cream cheese, milk, and powdered sugar at medium speed with an electric mixer until creamy. Add pudding mix, rind, and juice; beat until blended. Spread half of lemon mixture evenly into crust.
• Stir together blueberries and preserves; spread evenly over lemon mixture. Spread remaining lemon mixture over blueberry mixture; cover and chill 2 hours or until set.
• Beat whipping cream with an electric mixer until soft peaks form, and spread around outer edge of pie, forming a 3-inch border. Garnish, if desired. Yield: 8 servings.

*Jan Moon*
Former Test Kitchens Professional

*cook's secret...* Vanilla instant pudding works well as a substitute for lemon pudding in this pie; the flavor simply won't be as tart.

Linda Morten has been cooking since she was a teenager. "My mother was an avid cook who entertained a lot," she says. Linda prepares simple, quick meals during the week and more involved meals on the weekend. She developed this pie from her favorite dessert. "I love tiramisù. I was trying to make it a little different, so I used a ready-made pound cake to create a different crust," she says. Her recipe was the Grand Prize Winner in our 2000 *Southern Living* Holiday Recipe Contest.

*contest winner*

## Tiramisù Toffee Trifle Pie

| | |
|---|---|
| 1½  tablespoons instant coffee granules | ½  cup powdered sugar |
| ¾  cup warm water | ½  cup chocolate syrup |
| 1  (10.75-ounce) frozen pound cake, thawed | 1  (12-ounce) container frozen whipped topping, thawed and divided |
| 1  (8-ounce) package mascarpone or cream cheese, softened | 2  (1.4-ounce) English chocolate-covered toffee candy bars, coarsely chopped |

• Stir together coffee granules and ¾ cup warm water until coffee is dissolved. Cool.
• Cut cake into 14 slices. Cut each slice in half diagonally. Place triangles in bottom and up sides of a 9-inch deep-dish pieplate. Drizzle coffee mixture over cake.
• Beat mascarpone cheese, sugar, and chocolate syrup at medium speed with an electric mixer until smooth. Add 2½ cups whipped topping, and beat until light and fluffy.
• Spread cheese mixture evenly over cake. Dollop remaining whipped topping around edges of pie. Sprinkle with candy. Chill 8 hours. Yield: 8 to 10 servings.

*Linda Morten*
Katy, Texas

*cook's secret*... To save a few fat grams, use Neufchâtel cheese instead of mascarpone and reduced-fat frozen whipped topping. But don't skimp on the candy bars!

Test Kitchens Professionals Rebecca Kracke Gordon and Pam Lolley used fresh lemons to create this refreshing pie filling, but they also found that fresh frozen lemon juice (the kind in the yellow plastic bottle) works equally well.

# Lemon Meringue Pie

| | | | |
|---|---|---|---|
| 1 | (15-ounce) package refrigerated piecrusts | 6 | egg whites |
| | Lemon Meringue Pie Filling | ½ | teaspoon vanilla extract |
| | | 6 | tablespoons sugar |

• Unfold and stack piecrusts on a lightly floured surface. Roll into 1 (12-inch) circle. Fit piecrust into a 9-inch pieplate (about 1 inch deep); fold edges under, and crimp. Prick bottom and sides of piecrust with a fork. Freeze 10 minutes.

• Line piecrust with parchment paper; fill with pie weights or dried beans.

• Bake at 425° for 10 minutes. Remove weights and parchment paper; bake 12 to 15 more minutes or until crust is lightly browned. (Shield edges with aluminum foil if they brown too quickly.)

• Prepare Lemon Meringue Pie Filling; pour into piecrust. Cover with plastic wrap, placing directly on filling. (Proceed immediately with next step to ensure that the meringue is spread over the pie filling while it is still warm.)

• Beat egg whites and vanilla extract at high speed with an electric mixer until foamy. Add sugar, 1 tablespoon at a time, and beat 2 to 4 minutes or until stiff peaks form and sugar dissolves.

• Remove plastic wrap from pie, and spread meringue evenly over warm Lemon Meringue Pie Filling, sealing edges.

• Bake at 325° for 25 minutes or until golden brown. Cool pie completely on a wire rack. Store leftovers in the refrigerator. Yield: 8 to 10 servings.

## Lemon Meringue Pie Filling:

| | | |
|---|---|---|
| 1 | cup sugar | |
| ¼ | cup cornstarch | |
| ⅛ | teaspoon salt | |
| 4 | large egg yolks | |
| 2 | cups milk | |

| | |
|---|---|
| ⅓ | cup fresh lemon juice |
| 3 | tablespoons butter or margarine |
| 1 | teaspoon grated lemon rind |
| ½ | teaspoon vanilla extract |

• Whisk together first 3 ingredients in a heavy, nonaluminum medium saucepan. Whisk together egg yolks, milk, and lemon juice in a bowl; whisk into sugar mixture in pan over medium heat. Bring to a boil, and boil, whisking constantly, 1 minute. Remove pan from heat; stir in butter, lemon rind, and vanilla extract until smooth. Yield: enough filling for 1 (9-inch) pie.

*cook's secret...* Sealing meringue to the outer edge of crust over a hot filling helps keep the meringue from shrinking after it's cooked.

### Secrets to Mastering Meringue

A perfect meringue is easy when you follow these step-by-step instructions.

**1.** Let egg whites stand at room temperature 30 minutes before beating. A copper, stainless-steel, or glass bowl will work best. Beat egg whites and vanilla until foamy (as shown). Gradually add sugar, 1 tablespoon at a time.

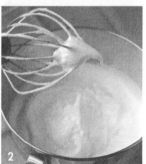

**2.** Beat egg whites and vanilla until stiff peaks form and sugar dissolves—about 2 to 4 minutes. A high-powered mixer will do the job more quickly than a handheld one.

Cobblers are old-fashioned Southern treasures. Soft doughs and crumbly drop biscuits add richness atop both sweet and savory fillings. Our Test Kitchens staff says the key is to use a light touch in preparing the delicate toppings, being careful not to overknead the dough or stir any longer than necessary. Cobblers may be long on ingredients, but they assemble quickly.

## Apple-Vinegar Biscuit Cobbler

| | | | |
|---|---|---|---|
| 8 | Granny Smith apples, peeled and cut into wedges | ¼ | cup butter or margarine |
| 2 | cups sugar | ⅓ | cup cider vinegar |
| 1 | (3-ounce) package cream cheese | 1 | teaspoon grated lemon rind |
| ⅓ | cup butter or margarine, cut into pieces | 1 | teaspoon ground cinnamon |
| 2½ | cups self-rising flour | 1 | teaspoon ground allspice |
| 1 | cup milk | ¼ | teaspoon ground cloves |
| | | | Vanilla ice cream (optional) |

• Combine apple and sugar; set aside.

• Cut cream cheese and ⅓ cup butter into flour with a fork or pastry blender until crumbly; stir in milk.

• Turn dough out onto a lightly floured surface; knead 3 or 4 times. Pat or roll dough to ½-inch thickness. Cut with a 2½-inch round cutter; set aside.

• Melt ¼ cup butter in a large skillet over medium-high heat; add apple mixture. Cook, stirring often, 20 minutes or until apple is tender and syrup thickens slightly. Stir in next 5 ingredients. Pour into a lightly greased 11- x 7-inch baking dish; place dish on an aluminum foil–lined baking sheet. Arrange 12 biscuits over hot mixture. Place remaining biscuits on a baking sheet.

• Bake cobbler at 425° for 20 minutes or until biscuits are golden. Bake remaining biscuits at 425° for 12 to 15 minutes. Serve cobbler with ice cream, if desired. Yield: 6 to 8 servings.

## cook's secret... Vinegar adds a sweet-sour dimension to this cobbler.
If you don't have cider vinegar, white vinegar will work, but the flavor won't be as full-bodied.

# Blackberry Cobbler

*We loved the bumpy "cobbled" top on this juicy fruit dessert.*
*You can use fresh or frozen berries.*

5 cups fresh blackberries or 2 (14-ounce)
    packages frozen blackberries,
    thawed and drained
1 cup sugar
3 to 4 tablespoons all-purpose flour

1 tablespoon lemon juice
Crust
2 tablespoons butter or margarine, melted
1 teaspoon sugar
Vanilla ice cream (optional)

• Combine first 4 ingredients; toss well. Spoon mixture into a lightly greased 8- or
9-inch square pan.
• Prepare Crust, and spoon 9 mounds over blackberries. Brush with butter, and sprinkle
with 1 teaspoon sugar.
• Bake, uncovered, at 425° for 30 minutes or until browned and bubbly. Serve warm with
ice cream, if desired. Yield: 9 servings.
**NOTE:** *If you use frozen berries, increase the flour to ⅓ cup.*

## Crust:

1¾ cups all-purpose flour
3 tablespoons sugar
1½ teaspoons baking powder
¾ teaspoon salt

¼ cup shortening
⅓ cup whipping cream
⅓ cup buttermilk

• Combine first 4 ingredients; cut in shortening with a pastry blender until mixture is
crumbly. Stir in whipping cream and buttermilk just until blended. Yield: enough topping
for 1 cobbler.

*cook's secret*... Slip a baking sheet or aluminum foil under a cobbler
or any juicy fruit dessert when baking to catch any overflow.

# Pear-Ginger Cobbler

8 large red or green Anjou pears, sliced
2 tablespoons lemon juice
½ cup apple cider
½ cup maple syrup
¼ cup firmly packed brown sugar
2 tablespoons all-purpose flour
1 teaspoon ground cinnamon

¼ teaspoon ground nutmeg
3 tablespoons butter or margarine,
   cut into pieces
Ginger-Almond Topping
2 tablespoons granulated sugar
Whipped cream
Crystallized ginger (optional)

• Toss together pears and lemon juice.
• Whisk together apple cider and next 5 ingredients in a large bowl; add pears, tossing to coat. Pour mixture into a 2-quart baking dish; dot with butter.
• Spread Ginger-Almond Topping over mixture; sprinkle with granulated sugar.
• Bake at 350° for 45 to 50 minutes or until golden. Serve with whipped cream; sprinkle with crystallized ginger, if desired. Yield: 6 to 8 servings.

## Ginger-Almond Topping:

1½ cups all-purpose flour
1 tablespoon sugar
2 teaspoons baking powder
½ teaspoon salt

⅓ cup shortening
1 to 2 teaspoons ground ginger
½ cup chopped almonds, toasted
1 to 1¼ cups milk

• Combine first 4 ingredients; cut in shortening with a fork or pastry blender until crumbly. Stir in ground ginger, toasted almonds, and enough milk to make a soft dough. Yield: enough topping for 2-quart dish.

*cook's secret*... Use real maple syrup instead of pancake syrup for the best flavor in this cobbler.

# Sweet Potato Cobbler

| | | | |
|---|---|---|---|
| ½ | cup butter or margarine | 2 | large sweet potatoes, peeled and thinly sliced (about 1½ pounds) |
| 2 | tablespoons whipping cream | ⅓ | cup butter or margarine |
| 1 | cup granulated sugar | 1⅔ | cups self-rising flour |
| ¼ | cup firmly packed light brown sugar | ½ | cup buttermilk |
| 1 | teaspoon ground cinnamon | | Streusel Topping |
| ¼ | teaspoon salt | | |
| ¼ | teaspoon ground nutmeg | | |

• Melt ½ cup butter in a 10½-inch cast-iron skillet over medium heat. Whisk in whipping cream and next 5 ingredients. Remove from heat.

• Layer sweet potato slices evenly in cream mixture. Cover with aluminum foil, and place on a baking sheet.

• Bake at 350° for 20 minutes. Uncover.

• Cut ⅓ cup butter into flour with a fork or pastry blender until crumbly; stir in buttermilk until moistened. Turn dough out onto a lightly floured surface; knead 3 or 4 times. Pat or roll dough into a 10½-inch circle; place over cobbler. Sprinkle with Streusel Topping.

• Bake, uncovered, at 350° for 25 minutes or until golden. Yield: 6 servings.

## Streusel Topping:

| | | | |
|---|---|---|---|
| ⅓ | cup uncooked regular oats | 3 | tablespoons butter or margarine, cut into pieces |
| ⅓ | cup all-purpose flour | | |
| ⅓ | cup firmly packed light brown sugar | ⅓ | cup chopped pecans |

• Combine first 3 ingredients; cut in butter with a fork or pastry blender until crumbly. Stir in pecans. Yield: 1⅓ cups.

*cook's secret*... Serve this cobbler at the table right from the cast-iron skillet to add to the rustic nature of the recipe.

I have Penny P. Patrick's Praline Parlor to thank for my love of caramel apples. While working at this shop within Six Flags Great America amusement park, I made well over fifty thousand of them. The many hours spent leaning over a huge cauldron of hot caramel taught me a few tricks of the trade. Find them in the box at right.

*James Schend*
Assistant Test Kitchens Director

# Caramel Apples

| | |
|---|---|
| 6 large Granny Smith apples | 1 tablespoon water |
| 6 wooden craft sticks | 2 cups chopped pecans, toasted |
| 1 (14-ounce) package caramels, unwrapped | 1 (12-ounce) package semisweet chocolate morsels |
| 1 tablespoon vanilla extract | Pecan halves (optional) |

• Wash and dry apples; remove stems. Insert craft sticks into stem end of each apple; set aside.

• Combine caramels, vanilla, and 1 tablespoon water in a microwave-safe glass bowl. Microwave at HIGH 1½ minutes or until melted, stirring twice.

• Dip each apple into the caramel mixture quickly, allowing excess caramel to drip off. Roll in chopped pecans; place on lightly greased wax paper. Chill at least 15 minutes.

• Microwave chocolate morsels at HIGH 1½ minutes or until melted, stirring twice; cool 5 minutes. Pour chocolate where craft sticks and apple meet, allowing chocolate to drip down sides of apples. Press pecan halves onto chocolate, if desired. Chill 15 minutes or until set. Yield: 6 apples.

**NOTE:** *For testing purposes only, we used Kraft Caramels.*

**Calypso Caramel Apples:** Substitute 1 cup chopped toasted macadamia nuts and 1 cup toasted coconut for pecans.

**Georgian Caramel Apples:** Substitute 2 cups chopped toasted peanuts for pecans.

**Black-and-White Caramel Apples:** Microwave 1 cup white chocolate morsels at HIGH 60 seconds or until melted, stirring once; drizzle evenly over semisweet chocolate.

*James Schend*
Assistant Test Kitchens Director

## Secrets to Super Caramel Apples

● Lightly scrub apples with mild soap and a soft scrub brush to remove waxy coating.

● Hot caramel won't stick to wet apples, so make sure apples are thoroughly dry.

● Don't get caramel too hot, or you'll end up with only a thin layer on your apples and the rest sliding off.

● Scrape excess caramel off the sides of your apples before rolling in nuts or other coating. Don't forget to scrape the bottom of the apples, too.

# The Best-Ever Caramel Sauce

½  cup butter or margarine

1  cup firmly packed light brown sugar

½  cup whipping cream

1  tablespoon vanilla extract

Apple slices

● Cook butter and sugar in a heavy saucepan over medium heat, stirring occasionally, until sugar melts.

● Stir in ½ cup whipping cream, stirring occasionally. Bring to a boil, stirring occasionally. Remove from heat. Stir in vanilla. Serve with apple slices. Yield: 1¼ cups.

Adapted from *Discover Dinnertime: Your Guide to Building Family Time Around the Table* (Wimmer Cookbooks)

*cook's secret*... Toss apple slices in pineapple juice before serving to prevent browning.

# Peanut Butter Pudding

½  cup sugar
2  tablespoons cornstarch
¼  teaspoon salt
1½  cups milk

½  cup half-and-half
¾  cup creamy peanut butter
1  teaspoon vanilla extract
Garnishes: whipped cream, chocolate curls

• Combine first 3 ingredients in a medium-size heavy saucepan; gradually whisk in milk and half-and-half.
• Bring to a boil over medium heat, whisking constantly. Boil, whisking constantly, 1 minute. Remove from heat. (Pudding will be thin.) Add peanut butter and vanilla, whisking until smooth. Pour into a bowl; place plastic wrap directly over warm pudding. Chill 2 hours. Garnish, if desired. Yield: 2½ cups.

*Ellie Wells*
Lakeland, Florida

### Secrets to Perfect Puddings

• For the smoothest texture, stir with a whisk.
• Don't boil the mixture more than 1 minute, or the cornstarch will break down and the pudding will be thin.
• Air is the enemy of pudding; it forms a skin on top. To prevent the skin, press plastic wrap directly onto the pudding's surface before chilling.

*Lyda Jones*
Test Kitchens Director

# Vanilla Cream

*This recipe was the filling for a classic vanilla cream pie recipe we published in 1984. We made slight adjustments for an updated treat.*

¾ cup sugar

¼ cup plus 1 tablespoon cornstarch

⅛ teaspoon salt

3 egg yolks

3 cups milk or half-and-half

2 tablespoons butter or margarine

1 teaspoon vanilla extract

• Combine first 3 ingredients in a medium-size heavy saucepan. Whisk together egg yolks and milk; gradually add to sugar mixture. Whisk until smooth.

• Bring to a boil over medium heat, whisking constantly. Boil, whisking constantly, 1 minute. Remove from heat; whisk in butter and vanilla. Pour into a bowl; place plastic wrap directly over warm pudding. Cool 30 minutes. Chill 2 hours. Yield: 4 cups.

**Coffee Cream:** Add ½ cup strong brewed coffee to egg yolk mixture; proceed as directed. Yield: 4½ cups.

**Coconut Cream:** Decrease milk to 2 cups. Whisk together egg yolks, 2 cups milk, ½ cup cream of coconut, and ¾ cup pineapple juice; proceed as directed. Omit vanilla extract, and substitute 1 (6-ounce) package frozen coconut, thawed. Yield: 5 cups.

**Almond Cream:** Decrease milk to 1 cup. Whisk together egg yolks, 2 cups half-and-half, and 1 cup milk; proceed as directed. Substitute 1 teaspoon almond extract for vanilla. Garnish with toasted almond slices. Yield: 4 cups.

**Orange Cream:** Decrease milk to 2 cups. Whisk together egg yolks, 2 cups milk, 1 tablespoon grated orange rind, and 1 cup fresh orange juice; proceed as directed. Substitute 2 tablespoons orange liqueur for vanilla. Garnish with orange rind curls. Yield: 4 cups.

*cook's secret...* Don't stir the pudding after it has chilled, or it will lose its body.

# Graham Banana Pudding

| | | | | |
|---|---|---|---|---|
| 4 | cups half-and-half | | 2 | teaspoons vanilla extract |
| 4 | large egg yolks | | 1 | (4.8-ounce) package graham crackers, divided |
| 1½ | cups sugar | | | |
| ¼ | cup cornstarch | | 4 | large ripe bananas, sliced and divided |
| ¼ | teaspoon salt | | 2 | cups whipping cream |
| 3 | tablespoons butter or margarine | | 2 | tablespoons sugar |

• Whisk together first 5 ingredients in a large saucepan over low heat; cook, whisking constantly, 8 to 10 minutes or until thickened. Remove from heat, and stir in butter and vanilla.

• Layer 5 graham crackers, half of bananas, and half of pudding in a 13- x 9-inch baking dish. Repeat layers. Cover pudding, and chill 6 hours.

• Beat whipping cream and 2 tablespoons sugar at medium speed with an electric mixer until soft peaks form. Spread over pudding. Chill until ready to serve. Yield: 6 to 8 servings.

*Dorsella Utter*
Louisville, Kentucky

*cook's secret...* This pudding will give traditional banana pudding a run for its money. This recipe is very forgiving: In a pinch, you can substitute vanilla wafers for the graham crackers.

# Flan Almendra

½ cup sugar
1⅔ cups sweetened condensed milk
1 cup milk
1 cup slivered almonds

3 eggs
3 egg yolks
1 teaspoon vanilla extract
Strawberry halves

• Sprinkle sugar in a 9-inch round cakepan; place over medium heat. Using oven mitts, caramelize sugar by shaking pan occasionally until sugar melts and turns a light golden brown; cool. (Mixture may crack slightly as it cools.)

• Combine next 6 ingredients in container of an electric blender; process at high speed 15 seconds. Pour over caramelized sugar; cover pan with aluminum foil, and place in a large shallow pan. Pour hot water to a depth of 1 inch into a larger pan. Bake at 350° for 55 minutes or until a knife inserted near center comes out clean.

• Remove pan from water and uncover; let cool on a wire rack at least 30 minutes. Loosen edges with a spatula. Invert flan onto plate, and arrange strawberries around sides. Yield: 6 servings.

**Individual Flans Almendra:** Place 1 cup sugar in a heavy saucepan; place over medium heat. Using oven mitts, caramelize sugar by shaking pan occasionally until sugar melts and turns a light golden brown. Remove from heat, and pour hot caramel mixture into 6 (10-ounce) custard cups. Let cool. Pour flan mixture evenly into custard cups, making sure mixture is evenly divided; cover with aluminum foil. Place custard cups in a broiler pan; pour hot water to a depth of 1 inch into pan. Bake at 350° for 35 to 40 minutes or until a knife inserted near center comes out clean. Remove cups from water, and cool. To serve, loosen edges of custards with a spatula; invert onto plates.

*cook's secret...* If a gas burner is used, a little stirring may be necessary when caramelizing the sugar.

# Key Lime Bars

*You can purchase bottled Key lime juice in many supermarkets,*
*or find it online at www.keylimejuice.com.*

| | | | |
|---|---|---|---|
| 2 | cups all-purpose flour | 2 | tablespoons Key lime juice |
| ⅔ | cup macadamia nuts | 1 | (14-ounce) can sweetened condensed |
| ½ | cup sugar | | milk |
| ½ | cup butter, melted | 1 | teaspoon grated lime rind |
| ¾ | cup sugar | 2½ | cups whipping cream, whipped |
| ½ | cup Key lime juice | | Garnish: lime slices, chopped macadamia |
| 1 | envelope unflavored gelatin | | nuts |

• Process first 4 ingredients in a food processor until nuts are coarsely chopped. Press mixture into a greased aluminum foil–lined 13- x 9-inch pan.

• Bake at 350° for 20 minutes or until crust is golden. Cool in pan on a wire rack.

• Cook ¾ cup sugar and ½ cup lime juice in a saucepan over low heat, stirring until sugar dissolves. Remove from heat, and set aside.

• Sprinkle gelatin over 2 tablespoons lime juice in a medium bowl; stir mixture, and let stand 3 to 5 minutes.

• Add sugar mixture to gelatin mixture; stir until gelatin dissolves. Whisk in sweetened condensed milk and lime rind. Place bowl in a larger bowl filled with ice; whisk mixture 10 minutes or until partially set.

• Fold lime mixture into whipped cream. Pour evenly over prepared crust; cover and chill 8 hours. Cut into squares. Garnish, if desired. Yield: 2 dozen bars.

*cook's secret...* You can substitute regular lime juice if you can't find Key lime juice, but the flavor won't be as tart.

# Watermelon Sorbet

| | | | |
|---|---|---|---|
| 3 | cups water | 4 | cups seeded, chopped watermelon |
| 1 | cup sugar | ¼ | cup lime juice |

• Bring 3 cups water and sugar just to a boil in a medium saucepan over high heat, stirring until sugar dissolves. Remove from heat. Cool.

• Process sugar syrup and watermelon, in batches, in a blender until smooth. Stir in lime juice. Cover and chill 2 hours.

- Pour mixture into freezer container of a 1-gallon hand-turned or electric freezer, and freeze according to manufacturer's instructions. Yield: about ½ gallon.

**Grapefruit Sorbet:** Substitute 3 cups fresh grapefruit juice and 1 teaspoon chopped fresh mint for watermelon and lime juice. Proceed as directed.

**Pineapple Sorbet:** Substitute 2 cups chopped pineapple for watermelon and lime juice. Strain and discard pulp after processing mixture in blender, if desired. Proceed as directed.

**Lemon Sorbet:** Substitute ½ cup fresh lemon juice and 2 teaspoons grated lemon rind for watermelon and lime juice. Proceed as directed.

**Orange Sorbet:** Substitute 3 cups fresh orange juice and 2 teaspoons grated orange rind for watermelon and lime juice. Proceed as directed.

**Strawberry Sorbet:** Substitute 5 cups fresh or frozen strawberries and 2 tablespoons lemon juice for watermelon and lime juice. Proceed as directed.

**Cantaloupe Sorbet:** Substitute 4 cups chopped cantaloupe for watermelon and lime juice. Proceed as directed.

**Cherry Sorbet:** Substitute 1 (6-ounce) can frozen lemonade concentrate, prepared, and 1 (16-ounce) jar maraschino cherries, drained, for watermelon and lime juice. Strain and discard pulp, if desired. Proceed as directed.

**Raspberry Sorbet:** Substitute 5 cups fresh or frozen raspberries for watermelon and lime juice. Proceed as directed.

*cook's secret...* Sugar is the key to a good sorbet: Too little and the crystals will be too big; too much and the sorbet will be slushy. Select the ripest, most fragrant fruits to add even more punch. Cover leftover sorbet in plastic wrap (directly on the surface), and store in a plastic container in the freezer for up to 2 weeks.

*Scott Jones*
Foods Editor

D onna Thomas's recipe was the Signature Desserts winner in the 2002 *Southern Living* Cook-Off. Donna says that she created this recipe when she was trying to make a new flavor of ice cream. "I made a gallon a day for twenty days until I got the base right," she says. "Homemade ice cream was a big part of growing up in Texas, and just like with barbecue sauce, you want bragging rights!"

*contest winner*

## Pecan–Caramel Crunch Ice Cream

| | |
|---|---|
| 1 cup chopped pecans | ½ teaspoon salt |
| ¾ cup quick-cooking oats | 4 egg yolks |
| ¼ cup all-purpose flour | 4 cups whipping cream |
| ¼ cup firmly packed light brown sugar | 1 (14-ounce) can sweetened condensed milk |
| ¼ cup butter, melted | |
| 2 cups firmly packed light brown sugar | 2 tablespoons vanilla extract |
| 3 cups milk | 1 (20-ounce) bottle caramel topping |
| 1 (12-ounce) can evaporated milk | Garnish: waffle cone pieces |

• Preheat oven to 350°. Stir together first 5 ingredients; spread mixture in a thin layer on a baking sheet.

• Bake at 350° for 15 minutes; cool completely on a wire rack. Process in a food processor until finely chopped; set aside.

• Stir together 2 cups brown sugar and next 3 ingredients in a large saucepan over low heat, and simmer, stirring often, 1 minute. (Do not boil.)

• Beat egg yolks until thick and lemon-colored. Gradually stir 1 cup hot brown sugar mixture into yolks. Add egg yolk mixture to remaining hot mixture; cook, stirring constantly, over low heat 2 minutes or until mixture begins to thicken. Remove pan from heat; stir in cream, condensed milk, and vanilla. Let cool to room temperature.

• Pour mixture into freezer container of a 6-quart hand-turned or electric freezer, and freeze according to manufacturer's instructions 5 to 7 minutes or until partially frozen. Layer top of ice cream evenly with oat mixture and caramel topping. Freeze according to manufacturer's instructions plus 10 to 15 more minutes or until mixture is frozen. Garnish, if desired. Yield: 4 quarts.

*Donna Thomas*
Dallas, Texas

# Summertime Peach Ice Cream

4 cups peeled, diced fresh peaches
   (about 8 small ripe peaches)
1 cup sugar
1 (12-ounce) can evaporated milk
1 (3.4-ounce) package vanilla instant
   pudding mix

1 (14-ounce) can sweetened condensed
   milk
4 cups half-and-half

• Combine peaches and sugar, and let stand 1 hour.
• Process peach mixture in a food processor until smooth, stopping to scrape down sides.
• Stir together evaporated milk and pudding mix in a large bowl; stir in peach puree, condensed milk, and half-and-half.
• Pour mixture into freezer container of a 4-quart hand-turned or electric freezer, and freeze according to manufacturer's instructions. Spoon into an airtight container, and freeze until firm. Yield: 2 quarts.

*Carol S. Noble*
Burgaw, North Carolina

J eanne Wood says she loves to bake cookies during the holidays. In fact, in her neighborhood she's known as "The Cookie Queen." She jokes, "Now, my friends have come to expect a box each year, and I keep telling them they're going to bake me into my grave."

# English Rocks

| | | | | |
|---|---|---|---|---|
| ¾ | cup firmly packed light brown sugar | | ¼ | teaspoon ground allspice |
| ½ | cup butter or margarine, softened | | ¼ | cup brandy* |
| 2 | large eggs | | 2 | cups chopped pecans |
| 1½ | cups all-purpose flour | | ½ | pound candied cherries, halved |
| 1 | teaspoon ground cinnamon | | ½ | pound candied pineapple, chopped |
| ½ | teaspoon baking soda | | 1 | cup pitted dates, chopped |
| ¼ | teaspoon salt | | 1 | cup raisins |
| ¼ | teaspoon ground cloves | | | |

• Beat brown sugar and butter at medium speed with an electric mixer until smooth. Add eggs, beating until mixture is blended.

• Combine flour and next 5 ingredients; gradually add to butter mixture, beating until blended. Add brandy, beating until blended.

• Combine pecans and remaining 4 ingredients in a large bowl. Pour batter over pecan mixture, and stir until blended.

• Drop dough by rounded teaspoonfuls 2 inches apart onto lightly greased baking sheets.

• Bake at 325° for 20 minutes or until lightly browned. Cool on baking sheets 2 to 3 minutes. Remove to wire racks to cool completely. Yield: 4 dozen.

*½ cup apple juice may be substituted.

*Jeanne Wood*
New Orleans, Louisiana

*cook's secret...* If you want to make these gems year-round, freeze containers of candied cherries and pineapple when they're available during the winter holidays.

Susan Spray traces her love of Christmas cookies back many years. "I started baking a wide variety when I was eighteen, and I've been doing it ever since," she says.

## Swedish Holiday Cookies

| | | | |
|---|---|---|---|
| 1 | cup butter or margarine, softened | 1 | tablespoon water |
| ¾ | cup sugar | 1 | teaspoon baking powder |
| 1½ | tablespoons dark molasses | 2½ | cups all-purpose flour |
| 2 | teaspoons ground cinnamon | 2 | egg whites, lightly beaten |
| ½ | teaspoon ground cardamom | | Sugar |

• Beat butter at medium speed with an electric mixer until creamy. Add ¾ cup sugar, beating until smooth. Add molasses, cinnamon, and cardamom, beating until blended.
• Combine 1 tablespoon water and baking powder, stirring until baking powder is dissolved; add to butter mixture. Gradually add flour to butter mixture, beating until blended. Cover; chill 8 hours.
• Turn dough out onto a lightly floured surface; roll to ¼-inch thickness. Cut with a 2-inch round or other desired shape cutter. Place 2 inches apart on lightly greased baking sheets. Brush evenly with egg white, and sprinkle with sugar.
• Bake at 375° for 8 minutes or until lightly browned. Cool on baking sheets 5 to 6 minutes. Remove to wire racks to cool completely. Yield: about 5 dozen.

*Susan Spray*
Little Rock, Arkansas

*cook's secret...* If you don't have cardamom, just leave it out of this recipe because there's really no substitute for its exotic sweet flavor. The cookies will still be nicely scented and spiced by the cinnamon.

Dick Jack's son, Craig, gave us a heads-up on his father in a letter that opened, "I think you need an article about 'The Cookie King.' My dad makes about 330 dozen cookies every holiday season. (One year the total came to 541 dozen!) I can attest to the taste of his cookies, and there's nothing better." Here are two of his specialties.

## Crunchy Lace Cookies

|  |  |  |  |
|---|---|---|---|
| 2 | tablespoons hot water | 1½ | cups uncooked regular oats |
| 1½ | teaspoons baking soda | 1½ | cups firmly packed light brown sugar |
| ¾ | cup butter or margarine, melted | 1½ | cups all-purpose flour |
| 1 | tablespoon light corn syrup | 1½ | cups sweetened flaked coconut |

• Stir together 2 tablespoons hot water and baking soda in a large bowl until baking soda is dissolved. Add butter and syrup, stirring until blended.
• Combine 1½ cups oats and remaining 3 ingredients; stir into butter mixture, stirring until blended.
• Shape dough into ¾-inch balls, and place 3 inches apart on lightly greased baking sheets. Slightly flatten dough balls.
• Bake at 350° for 7 to 8 minutes or until golden brown. Remove to wire racks to cool completely. Yield: 2 dozen.

*Dick Jack*
Galena, Missouri

*cook's secret...* Quick oats are not a substitute in this recipe. They are finer, measure more cup-for-cup, and would change the consistency of these cookies.

# Date Moons

| | |
|---|---|
| ½  cup butter or margarine, softened | ¼  cup granulated sugar |
| 1  (3-ounce) package cream cheese, softened | ¼  cup water |
| 1  cup all-purpose flour | ½  cup chopped walnuts |
| ⅛  teaspoon salt | 1  teaspoon grated orange rind |
| 1  cup chopped dates | ½  cup powdered sugar |

• Beat butter and cream cheese at medium speed with an electric mixer until smooth. Add flour and salt, and beat until blended.

• Shape dough into a ball; cover with wax paper, and chill 1 hour.

• Cook dates, granulated sugar, and ¼ cup water in a saucepan over medium heat 3 to 5 minutes or until thickened. Remove from heat; stir in walnuts and orange rind, and let cool.

• Divide dough in half. Place 1 portion on a lightly floured surface, and roll to ⅛-inch thickness. Cut dough with a 2½-inch round cutter, and place on a lightly greased baking sheet. Spoon ½ teaspoon date mixture in center of each cookie. Repeat procedure with remaining dough.

• Fold dough over filling, pressing edges with tines of a fork to seal.

• Bake at 375° for 15 minutes or until lightly browned. Sprinkle with powdered sugar. Yield: 3 dozen.

*Dick Jack*
Galena, Missouri

*cook's secret...* When grating orange rind, a fine-tooth grater makes the tiniest shreds. Be careful to just grate the rind, as the white part underneath is bitter.

When Betty Sims entertains her friends, they know that the food will be wonderful and the setting will be lovely, since she's a former caterer. This recipe for Chocolate Chubbies is adapted from her cookbook *Southern Scrumptious: How to Cater Your Own Party*.

# Chocolate Chubbies

| | | | |
|---|---|---|---|
| 6 | (1-ounce) semisweet chocolate baking squares, chopped | ¼ | cup all-purpose flour |
| | | ½ | teaspoon baking powder |
| 2 | (1-ounce) unsweetened chocolate baking squares, chopped | ⅛ | teaspoon salt |
| | | 2 | cups semisweet chocolate morsels |
| ⅓ | cup butter | 2 | cups coarsely chopped pecans |
| 3 | large eggs | 2 | cups coarsely chopped walnuts |
| 1 | cup sugar | | |

• Combine first 3 ingredients in a heavy saucepan; cook, stirring often, over low heat until chocolate melts. Remove from heat; cool slightly.

• Beat eggs and sugar at medium speed with an electric mixer until smooth; add chocolate mixture, beating well.

• Combine flour, baking powder, and salt; add to chocolate mixture, stirring just until dry ingredients are moistened. Fold in chocolate morsels, pecans, and walnuts.

• Drop batter by tablespoonfuls 2 inches apart onto lightly greased baking sheets.

• Bake at 325° for 12 to 15 minutes or until done. Cool cookies on baking sheet 1 minute. Remove to wire racks; cool. Yield: 3½ dozen.

*Betty Sims*
Decatur, Alabama
Adapted from *Southern Scrumptious: How to Cater Your Own Party*
(Betty Sims)

*cook's secret...* Coarsely chopping the nuts contributes to the chunky, "chubby" quality the cookies' name describes.

Young guests bring batches of homemade cookies (prepared with their mothers' help) to Hosetta Coleman's annual mother-daughter Christmas party. They gather around the dining room table to share their creations and introduce their mothers. As one mom says, "What's most fun about making cookies is just being together and sharing in the mommy-daughter experience." Here, and on the next two pages, we share some favorite recipes from a recent gathering.

## Ginger Cookies

| | |
|---|---|
| 1 cup sugar | 2 teaspoons baking soda |
| ¾ cup shortening | 1 teaspoon ground cloves |
| ¼ cup molasses | 1 teaspoon ground cinnamon |
| 1 large egg | 1 teaspoon ground ginger |
| 2 cups all-purpose flour | 2 tablespoons sugar |

• Beat first 3 ingredients at medium speed with an electric mixer until blended. Add egg, beating until blended.
• Combine flour and next 4 ingredients; gradually add to shortening mixture, beating just until blended.
• Roll dough into 1-inch balls, and dip into 2 tablespoons sugar. Place on lightly greased baking sheets, and flatten slightly with the bottom of a glass.
• Bake at 375° for 10 minutes or until golden brown. Remove to wire racks to cool. Yield: 4 dozen.

*Hosetta Coleman*
Temple Terrace, Florida

*cook's secret*... 1 tablespoon allspice will substitute for the trio of spices in these cookies.

# Buttery Oat Tea Cookies

| | |
|---|---|
| 1 cup butter, softened | ½ teaspoon vanilla extract |
| 1½ cups sugar | 1½ cups self-rising flour |
| 1 large egg | 1 cup uncooked regular oats |

• Beat butter and sugar at medium speed with an electric mixer until fluffy. Add egg and vanilla; beat until blended. Stir in flour.

• Shape into 1-inch balls, and roll each ball in oats. Place on baking sheets, and flatten slightly with the bottom of a glass.

• Bake at 350° for 12 to 15 minutes or until golden brown. Remove to wire racks to cool. Yield: 4 dozen.

*Joan Wagner*
Apollo Beach, Florida

*cook's secret...* Chill the dough just a little if the dough's too soft to roll into balls.

# Chewy Apple Brownies

*These blond brownies are great for sneaking fruit into your children's diet.*

| | |
|---|---|
| 2 cups all-purpose flour | 2 large eggs |
| 1 teaspoon baking soda | 1 teaspoon vanilla extract |
| 1 teaspoon baking powder | 2 cups peeled and diced Granny Smith |
| 1 teaspoon ground cinnamon | apples |
| ½ teaspoon salt | ½ cup chopped pecans or walnuts |
| 1 cup butter or margarine, softened | Vanilla ice cream (optional) |
| 1¾ cups sugar | |

• Combine first 5 ingredients; set aside.

• Beat butter and next 3 ingredients at medium speed with an electric mixer until fluffy.

• Gradually stir flour mixture into butter mixture. Stir in apples and pecans. (Mixture will be thick.) Spread dough into a lightly greased 9-inch square pan.

• Bake at 350° for 1 hour, shielding with foil after 35 minutes to prevent excessive browning. Cool on a wire rack, and cut into squares. Serve with ice cream, if desired. Yield: 16 bars.

*Joyce Sawyer*
Brandon, Florida

# Chocolate-Dipped Butter Cookies

1 cup butter, softened
⅔ cup sugar
1 large egg
1 teaspoon orange extract

2½ cups all-purpose flour
½ teaspoon baking powder
2 (2-ounce) chocolate bark coating squares
Chocolate candy sprinkles

- Beat butter and sugar at medium speed with an electric mixer until fluffy. Add egg and extract; beat until blended.
- Combine flour and baking powder; gradually add to butter mixture, beating until blended.
- Use a cookie press fitted with a bar-shaped disk to shape dough into straws, following manufacturer's instructions. Press onto ungreased baking sheets.
- Bake at 350° for 10 to 12 minutes or until lightly browned. Transfer cookies to wire racks to cool.
- Microwave chocolate squares in a small bowl at HIGH, stirring twice, 1½ minutes or until melted.
- Dip ends of cookies in melted chocolate; sprinkle with candy sprinkles. Place on wax paper, and let stand until chocolate is firm. Yield: 6 dozen.

*Laura McGowan*
Tampa, Florida

## Cookie Press Secrets

- For best results, use a cookie press that portions dough for each cookie.
- Fill the press with room-temperature dough.
- Pressing cookies onto ungreased baking sheets allows the dough a clean release for perfect shapes.
- If at first you don't succeed, try again. It may take a few tries with a cookie press to get the hang of it, but practice makes perfect. Just move slowly, and be patient.

*Rebecca Kracke Gordon*
Test Kitchens Professional

The secret to great bar cookies is to spread the batter evenly in the correct-size pan; using a smaller pan makes gummy cookies, while a larger pan produces dry ones. After baking, most cookies should be cooled completely in the pan on a wire rack before cutting. Here are three tasty recipes from our bar-cookie expert, Alison Lewis.

## Layered Apricot Bars

| | | | |
|---|---|---|---|
| 1 | (6-ounce) package dried apricots | ½ | teaspoon baking powder |
| ½ | cup butter or margarine, softened | ¼ | teaspoon salt |
| ¼ | cup granulated sugar | ½ | cup chopped walnuts |
| 1⅓ | cups all-purpose flour, divided | 1 | teaspoon vanilla extract |
| 2 | large eggs | | Powdered sugar |
| ¾ | cup firmly packed brown sugar | | |

• Bring apricots and water to cover to a boil in a small saucepan. Reduce heat, and simmer, uncovered, 15 minutes or until tender. Drain and coarsely chop apricots; set aside.
• Beat butter at medium speed with an electric mixer until creamy; gradually add ¼ cup granulated sugar, beating well. Stir in 1 cup flour, and press mixture into a lightly greased aluminum foil–lined 9-inch square pan.
• Bake at 350° for 15 to 20 minutes or until lightly browned.
• Beat eggs at medium speed until thick and pale; gradually add brown sugar, beating well. Add remaining ⅓ cup flour, baking powder, and salt, beating well. Stir in chopped apricot, walnuts, and vanilla; spread mixture evenly over crust.
• Bake at 325° for 45 minutes. Let cool completely in pan on a wire rack. Cut into bars; sprinkle with powdered sugar. Yield: 1½ dozen.

*Alison Lewis*
Former Assistant Foods Editor

*cook's secret...* You can omit the step to grease the foil by using the new nonstick aluminum foil on the market.

# Lemon Bars

2¼ cups all-purpose flour, divided
½ cup powdered sugar
1 cup butter or margarine, softened
4 large eggs

2 cups granulated sugar
⅓ cup lemon juice
½ teaspoon baking powder
Powdered sugar

- Combine 2 cups flour and ½ cup powdered sugar.
- Cut butter into flour mixture with a fork or pastry blender until crumbly. Firmly press mixture into a lightly greased 13- x 9-inch pan.
- Bake at 350° for 20 to 25 minutes or until lightly browned.
- Whisk eggs in a large bowl; whisk in 2 cups granulated sugar and lemon juice. Combine remaining ¼ cup flour and baking powder; whisk into egg mixture. Pour batter over crust.
- Bake at 350° for 25 minutes or until set. Let cool completely in pan on a wire rack. Cut into bars, and sprinkle with additional powdered sugar. Yield: 2½ dozen.

*Alison Lewis*
Former Assistant Foods Editor

*cook's secret...* The secret to making the most delectable lemon bars is to use fresh juice. Bottled substitutes lack the spunk of fresh.

# Crispy Peanut Squares

1 cup sugar
1 cup light corn syrup
1 cup creamy peanut butter

1 teaspoon vanilla extract
6 cups crisp rice cereal squares
1 cup peanuts

- Combine first 3 ingredients in a glass bowl; microwave at HIGH 3 to 4 minutes or until melted, stirring once. Stir in vanilla. Fold in cereal and peanuts. Spread mixture into a lightly greased 13- x 9-inch pan. Cover and chill 1 hour or until set; cut into small squares. Yield: 4 dozen.

*Alison Lewis*
Former Assistant Foods Editor

*cook's secret...* For a neat way to cut bar cookies, line a baking pan with aluminum foil, allowing several inches to extend over the sides; lightly grease the foil. Spread batter in the pan; bake and cool. Lift cookies from the pan using the foil; press the foil edges down, and cut the cookies into the desired size.

For as long as I can remember, cookies have been a tradition in the Kracke family. One Christmas, my mom and I spent extra time on the sweet treats by making them into ornaments. Back then, gingerbread cutouts were my favorite to decorate. Nowadays, I prefer sugary stars and bells. And with the memories of our baking and decorating still so warm, I want to share this recipe with you. Even when you're baking cookies to decorate later with family and friends, be sure to make enough so that you can eat some immediately. These are especially good right from the oven.

*Rebecca Kracke Gordon*
Test Kitchens Professional

# Glazed Sugar Cookies

| | |
|---|---|
| 1 cup butter or margarine, softened | ¼ teaspoon salt |
| 1 cup sugar | Glaze |
| 1 large egg | Royal Icing |
| 1 teaspoon vanilla extract | Edible gold dust |
| 3 cups all-purpose flour | Clear vanilla extract |

• Beat butter and sugar at medium speed with an electric mixer until fluffy. Add egg and vanilla, beating well. Gradually add flour and salt, beating until blended. Divide dough in half; cover and chill 1 hour.

• Roll each portion of dough to ¼-inch thickness on a lightly floured surface. Cut dough into desired shapes with a 3½-inch cutter, and place on lightly greased baking sheets.

• Bake at 350° for 8 to 10 minutes or until edges are lightly browned. Remove to wire racks to cool. Dip cookies in Glaze, and place on wax paper to dry. Decorate cookies as desired with Royal Icing.

• Combine ¼ teaspoon gold dust and ¼ teaspoon clear vanilla extract with a small paintbrush. Working quickly, brush on gold accents; add 1 drop vanilla at a time to mixture, as needed, to moisten gold dust. Sprinkle on gold dust, if desired. Yield: 1 dozen.

**NOTE:** *Cookies may also be cut with a 2½-inch cutter. Decorator sugar crystals may be substituted for gold dust mixture. Yield: 3 dozen.*

**Candy Cane Cookies:** To shape candy canes instead of using cookie cutters, divide each dough portion into eighths; roll into 12- x ½-inch logs. Shape into candy canes on lightly greased baking sheets. Bake at 350° for 18 to 20 minutes or until lightly browned. Remove to wire racks to cool. Dip cookies in Glaze, and garnish with red decorator sugar crystals. Place on wax paper to dry. Yield: 16 cookies.

## Glaze:

| | |
|---|---|
| 1 (16-ounce) package powdered sugar | 4 to 6 tablespoons hot water |

• Stir together powdered sugar and hot water until smooth. Yield: 1⅓ cups.

## Royal Icing:

| | |
|---|---|
| 1 (16-ounce) package powdered sugar | 6 tablespoons hot water |
| 3 tablespoons meringue powder | Food coloring (optional) |

• Stir together first 3 ingredients until smooth. Stir in food coloring, if desired. Pour into a zip-top freezer bag. Snip a tiny hole in 1 corner of bag, and squeeze desired designs on cookies. Yield: 1⅔ cups.

*cook's secret...* To make the rolling easier, divide the dough and form it into a flat disk instead of a ball. If the dough becomes difficult to handle and tears easily, place it in the refrigerator to chill again. Cut preparation time in half by chilling dough in the freezer.

*Rebecca Kracke Gordon*
Test Kitchens Professional

# Classic Peanut Brittle

1 cup sugar
½ cup light corn syrup
⅛ teaspoon salt
1 cup dry-roasted or shelled raw peanuts

2 tablespoons butter
1 teaspoon baking soda
2 teaspoons vanilla extract

• Cook first 3 ingredients in a medium-size heavy saucepan over medium heat, stirring constantly, until mixture starts to boil. Boil, without stirring, 5 minutes or until a candy thermometer reaches 310° (photo 1). Add peanuts, and cook 2 to 3 more minutes or to 280°. (Mixture should be golden brown.) Remove from heat, and stir in butter and remaining ingredients (photo 2).
• Immediately pour mixture into a buttered 15- x 10-inch jellyroll pan (photo 3). Spread mixture thinly with the back of a wooden spoon. Allow to stand 5 minutes or until hardened. Break into pieces (photo 4). Yield: 1 pound.

**Microwave Brittle:** Combine first 3 ingredients in a large glass bowl. Microwave at HIGH 5 minutes, add peanuts, and microwave 2 more minutes with 1,000-watt microwave. (Microwave 4 more minutes if using a 700-watt microwave.) Stir in remaining ingredients. Pour into a buttered 15- x 10-inch jellyroll pan; shake pan to spread thinly. Cool until firm, and break into pieces. Store in an airtight container.

**Pecan Brittle:** Substitute 1 cup chopped pecans for peanuts.

**Chocolate-Dipped Peanut Brittle:** Prepare peanut brittle as directed. Melt 2 (2-ounce) chocolate bark coating squares; dip peanut brittle pieces into melted chocolate. Place on wax paper, and let harden.

**Popcorn Peanut Brittle:** Prepare brittle as directed. Stir in 1 cup popped popcorn before pouring into pan.

*cook's secret...* Choose a sunny, dry day to make this candy because it's sensitive to humidity. Store peanut brittle in an airtight tin to keep it crisp and crunchy, not sticky to the touch.

*Cybil Talley*
Former Assistant Foods Editor

## Secrets to Making Classic Peanut Brittle

**1.** Combine sugar, corn syrup, and salt in a heavy nonaluminum saucepan. Insert the candy thermometer. Boil, without stirring, until the mixture reaches 310°.

**2.** Add peanuts, and cook until the thermometer reads 280° and mixture has a rich golden brown color. Remove from heat, and add butter, baking soda, and vanilla extract.

**3.** Immediately pour hot mixture into a shallow pan that has been greased with softened butter.

**4.** Spread mixture thinly with the back of a wooden spoon. Cool. Break candy into pieces with your hands, or use a rolling pin.

# Cherry Divinity

2½ cups sugar
½ cup water
½ cup light corn syrup

2 egg whites
1 teaspoon vanilla extract
1 cup finely chopped red candied cherries

• Combine first 3 ingredients in a 3-quart saucepan, and cook over low heat, stirring constantly, until sugar dissolves. Cover and cook over medium heat 2 to 3 minutes to wash down sugar crystals from sides of pan. Uncover and cook over medium heat, without stirring, until a candy thermometer registers 260° (hard ball stage). Remove from heat (photo 1).

• Beat egg whites in a large mixing bowl at high speed with an electric mixer until stiff peaks form. Pour hot sugar mixture in a heavy stream over beaten egg whites while beating constantly at high speed (photo 2). Add vanilla, and continue beating just until mixture holds its shape (3 to 4 minutes). Stir in chopped cherries (photo 3).

• Working quickly, drop divinity by rounded teaspoonfuls onto wax paper; cool. Peel from wax paper. Yield: 3 dozen (1½ pounds).

*cook's secret...* Once divinity holds its shape upon beating, it firms up quickly. Once you stir in the cherries, immediately spoon it out by teaspoonfuls onto wax paper.

### Secrets to Making Divinity

**1.** Cook the candy mixture, without stirring, to 260°. Do not let the candy thermometer touch the bottom of pan. Remove from heat.

**2.** Pour the hot sugar mixture in a heavy stream over the beaten egg whites while beating constantly.

**3.** Add vanilla, and continue beating just until mixture holds its shape (3 to 4 minutes). Stir in cherries.

This recipe from David Garrido, Executive Chef at Jeffrey's in Austin, adds a delightful finish to any meal.

*chef recipe*

# Hazelnut-Chocolate Truffles

| | |
|---|---|
| ¾ cup whipping cream | 2 tablespoons hazelnut liqueur |
| 1 cup finely chopped bittersweet chocolate | ¾ cup hazelnuts |
| 1 tablespoon unsalted butter | 1 (3-ounce) dark chocolate bar, chopped* |

• Bring cream to a boil in a medium saucepan over medium-high heat; whisk in bittersweet chocolate, butter, and hazelnut liqueur until well combined. Chill at least 2 hours.
• Place hazelnuts on a baking sheet. Bake at 350° for 10 minutes or until hazelnuts are toasted. Place warm hazelnuts in a dish towel, and rub vigorously to remove skins.
• Process toasted hazelnuts in a food processor until ground. Place in a shallow dish.
• Shape chocolate mixture into 1-inch balls. Melt chopped dark chocolate bar in a small saucepan over low heat. Roll each ball in 1 teaspoon melted dark chocolate, and immediately roll in toasted, ground hazelnuts.
• Cover and chill truffles until ready to serve. Yield: 20 truffles.

*½ cup semisweet morsels may be substituted for dark chocolate bar.*

**NOTE:** *For testing purposes only, we used Ghirardelli Dark Chocolate for dark chocolate bar.*

*Executive Chef David Garrido*
*Austin, Texas*

*cook's secret...* When testing this recipe, Test Kitchens Professional Angela Sellers wore plastic gloves so that she could roll each truffle in melted chocolate in her palm.

Few confections are so readily identified with the South as pralines, those irresistible nuggets of caramel and pecans. Pralines aren't difficult to make, but they can be somewhat tricky. The requirements are plenty of stirring, patience, and careful attention.

Two big questions usually come up during preparation: When should you remove the candy mixture from the heat? And when should you stop beating and start spooning it? If the mixture gets too hot, the candy will be dry and crumbly. If it isn't cooked long enough, the mixture will be runny and sticky.

Here are some secrets learned after making several batches in our Test Kitchens:

• A candy thermometer gives the best temperature reading and takes out most of the guesswork. We like to use two thermometers for accuracy.

• Beat the mixture with a wooden spoon just until it begins to thicken. You'll feel the mixture become heavier, and its color will become lighter when it's ready to spoon out into pralines. Often, the last few pralines that you spoon will be thicker and less perfectly shaped than the first several, but they'll still taste just as good.

• The candy tastes best if eaten within 1 or 2 days; pralines become sugary and gritty with age.

• Store them in an airtight container (a metal tin works well).

# Pralines

| | |
|---|---|
| 1½ cups granulated sugar | ¼ cup butter or margarine |
| 1½ cups firmly packed brown sugar | 2 cups pecan halves, toasted |
| 1 cup evaporated milk | 1 teaspoon vanilla extract |

• Bring sugars and milk to a boil in a Dutch oven, stirring often. Cook over medium heat, stirring often, 11 minutes or until a candy thermometer registers 228° (thread stage; photo 1).

• Stir in butter and pecans; cook, stirring constantly, until candy thermometer registers 236° (soft ball stage; photo 2).

• Remove from heat; stir in vanilla. Beat with a wooden spoon 1 to 2 minutes or just until mixture begins to thicken. Quickly drop by heaping tablespoonfuls onto buttered wax paper or parchment paper (photo 3); let stand until firm. Yield: about 2½ dozen.

## Secrets to Preparing Pralines

**1.** Bring sugars and milk to a boil in a Dutch oven, stirring often, until a candy thermometer registers 228°.

**2.** Add butter and pecans, stirring constantly. Cook the mixture until a candy thermometer registers 236° (soft ball stage).

**3.** Add vanilla, and beat as directed. Drop mixture by tablespoonfuls onto buttered wax paper, working rapidly before mixture cools.

*cook's secret*... If your pralines don't turn out right the first time, simply create a new dessert—fold them into softened vanilla ice cream. Or if they're too soft, scrape up the mixture, chill it, and roll it into 1-inch balls. Then dip the balls into melted chocolate to make truffles. If the candy mixture hardens in the pot, break it into pieces, and sprinkle it over a hot apple pie, cheesecake, or ice cream.

*Peggy Smith*
Former Associate Foods Editor

My grandmother Ruth Pilgrim taught my mother, Anne Kracke, how to make this fudge; my mother, in turn, taught me. This decadent goody is a staple gift during the holidays for treating teachers, neighbors, and friends.

*Rebecca Kracke Gordon*
Test Kitchens Professional

# Mama's Fudge

| | |
|---|---|
| 2 cups sugar | ¼ teaspoon salt |
| ⅔ cup milk | 3 tablespoons butter |
| ¼ cup unsweetened cocoa | 1 teaspoon vanilla extract |
| 1 tablespoon corn syrup | |

• Stir together first 5 ingredients in a 2-quart saucepan. Bring mixture to a boil over medium-high heat, and cook until a candy thermometer registers 240° (soft ball stage). Remove mixture from heat; add butter, and let melt. (Do not stir.) Let cool 10 to 15 minutes or until pan is cool to the touch. Stir in vanilla.

• Beat mixture at medium-low speed with an electric mixer 2 to 3 minutes or just until mixture begins to lose its gloss. Working quickly, pour fudge onto a buttered 11- x 7-inch platter. Let cool 15 minutes. Cut into 1-inch pieces. Yield: about 20 (1-inch) pieces.

*Anne Kracke*
Birmingham, Alabama

*cook's secret...* Be careful with the beating step. Beat the mixture just until it loses its gloss. Beat it too long, and you won't be able to pour it. If this happens, knead small portions with your fingers and shape it into logs or balls.

# Mini Tiramisù Éclairs

⅓ cup hot water
2 tablespoons granulated sugar
2 teaspoons instant coffee granules
2 (3-ounce) packages ladyfingers, split
1 (8-ounce) package mascarpone cheese

1½ cups powdered sugar, divided
2 tablespoons chocolate syrup
½ cup semisweet chocolate morsels
1 tablespoon butter
1 tablespoon whipping cream

• Stir together first 3 ingredients until sugar is dissolved; set aside 2 tablespoons coffee mixture. Brush cut sides of ladyfingers evenly with remaining coffee mixture.
• Stir together mascarpone cheese, ½ cup powdered sugar, and chocolate syrup until blended. Spoon or pipe mascarpone cheese mixture evenly onto 24 cut sides of ladyfinger halves; top with remaining ladyfinger halves, cut sides down.
• Microwave chocolate morsels, butter, and cream at HIGH 30 seconds or until melted, stirring twice. Place chocolate mixture in a small zip-top freezer bag; seal bag. Snip a tiny hole in 1 corner of bag, and drizzle over éclairs. Let stand until firm.
• Stir together reserved coffee mixture and remaining 1 cup powdered sugar, stirring until blended. Place coffee–powdered sugar mixture in a small zip-top freezer bag; seal bag. Snip a tiny hole in 1 corner of bag. Drizzle éclairs evenly with coffee–powdered sugar mixture. Place on a serving platter, cake stand, or in candy boxes, if desired. Yield: 2 dozen.

*Jan Moon*
Former Test Kitchens Professional

*cook's secret*... Substitute 1 (8-ounce) package cream cheese, softened, for mascarpone, if desired.

My proudest moment in a cooking class came when I pulled my éclair pastries from the oven. "Those are beautiful!" the teacher gasped. I glowed with pride and realized that if *I* could make éclairs, anyone could.

*Donna Florio*
Senior Writer

# Vanilla Cream-Filled Éclairs

*Choux is the French name for this tender pastry.*
*We've simplified the recipe by using piecrust mix.*

| | |
|---|---|
| 1⅓ cups water | 2 egg whites |
| 1 (11-ounce) package piecrust mix | Vanilla Pastry Cream |
| 3 large eggs | Chocolate Glaze |

• Bring 1⅓ cups water to a boil in a 3-quart saucepan over medium-high heat. Stir in piecrust mix, beating vigorously with a wooden spoon 1 minute or until mixture leaves sides of pan.

• Place dough in bowl of a heavy-duty electric stand mixer; cool 5 minutes. Beat dough at medium speed with electric mixer using paddle attachment. Add eggs and egg whites, 1 at a time, beating until blended after each addition. (If desired, eggs and egg whites may be added, 1 at a time, and beaten vigorously with a wooden spoon instead of a mixer.)

• Spoon dough into a large zip-top freezer bag. (A large pastry bag may also be used.) Cut a 1½-inch opening across 1 corner of the bag. Pipe 4-inch-long strips of dough 2 inches apart onto ungreased baking sheets. Bake at 425° for 20 to 25 minutes or until puffed and golden. (Do not underbake.) Remove from oven, and cut a small slit in side of each éclair to allow steam to escape. Cool on wire racks.

• Split éclairs using a serrated knife, starting at 1 long side without cutting through opposite side. Pull out and discard soft dough inside. Carefully spoon about ¼ cup Vanilla Pastry Cream into each éclair; close top of each éclair over filling. Top evenly with Chocolate Glaze. Chill 2 hours, or freeze up to 1 month. Yield: 1 dozen.

**NOTE:** *For testing purposes only, we used Betty Crocker piecrust mix.*

**Peanut Butter–Chocolate Éclairs:** Follow recipe for Vanilla Cream-Filled Éclairs, substituting Peanut Butter Pastry Cream for Vanilla Pastry Cream.

**Mocha Éclairs:** Follow recipe for Vanilla Cream-Filled Éclairs, substituting Coffee Pastry Cream for Vanilla Pastry Cream.

**Banana-Chocolate Éclairs:** Follow recipe for Vanilla Cream-Filled Éclairs, adding 3 medium bananas, quartered lengthwise and thinly sliced, to Vanilla Pastry Cream after chilling 4 hours.

**Strawberry Cream Éclairs:** Follow recipe for Vanilla Cream-Filled Éclairs, substituting Grand Marnier Pastry Cream for Vanilla Pastry Cream. Slice 1 quart strawberries, and spoon evenly into éclairs before filling with pastry cream. Top with White Chocolate Glaze; drizzle with Chocolate Glaze.

## Vanilla Pastry Cream:

| | |
|---|---|
| 2 large eggs | 2 cups half-and-half |
| 2 egg yolks | 2 tablespoons butter, softened |
| ½ cup sugar | 2 teaspoons vanilla extract |
| ⅓ cup cornstarch | |

• Whisk together first 4 ingredients in a 3-quart saucepan. Gradually whisk in half-and-half. Cook over medium heat, whisking constantly, until mixture comes to a boil. Cook 1 minute or until mixture is thickened and bubbly. Remove from heat; whisk in butter and vanilla. Cover and chill 4 hours. Yield: 3 cups.

**Peanut Butter Pastry Cream:** Omit 2 tablespoons butter, and stir in ⅓ cup creamy peanut butter.

**Coffee Pastry Cream:** Stir 1 tablespoon instant coffee granules in with half-and-half.

**Grand Marnier Pastry Cream:** Omit vanilla extract, and stir in 2 tablespoons orange liqueur.

## Chocolate Glaze:

| | |
|---|---|
| 1 cup semisweet chocolate morsels | 2 tablespoons butter, softened |
| ¼ cup whipping cream | |

• Microwave morsels and whipping cream at HIGH in a 2-cup glass measuring cup 30 seconds to 1 minute or until melted, stirring twice. Whisk in butter until blended, and spoon immediately over éclairs. Yield: 1⅓ cups.

**White Chocolate Glaze:** Substitute 4 ounces chopped white chocolate for semisweet chocolate morsels.

*Mary Allen Perry*
Associate Foods Editor

main dishes

# Top 10 Best Kept Main Dish Secrets

**1.** To serve perfectly cooked, tender shrimp, don't boil them. Drop them into a large pot of boiling water, and bring the water back to a boil. Cover and remove the pot from the heat; let the shrimp stand 3 to 5 minutes (depending on the size) or until shrimp turn pink.

**2.** Take advantage of refrigerated bread doughs in the dairy case. Crescent rolls, breadsticks, pizza crusts, and biscuits offer convenient ways to top casseroles or wrap leftovers.

**3.** Lightly sprinkle beef and chicken strips with 1 or 2 tablespoons of cornstarch before stir-frying them. It helps the meat to brown beautifully and quickly. The velvety texture of the completed recipe is a bonus.

**4.** Rotisserie chicken is terrific when you need chopped chicken for a recipe. Remove the meat from the bones while it's still warm, and freeze in a zip-top freezer bag. One chicken yields about 3 cups of chopped meat.

**5.** For a speedy "home-cooked" entrée, purchase sliced, cooked beef brisket by the pound from your favorite barbecue restaurant. Arrange in a baking dish, and cover with equal parts barbecue sauce and beef broth. Bake, covered, at 350° for 30 minutes or until thoroughly heated.

**6.** Add fresh herbs to coals when grilling for flavorful meats and vegetables (dampen the herbs with water first so they don't burn).

**7.** After grilling, wrap meat in aluminum foil, and allow it to rest for 15 minutes. The internal temperature may climb another 5 to 10 degrees, cooking the meat further.

**8.** There's not much difference between a fresh or frozen turkey. Fresh is more convenient if you're pushed for time, but it will cost more per pound than frozen. If purchasing frozen, keep in mind that two small birds will thaw and cook quicker than one large.

**9.** Slices of country ham or smoked turkey pack a punch in soups and casseroles. Pack ham or turkey leftovers in small zip-top freezer bags with just enough meat to season one recipe; freeze them in one large zip-top freezer bag. You'll have exactly the amount you need for a recipe without prying small portions from a large frozen block.

**10.** Casseroles are some of the easiest recipes to double. However, don't automatically double the salt, pepper, herbs, and spices; taste and adjust the seasonings carefully.

According to Jeff Shivers, native Texan and Executive Director of the International Bar-b-que Cookers Association, "Some folks in other parts of the country don't even know what brisket is. It's just now starting to become more popular in places other than Texas."

*Southern Living* Assistant Garden Design Editor Troy Black isn't from Texas, but you wouldn't know it by his brisket. Troy's recipe contains all the prerequisites of a true Texas brisket—a great rub, a juicy mop, and a long, slow smoking time. He's got the technique down to a science, too.

*regional favorite*

# Troy's Traditional Brisket

| | |
|---|---|
| 1 (5¾-pound) trimmed beef brisket flat | Brisket Mopping Sauce |
| Brisket Rub | Mop |
| Hickory smoking chips | Brisket Red Sauce (optional) |

• Sprinkle each side of beef with ¼ cup Brisket Rub; rub thoroughly into meat. Wrap brisket in plastic wrap, and chill 8 hours.
• Soak hickory chips in water for 8 hours. Drain.
• Prepare smoker according to manufacturer's directions, regulating temperature with a thermometer to 225°; allow it to maintain that temperature for 1 hour before adding beef.
• Remove beef from refrigerator, and let stand 30 minutes.
• Place brisket on smoker rack, fat side up. Insert thermometer horizontally into thickest portion of beef brisket. Maintain smoker temperature between 225° and 250°.
• Add a handful (about ¼ cup) of hickory chips about every hour.
• Brush beef liberally with Brisket Mopping Sauce when beef starts to look dry (internal temperature will be about 156°). Mop top of brisket every hour. When internal temperature reaches 170°, place brisket on a sheet of heavy-duty aluminum foil; mop liberally with Brisket Mopping Sauce. Wrap tightly, and return to smoker.
• Remove brisket from smoker when internal temperature reaches 190° with an instant-read thermometer. Let stand 1 hour. Cut into very thin (⅛- to ¼-inch-thick) slices. Serve with Brisket Red Sauce, if desired. Yield: 8 servings.

**NOTE:** *Mops may be found in the grilling supply section of supermarkets, in restaurant-supply stores, and in the grilling accessory section of sporting-goods stores. For testing purposes only, we used the Weber Smokey Mountain Cooker Smoker.*

## Brisket Rub:

*This makes enough for about three briskets.*

| | |
|---|---|
| ¾ cup paprika | 2 tablespoons garlic salt |
| ¼ cup kosher salt | 2 tablespoons onion powder |
| ¼ cup sugar | 2 tablespoons chili powder |
| ¼ cup black pepper | 2 teaspoons ground red pepper |
| 2 tablespoons garlic powder | |

• Combine all ingredients. Store in an airtight container. Yield: 2 cups.

## Brisket Mopping Sauce:

*This is enough sauce for about two briskets, so half the recipe if you're preparing just one.*

| | |
|---|---|
| 1 (12-ounce) bottle beer | ½ cup water |
| 1 cup apple cider vinegar | ½ cup Worcestershire sauce |
| 1 onion, minced | ¼ cup vegetable oil |
| 4 garlic cloves, minced | 2 tablespoons Brisket Rub |

• Stir together all ingredients until blended. Yield: 4 cups.

## Brisket Red Sauce:

| | |
|---|---|
| 1½ cups apple cider vinegar | ½ teaspoon onion powder |
| 1 cup ketchup | ½ tablespoon garlic powder |
| ½ teaspoon ground red pepper | ½ tablespoon ground cumin |
| ¼ cup Worcestershire sauce | 2 tablespoons unsalted butter, melted |
| 1 teaspoon salt | ½ cup firmly packed brown sugar |
| ½ teaspoon black pepper | |

• Stir together all ingredients until blended. Serve sauce heated or at room temperature. Yield: 3½ cups.

*Troy Black*
Assistant Garden Design Editor

*cook's secret...* A good rule of thumb is to smoke brisket 1 hour and 15 minutes per pound at 225° to 250° until the internal temperature reaches 190°. That's much longer than really is needed as far as the meat being safe to eat, but that's the temperature that makes this cut of meat melt-in-your-mouth tender.

# Smoky Barbecue Brisket

*Here's an easy indoor version of*
*spicy barbecue brisket.*

| | |
|---|---|
| 1 (4- to 6-pound) beef brisket, trimmed | 1 to 2 teaspoons salt |
| 1 (5-ounce) bottle liquid smoke | ⅓ cup Worcestershire sauce |
| 1 onion, chopped | 1 (12- to 18-ounce) bottle barbecue sauce |
| 2 teaspoons garlic salt | |

• Place brisket in a large shallow dish or extra-large zip-top freezer bag; pour liquid smoke over brisket. Sprinkle evenly with onion, garlic salt, and salt. Cover or seal, and chill 8 hours, turning occasionally.
• Remove brisket, and place on a large piece of heavy-duty aluminum foil, discarding liquid smoke mixture. Pour Worcestershire sauce evenly over brisket, and fold foil to seal; place wrapped brisket in a roasting pan.
• Bake at 275° for 5 hours. Unfold foil; pour barbecue sauce evenly over brisket. Bake 1 more hour, uncovered. Yield: 8 servings.

*Linda Pugliano*
*Fort Worth, Texas*

*cook's secret...* This is even better if it stays in the refrigerator a day after cooking to absorb the flavors. Slice and reheat it in the oven or microwave. Serve with extra barbecue sauce and Texas toast for dipping.

# Peppered Rib-Eye Roast

*Sprinkle on flavor and stir in color with this well-known*
*ingredient: pepper. Having captured the hearts of many Southern cooks,*
*pepper has great merit due to its numerous varieties.*

| | |
|---|---|
| 1 cup soy sauce | ½ teaspoon ground cardamom |
| ¾ cup red wine vinegar | 1 (5- to 6-pound) eye of round roast, |
| 1 tablespoon tomato paste | trimmed |
| 3 garlic cloves, minced | ¼ cup water |
| 1 teaspoon paprika | 1½ tablespoons cornstarch |
| ½ cup assorted coarsely ground peppercorns | Sautéed sliced mushrooms (optional) |

- Stir together first 5 ingredients.
- Combine peppercorns and ground cardamom; press into roast. Place roast in a shallow dish; pour marinade over roast. Cover and chill 8 hours, turning roast occasionally.
- Remove roast from marinade, reserving 1 cup marinade. Wrap roast in aluminum foil, sealing well; place in a shallow roasting pan.
- Bake at 300° for 2 hours or until done. Remove from oven; unwrap foil, and drain, reserving juices. Increase oven temperature to 350°; return roast to pan, and bake 15 minutes.
- Combine ¼ cup water and cornstarch in a saucepan, stirring until mixture is smooth. Stir in reserved juices and reserved 1 cup marinade.
- Bring to a boil over medium heat, stirring constantly; boil, stirring constantly, 1 minute. Stir in mushrooms, if desired. Serve with roast. Yield: 10 to 12 servings.

*Sandra F. Alsup*
Knoxville, Tennessee

*cook's secret...* To keep pepper at its freshest, store whole dried peppercorns in a cool, dark place for up to a year. Store ground pepper no longer than 4 months.

## Pepper Picks

Peppercorns are berries that grow in grapelike clusters on climbing vines (*Piper nigrum*). The pepper plant's berry is processed into three basic types.

- Black peppercorns, the most common variety, are picked when the berry is not quite ripe, and then dried. This pepper is the most intensely flavored: slightly hot with a trace of sweetness.
- White peppercorns are less pungent and have been allowed to ripen. They are often used for appearance so that the specks won't stand out in foods.
- Green peppercorns are soft, underripe berries that have a less sharp flavor.
- Pink peppercorns, which add a touch of color and a slightly sweet flavor to your recipes, aren't true peppercorns. They're actually expensive dried berries from the *Baies* rose plant.

enry Bain Sauce originated with the headwaiter at the Pendennis Club in Louisville in the 1880s. The club has never revealed the official recipe; however, Jean Briscoe's version—a favorite at the annual Derby party she hosts with her husband, John—received our Test Kitchens' highest rating.

*editor's choice*

# Beef Tenderloin with Henry Bain Sauce

| | |
|---|---|
| 1 (8-ounce) bottle chutney | ¼ cup butter or margarine, softened |
| 1 (14-ounce) bottle ketchup | 2 teaspoons salt |
| 1 (12-ounce) bottle chili sauce | 1 teaspoon freshly ground pepper |
| 1 (11-ounce) bottle steak sauce | 1 (4½- to 5-pound) beef tenderloin, |
| 1 (10-ounce) bottle Worcestershire sauce | trimmed |
| 1 teaspoon hot sauce | |

• Process chutney in a blender or food processor until smooth. Add ketchup and next 4 ingredients, and process until blended. Chill at least 2 hours.

• Stir together butter, salt, and pepper; rub over tenderloin. Place on a lightly greased rack in a jellyroll pan. Fold under 4 to 6 inches of narrow end of tenderloin to fit onto rack.

• Bake at 500° for 30 to 35 minutes or to desired degree of doneness. Let stand 15 minutes before serving. Serve tenderloin with sauce. Yield: 10 to 12 servings.

**NOTE:** *For testing purposes only, we used Major Grey's Chutney and A1 Steak Sauce.*

*Jean Briscoe*
*Louisville, Kentucky*

*cook's secret...* At about $13 to $20 a pound, beef tenderloin is a special-occasion purchase. Sometimes you can find a great deal on the whole tenderloin. Also known as the short loin, whole tenderloin can vary between 3 and 6 pounds. Ask the butcher to cut it into 2 or more tenderloins or steaks (also known as filets mignons).

If you've got a nice dinner planned or just want to stock up, call the meat department at your local supermarket to find the best price. (Whole tenderloins are often as low as $8 a pound.) This cut takes well to broiling, grilling, or sautéing. Savory rubs and simple marinades lend vibrant flavor without a lot of work.

Angela Kotowicz and her husband, Chris, serve this 2001 *Southern Living* Holiday Recipe Contest Grand Prize Winner on special occasions. "Every time we have made it, we have adapted the sauce to our liking, adding and changing things," Angela says.

## Pepper-Seared Beef Tenderloin with Horseradish Cream Sauce

| | | | |
|---|---|---|---|
| 4 | (6-ounce) beef tenderloin fillets | ¼ | teaspoon ground pepper |
| ¾ | teaspoon salt, divided | ⅔ | cup whipping cream |
| 1 | tablespoon cracked pepper | 2 | tablespoons prepared horseradish |
| ½ | cup butter or margarine, divided | 1 | teaspoon Dijon mustard |
| 2 | teaspoons all-purpose flour | | |

• Sprinkle fillets evenly with ½ teaspoon salt; press cracked pepper into all sides of fillets.
• Melt ¼ cup butter in a large heavy skillet over medium-high heat; add beef, and cook for 3 to 4 minutes on each side or until beef is desired degree of doneness.
• Melt remaining ¼ cup butter in a saucepan over medium heat. Whisk in flour, remaining ¼ teaspoon salt, and ground pepper until blended; cook, whisking constantly, 1 minute. Add cream, and cook, whisking constantly, 1 minute or until thickened and bubbly. Stir in horseradish and mustard. Drizzle over fillets. Yield: 4 servings.

*Angela M. Kotowicz*
St. Louis, Missouri

*cook's secret*... Prepared horseradish loses its hotness after it's opened. Store it in the refrigerator, and replace it after 3 or 4 months.

# Mini Beef Wellingtons

| | |
|---|---|
| 5 tablespoons butter or margarine, divided | 2 tablespoons dry sherry or beef broth |
| 8 (3-ounce) beef tenderloin fillets, 1 inch thick | 1 (17.3-ounce) package frozen puff pastry sheets, thawed |
| ¼ teaspoon salt | 1 egg white, lightly beaten |
| ¼ teaspoon pepper | 1½ tablespoons butter or margarine |
| 3 large fresh mushrooms, chopped | 1½ tablespoons all-purpose flour |
| 1 (8-ounce) package fresh mushrooms, chopped | 1 tablespoon tomato paste |
| | 2 (14-ounce) cans beef broth |
| | 1 bay leaf, crushed |

• Melt 3 tablespoons butter in a large skillet over medium heat; add beef, and cook 3 minutes on each side or until browned. Remove from skillet; sprinkle with salt and pepper, and let cool.

• Melt remaining 2 tablespoons butter in skillet; add mushrooms, and sauté 5 minutes. Stir in sherry.

• Unfold pastry sheets on a lightly floured surface; roll to ⅛-inch thickness, and cut into fourths. Place 1 fillet in center of each square; top with mushroom mixture. Bring opposite corners of squares together over beef, gently pressing to seal. Place on a baking sheet; brush with egg white.

• Bake at 425° on the lowest oven rack for 25 to 30 minutes or until golden.

• Melt 1½ tablespoons butter in skillet; whisk in flour. Cook, whisking constantly, 2 to 3 minutes or until lightly browned. Add tomato paste; cook, stirring constantly, 1 to 2 minutes. Gradually whisk in broth. Add bay leaf; simmer 20 minutes. Pour through a wire-mesh strainer into a bowl. Serve sauce with Beef Wellingtons. Yield: 8 servings.

*Sue Siegel*
Seminole, Florida

### Puffed to Perfection

• Thaw frozen puff pastry 20 minutes at room temperature before using, but keep refrigerated until ready to fill.

• Dust countertop lightly with flour when using puff pastry.

• Avoid placing a hot filling on buttery puff pastry.

*Cybil Talley*
Former Assistant Foods Editor

# Simple Pepper Steak

*Turn this dish into a hearty meal with hot cooked rice or noodles and a spinach salad.*

¼ cup cornstarch, divided
½ teaspoon ground ginger
1 (10½-ounce) can beef broth
2 tablespoons soy sauce
½ teaspoon dried crushed red pepper (optional)
½ teaspoon salt
½ teaspoon black pepper

1 pound boneless top sirloin steak, cut into thin slices
1 tablespoon vegetable oil
2 teaspoons sesame oil
1 garlic clove, pressed
1 green bell pepper, sliced
1 medium onion, sliced
Hot cooked rice

• Whisk together 2 tablespoons cornstarch, ginger, beef broth, soy sauce, and, if desired, red pepper; set aside.

• Combine remaining 2 tablespoons cornstarch, salt, and black pepper; dredge steak in mixture.

• Heat vegetable oil and sesame oil in a large skillet over high heat 3 minutes; add steak and garlic, and sauté 4 minutes or until browned.

• Add bell pepper and onion; sauté 8 minutes or until tender. Stir in broth mixture; reduce heat, and simmer 3 to 5 minutes or until thickened. Serve over hot cooked rice. Yield: 6 servings.

*Elizabeth Ann Duncan*
Arden, North Carolina

*cook's secret...* Searing is a simple cooking method that seals in juices and the flavor of meat or fish. Pat meat as dry as possible, and then place it in a sizzling skillet. Don't turn the meat until a rich brown crust has formed; then brown the other side. This quickly locks in the juices, as this pepper steak exemplifies.

Chicken-fried steak might just be the national entrée of Texas. Dinner plates laden with fried steaks, potatoes, and gravy are as much a part of the Lone Star State's persona as tumbleweeds and cowboy hats. Though historians stand divided on whether the dish appeared first as a chuckwagon creation or a takeoff on German *Wiener schnitzel*, all agree that it is a fine way to enjoy some of the less tender cuts of beef.

The dish begins with round steak that has been pounded with a meat mallet or run though a cubing machine. Thus tenderized, it's breaded, fried, and served with cream gravy made from the pan drippings. On this last point, Texas cooks are adamant because it separates chicken-fried steak from country-fried. "This is not brown gravy, it's cream gravy," says Annetta White of Austin's Broken Spoke restaurant. And mashed or fried potatoes on the plate are a must, but beyond that, the side dishes become a free-for-all.

"At my parents' house, no vegetable except mashed potatoes goes on the plate unless Mom requires it," says Vanessa McNeil of our Test Kitchens. Vanessa is a Texan who, as a teenager, made it her mission to find a great chicken-fried recipe.

*cook's secret...* "My Dad wanted to have chicken-fried steak at home, but we didn't know how to do it," recalls Vanessa McNeil. "Then I visited Austin, which has lots of places that serve it, and I met someone who worked in one of the kitchens. He told me the secret is crumbled saltine crackers—they give chicken-fried steak a great crust."

# Chicken-Fried Steak

*Serve chicken-fried steak with its classic counterpart: mashed potatoes.*

¼ teaspoon salt

¼ teaspoon black pepper

4 (4-ounce) cube steaks

38 saltine crackers (1 sleeve), crushed

1¼ cups all-purpose flour, divided

½ teaspoon baking powder

2 teaspoons salt, divided

1½ teaspoons black pepper, divided

½ teaspoon ground red pepper

4¾ cups milk, divided

2 large eggs

3½ cups peanut oil

Garnish: chopped fresh parsley

• Sprinkle salt and ¼ teaspoon black pepper evenly over steaks. Set aside.

• Combine cracker crumbs, 1 cup flour, baking powder, 1 teaspoon salt, ½ teaspoon black pepper, and red pepper.

• Whisk together ¾ cup milk and eggs. Dredge steaks in cracker crumb mixture; dip in milk mixture, and dredge in cracker mixture again.

• Pour oil into a 12-inch skillet; heat to 360°. (Do not use a nonstick skillet.) Fry steaks 10 minutes. Turn and fry 4 to 5 more minutes or until golden brown. Remove to a wire rack on a jellyroll pan. Keep steaks warm in a 225° oven. Carefully drain hot oil, reserving cooked bits and 1 tablespoon drippings in skillet.

• Whisk together remaining ¼ cup flour, 1 teaspoon salt, 1 teaspoon black pepper, and 4 cups milk. Pour mixture into reserved drippings in skillet; cook over medium-high heat, whisking constantly, 10 to 12 minutes or until thickened. Serve gravy with steaks and mashed potatoes. Sprinkle with parsley, if desired. Yield: 4 servings.

*Vanessa McNeil*
Test Kitchens Specialist

## Vanessa's Tips

• Firmly push the cube steak down into the cracker crumbs; the crumbs will fill the crevices and keep the steak from shrinking as it cooks.

• It's time to turn the steak when you see juice oozing out of the top.

*S*paghetti-and-Spinach Casserole travels well, so it's a good choice for a covered-dish dinner.

## Spaghetti-and-Spinach Casserole

| | | | | |
|---|---|---|---|---|
| 1½ | pounds ground beef | 2 | cups (8 ounces) shredded Monterey Jack cheese | |
| 2 | garlic cloves, minced | | | |
| ½ | teaspoon salt | 1½ | cups sour cream | |
| ½ | teaspoon pepper | 1 | large egg, lightly beaten | |
| 1 | (26-ounce) jar spaghetti sauce | 1 | teaspoon garlic salt | |
| 1 | teaspoon Italian seasoning | 8 | ounces wide egg noodles, cooked | |
| 1 | (10-ounce) package frozen chopped spinach, thawed and drained | 1½ | cups shredded Parmesan cheese | |

• Cook first 4 ingredients in a large nonstick skillet over medium heat, stirring until beef crumbles and is no longer pink. Drain and return to skillet. Stir in spaghetti sauce and Italian seasoning.

• Combine spinach and next 4 ingredients. Fold in noodles, and spoon mixture into a lightly greased 13- x 9-inch baking dish. Sprinkle with half of Parmesan cheese; top with beef mixture and remaining Parmesan cheese.

• Bake at 350° for 30 minutes or until bubbly and golden. Yield: 8 to 10 servings.

*Susanne Pettit*
Memphis, Tennessee

*cook's secret*... This Italian-inspired casserole freezes well. Bake it as directed, and then let it cool; cover and freeze. Thaw overnight in the refrigerator. Bake, covered, at 350° for 30 minutes; uncover and bake 10 more minutes.

## Potluck Pointers

Here are some tips to help make hosting a potluck easy and fun.

### Planning and More

• Decide which type of food you want to serve ahead of time. Be as specific as possible when assigning dishes; communicate which kinds you want and how many people you'll serve.

• Monitor the menu by selecting dishes with a variety of tastes and textures. (Go for opposites: crunchy/smooth, spicy/mild, soft/firm.)

• Plan a menu that can be served at room temperature if you're worried about having to keep items warm. If not, foods that should be kept hot or cold should not enter the "danger zone" (temperatures between 40° and 140°) for more than 2 hours. Use small platters, and replenish as needed.

• Stack mix-and-match plates and napkins to add a colorful element to your buffet table.

• Place food on pedestals for visual appeal; fill vertical space with flowers or breadsticks.

• Enhance the serving table with one or more centerpieces. Use votives or lanterns to avoid open flames from candlesticks.

• Collect containers suitable for instant flower arranging. Simple vases or bottles will work, as well as planters, galvanized buckets, or hurricane lanterns.

### Creative Containers

• Look for unique plates and serving dishes at local outlets or discount stores. For example, you can place a cake on a terra-cotta plate or put a salad in a similar pot.

• Serve cookies or brownies in decorative gift bags.

• Line a basket with a bandanna or colorful tea towels to hold croissants, rolls, or muffins.

• Use a decorative ice bucket for cold foods, such as potato salad or coleslaw. Fill with ice, and place a bowl or container of your chilled side dish in the bucket. Then serve from on top of the ice.

Charlotte Skelton serves great-tasting meals without a lot of fuss. Her secret: stocking her freezer with one-dish meals. In fact, she's built a career around it. Her A la Carte Alley is home to one of The Delta's most popular restaurants. Though the business has grown, the thing that hasn't changed is her love of recipes she can make ahead, freeze, and reheat.

*make–ahead*

# Beef Lombardi

| | | | |
|---|---|---|---|
| 1 | pound lean ground beef | ½ | (12-ounce) package medium egg noodles |
| 1 | (14.5-ounce) can diced tomatoes | 6 | green onions, chopped (about ½ cup) |
| 1 | (10-ounce) can diced tomatoes and green chiles | 1 | cup sour cream |
| 2 | teaspoons sugar | 1 | cup (4 ounces) shredded sharp Cheddar cheese |
| 2 | teaspoons salt | 1 | cup shredded Parmesan cheese |
| ¼ | teaspoon pepper | 1 | cup (4 ounces) shredded mozzarella cheese |
| 1 | (6-ounce) can tomato paste | | |
| 1 | bay leaf | **Garnish: fresh parsley sprigs** | |

• Cook ground beef in a large skillet over medium heat 5 to 6 minutes, stirring until it crumbles and is no longer pink. Drain.

• Stir in tomatoes and next 4 ingredients; cook 5 minutes. Add tomato paste and bay leaf, and simmer 30 minutes. Discard bay leaf.

• Cook egg noodles according to package directions; drain.

• Stir together cooked egg noodles, chopped green onions, and sour cream until blended.

• Place noodle mixture in bottom of a lightly greased 13- x 9-inch baking dish. Top with beef mixture; sprinkle evenly with cheeses.

• Bake, covered with aluminum foil, at 350° for 35 minutes. Uncover casserole, and bake 5 more minutes. Garnish, if desired. Yield: 6 servings.

**NOTE:** *Freeze up to 1 month, if desired. Thaw in refrigerator overnight. Bake as directed.*

*Charlotte Skelton*
Cleveland, Mississippi

*cook's secret...* Most reduced-fat products lighten foods while giving better flavor and texture results than nonfat products. To lighten this recipe, substitute low-fat sour cream and 2% reduced-fat Cheddar cheese. Reduce amount of cheeses on top to ½ cup each.

I'm a casserole person," declares Christina Valenta. "I came up with this dish in a New York minute from leftovers." Christina's recipe for Mexican Lasagna was a Runner Up in the 2001 *Southern Living* Holiday Recipe Contest.

*contest winner*

# Mexican Lasagna

| | | | |
|---|---|---|---|
| ½ | pound mild ground pork sausage | 1 | (10¾-ounce) can cream of mushroom soup, undiluted |
| ½ | pound ground beef | 1 | (10-ounce) can enchilada sauce |
| 1 | (15-ounce) can jalapeño ranch-style pinto beans, drained | 9 | (6-inch) corn tortillas |
| ⅔ | cup canned diced tomatoes and green chiles | 2 | cups (8 ounces) shredded Cheddar cheese |
| 1 | teaspoon garlic powder | 1 | cup (4 ounces) shredded Monterey Jack cheese |
| 1 | teaspoon ground cumin | | |
| ½ | teaspoon salt | 1 | medium tomato, seeded and diced |
| ½ | teaspoon pepper | 4 | green onions, chopped |
| 1 | (10¾-ounce) can cream of celery soup, undiluted | ¼ | cup chopped fresh cilantro |
| | | 1 | medium avocado, chopped |

- Cook sausage and ground beef in a large skillet over medium-high heat, stirring until meat crumbles and is no longer pink. Drain. Stir in beans and next 5 ingredients; cook until thoroughly heated.
- Stir together soups and enchilada sauce in a saucepan; cook until thoroughly heated.
- Spoon one-third of sauce onto bottom of a lightly greased 13- x 9-inch baking dish; top with 3 tortillas. Spoon half of beef mixture and one-third of sauce over tortillas; sprinkle with half of Cheddar cheese. Top with 3 tortillas; repeat beef, sauce, and Cheddar cheese layers, and end with tortillas. Sprinkle with Monterey Jack cheese and next 3 ingredients.
- Bake at 350° for 30 minutes. Top with avocado. Yield: 6 to 8 servings.

*Christina Valenta*
*Friendswood, Texas*

*cook's secret...* An easy way to seed a tomato is to slice it in half crosswise; then take each half in your hand and squeeze gently, removing the seeds with your fingers or a spoon.

# Sweet 'n' Saucy Meat Loaf

| | |
|---|---|
| 1 pound lean ground beef | 2 garlic cloves, chopped |
| 1 pound lean ground pork sausage | 1 tablespoon chopped fresh parsley |
| 1 cup fine, dry breadcrumbs | 1 tablespoon curry powder |
| 1 large egg, lightly beaten | 1 teaspoon salt |
| 1 medium onion, diced | ½ teaspoon pepper |
| ½ cup milk | Sweet 'n' Saucy Sauce |

• Combine first 11 ingredients. Shape into a loaf, and place in a lightly greased 9- x 5-inch loafpan.

• Bake at 375° for 30 minutes. Pour half of Sweet 'n' Saucy Sauce over meat loaf; bake 45 more minutes. Remove from pan; serve with remaining sauce. Yield: 6 servings.

## Sweet 'n' Saucy Sauce:

| | |
|---|---|
| 2 tablespoons butter or margarine | ¼ cup beef broth |
| 1 small onion, diced | ¼ cup Worcestershire sauce |
| ½ cup ketchup | 1 tablespoon instant coffee granules |
| ¼ cup firmly packed brown sugar | 2 tablespoons rice vinegar |
| ¼ cup water | 2 teaspoons lemon juice |

• Melt butter in a large skillet over medium-high heat; add onion, and sauté 5 minutes or until tender. Stir in ½ cup ketchup and remaining ingredients. Bring to a boil, stirring constantly; reduce heat, and simmer 10 minutes. Yield: 1½ cups.

*Marion Hall*
Knoxville, Tennessee

### Making Meat Loaf

• Bake meat loaf on a rack in a roasting pan to keep it out of the fatty drippings.

• Prevent meat loaf from sticking and speed cleanup by spraying the pan with vegetable cooking spray.

• Use a meat thermometer to be sure your meat loaf is done. It should register 160°, the meat should have no pinkness, and the juices should run clear.

• Meat loaf freezes well, so make 2 loaves at a time, and freeze 1 loaf for later use.

Drawn from an old family recipe, former NFL star Dan Pastorini's delicious Italian Meat Sauce is a guaranteed crowd-pleaser. Dan and his fellow volunteer firemen in Chappell Hill, Texas, enjoy cooking firehouse-size dinners. "We're totally self-sufficient, so we have quite a few fund-raisers throughout the year. These give us a chance to showcase our cooking and barbecuing skills," Dan says, with a grin.

## Italian Meat Sauce

| | |
|---|---|
| 1 pound ground pork* | 2 (15-ounce) cans tomato sauce |
| 1 pound ground beef | 1 (14-ounce) can beef broth |
| 1 medium onion, diced | 1 (10¾-ounce) can tomato puree |
| 2 celery ribs, diced | 1 (6-ounce) can Italian-style tomato paste |
| 2 small carrots, diced | 1 tablespoon chopped fresh thyme |
| 3 garlic cloves, minced | 1 tablespoon chopped fresh oregano |
| 1 teaspoon salt | 1 tablespoon chopped fresh basil |
| 1 teaspoon pepper | 1 (20-ounce) package refrigerated cheese-filled ravioli, cooked |
| 1 (8-ounce) package sliced fresh mushrooms | Garnish: chopped fresh basil |

- Cook first 8 ingredients in a large Dutch oven over medium heat, stirring until meat crumbles and is no longer pink. Drain.
- Stir in mushrooms and next 6 ingredients; simmer 3 hours. Stir in 1 tablespoon basil just before serving; serve over ravioli. Garnish, if desired. Yield: 10 cups.

*1 pound ground beef may be substituted.

Dan Pastorini
Chappell Hill, Texas

*cook's secret...* Refrigerated ravioli is a novel noodle on which to serve a spicy Italian meat sauce. It cooks in just a couple of minutes, so put it on at the last minute so that it's hot and fresh.

Jacques Haeringer, chef and author of *Two for Tonight* (Bartleby Press), feels the preparation of food is an act of love. "Most of our memorable moments are celebrated with festive meals," says Jacques. "The pleasures of fine food and wine are essential parts of a passionate life."

*chef recipe*

# Dijon Rack of Lamb

2  (8-rib) lamb rib roasts (2 to 2½ pounds each), trimmed
1  teaspoon salt
3  teaspoons pepper

3  tablespoons olive oil
3  tablespoons Dijon mustard
1  cup fresh herb focaccia breadcrumbs*

- Rub lamb evenly with salt and pepper.
- Cook lamb in hot oil in a large skillet over high heat 3 minutes on each side or until browned. Place lamb, fat side up, on a rack in a broiling pan.
- Bake at 425° for 20 minutes or until a meat thermometer inserted into thickest portion registers 145°.
- Remove lamb from oven, leaving oven on. Cover lamb loosely with aluminum foil, and let stand 10 minutes or until meat thermometer registers 150°.
- Brush lamb with mustard; cover with breadcrumbs. Return lamb to oven, and bake 4 to 5 minutes or until golden. Cut into chops, and serve. Yield: 8 servings.

*1 cup fresh French breadcrumbs may be substituted. Focaccia is a flat Italian bread that can be found in the bakery section of grocery stores.*

**NOTE:** *When Jacques prepares this dish, he prefers to cook the lamb until a meat thermometer inserted into the thickest portion registers 135°.*

Chef Jacques Haeringer
Great Falls, Virginia

*cook's secret...* "To ignite your passionate life, include your loved ones when you cook; you'll bring more to the table," says Jacques. He suggests planning ahead so everyone will be prepared. Select and assign recipes according to skill levels so you don't leave anyone out. Those who finish first may assist others or work on table decor.

Giuliano Hazan promises easy recipes for fresh, healthy food in his cookbook *Every Night Italian*. His approach to cooking—few ingredients, simple directions, and impressive taste—is illustrated in this recipe adapted from his cookbook.

*chef recipe*

## Lamb Shanks Braised with Tomatoes

*Giuliano's recipe calls for lamb shoulder, but we found shanks were more readily available.*

3 pounds bone-in lamb shanks, cut into
   1- to 1½-inch-thick slices
1 teaspoon salt
1 teaspoon pepper
2 tablespoons olive oil
½ cup dry white wine

1 teaspoon chopped fresh rosemary leaves
3 garlic cloves, finely chopped
1 (28-ounce) can whole peeled tomatoes,
   coarsely chopped
2 bay leaves

• Sprinkle lamb with salt and pepper. Brown lamb on all sides in hot oil in a skillet over medium-high heat. Stir in wine, rosemary, and garlic; cook 3 minutes. Add tomatoes and bay leaves.

• Cover, reduce heat, and simmer 1 to 1½ hours, turning lamb every 15 to 20 minutes or until tender.

• Remove lamb to a serving platter. Discard bay leaves, and serve lamb with sauce from pan. Yield: 4 to 6 servings.

*Chef Giuliano Hazan*
Sarasota, Florida
Adapted from *Every Night Italian* (Scribner)

*cook's secret...* Shallow bowls are great for serving these brothy lamb shanks because you can enjoy all the juices.

As a child, Danny Henderson spent lots of time in the kitchen watching his mom cook. Today, he rekindles that culinary spirit with an annual New Year's Day barbecue. "It's a chance for us to get together, think about the past year's blessings, wish each other good luck for the coming year, and spend the day eating great barbecue," he says.

Danny has been perfecting his barbecue techniques for years. He stresses the importance of supplying oxygen to the coals—especially in cold weather—to maintain the heat and keep the meat cooking evenly.

*regional favorite*

## Barbecue Pork Shoulder

| | |
|---|---|
| 1 (2-pound) package hickory wood chunks, divided | ½ cup firmly packed brown sugar |
| 2 quarts white vinegar | ¼ cup ground black pepper |
| ½ cup ground red pepper, divided | 2 tablespoons lemon juice |
| 5 oranges, quartered and divided | ¼ cup liquid smoke |
| 5 lemons, quartered and divided | 1 (7- to 8-pound) pork shoulder roast |

• Soak 1 pound of wood chunks in water 30 minutes to 1 hour.

• Bring vinegar, ¼ cup ground red pepper, 3 oranges, and 3 lemons to a boil in a Dutch oven over medium heat; cook 10 minutes. Remove vinegar mixture from heat, and cool.

• Combine remaining ¼ cup ground red pepper, brown sugar, and next 3 ingredients. Rub evenly over pork. Drizzle 1 cup vinegar mixture over pork; set aside 2 cups vinegar mixture for basting, and reserve remaining mixture to fill the water pan.

• Prepare charcoal fire in smoker; let burn 15 to 20 minutes.

• Drain wood chunks, and place on coals. Place water pan in smoker; add vinegar mixture and remaining 2 oranges and 2 lemons to depth of fill line. Place pork on lower food rack; cover with smoker lid.

• Cook pork roast 6 to 7 hours or until a meat thermometer inserted into the thickest part of roast registers 170°. Baste with reserved vinegar mixture every hour after pork roast has cooked 3 hours. Add more charcoal, remaining 1 pound wood chunks, and vinegar mixture to smoker as needed. Yield: 10 servings.

*Danny Henderson*
Huntsville, Alabama

My husband, John, loves to be outside next to his smoker or grill. He realized some time ago that he could stay outdoors longer, avoiding inside chores, if he chose to smoke meats rather than grill them. His many years of practice bring fabulous results.

*Kate Nicholson*
Associate Foods Editor

# Smoked Boston Butt

1 (10-ounce) bottle teriyaki sauce
1 cup honey
½ cup cider vinegar
2 tablespoons black pepper
2 tablespoons garlic powder

1 teaspoon dried crushed red pepper
1 (6-pound) Boston butt pork roast
Hickory wood chunks
Barbecue sauce

• Combine first 6 ingredients in a shallow dish or large zip-top freezer bag. Cut deep slits in roast using a paring knife; add roast to marinade. Cover or seal, and chill 8 hours, turning occasionally.
• Soak wood chunks in water 1 hour.
• Prepare charcoal fire in smoker; let burn 15 to 20 minutes.
• Drain wood chunks, and place on coals. Place water pan in smoker; add water to depth of fill line. Place roast in center of lower food rack.
• Cook, covered, 6 to 8 hours or until a meat thermometer inserted into thickest portion registers 165°, adding additional water, if necessary. Remove from smoker; cool slightly. Chop or shred; serve with barbecue sauce. Yield: 6 to 8 servings.

*John Nicholson*
Birmingham, Alabama

*cook's secret...* To take the chill off the roast, let it stand at room temperature for 30 minutes before cooking.

Present pinwheel slices of this Madeira-and-fig-infused roast on a bed of Italian parsley sprigs rather than the usual mixed greens.

# Fig-Balsamic Roasted Pork Loin

½ pound ground pork sausage
1¾ cups herb-seasoned stuffing mix
1 large ripe Bartlett pear, peeled and
   chopped
½ red bell pepper, finely chopped
½ cup hot chicken broth
⅓ cup chopped dried figs
1 tablespoon fresh minced thyme
1 (4-pound) boneless pork loin roast

1 teaspoon salt
1 to 2 tablespoons cracked pepper
1 (11.5-ounce) jar fig preserves
1 cup Madeira wine
2 tablespoons balsamic vinegar
¼ cup butter or margarine
¼ cup all-purpose flour
Garnishes: dried figs, Bartlett pear slices,
   fresh parsley sprigs

• Cook sausage in a large skillet over medium-high heat, stirring often, 4 to 5 minutes or until lightly browned. Drain well. Stir together sausage, stuffing mix, and next 5 ingredients. Set aside.

• Butterfly pork loin roast by making a lengthwise cut down center of 1 flat side, cutting to within ½ inch of the bottom. (Do not cut all the way through roast.) Open roast, forming a rectangle, and place between 2 sheets of heavy-duty plastic wrap. Flatten to ½-inch thickness, using a meat mallet or rolling pin (photo 1). Sprinkle evenly with salt and pepper. Spoon sausage mixture evenly over pork loin roast, leaving a ½-inch border. Roll up roast (photo 2), and tie with string at 1½-inch intervals (photo 3). Place roast, seam side down, in a greased shallow roasting pan.

• Bake at 375° for 55 to 60 minutes or until a meat thermometer inserted into thickest portion registers 145°. Remove roast from pan, reserving drippings in pan.

• Stir together fig preserves, Madeira, and balsamic vinegar. Spoon half of preserves mixture evenly over roast.

• Bake at 375° for 20 to 30 more minutes or until meat thermometer registers 160°. Let roast stand 15 minutes before slicing.

• Melt butter in a medium saucepan; whisk in flour until smooth. Cook, whisking constantly, 3 minutes. Whisk in reserved pan drippings and remaining fig preserves mixture, and cook over medium-high heat 5 minutes. Serve sauce with roast; garnish, if desired. Yield: 8 to 10 servings.

## Preparing the Perfect Pork Tenderloin

**1.** Pounding the pork loin with the flat, smooth side of a meat mallet or rolling pin to a ½-inch thickness produces an even surface and allows for easier rolling of the stuffed meat.

**2.** Leave a ½-inch border on the edge of the meat to prevent the stuffing from spilling out of the sides. The stuffing will expand as you roll it jellyroll style.

**3.** Using butcher's twine, tie the roast at 1½-inch intervals. The twine is available at kitchen specialty shops and at grocery stores in the cooking utensils aisle.

*cook's secret...* Purchase a pork loin roast, not a rolled pork loin roast (which has 2 loins tied together with netting). Don't trim the entire fat cap on top of the loin; this layer prevents the meat from drying out.

Carved from an area where there's little fat surrounding or running through the meat, the tenderloin is leaner than many other choices. Keep the cooking time relatively short; you don't want to dry out this prize delicacy.

*editor's choice*

## Pork Medaillons with Blackberry Sauce

2 (1-pound) pork tenderloins
1 teaspoon salt
1 teaspoon coarsely ground pepper
1 teaspoon coarsely ground whole allspice
¼ cup butter or margarine, divided
½ cup diced shallots (about 3 large)

⅔ cup dry white wine
3 tablespoons seedless blackberry fruit spread
Garnishes: fresh blackberries, fresh thyme sprigs

• Sprinkle pork evenly with salt, pepper, and allspice. Cover and chill 30 minutes.
• Grill pork over medium-high heat (350° to 400°) 20 minutes or until a meat thermometer inserted into thickest portion registers 160°, turning pork once. Remove from grill, and let stand 10 minutes.
• Melt 2 tablespoons butter in a small saucepan over medium-high heat while pork stands. Add shallots, and sauté 5 minutes or until tender. Add wine; cook 13 minutes or until liquid is reduced by half. Reduce heat to low; whisk in fruit spread and remaining 2 tablespoons butter. Cook 2 minutes or until slightly thickened.
• Cut pork into ¼-inch-thick slices. Drizzle blackberry sauce over pork. Garnish, if desired. Yield: 6 servings.

**NOTE:** *For testing purposes only, we used Polaner All Fruit for blackberry fruit spread.*

*Kathy Hunt*
*Dallas, Texas*

*cook's secret...* Pork tenderloin usually comes in packages of 2 loins weighing between 2 and 3 pounds; some markets sell it individually packaged. It's a terrific choice for busy folks because it cooks quickly and pairs well with sweet or savory flavors. Serve roasted or grilled and then sliced.

E‌xecutive Foods Editor Susan Dosier says Red Wine Sauce adds an extra layer of flavor to this tenderloin. She promises, "The sauce is not as tricky as making gravy. If you can boil water, you can make this sauce."

## Molasses Pork Tenderloin with Red Wine Sauce

| | |
|---|---|
| 1¼ cups molasses | 3 tablespoons minced fresh ginger |
| 1 cup reduced-sodium soy sauce | 2 large garlic cloves, minced |
| ¼ cup fresh lemon juice | 3 (¾-pound) pork tenderloins |
| ¼ cup olive oil | Red Wine Sauce (optional) |

• Combine first 6 ingredients in a shallow dish or zip-top freezer bag; add tenderloins. Cover or seal, and chill 8 hours.
• Remove tenderloins from marinade, discarding marinade. Grill tenderloins, covered with grill lid, over medium-high heat (350° to 400°), turning occasionally, 20 minutes or until a meat thermometer inserted into thickest portion registers 160°. Let stand 10 minutes before slicing. Serve with Red Wine Sauce, if desired. Yield: 6 to 8 servings.

### Red Wine Sauce:

| | |
|---|---|
| ½ small sweet onion, minced | 1 (14-ounce) can beef broth |
| 2 tablespoons butter | ¼ cup water |
| ½ cup dry red wine | 2 tablespoons cornstarch |

• Sauté onion in butter in a saucepan over medium-high heat 3 minutes. Add wine; cook 3 minutes. Add beef broth; bring to a boil, and cook 5 minutes.
• Stir together ¼ cup water and cornstarch; add to broth mixture and cook, stirring constantly, 1 minute or until mixture thickens. Remove from heat, and serve over tenderloin. Yield: about 1¼ cups.

*Susan Dosier*
Executive Foods Editor

*cook's secret...* To free up oven space for other dishes, grill the tenderloin and have it ready about 30 minutes before you're ready to sit down. "Wrap it in heavy-duty plastic wrap; then wrap it in foil. This will allow it to rest longer without getting cold. As the meat rests, the flavorful juices are reabsorbed, making for moist slices," Susan says. Once the Red Wine Sauce is finished, unwrap the pork and slice it on a clean cutting board.

This recipe from Bob Gadsby was a finalist in the Taste of the South category in the 2002 *Southern Living* Cook-Off. Bob, who works full-time for the U.S. Customs Service, loves experimenting with food. His dish is a combination of inspirations. "When it comes to barbecue, pork is my meat of choice," he says. "Smoked Gouda—one of my favorite cheeses—seemed like a natural with grits. As for the Sweet Onion Applesauce, it started out as a compote I couldn't stop messing with."

*contest winner*

# Maple-Chipotle Pork on Smoked Gouda Grits with Sweet Onion Applesauce

| | |
|---|---|
| ½ cup barbecue sauce | 2 (1-pound) pork tenderloins |
| ½ cup maple syrup | Salt and pepper to taste |
| 2 chipotle peppers in adobo sauce, seeded and minced | Smoked Gouda Grits |
| 1 teaspoon adobo sauce from can | Sweet Onion Applesauce |

- Preheat oven to 375°. Whisk together first 4 ingredients.
- Place pork in greased jellyroll pan; sprinkle evenly with salt and pepper to taste. Pour half of chipotle mixture over pork; reserve remaining chipotle mixture.
- Bake at 375° for 20 to 30 minutes or until a meat thermometer inserted into thickest portion registers 160°, basting occasionally with pan drippings. Remove pork to a wire rack, and let stand 10 minutes. Cut into ½-inch-thick slices.
- Spoon Smoked Gouda Grits evenly onto 6 serving plates; top with pork slices, and drizzle with remaining chipotle mixture. Dollop Sweet Onion Applesauce around Smoked Gouda Grits. Yield: 6 servings.

## Smoked Gouda Grits:

| | | | |
|---|---|---|---|
| 4 | cups low-sodium chicken broth or water | 1¼ | cups uncooked regular grits |
| 3 | cups milk | 1½ | cups (6 ounces) shredded smoked |
| 2 | teaspoons salt | | Gouda cheese |
| ½ | teaspoon ground white pepper | 2 | to 3 tablespoons unsalted butter |

• Bring first 4 ingredients to a boil in a medium saucepan; gradually whisk in grits. Cover, reduce heat, and simmer, stirring occasionally, 20 minutes or until thickened. Add cheese and butter, stirring until melted. Yield: 6 to 8 servings.

## Sweet Onion Applesauce:

| | | | |
|---|---|---|---|
| 1 | medium-size sweet onion, finely chopped | 1 | tablespoon cider vinegar |
| 1 | tablespoon vegetable oil | 1 | cup applesauce |
| 1 | tablespoon granulated sugar | 1 | teaspoon thyme leaves |
| 1 | medium Golden Delicious apple, peeled and chopped | | |

• Sauté onion in hot oil in skillet over medium-high heat 8 to 10 minutes or until golden. Sprinkle with sugar, and cook, stirring often, 2 minutes. Add apple and vinegar, and cook, stirring often, 3 minutes. Stir in applesauce and thyme. Cover and chill until ready to serve. Yield: 1 cup.

*Bob Gadsby*
Great Falls, Montana

*cook's secret...* Use a wire whisk instead of stirring with a spoon for lump-free grits.

ark Kerr's perpetual search for interesting salsas, exotic chiles, and spicy condiments keeps him circling the globe. His passion for chiles—from smoky chipotles to mild Anaheims—fuels the selection of salsas and hot stuff at his El Paso Chile Company, a thriving mail-order business.

This true love of hot stuff surfaces in his cooking and entertaining. He uses a variety of peppers to deliver big flavors—not just scorching heat—that everyone can enjoy.

## Adobo Grilled Pork Tacos with Cucumber-Radish Salsa

| | |
|---|---|
| 1 (2-ounce) package dried mild New Mexico chiles, divided | ¼ teaspoon salt |
| 2 teaspoons cumin seeds | ¼ teaspoon ground red pepper |
| 1 tablespoon dried oregano | 2 (¾-pound) pork tenderloins |
| 3 garlic cloves | 1 (8-ounce) container sour cream |
| 2 tablespoons cider vinegar | Cucumber-Radish Salsa |
| 1 teaspoon sugar | 24 corn or flour tortillas, warmed |
| | Garnishes: lime wedges, fresh cilantro |

• Slice chiles in half lengthwise. Remove and discard stems and seeds. Place chiles in a bowl, and add boiling water to cover. Let stand 20 minutes or until chiles are softened. Drain chiles, reserving liquid.

• Cook cumin seeds in a skillet over medium heat 30 seconds. Add oregano, and cook, stirring constantly, 30 seconds or until cumin is toasted.

• Process cumin mixture, soaked chiles, 1 cup reserved liquid, garlic, and next 4 ingredients in a blender or food processor until smooth, adding more reserved liquid if needed.

• Place pork in a shallow dish or zip-top freezer bag. Pour half of chile mixture over meat. Cover or seal, and chill for 30 minutes. Remove pork from marinade, discarding marinade.

• Stir together sour cream and ½ cup Cucumber-Radish Salsa; cover and chill until ready to serve.

• Grill pork, covered with grill lid, over medium-high heat (350° to 400°), turning occasionally and basting with reserved chile mixture, 20 minutes or until a meat thermometer inserted into thickest portion registers 160°. Remove from grill; let stand 10 minutes. Coarsely chop pork. Serve in warm tortillas with remaining Cucumber-Radish Salsa and sour cream mixture. Garnish, if desired. Yield: 24 servings.

## Cucumber-Radish Salsa:

2 cucumbers, peeled, seeded, and chopped
1 (6-ounce) package radishes, grated
1 small onion, minced
¼ cup lime juice

2 tablespoons chopped fresh cilantro
½ teaspoon salt
¼ teaspoon ground red pepper
Garnish: whole radish

• Stir together first 7 ingredients. Cover and chill, if desired. Garnish, if desired. Yield: 3 cups.

*Park Kerr*
El Paso, Texas

*cook's secret...* Park tends the grill while enjoying what he calls **Rio Grand Limeade.** Stir together 1 (12-ounce) can frozen limeade concentrate, thawed; 1½ cups tequila; 1½ cups water; 1 cup orange liqueur; and ½ cup fresh lime juice. Chill 8 hours, and serve over ice.

## Slow-Cooker Barbecue Ribs

4 pounds bone-in country-style pork ribs
2 teaspoons salt, divided
1 medium onion, chopped
1 cup firmly packed light brown sugar
1 cup apple butter
1 cup ketchup

½ cup lemon juice
½ cup orange juice
1 tablespoon steak sauce
1 teaspoon coarsely ground pepper
1 teaspoon minced garlic
½ teaspoon Worcestershire sauce

• Cut ribs apart, if necessary, and trim; sprinkle 1 teaspoon salt evenly over ribs, and set aside.
• Stir together remaining 1 teaspoon salt, chopped onion, and remaining 9 ingredients until blended. Pour half of mixture into a 5-quart slow cooker. Place ribs in slow cooker, and pour remaining mixture over ribs.
• Cover and cook at HIGH 6 to 7 hours. Yield: 6 to 8 servings.
**NOTE:** *For testing purposes only, we used A1 Steak Sauce.*

*Allison Sinclair*
Westfield, North Carolina

*cook's secret...* Put these ribs on before you leave for work, or cook them overnight and refrigerate until dinnertime. If you reheat in the microwave, use 50% power.

When it comes to preparing weeknight meals, speed and ease are important, and braising offers both qualities. *Braising* refers to cooking meat or vegetables in a small amount of liquid in an ovenproof container with a tight-fitting lid. Tough, generally inexpensive cuts of meat are magically transformed into something fall-off-the-bone tender with very little effort. Braises are even better when prepared 1 or 2 days in advance, allowing the flavors to really come together. When starting early, store meat in the sauce to keep it from drying out.

*editor's choice*

# Braised Short Ribs

2¼ cups dry red wine, divided
2¼ cups beef broth, divided
　2 garlic cloves, chopped
　1 teaspoon ground allspice
　½ teaspoon ground ginger
　4 pounds beef short ribs, trimmed and
　　　cut in half
　1 teaspoon salt

　1 teaspoon pepper
　½ cup all-purpose flour
　3 tablespoons olive oil
　1 carrot, chopped
　½ onion, chopped
　1 celery rib, chopped
　2 tablespoons tomato paste
Roasted red potatoes

• Combine ¼ cup wine, ¼ cup broth, garlic, allspice, and ginger in a shallow dish; add ribs, turning to coat. Cover and chill ribs 4 to 6 hours, turning occasionally.
• Remove ribs from marinade, reserving marinade. Sprinkle ribs with salt and pepper; dredge in flour. Cook ribs, in batches, in hot oil in a Dutch oven over medium-high heat 15 minutes or until browned (photo 1). Remove ribs, and set aside.
• Reduce heat to medium; add carrot, onion, and celery, and sauté 7 minutes or until browned. Add tomato paste; cook, stirring constantly, 3 minutes.
• Return ribs to pan. Stir in reserved marinade and remaining 2 cups wine and 2 cups broth (photo 2); bring mixture to a boil, and tightly cover. Bake at 300° for 3 hours (photo 3). Remove ribs.
• Skim fat from sauce and discard; simmer sauce for 12 to 15 minutes or until reduced by half. Serve with ribs over roasted potatoes. Yield: 6 servings.

*Mildred Bickley*
Bristol, Virginia

## Braising Meat

**1.** When braising meat, dredge in flour and brown in batches.

**2.** Add liquid to cover meat by about two-thirds.

**3.** Bring liquid to a boil, cover tightly, and bake as directed.

*cook's secret...* Dredging meat in flour and browning it before braising adds color and thickening power to the resulting sauce—a hearty, delicious, nutrient-rich bonus to the meat slowly and gently cooking in its own juices.

## Best Meat Cuts for Braising

Braising works well for tough cuts of meat because it tenderizes them. These cuts will end up especially fall-off-the-bone tender using this technique.

**Pork:** picnic shoulder, Boston butt

**Lamb:** shanks, leg of lamb

**Veal:** shanks

**Beef:** short ribs, bottom round, eye of round, chuck

*regional favorite*

# Smoky Chipotle Baby Back Ribs

*Grilling ribs doesn't have to be an all-day affair.*
*You can grill them in 3 hours flat.*

| | |
|---|---|
| 3 slabs baby back pork ribs (about 5½ pounds) | Chipotle Rub |
| 2 oranges, halved | Smoky Chipotle 'Cue Sauce |

- Rinse and pat ribs dry. If desired, remove thin membrane from back of ribs by slicing into it with a knife and then pulling it off (this will make ribs more tender).
- Rub meat with cut sides of oranges, squeezing as you rub. Massage Chipotle Rub into meat, covering all sides. Wrap tightly with plastic wrap, and place in a zip-top freezer bag or 13- x 9-inch baking dish; chill 8 hours. Let ribs stand at room temperature 30 minutes before grilling. Remove plastic wrap.
- **To grill on a charcoal grill:** Prepare hot fire by piling charcoal on one side of grill, leaving the other side empty. Place food grate on grill; position rib rack on grate over unlit side. Place slabs in rack. Grill, covered with grill lid, over medium-high heat (350° to 400°) 1 hour. Reposition rib slabs, placing the one closest to the heat source away from heat and moving other slabs closer. Grill 1 more hour or until meat is tender. Grill 30 more minutes over medium heat (300° to 350°), basting with half of Smoky Chipotle 'Cue Sauce. Remove ribs from grill, and let stand 10 minutes. Cut ribs, slicing between bones. Serve with remaining sauce.
- **To grill on a gas grill:** Light only one side. Coat food grate with vegetable cooking spray, and place on grill; position rib rack on grate over unlit side. Place rib slabs in rack. Grill, covered with grill lid, over medium-high heat (350° to 400°) 1 hour. Reposition rib slabs, placing the one closest to the heat source away from heat and moving other slabs closer. Grill 1 more hour or until meat is tender. Lower temperature to medium heat (300° to 350°), and cook ribs 30 more minutes, basting with half of Smoky Chipotle 'Cue Sauce. Remove ribs from grill, and let stand 10 minutes. Cut ribs, slicing between bones. Serve ribs with remaining sauce. Yield: 6 servings.

## Chipotle Rub:

| | |
|---|---|
| 2 to 3 canned chipotle chile peppers | 1 tablespoon chili powder |
| ¼ cup firmly packed brown sugar | 1 teaspoon salt |

- Chop chipotle chile peppers; stir together peppers, brown sugar, chili powder, and salt to form a paste. Yield: ⅓ cup.

## Smoky Chipotle 'Cue Sauce:

- 2 (18-ounce) bottles barbecue sauce
- 2 canned chipotle chili peppers
- 2 tablespoons brown sugar
- 1 teaspoon chili powder

- Process barbecue sauce, chipotle chile peppers, brown sugar, and chili powder in a blender until smooth. Pour into a saucepan, and bring to a boil over medium-high heat. Reduce heat, and simmer 30 minutes. Yield: about 2½ cups.

**NOTE:** *For testing purposes only, we used Stubb's Original Bar-B-Q Sauce.*

*Joe Batric*
Birmingham, Alabama

*cook's secret...* Baby back ribs are meatier and more tender than spare ribs and are worth the extra money. Grill them upright in a rib rack (about a $15 investment).

### How to Grill Baby Back Ribs

- Don't skip rubbing the ribs with citrus fruit halves; the juice adds a perky zip to the flavor. You will find the canned chipotle chile peppers at the grocery story alongside other ethnic ingredients (photo 1).
- Remove the thin membrane on the back, or bone side, of each rib rack if you want the meat to almost fall off. Leave it on if you like the crispy texture that results from grilling or want to save prep time.

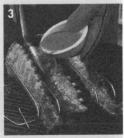

- For best flavor, wrap seasoned ribs in plastic wrap to hold rub moisture close to the meat. Place each slab in a separate 2-gallon-size zip-top freezer bag, and refrigerate overnight. When ready to grill, unwrapping the ribs can be messy. To minimize the mess, hang a zip-top plastic bag on the grill handle, being careful that it doesn't touch the hot grill. Unwrap ribs over the bag, discarding the plastic wrap into the bag (photo 2). Slide the ribs into the rib rack. Immediately remove the bag from the handle, and discard. Ribs can also be placed directly on the food grate—however, expect to turn the ribs and manage the fire more often. Place an oven thermometer on the unlit cooking area of the grill. To maintain temperature, stoke the fire, and make sure vents are open.

- When the meat is tender and done, bones should wiggle easily when moved, and the meat will be shrunk down from the bones. Slow the fire by partially or fully closing vents before basting. Pour sauce over ribs, guiding it to cover with a grill brush (photo 3).

*Vanessa McNeil*
Test Kitchens Specialist

oevis and Charles McKay feel close to their North Carolina roots despite having lived in Manhattan for many years. Roevis's recipe for baked ham is so good it's included in our Recipe Hall of Fame.

# Baked Ham with Bourbon Glaze

1 cup honey
½ cup molasses
½ cup bourbon
¼ cup orange juice

2 tablespoons Dijon mustard
1 (6- to 8-pound) smoked ham half
Garnish: fresh herb sprigs

• Microwave honey and molasses in a 1-quart microwave-safe dish at HIGH 1 minute; whisk to blend. Whisk in bourbon, orange juice, and mustard.
• Remove skin and excess fat from ham, and place ham in a roasting pan.
• Bake at 325° on lower oven rack for 1½ hours or until a meat thermometer inserted into thickest portion registers 140°, basting occasionally with honey mixture.
• Bring drippings and remaining glaze to a boil in a small saucepan. Remove from heat, and serve with sliced ham. Garnish, if desired. Yield: 12 to 14 servings.

*Roevis McKay*
*New York, New York*

*cook's secret...* Use the microwave to quickly blend the flavors of the honey and molasses for the glaze; then simply whisk in the other ingredients.

### Carving a Ham

Hold a sharp carving knife perpendicular to the bone. Cut full slices just until you feel the knife touching the bone (photo 1). Then place the knife at a 90-degree angle to the slices, parallel to the bone, and cut to release the slices (photo 2). Once all the meat has been cut from this side, turn the ham over, and repeat the procedure.

M ichelle Weaver is a sous-chef at the Charleston Grill in the Charleston Place Hotel. Her Baked Ham is traditionally the star of the family's New Year's Day meal. She rounds out the menu with black-eyed peas, rice, cheese grits, and collard greens.

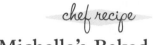

## Michelle's Baked Ham

| | |
|---|---|
| 1 (10-pound) smoked ham | ¼ cup stone-ground mustard |
| 1 (13-ounce) jar orange marmalade | 1 tablespoon chopped fresh thyme |

• Wrap ham in aluminum foil, and place in a lightly greased 13- x 9-inch pan; bake at 300° for 2 hours.

• Remove ham from oven, and unwrap. Remove skin and excess fat from ham. Score fat on ham in a diamond pattern.

• Stir together marmalade and remaining ingredients in small bowl. Spoon glaze over ham, and bake 1 hour, basting every 15 minutes or until a meat thermometer inserted into the thickest portion registers 140°. Let stand 15 minutes before slicing. Yield: 16 to 20 servings.

*Chef Michelle Weaver*
Charleston, South Carolina

*cook's secret*... Since smoked ham is already cooked, you don't have to cook it again, but it's more tender and juicy when reheated to 140°.

The first time that I ventured to prepare a ham, I ended up buying a mega-size orb with not a clue as to how much I needed, how long to bake it, or how to carve it. I've wised up since then after a few talks with more seasoned cooks. If your experience is similar to mine, this information will ease your mind about tackling this cut of meat. Let us help you prepare a ham that's stellar enough for an Easter buffet and so good you won't mind leftovers. Peruse the three recipes that follow this one for ways to use the leftovers.

*Cybil Talley*
Former Assistant Foods Editor

*special occasion*

## Pineapple-Glazed Ham

*Layered with brown sugar and Dijon mustard, Pineapple-Glazed Ham boasts just the right balance of sweetness and saltiness.*

4   cups pineapple juice
1   (1-inch) piece fresh ginger, peeled and sliced
4   garlic cloves, pressed
1   (7- to 9-pound) bone-in smoked fully cooked ham

12   to 16 whole cloves
¼   cup Dijon mustard
1   cup firmly packed light brown sugar
1   (20-ounce) can pineapple slices in juice, drained
10   maraschino cherries, halved

• Stir together first 3 ingredients in a saucepan; bring to a boil. Reduce heat to medium-low, and simmer 25 minutes or until liquid is reduced by half. Pour mixture through a wire-mesh strainer into a bowl, discarding solids.
• Remove skin and excess fat from ham. Make ¼-inch-deep cuts in a diamond design, and insert cloves at 1-inch intervals. Place ham in an aluminum foil-lined roasting pan. Spread Dijon mustard evenly over ham. Pat brown sugar on top of the mustard. Pour pineapple juice mixture into pan.
• Arrange pineapple and cherries evenly over brown sugar layer on ham; secure with wooden picks.
• Bake at 325° for 1 hour. Shield with aluminum foil after 1 hour to prevent excess browning, and bake 1 to 1½ more hours or until a meat thermometer inserted into thickest portion registers 140°, basting every 30 minutes with pan juices. Let stand 15 minutes before slicing.

• Remove from pan, reserving drippings. Cover ham, and chill, if desired. Chill reserved drippings.

• Remove and discard fat from drippings. Bring drippings to a boil in a small saucepan. Serve warm with ham. Yield: 14 to 18 servings.

*Annette B. Chance*
*Cape Charles, Virginia*

*cook's secret*... Peel fresh ginger with a vegetable peeler or paring knife. Peel as much as is needed, and then wrap the remainder until it's airtight and freeze up to 2 months.

### Buying a Ham

• Plan to purchase a ham large enough to serve for both dinner and multiple meals later. For example, let's say you want to serve dinner for 8 people. Allotting 2 to 3 servings per pound for a bone-in ham, you'll need to buy a 7- to 9-pound ham.

• We find the taste and texture of a bone-in ham to be the best. Plus, this will leave you with the ham bone. Save this premium ingredient for your next pot of beans, greens, or soup.

• You'll also find half-hams cut into shank and butt portions. Though pricier, the butt portion offers more meat because there's not as much bone as in the shank. Also available are spiral-sliced hams; they're easier to serve, but you'll pay for this convenience.

• The label on the ham tells you whether it's ready to eat or should be cooked. For the best flavor, we recommend that you bake a fully cooked ham at 325° for 15 to 20 minutes per pound or until it reaches an internal temperature of 140°. Uncooked hams should be baked at 325° for 18 to 22 minutes per pound or until a meat thermometer registers 160°.

• If you don't plan on using the remaining meat within 4 to 5 days, slice or cube it, and then wrap tightly in heavy-duty plastic wrap. Freeze it in an airtight container up to 2 months, but don't store it any longer because its texture and flavor will change.

# Ham-Broccoli Pot Pie

1 (10-ounce) package frozen chopped
  broccoli, thawed
1 (11-ounce) can sweet whole kernel corn,
  drained
1 (10¾-ounce) can cream of mushroom
  soup, undiluted
2 cups diced cooked ham

2 cups (8 ounces) shredded colby-Jack
  cheese blend
1 (8-ounce) container sour cream
½ teaspoon pepper
½ teaspoon dry mustard
½ (15-ounce) package refrigerated
  piecrusts

- Arrange chopped broccoli in a lightly greased 11- x 7-inch baking dish.
- Stir together corn and next 6 ingredients. Spoon over broccoli.
- Unfold piecrust; pat or roll into an 11- x 7-inch rectangle, and place over ham mixture. Crimp edges, and cut 4 slits for steam to escape.
- Bake at 400° for 30 to 35 minutes or until golden. Yield: 6 servings.

*Cindy Enfinger*
*Okeechobee, Florida*

*cook's secret...* Substitute chopped cooked chicken for ham, and you'll have a **Chicken Divan Pot Pie.**

*make-ahead*

# Ham-and-Greens Pot Pie with Cornbread Crust

*Associate Foods Editor Mary Allen Perry streamlined an all-time favorite pot pie recipe by adding frozen vegetables and replacing a labor-intensive crust with a batter that is quickly stirred together.*

4 cups chopped cooked ham
2 tablespoons vegetable oil
3 tablespoons all-purpose flour
3 cups chicken broth
1 (16-ounce) package frozen seasoning
  blend

1 (16-ounce) package frozen chopped
  collard greens
1 (15.8-ounce) can black-eyed peas, rinsed
  and drained
½ teaspoon dried crushed red pepper
Cornbread Crust Batter

- Sauté ham in hot oil in a Dutch oven over medium-high heat 5 minutes or until lightly browned. Add flour, and cook, stirring constantly, 1 minute. Gradually add chicken broth, and cook, stirring constantly, 3 minutes or until broth begins to thicken.
- Bring mixture to a boil, and add seasoning blend and collard greens; return to a boil, and cook, stirring often, 15 minutes. Stir in black-eyed peas and crushed red pepper; spoon hot mixture into a lightly greased 13- x 9-inch baking dish. Pour Cornbread Crust Batter evenly over hot filling mixture.
- Bake at 425° for 20 to 25 minutes or until cornbread is golden brown and set. Yield: 8 to 10 servings.

**NOTE:** *For testing purposes only, we used McKenzie's Seasoning Blend.*

## Cornbread Crust Batter:

| | |
|---|---|
| 1½ cups white cornmeal mix | 2 large eggs, lightly beaten |
| ½ cup all-purpose flour | 1½ cups buttermilk |
| 1 teaspoon sugar | |

- Combine first 3 ingredients; make a well in the center of mixture. Add eggs and buttermilk to cornmeal mixture, stirring just until moistened. Yield: 1 (13- x 9-inch) crust.

*Mary Allen Perry*
Associate Foods Editor

*cook's secret...* Sautéing the cooked ham a bit caramelizes the edges and releases flavorful juices for the saucy combo.

••• To ensure even cooking, the filling should be hot before the crust batter is added.

••• The filling can be made ahead. Simply reheat it, and add the crust batter.

••• Seasoning blends may be convenient to use, but salt content among brands can vary dramatically. Choose a blend that best suits your needs. For our Ham-and-Greens Pot Pie, we used a salt-free blend.

Our Test Kitchens staff came up with a nifty idea for dressing up this one-dish meal for a special occasion. Cut white bread slices with your favorite 3-inch cookie cutters. Brush with a lightly beaten egg; sprinkle with chopped fresh parsley and diced pimientos. Bake at 350° for 15 minutes or until toasted. Arrange the cutouts atop Lynette Granade's hearty bacon-and-ham casserole.

## Cheesy Bacon-and-Ham Casserole

| | | | | |
|---|---|---|---|---|
| ½ | pound bacon | | ¼ | cup butter or margarine |
| ½ | pound chopped cooked ham | | 6 | large eggs, lightly beaten |
| ¾ | cup quick-cooking grits | | ½ | cup milk |
| 1 | (16-ounce) loaf prepared pasteurized cheese product, cubed | | 2 | teaspoons baking powder |
| | | | ½ | teaspoon freshly ground pepper |

• Cook bacon in a large skillet until crisp; remove bacon, and drain on paper towels, reserving 1 tablespoon drippings in skillet. Crumble bacon, and set aside.
• Cook ham in reserved drippings in skillet over medium heat until browned.
• Cook grits according to package directions. Remove from heat; stir in cheese and butter until melted. Stir in bacon, ham, eggs, and remaining ingredients. Pour into a lightly greased 13- x 9-inch baking dish.
• Bake at 350° for 45 minutes or until set. Yield: 8 servings.

*Lynette S. Granade*
Mobile, Alabama

*cook's secret...* This casserole may be prepared a day ahead; cover and chill. Remove from the refrigerator the following day, and let stand at room temperature 30 minutes. Bake as directed.

Charlotte Skelton, restaurant owner and author of the cookbook *Absolutely a la Carte* (A la Carte Alley), developed this uniquely Southern recipe that works as a tasty appetizer cut into small squares or as a main dish served with a tossed green salad.

*make–ahead*

# One-Dish Black-Eyed Pea Cornbread

| | |
|---|---|
| 1 pound spicy ground pork sausage | ½ cup vegetable oil |
| 1 medium onion, diced | 1 (15.8-ounce) can black-eyed peas, drained |
| 1 cup white cornmeal | |
| ½ cup all-purpose flour | 2 cups (8 ounces) shredded Cheddar cheese |
| 1 teaspoon salt | |
| ½ teaspoon baking soda | ¾ cup cream-style corn |
| 2 large eggs, lightly beaten | ¼ cup chopped pickled jalapeño peppers |
| 1 cup buttermilk | 1 (4.5-ounce) can chopped green chiles |

- Cook sausage and onion in a large skillet over medium-high heat 5 minutes, stirring until sausage crumbles and is no longer pink. Drain.
- Combine cornmeal, flour, salt, and baking soda.
- Stir together eggs, buttermilk, and oil until combined. Add to dry ingredients, stirring just until moistened. (Batter will not be smooth.) Add sausage mixture, peas, and remaining ingredients to batter, stirring well.
- Pour into a greased 13- x 9-inch baking dish.
- Bake, uncovered, at 350° for 1 hour or until golden and set. Yield: 12 appetizers or 6 main-dish servings.

**NOTE:** *Freeze baked cornbread up to 1 month, if desired. Thaw in refrigerator overnight. Bake, covered, at 350° for 30 minutes. Uncover and bake 10 more minutes or until thoroughly heated. To reheat directly from the freezer, bake, covered, at 350° for 1 hour. Uncover and bake 10 more minutes or until thoroughly heated.*

*Charlotte Skelton*
*Cleveland, Mississippi*

*cook's secret...* To lighten this recipe, substitute 1 (12-ounce) package reduced-fat sausage, ½ cup egg substitute, fat-free buttermilk, and 2% reduced-fat Cheddar cheese. Reduce oil to 2 tablespoons. Prepare and bake as directed.

I love to cook, and cooking for one can be fun. I make things I like, and I keep them simple," says Jan Karon, best-selling author of the Mitford books series. Here, she shares a couple of her favorite comfort-food recipes.

# Jan's Roasted Chicken

| | |
|---|---|
| 1 (3- to 4-pound) whole chicken | 1 tablespoon coarsely ground pepper |
| 3 tablespoons olive oil, divided | 3 sprigs fresh rosemary |
| 3 garlic cloves, halved | 1 lemon, quartered |
| 1 teaspoon salt | |

• Rub chicken and cavities with 2 tablespoons olive oil, garlic cloves, salt, and pepper.
• Tuck chicken wings under; tie legs together with string, if desired. Pour remaining 1 tablespoon oil into a large cast-iron skillet; place chicken, breast side up, in skillet.
• Place 1 rosemary sprig and 2 lemon quarters into neck cavity of chicken; repeat in lower cavity. Place remaining rosemary sprig underneath skin.
• Bake, uncovered, at 450° for 30 minutes; reduce heat to 350°, and cook 1 hour. Serve with Jan's Roasted Potatoes. Yield: 4 servings.

*cook's secret...* Cooking this chicken in cast iron holds the high heat and cooks the chicken evenly, making it tender and golden.

# Jan's Roasted Potatoes

| | |
|---|---|
| 8 medium new potatoes, halved | 1 teaspoon salt |
| 3 tablespoons butter or margarine, melted | 1 teaspoon pepper |

• Place potatoes on a baking sheet. Drizzle with butter; sprinkle with salt and pepper.
• Bake, uncovered, at 350° for 1 hour, turning every 20 minutes. Yield: 4 servings.

*Jan Karon*
Blowing Rock, North Carolina
From *Jan Karon's Cookbook and Kitchen Reader*
(Viking, November 2004)

Curtis Aikens's undeniable talent in the kitchen landed him a spot on the Food Network in 1993. To his credit, Curtis has never lost sight of his Southern upbringing and the tremendous influence both his immediate and extended families have had on his career. He and his family gather in his hometown of Conyers, Georgia, to enjoy the kinds of home-cooked meals he so fondly remembers from his childhood. Once the food is blessed and the dishes are passed, Curtis sits back and reflects, "There's nothing like family and a home-cooked meal." This recipe is often on their dinner table.

*chef recipe*

## Mama's Fried Chicken

1　(3- to 4-pound) whole chicken, cut into
　　pieces
1　teaspoon salt
1　teaspoon pepper

2　cups buttermilk
　　Self-rising flour
　　Vegetable oil

• Sprinkle chicken with salt and pepper. Place chicken in a shallow dish or zip-top plastic bag, and add buttermilk. Cover or seal, and chill at least 2 hours.
• Remove chicken from buttermilk, discarding buttermilk. Dredge chicken in flour.
• Pour oil to a depth of 1½ inches into a deep skillet or Dutch oven; heat to 360°. Add chicken, a few pieces at a time; cover and cook 6 minutes. Uncover chicken, and cook 9 minutes. Turn chicken; cover and cook 6 minutes. Uncover and cook 5 to 9 minutes, turning chicken the last 3 minutes for even browning, if necessary. Drain on paper towels. Yield: 4 to 6 servings.

*Chef Curtis Aikens*
Conyers, Georgia

*cook's secret...* The leavenings in the self-rising flour used for breading the chicken make it fry up extra crispy.

Believe it or not, chicken grilled over a can of cola or beer is tender, moist, and full of flavor. It's incredibly easy, too. These recipes are adapted from Steven Raichlen's book *Beer-Can Chicken*.

# Basic Beer-Can Chicken

| | |
|---|---|
| 2 tablespoons All-Purpose Barbecue Rub, divided | 1 tablespoon vegetable oil |
| 1 (3½- to 4-pound) whole chicken | 1 (12-ounce) can beer |

• Sprinkle 1 teaspoon All-Purpose Barbecue Rub inside body cavity and ½ teaspoon inside neck cavity of chicken.

• Rub oil over skin. Sprinkle with 1 tablespoon All-Purpose Barbecue Rub, and rub over skin.

• Pour out half of beer (about ¾ cup), and reserve for another use, leaving remaining beer in can. Make 2 additional holes in top of can. Spoon remaining 1½ teaspoons rub into beer can. Beer will start to foam.

• Place chicken upright onto the beer can, fitting can into cavity. Pull legs forward to form a tripod, allowing chicken to stand upright.

• Prepare a fire by piling charcoal on one side of grill, leaving other side empty. (For gas grills, light only one side.) Place a drip pan on unlit side, and place food grate on grill. Place chicken upright over drip pan. Grill, covered with grill lid, 1 hour and 15 minutes or until golden and a meat thermometer in thigh registers 180°.

• Remove chicken from grill, and let stand 5 minutes; carefully remove can. Yield: 2 to 4 servings.

## All-Purpose Barbecue Rub:

| | |
|---|---|
| ¼ cup coarse salt | ¼ cup sweet paprika |
| ¼ cup dark brown sugar | 2 tablespoons pepper |

• Combine all ingredients. Store mixture in an airtight jar, away from heat, up to 6 months. Yield: about 1 cup.

*cook's secret...* Never place cooked chicken on the same platter that held the uncooked meat. For example, take the chicken to the grill on one platter; then clean or replace that platter before bringing in the grilled chicken.

# Cola-Can Chicken

| | |
|---|---|
| 2 tablespoons Barbecue Rub, divided | 1 (12-ounce) can cola |
| 1 (3½- to 4-pound) whole chicken | Cola Barbecue Sauce |
| 3 tablespoons vegetable oil | |

• Sprinkle 1 teaspoon Barbecue Rub inside body cavity and ½ teaspoon inside neck cavity of chicken. Rub oil over skin. Rub 1 tablespoon Barbecue Rub over skin.

• Pour out ¾ cup cola, and reserve for barbecue sauce, leaving remaining cola in can. Make 2 more holes in top of can. Spoon remaining 1½ teaspoons rub into can. Cola will foam.

• Place chicken upright onto the cola can, fitting can into cavity. Pull legs forward to form a tripod, allowing chicken to stand upright.

• Prepare fire by piling charcoal on one side of grill, leaving other side empty. (For gas grills, light only one side.) Place a drip pan on unlit side, and place food grate on grill. Place chicken upright over drip pan. Grill, covered with grill lid, 1 hour and 15 minutes or until golden and a meat thermometer in thigh registers 180°. Remove chicken from grill, and let stand 5 minutes; carefully remove can. Serve with Cola Barbecue Sauce. Yield: 2 to 4 servings.

## Barbecue Rub:

| | |
|---|---|
| 1 tablespoon mild chili powder | 1 teaspoon ground cumin |
| 2 teaspoons salt | ½ teaspoon garlic powder |
| 2 teaspoons light brown sugar | ¼ teaspoon ground red pepper |
| 1 teaspoon pepper | |

• Combine all ingredients. Yield: 3 tablespoons.

## Cola Barbecue Sauce:

| | |
|---|---|
| ½ small onion, minced | 2 tablespoons fresh lemon juice |
| 1 tablespoon minced fresh ginger | 2 tablespoons Worcestershire sauce |
| 1 garlic clove, minced | 2 tablespoons steak sauce |
| 1 tablespoon butter, melted | ½ teaspoon pepper |
| ¾ cup reserved cola | ½ teaspoon liquid smoke |
| ¾ cup ketchup | Salt to taste |
| ½ teaspoon grated lemon rind | |

• Sauté first 3 ingredients in butter in a heavy saucepan 3 minutes or until tender. Stir in cola and remaining ingredients; bring to a boil. Reduce heat; simmer 5 minutes. Yield: 1½ cups.

*Steven Raichlen*
Coconut Grove, Florida
Adapted from *Beer-Can Chicken* (Workman Publishing Company)

# Chicken with White Barbecue Sauce

1   cup mayonnaise
½   cup white vinegar
1   tablespoon lemon juice
1   teaspoon salt
1   teaspoon pepper

Hickory wood chips
2   (2½-pound) whole chickens
1   teaspoon salt
1   teaspoon pepper
2   lemons, cut in half

• Stir together first 5 ingredients; cover and chill 8 hours.
• Soak wood chips in water at least 30 minutes.
• Prepare charcoal fire in smoker; let burn 15 to 20 minutes.
• Rinse chickens, and pat dry. Sprinkle each chicken with ½ teaspoon salt and ½ teaspoon pepper. Place 2 lemon halves into the cavity of each chicken.
• Drain chips, and place on coals. Place water pan in smoker; add water to depth of fill line. Place chickens on lower food rack; cover with smoker lid.
• Cook 1 hour and 30 minutes to 2 hours or until a meat thermometer inserted into thickest portion of thigh registers 180°. Serve chicken with sauce. Yield: 8 servings.

*cook's secret...* When the proper internal temperature is reached, the outside of large pieces of meat may be quite dark; the interior may appear slightly red or pink, but it's perfectly safe. Smoked meats retain some of their internal pink color.

*Andria Scott Hurst*
Foods Editor

## Smoke Signals
• Soak your favorite wood chips in water at least 30 minutes and chunks at least an hour before using. (The wet wood will smoke slowly; dry wood will flame and quickly burn out.) Hickory and mesquite are the most popular in the South, but apple, cherry, and pecan impart great flavor, too.
• Add wine, broth, or fresh herbs to the water pan for more flavor.
• Electric, gas, and charcoal smokers work equally well.
• If you're using a charcoal grill, arrange hot coals and wood chips on one side. (For a gas grill, light only one side.) Position a small pan of water on the unlit side. Place the food rack on the grill; arrange food over the water pan. Close the lid, leaving a small vent open to keep the coals alive.
• Use an instant-read thermometer to check for doneness of smoked foods. Don't depend on appearance alone.

M ary Cale's daughter-in-law was so convinced this recipe was a winner that she submitted it to the 2001 *Southern Living* Holiday Recipe Contest on behalf of her mother-in-law. Mary says, "It's just an old country recipe I've been making for a few years, and it's one of our family's favorites. It's also a good dish to give to people in the church or take to a party." Mary's recipe was the One-Dish Meals Grand Prize Winner.

*contest winner*

# Chicken Pot Pie

| | | | |
|---|---|---|---|
| 1 | (3½-pound) whole chicken | 3 | carrots, cooked and diced |
| 5 | cups water | 1 | (8.5-ounce) can sweet green peas, drained |
| 2 | celery stalk tops with leaves | | |
| 1¼ | teaspoons salt | 1 | teaspoon salt |
| ¼ | teaspoon pepper | ¼ | teaspoon pepper |
| 3 | to 4 bacon slices | ⅛ | teaspoon dried thyme |
| 3 | green onions, sliced | ½ | (15-ounce) package refrigerated piecrusts |
| 2 | large celery ribs, chopped | | |
| ½ | cup all-purpose flour | | Cranberry sauce |
| 3 | hard-cooked eggs, sliced | | |

• Bring first 5 ingredients to a boil in a large Dutch oven; reduce heat, and simmer mixture 1½ hours or until chicken is done.
• Remove chicken, reserving 3½ cups broth in Dutch oven; discard celery tops. Let chicken cool; skin, bone, and cut into bite-size pieces. Set aside.
• Cook bacon in a large skillet until crisp; remove bacon, and drain on paper towels, reserving 3 tablespoons drippings in skillet. Crumble bacon, and set aside.
• Sauté green onions and chopped celery in hot drippings in skillet over medium heat 5 minutes or until tender. Gradually whisk in flour until blended. Gradually add reserved broth; cook, whisking constantly, 3 minutes or until thickened and bubbly. Stir in chicken, bacon, eggs, and next 5 ingredients.
• Spoon mixture into a 3-quart baking dish, and top with refrigerated piecrust.
• Bake, uncovered, at 450° for 25 minutes or until golden and bubbly. Serve with cranberry sauce. Yield: 6 to 8 servings.

*Mary Cale*
Birmingham, Alabama

Southerners are both passionate and opinionated about chicken and dumplings. The dumplings *must* be rolled, or they *must* be dropped. Celery is either the salvation or the ruination of the broth. And don't even think about asking if you could use a package of chicken breasts instead of the whole bird.

## Chicken and Dumplings

| | | | |
|---|---|---|---|
| 1 | (2½-pound) whole chicken, cut into pieces | 1 | teaspoon chicken bouillon granules |
| 2½ | teaspoons salt, divided | 3 | cups self-rising flour |
| ¾ | teaspoon black pepper, divided | ½ | teaspoon poultry seasoning |
| ½ | teaspoon garlic powder | ⅓ | cup shortening |
| ½ | teaspoon dried thyme | 2 | teaspoons bacon drippings |
| ¼ | teaspoon ground red pepper | 1 | cup milk |

• Cover chicken with water, and bring to a boil in a large Dutch oven. Add 1½ teaspoons salt, ½ teaspoon black pepper, and next 3 ingredients; cover, reduce heat, and simmer 1 hour. Remove chicken, reserving broth in Dutch oven; cool chicken. Skim fat from broth; bring broth to a simmer. Skin, bone, and coarsely chop chicken. Add chicken, bouillon, and remaining salt and black pepper to broth. Return to simmer.
• Combine flour and poultry seasoning in a bowl. Cut in shortening and bacon drippings with a pastry blender until mixture is crumbly. Add milk, stirring until dry ingredients are moistened. Turn dough out onto a lightly floured surface. Roll out to ⅛-inch thickness; cut into 1-inch pieces.
• Bring broth mixture to a boil. Drop dumplings, a few at a time, into broth, stirring gently. Reduce heat, cover, and simmer, stirring often, for 25 minutes. Yield: 8 servings.

*cook's secret...* Test Kitchens Director Lyda Jones offers a few tips for making this classic dish perfect every time.
• Boil the chicken the night before and refrigerate the broth. All the fat will collect on the surface, making it easier to remove.
• Break shortening into small pieces, and use solidified bacon drippings. They'll cut into the flour more evenly.
• As soon as you have a moist ball of dough, resist the urge to keep working it. The more you handle the dough, the tougher the dumplings will be.

# Chicken with Green Olives

| | |
|---|---|
| 5 anchovy fillets | 4 garlic cloves, peeled and crushed |
| 1½ cups (8 ounces) green olives, slivered and divided | ½ cup dry white wine |
| | 3 tablespoons red wine vinegar |
| 3 pounds chicken legs, thighs, and wings | 2 tablespoons water |
| ½ teaspoon salt | 3 tablespoons lemon juice |
| ½ teaspoon pepper | 3 tablespoons finely chopped fresh Italian parsley |
| 2 tablespoons olive oil | |

• Process anchovy fillets and ¾ cup green olives in a food processor until chopped, stopping to scrape down sides; set aside.

• Sprinkle chicken with salt and pepper. Brown chicken on all sides in hot oil in a large skillet over medium-high heat. Remove chicken, reserving 2 teaspoons drippings in skillet; add garlic, and sauté 1 minute. Add white wine and vinegar; cook 2 minutes, stirring to loosen browned bits from bottom of skillet. Stir in anchovy mixture and 2 tablespoons water.

• Return chicken to skillet, turning to coat pieces in sauce.

• Cook, covered, over medium-low heat 45 minutes or until chicken is tender. (Stir in additional water if needed.)

• Add 3 tablespoons lemon juice, Italian parsley, and remaining ¾ cup green olives; cook 1 to 2 more minutes. Serve immediately. Yield: 4 to 6 servings.

*Chef Giuliano Hazan*
Sarasota, Florida
Adapted from *Every Night Italian* (Scribner)

*cook's secret...* Smash the garlic cloves with the flat edge of a chef's knife, and you can easily pull away the peel with your fingers.

When Monique Wells moved to Paris, the last thing the Houston native thought she'd miss was home, let alone the food of her childhood. However, after having "wallowed in the wealth of French cuisine for several months," Monique had a revealing experience. "I woke up one morning and realized that I didn't want a croissant for breakfast. What I wanted was grits. In that moment, my mind was flooded with memories of food from home, such as fresh biscuits and cane syrup," she says.

In 2000, Monique published *Food for the Soul* (Elton-Wolf Publishing), a collection of Southern recipes that pay tribute to her Texas and Creole Louisiana roots. She realizes that our Southernness is connected to the foods we ate as children—good or bad. "Fortunately, mine are great memories," she says. "Food and family are the essence of life. As long as one takes meals with one's family, the two are irrevocably intertwined."

## Down-Home Chicken and Onions

| | | | |
|---|---|---|---|
| 2½ | pounds chicken legs, wings, and thighs | 3 | tablespoons butter or margarine |
| 1 | teaspoon salt | 2 | large onions, halved and sliced |
| 1 | teaspoon pepper | ½ | cup water |
| 1 | teaspoon seasoned salt (optional) | | Hot cooked rice |

• Sprinkle chicken evenly with salt, pepper, and, if desired, seasoned salt.
• Melt butter in a large skillet over medium heat. Add chicken pieces, and cook 5 minutes on each side or until browned. Remove chicken; keep warm.
• Add onions to skillet, and sauté 10 minutes or until tender. Return chicken to skillet; stir in ½ cup water. Cover and simmer, stirring occasionally, 30 minutes or until sauce thickens and chicken is done. Serve over hot cooked rice. Yield: 4 to 6 servings.

*Monique Wells*
*Paris, France*

*cook's secret...* If your chicken has been injected with a saline solution during processing, omit the seasoned salt, which is marked as optional. Otherwise, the dish will be too salty.

# Marinated Chicken Quarters

*Fresh herbs enliven these grilled chicken quarters*
*basted and served with lemon butter.*

½ cup butter or margarine, melted
½ cup lemon juice
1 tablespoon paprika
1 tablespoon dried oregano
1 teaspoon garlic salt
1 tablespoon chopped fresh cilantro
    or 1 teaspoon dried coriander

1 teaspoon ground cumin
1 (2½-pound) whole chicken, quartered
½ teaspoon salt
½ teaspoon pepper

- Combine first 7 ingredients; reserve ½ cup butter mixture.
- Sprinkle chicken evenly with salt and pepper. Place in shallow dishes or zip-top freezer bags; pour remaining butter mixture evenly over chicken. Cover or seal, and chill, along with reserved butter mixture, 8 hours.
- Remove chicken from marinade, discarding marinade.
- Grill, covered with grill lid, over medium-high heat (350° to 400°) 40 to 45 minutes or until done, basting often with reserved butter mixture and turning once. Yield: 4 servings.

*Gayle Millican*
Rowlett, Texas

*cook's secret...* Place chicken quarters on grill with bony sides down. The bones act as heat conductors.

## Chicken Pointers

- Cook until internal temperature reaches 180° in the thigh and 170° for bone-in parts. Juices should run clear when grilled chicken is pierced with a fork.
- Discard marinade in which uncooked chicken has soaked; never use it on cooked meat unless you boil it for 1 minute.
- Do not leave chicken at room temperature for more than 2 hours.
- Do not place cooked chicken on a plate where uncooked poultry has sat.

An easy menu allows Lynn and George O'Connor of Little Rock time to enjoy guests aboard their houseboat on Lake Ouachita. While Lynn adds finishing touches to the meal in the galley, George grills the chicken.

## Grilled Chicken with Basting Sauce

| | |
|---|---|
| ¼ cup butter or margarine | ½ teaspoon dried crushed red pepper |
| 2 tablespoons red wine vinegar | ½ teaspoon coarsely ground black pepper |
| 2 tablespoons Worcestershire sauce | 8 bone-in chicken breasts |
| 1 tablespoon sugar | 1 teaspoon salt |
| 1½ teaspoons lemon juice | ½ teaspoon black pepper |
| 1 garlic clove, chopped | |

• Cook first 8 ingredients in a saucepan over medium-low heat, stirring occasionally, until butter melts; set aside.
• Sprinkle chicken evenly with salt and pepper.
• Grill chicken, covered with grill lid, over medium-high heat (350° to 400°) 40 to 45 minutes or until done, turning occasionally and basting with sauce the last 10 minutes. Yield: 8 servings.

*Lynn and George O'Connor*
Little Rock, Arkansas

*cook's secret...* Basting with the sauce the last 10 minutes minimizes flare-ups on the grill caused by the butter in the recipe.

# Cheese-Stuffed Chicken in Phyllo

*Buttery layers of phyllo dress up ordinary chicken breast halves.*
*Look for phyllo, also sold as fillo dough leaves, in the freezer*
*section of your supermarket.*

| | | | |
|---|---|---|---|
| 8 | skinned and boned chicken breasts | ½ | cup (2 ounces) crumbled feta cheese |
| 1 | teaspoon salt | ½ | cup (2 ounces) shredded Cheddar cheese |
| ½ | teaspoon pepper | 1 | egg yolk, lightly beaten |
| 4 | cups chopped fresh spinach | 1 | tablespoon all-purpose flour |
| 1 | medium onion, chopped | ½ | teaspoon ground nutmeg |
| 2 | tablespoons olive or vegetable oil | ½ | teaspoon ground cumin |
| ½ | (8-ounce) package cream cheese, softened and cut into pieces | 16 | frozen phyllo pastry sheets, thawed |
| | | | Melted butter or margarine |
| 1 | cup (4 ounces) shredded mozzarella cheese | | Mixed salad greens (optional) |

• Place chicken between 2 sheets of heavy-duty plastic wrap, and flatten to ⅛-inch thickness, using a meat mallet or rolling pin. Sprinkle evenly with salt and pepper, and set aside.
• Sauté spinach and onion in hot oil in a large skillet over medium-high heat 3 to 4 minutes or until onion is tender. Remove from heat, and stir in cream cheese until blended. Stir in mozzarella cheese and next 6 ingredients.
• Spoon ¼ cup spinach mixture on center of each chicken breast half, and roll up, jelly-roll fashion.
• Unfold phyllo sheets on a lightly floured surface. Stack 2 phyllo sheets, brushing with melted butter between sheets. (Keep remaining phyllo sheets covered with plastic wrap to prevent drying out.) Place 1 chicken roll on short side of phyllo stack; gently roll up, folding in long side. Repeat procedure with remaining pastry, melted butter, and chicken. Place rolls in a shallow pan, and brush with melted butter.
• Bake, uncovered, at 350° for 35 to 40 minutes or until done. Serve on a bed of mixed greens, if desired. Yield: 8 servings.

*Betty Rake*
Plano, Texas

*cook's secret...* When working with frozen phyllo pastry, remember these tips:
• Thaw frozen phyllo completely in the refrigerator to avoid sticky dough.
• Cover phyllo sheets with plastic wrap and a damp towel until ready to use to prevent drying out.
• Cut down on calories by using butter-flavored cooking spray instead of brushing phyllo layers with melted butter.

# Chicken Sauté with Artichokes and Mushrooms

1 (6-ounce) jar marinated artichoke hearts
4 skinned and boned chicken breasts
¼ cup all-purpose flour
1 teaspoon seasoned salt
¼ teaspoon pepper
5 tablespoons butter, divided

12 fresh cremini or button mushrooms, halved
⅓ cup dry white wine
¼ cup chicken broth
2 tablespoons capers, drained

• Drain artichokes, reserving 2 tablespoons marinade; set artichokes and reserved marinade aside.

• Place chicken between 2 sheets of heavy-duty plastic wrap; flatten to ½-inch thickness, using a meat mallet or rolling pin. Combine flour, salt, and pepper in a shallow dish; dredge chicken in flour mixture, and set aside.

• Melt 3 tablespoons butter in a large skillet over medium-high heat; add mushrooms, and sauté 5 minutes. Push mushrooms to one side of pan, and melt 1 tablespoon butter in pan; add chicken. Cook chicken 5 to 6 minutes on each side. Remove chicken from pan.

• Add wine to skillet, and cook over medium-high heat, stirring to loosen browned bits from bottom of skillet. Add chicken broth, artichokes, and reserved artichoke marinade to skillet, and cook 3 minutes or until liquid is reduced by half. Remove from heat; add remaining 1 tablespoon butter and capers, stirring often until smooth. Serve sauce over chicken. Yield: 4 servings.

*Marie Rizzio*
Traverse City, Michigan

*cook's secret...* After you finish a meat or seafood sauté, you can make a great sauce from the browned bits in the skillet. Just add a liquid, such as wine or broth, to loosen the bits—this is called deglazing the pan—then boil briefly to reduce, or thicken, the sauce.

D enise Yennie's recipe for Chicken Florentine Panini was the $1,000,000 Grand Prize Winner in the 2002 Pillsbury Bake-Off®. Senior Writer Donna Florio attended the bake-off and knew from looking at Denise's cast-iron skillet that she was a Southern cook.

*contest winner*

# Chicken Florentine Panini

| | | | |
|---|---|---|---|
| 1 | (10-ounce) can refrigerated pizza crust | 1 | tablespoon sugar |
| 1 | (9-ounce) package frozen spinach | 1 | tablespoon balsamic vinegar |
| ¼ | cup light mayonnaise | 2 | skinned and boned chicken breasts |
| 2 | garlic cloves, minced and divided | ½ | teaspoon dried Italian seasoning |
| 1 | medium-size red onion, chopped | 4 | (4-inch) provolone cheese slices |
| 1 | tablespoon olive oil | | |

• Unroll crust; press into a 15- x 10-inch jellyroll pan. Bake at 375° for 10 minutes. Cool.
• Prepare spinach according to package directions. Drain well, pressing between paper towels. Set aside. Stir together mayonnaise and half of garlic in a bowl. Cover and chill.
• Sauté onion in hot oil in a saucepan over medium-high heat 2 to 3 minutes or until crisp-tender. Add sugar and vinegar. Reduce heat to low; simmer, stirring occasionally, 3 to 5 minutes or until almost all liquid evaporates.
• Place chicken between 2 sheets of heavy-duty plastic wrap or wax paper; flatten to ¼-inch thickness, using a meat mallet or rolling pin. Sprinkle with Italian seasoning and remaining garlic. Brown chicken in a large nonstick skillet coated with vegetable cooking spray over medium-high heat; cook 8 minutes, turning once.
• Cut pizza crust into 4 rectangles. Remove rectangles from pan; spread 1 side of each with 1 tablespoon garlic mayonnaise. Top 2 rectangles evenly with chicken, spinach, onion mixture, and cheese; top with remaining 2 rectangles, mayonnaise sides down.
• Cook sandwiches in a cast-iron skillet over medium-high heat. Top with a smaller skillet or press down with spatula to flatten slightly, cooking 2 to 3 minutes on each side or until golden and cheese melts. Cut each sandwich into fourths. Yield: 4 servings.

*Denise Yennie*
Nashville, Tennessee

*cook's secret*... Pound chicken breasts from end to end to even thickness for cooking. Thinly pounded breasts cook faster and sometimes require a larger skillet.

Charlotte Skelton, author of *Absolutely a la Carte,* is an on-the-go mother of three (including two teens) who juggles the responsibilities of an active family with a successful career. She also faces the universal challenge of serving her family a variety of great-tasting meals throughout the week. Charlotte's solution: stocking her freezer with convenient one-dish meals.

Charlotte's passion for Southwest flavors explodes in Chicken Enchiladas. "This is one of my standbys, especially when company's coming," she explains. This recipe freezes well and can be easily lightened.

*make–ahead*

## Chicken Enchiladas

| | |
|---|---|
| 2 tablespoons butter | 2 garlic cloves, minced |
| 2 large onions, thinly sliced | 2 teaspoons dried oregano |
| 2 cups chopped cooked chicken | 1 teaspoon ground cumin |
| ½ cup diced roasted red bell pepper | ½ teaspoon sugar |
| 2 (3-ounce) packages cream cheese, cubed | 1 (14-ounce) can chicken broth |
| ¼ teaspoon salt | ½ cup salsa |
| ¼ teaspoon black pepper | 10 (7-inch) flour tortillas |
| 4 (4.5-ounce) cans chopped green chiles | 2 cups (8 ounces) shredded Cheddar cheese |
| 1 small onion, chopped | |

• Melt butter in a large skillet over medium-high heat, stirring often; add sliced onions, and cook 20 minutes or until caramelized.

• Reduce heat to low; add chopped chicken and next 4 ingredients, stirring until combined. Set aside.

• Pulse chiles and next 5 ingredients in a blender or food processor several times until combined.

• Bring chile mixture and chicken broth to a boil in a saucepan over high heat; cook 5 minutes or until slightly thickened. (Mixture should be the consistency of a thin gravy.) Remove from heat, and stir in salsa.

• Spread one-third chile mixture evenly in a lightly greased 13- x 9-inch baking dish.

- Spoon chicken mixture evenly down center of each tortilla; roll up, and place seam side down in prepared baking dish. Top with remaining chile mixture; sprinkle with cheese.
- Bake at 375° for 20 to 25 minutes or until bubbly. Yield: 4 to 6 servings.

**NOTE:** *Freeze chile mixture and filled tortillas separately up to 1 month, if desired. Thaw in refrigerator overnight. Prepare and bake as directed.*

*Charlotte Skelton*
Cleveland, Mississippi

*cook's secret...* To lighten this recipe, substitute ⅓-less-fat cream cheese, 2% reduced-fat Cheddar cheese, and fat-free tortillas.

## Charlotte's Tips for Streamlined Meal Preparation

- Double the recipe when preparing such items as chili, gumbo, and spaghetti sauce. It doesn't take much time, and you can easily freeze the extra batch for heat-and-eat weeknight meals.
- For easy, uniform slices, freeze boneless, skinless chicken breasts, pork tenderloin, or steak for 10 minutes. Then slice for a stir-fry or quick sauté.
- Using simple garnishes, such as fresh chopped herbs, nuts, or slices of fruit, is an easy way to dress up weeknight recipes for company. Decorative serving dishes also provide a pop of color and visual interest.
- Set aside space in your refrigerator for a make-ahead dish before you prepare the recipe.
- If you plan to freeze a casserole, line the baking dish with aluminum foil. This makes removing and freezing the casserole easier and cuts down on cleanup.

# Smoked Turkey Breast

*This recipe received our Test Kitchens' highest rating.*

Hickory wood chunks

1 tablespoon salt

1 tablespoon garlic powder

1 tablespoon dried rosemary

1 tablespoon pepper

1 (5-pound) bone-in turkey breast

- Soak wood chunks in water 1 hour.
- Combine salt and next 3 ingredients; rub mixture over turkey breast.
- Prepare charcoal fire in smoker; let burn 15 to 20 minutes.
- Drain wood chunks, and place on coals. Place water pan in smoker; add water to depth of fill line. Place turkey in center of lower food rack.
- Cook, covered, 5 to 6 hours or until a meat thermometer inserted into thickest portion registers 170°, adding additional water to depth of fill line, if necessary. Remove from smoker; let stand 10 minutes before slicing. Yield: 6 to 8 servings.

*John Nicholson*
Birmingham, Alabama

*cook's secret...* Follow these tips for the tastiest turkey:

- If you buy frozen turkey, allow at least 1 day for every 5 pounds to thaw it, unwrapped, in the refrigerator. For a quicker method, leave the turkey in its unopened bag and thaw it, breast side down, in cold water, changing water every 30 minutes.
- Forget about the pop-up thermometer. A more accurate temperature reading comes from a meat thermometer inserted into the thigh meat. The meat is done when the thermometer registers 180°.
- Allow the bird to rest 15 minutes before carving; this makes for moister, more succulent slices of meat.

### John's Smoking Secrets

- Start with about one-fourth of a bag of hickory chunks in the smoker, and then add the same amount about 2 hours later. You may also need to add more charcoal about 4 hours into the smoking process. Insert additional hickory and charcoal through the small door of your smoker.
- Use hickory instead of mesquite wood because mesquite burns hotter and faster.
- Do not open the smoker lid before the minimum time has elapsed because the temperature will drop quickly, as with your oven.

# Orange-Glazed Turkey with Pan Gravy

*The cheesecloth covering acts as a blanket to lock in juices.*

| | |
|---|---|
| 2 (36-inch) squares cheesecloth | ½ cup orange marmalade, divided |
| 1½ cups orange juice | 3 tablespoons honey |
| 1 (12-pound) turkey | 2 teaspoons grated orange rind |
| 1 teaspoon salt | 1 tablespoon coarse-grained Dijon mustard |
| ½ teaspoon pepper | 1 (32-ounce) container chicken broth |
| ½ cup butter or margarine, melted | Pan Gravy |

- Soak cheesecloth squares in orange juice 5 minutes.
- Remove giblets and neck from turkey, and reserve for another use. Rinse turkey with cold water, and pat dry.
- Sprinkle cavity with salt and pepper. Place turkey, breast side up, in a large greased roasting pan.
- Stir together butter, ¼ cup marmalade, and next 3 ingredients; spoon ⅓ cup butter mixture into cavity, and brush top of turkey generously with remaining butter mixture.
- Tie ends of turkey legs together with string. Tuck wingtips under; wrap ends of legs with aluminum foil. Add chicken broth to pan.
- Remove cheesecloth from orange juice, reserving juice. Spread the soaked cheesecloth squares over most of the turkey, completely covering the legs and wings. Pour reserved orange juice over turkey.
- Bake on lowest oven rack at 350° for 2½ to 3 hours or until a meat thermometer inserted into turkey thigh reads 180°, basting occasionally with pan drippings. (Cheesecloth will become very brown as turkey roasts.) Remove and discard cheesecloth, string, and aluminum foil.
- Brush turkey with remaining ¼ cup orange marmalade, and let stand 15 minutes. Transfer to a serving platter, reserving drippings for Pan Gravy. Yield: 10 servings.

## Pan Gravy:

| | |
|---|---|
| Reserved pan drippings | 1 teaspoon browning-and-seasoning sauce |
| 3 tablespoons all-purpose flour | ½ teaspoon salt |
| ⅓ cup water | ½ teaspoon pepper |
| 2 cups chicken broth | |

- Skim fat from drippings. Add water to drippings to measure 3 cups.
- Stir together flour and ⅓ cup water in a large saucepan. Whisk in drippings, broth, and next 3 ingredients. Bring to a boil; reduce heat and simmer, whisking occasionally, 5 minutes or until thickened. Yield: 3 cups.

**NOTE:** *For testing purposes only, we used Kitchen Bouquet browning-and-seasoning sauce.*

In our Test Kitchens, we're always on the lookout for good ideas for potluck. This recipe is an ideal choice: It's attractive, has interesting flavor combinations, and travels well.

## Turkey Pot Pie with Cranberry-Pecan Crusts

*Turkey tenderloins, caramelized onions, and fresh spinach blend to make a perfect sweet/savory combination. The flavors hint of the holidays, but you'll enjoy the one-dish meal year-round.*

3 tablespoons butter, divided
2 large sweet onions, diced
½ cup all-purpose flour
1 teaspoon salt
1 teaspoon pepper
4 (12-ounce) turkey tenderloins, cut into 1½-inch cubes

2 tablespoons vegetable oil
1½ cups chicken broth
1 cup milk
1 (10-ounce) package fresh spinach, torn
Cranberry-Pecan Crusts

• Melt 1 tablespoon butter in a large skillet over medium-high heat; add onion, and sauté 15 minutes or until caramel-colored. Place onion in a bowl, and set aside.

• Combine flour, salt, and pepper; dredge turkey in flour mixture.

• Melt remaining 2 tablespoons butter with oil in skillet over medium-high heat; add turkey, and brown on all sides. Gradually stir in chicken broth and milk. Bring to a boil, and cook, stirring constantly, 1 minute or until thickened.

• Stir in onion. Add spinach, stirring just until wilted. Pour turkey mixture into a lightly greased 13- x 9-inch baking dish.

• Bake, covered, at 350° for 30 minutes. Remove from oven, and arrange desired amount of Cranberry-Pecan Crusts over pie before serving. Serve with any remaining Cranberry-Pecan Crusts on the side. Yield: 10 to 12 servings.

## Cranberry-Pecan Crusts:

*Reroll any leftover scraps of dough, and repeat the procedure.*

1 (15-ounce) package refrigerated  
   piecrusts

½ cup finely chopped pecans, toasted  
½ cup finely chopped dried cranberries

- Unfold each piecrust, and press out fold lines. Sprinkle 1 piecrust with pecans and cranberries; top with remaining piecrust. Roll into a 14-inch circle, sealing together piecrusts. Cut into desired shapes with a 2- to 3-inch cutter. Place pastry shapes on a lightly greased baking sheet.
- Bake at 425° for 8 to 10 minutes or until golden. Yield: 3 to 4 dozen.

*cook's secret*... You can make the crusts ahead. Simply store them separately so that they stay firm, and place them on the pie before serving.

### Travel Tips for Potluck Dinners

- Wrap casseroles with aluminum foil; cover with newspaper or towels to keep the food warm longer.
- Use lightweight, sealable serving containers. Shallow ones provide ample surface area to keep food cold and make packing easier.
- Pack perishable foods in a cooler. Avoid messes by using ice sealed in zip-top plastic bags or by using frozen gel packs.
- To keep dairy products, meats, fish, shellfish, poultry, cream pies, creamy salads, and custards at 40° or below, chill before placing in the cooler.
- Bring dishes in reusable disposable containers that the hostess can throw away or keep.

A gordita is a thick pancake made of masa; the edges are pinched up to hold a meat or bean filling and toppings. Dotty Griffith, dining editor and restaurant critic for *The Dallas Morning News,* shares her recipe for this Texas favorite.

*regional favorite*

## Gorditas with Turkey Mole

| | |
|---|---|
| 2 cups masa harina | 1 cup refried beans or 1 cup drained and |
| 1¼ cups chicken broth | mashed Buzz's Pot of Beans |
| ¼ cup shortening | Turkey Mole |
| ½ cup plus 1 tablespoon all-purpose flour | Toppings: 1 (15-ounce) can black beans, |
| ½ teaspoon salt | rinsed and drained; shredded lettuce; |
| 1 teaspoon baking powder | chopped tomato; sour cream |
| Vegetable oil | Garnishes: lime wedges, cilantro sprigs |

• Stir together masa harina and broth in a large mixing bowl. Cover and let stand 30 minutes. Add shortening, flour, salt, and baking powder; beat at medium speed with an electric mixer until smooth.

• Divide dough into 12 golf-size balls. Arrange on wax paper, and cover with damp towels. Pat each ball of dough into a 3-inch circle. (Lightly oil fingers to keep mixture from sticking.) Pinch edges of circles to form a ridge, and press a well in each center to hold toppings. Cover with a damp towel to prevent dough from drying.

• Pour oil to a depth of ¼ inch into a large skillet; heat to 350°. Fry gorditas, in batches, 2 minutes on each side, or until golden brown. Drain on paper towels.

• Dollop each gordita with 2 tablespoons refried beans; spoon 1 tablespoon Turkey Mole over beans on each gordita. (Reserve extra beans and mole for other uses.) Top gorditas with desired toppings, and garnish, if desired. Yield: 12 servings.

**NOTE:** *Fill a squirt bottle with sour cream. Squeeze onto top of gordita.*

*cook's secret...* Masa harina is corn flour traditionally used to make corn tortillas. It can be found in the ethnic foods section of large grocery stores.

## Buzz's Pot of Beans:

| | |
|---|---|
| 1 pound dried pinto beans | 3 bacon slices, cut into 1-inch pieces |
| ½ pound dried black beans | 3 chicken bouillon cubes |
| ½ pound dried red kidney beans | 3 tablespoons chili powder |
| 14 cups water | 1 tablespoon salt |
| 6 cups chopped onion, divided | 2 teaspoons ground black pepper |
| 10 garlic cloves | ½ to 1 teaspoon ground red pepper |

• Combine beans and water to cover 3 inches in a large Dutch oven; soak 8 hours. Drain.

• Combine beans, 14 cups water, 4 cups chopped onion, garlic, and remaining ingredients. Bring to a boil over high heat. Reduce heat, cover, and simmer, stirring occasionally, 1 hour. Add remaining chopped onion, and cook, covered, 2 hours or until beans are tender, adding more water, as needed. Yield: 12 servings.

## Turkey Mole:

| | |
|---|---|
| 1 (8¼-ounce to 9¼-ounce) can mole sauce | 1½ pounds cooked turkey, shredded (about 5 cups) |
| 1 (10-ounce) can enchilada sauce | ½ teaspoon salt |
| 4 cups chicken broth | |
| 1 tablespoon creamy peanut butter | |
| 2 (1-ounce) unsweetened dark chocolate baking squares | |

• Stir together mole and enchilada sauces in a medium saucepan, and add chicken broth. Bring mixture to a boil; reduce heat, and simmer 5 minutes.

• Stir in peanut butter and chocolate until melted and smooth. Stir in turkey and salt; cook until thoroughly heated. Yield: 6½ cups.

*Dotty Griffith*
Dallas, Texas
Adapted from *The Texas Holiday Cookbook*
(Gulf Publishing Company) and
*The Contemporary Cowboy Cookbook: From the Wild West to Wall Street*
(Lone Star Books)

*cook's secret...* Turkey Mole may also be spooned into taco shells or rolled in tortillas. Canned mole sauce may be found in the Mexican foods section of large supermarkets.

# Spicy Catfish with Vegetables and Basil Cream

*This recipe shows the versatility and creativity of sautéing.*

3 tablespoons butter, divided
1 (16-ounce) package frozen whole kernel
   corn, thawed
1 medium onion, chopped
1 medium-size green bell pepper, chopped
1 medium-size red bell pepper, chopped
¾ teaspoon salt
¾ teaspoon black pepper
½ cup all-purpose flour

¼ cup yellow cornmeal
1 tablespoon Creole seasoning
4 (6- to 8-ounce) catfish fillets
⅓ cup buttermilk
1 tablespoon vegetable oil
½ cup whipping cream
2 tablespoons chopped fresh basil
Garnish: fresh basil sprigs

• Melt 2 tablespoons butter in a large sauté pan over medium-high heat. Add corn, onion, and bell peppers; sauté 6 to 8 minutes or until tender. Stir in salt and black pepper; spoon onto serving dish, and keep warm.

• Combine flour, cornmeal, and Creole seasoning in a large shallow dish. Dip fillets in buttermilk, and dredge in flour mixture.

• Melt remaining 1 tablespoon butter with oil in sauté pan over medium-high heat. Cook fillets, in batches, 2 to 3 minutes on each side or until golden. Remove and arrange over vegetables.

• Add cream to sauté pan, stirring to loosen browned bits from bottom of pan. Add chopped basil, and cook, stirring often, 1 to 2 minutes or until thickened. Serve sauce with fillets and vegetables. Garnish, if desired. Yield: 4 servings.

*cook's secret...* A sauté pan is a straight-sided frying pan that allows food to be flipped and tossed with less spattering. A skillet has sides that flair outward. It's shallow with sloped sides that prevent steam from forming in the pan. Don't feel limited by the name of either pan. Most of our recipes can be done in either one.

# 6 Steps to Sauté Success

**1. Get Off to a Hot Start** To sauté in a small amount of fat means about ⅛ inch of fat. Butter adds great flavor, but it has a low smoke point, meaning it burns quickly. So when the milk solids (the white foam you see) just start to brown, add the food. Don't substitute margarine for butter. Because margarine contains water, it will steam the food rather than fry it. A great solution is to use vegetable oil and butter for heat control plus flavor. Vegetable and canola oil both have high smoke points and can withstand high cooking temperatures. Olive oils labeled "virgin" or "pure" also hold up to heat. Extra-virgin olive oil tends to burn quickly. When the oil in a hot pan shimmers, it's time to add the food.

**2. Take Your Time** When food is added, the skillet and oil temperatures fall. Add ingredients gradually, so you hear a constant sizzling sound.

**3. Beautifully Browned** For a crisp, browned crust, lightly dust meat or fish with flour, breadcrumbs, or cornmeal just before adding to the hot skillet. To sauté without breading, pat juicy meats, poultry, or seafood dry with paper towels (excess liquid will cause the oil to pop). Season with salt, pepper, or spices before cooking.

**4. Hear the Sizzle** Add the first piece of fish or meat pretty side down (skin side up on fish), and be sure to add the thickest portion first. You'll hear a fast sizzle that will slow as the temperature drops. Bubbles of oil or butter will form around the food. As the temperature rises, the sizzle increases. Add the next fillet (leave 1 inch of space around each; a crowded skillet steams rather than crisps). Expect splatters on the cooktop when the temperature is correct.

**5. Time to Turn** When the fillets look done around the top of the sides, it's time to turn. Give the pan a shake. Food should release and slide when it's ready to turn. Flip it with tongs or a spatula, and continue to cook until done. Then remove it from the skillet. If the food doesn't release easily, you skimped on the oil or the pan wasn't hot enough.

**6. Capture All the Flavor** Add a liquid, such as whipping cream, wine, or broth, to the hot skillet to loosen the browned bits from the bottom of the skillet. For a stronger flavor, boil the added liquid until the volume reduces by half. Add delicate herbs just before serving for fullest flavor.

Cherise Rembert, a nurse practitioner at a neurology clinic, had never entered a recipe contest before. With young children, she doesn't have much time for recipe testing. "I've never liked catfish just fried," she says. "It doesn't have much flavor. We have rosemary in our garden, so I thought of adding it to the breading." With her husband's encouragement, she sent in her entry the day before the contest deadline. It was a finalist in the Taste of the South category of our 2002 *Southern Living* Cook-Off.

*contest winner*

# Fried Lemon-Rosemary Catfish

| | |
|---|---|
| 1 large lemon | 4 (4- to 6-ounce) catfish fillets |
| ¼ cup milk | 2 cups yellow cornmeal |
| 2 medium eggs, lightly beaten | ¼ cup extra-virgin olive oil |
| 2 tablespoons chopped fresh rosemary | Garnishes: lemon slices, fresh rosemary |
| 2 tablespoons minced fresh garlic | sprigs |

• Grate lemon rind from lemon, avoiding the pale, bitter pith, into a large bowl; squeeze lemon juice into bowl. Stir in milk and next 3 ingredients until blended.

• Rinse fillets, and pat dry with paper towels. Add fillets to lemon mixture in bowl; cover and chill 1 hour.

• Place cornmeal on a large plate or in a large shallow dish. Turn fillets in lemon mixture until thoroughly coated; dredge in cornmeal, coating evenly.

• Cook fillets in hot oil in skillet over medium-high heat 4 minutes on each side or until browned. Remove from skillet. Garnish, if desired. Yield: 4 servings.

*Cherise Rembert*
Woodville, Alabama

*cook's secret*... Yellow cornmeal browns to make a prettier crust than white cornmeal.

# Baked Fish with Parmesan–Sour Cream Sauce

1½  pounds orange roughy fillets
1  (8-ounce) container sour cream
¼  cup shredded Parmesan cheese
½  teaspoon paprika
½  teaspoon salt

¼  teaspoon pepper
2  tablespoons Italian-seasoned
   breadcrumbs
2  tablespoons butter or margarine, melted

- Place fillets in a single layer in a lightly greased 13- x 9-inch pan.
- Stir together sour cream and next 4 ingredients; spread mixture evenly over fillets. Sprinkle with breadcrumbs, and drizzle with butter.
- Bake at 350° for 20 to 25 minutes or until fish flakes with a fork. Yield: 4 to 6 servings.

*Demetra Economos Anas*
*Potomac, Maryland*

*cook's secret...* Tilapia, flounder, or any other white fish works in place of orange roughy.

## Fish Facts

- Choose fish that has a fresh odor (not a strong one) and a moist appearance.
- Use fresh or thawed frozen fish within 1 or 2 days.
- Thaw frozen fish by rinsing with cold water 3 to 4 minutes.
- Dense, sturdy fish, such as salmon or tuna, can be prepared using any cooking method. Softer textured fish, such as orange roughy, tilapia, or snapper, should be baked or sautéed because it may fall apart when grilled or steamed.

*S*ejal Patel said she was thrilled when I asked her to share her family's traditional recipes with us. She quickly added, however, that if I wanted the really good stuff, I'd better talk to her mom, Ranjan Patel.

Once I received Ranjan's mouthwatering recipes, I asked if I could substitute more widely available ingredients for some of the less common ones that she uses. Sejal and I worked together and came up with a happy blend of Indian and Southern tastes in this recipe for Spicy Skillet Fish.

*Joy Zacharia*
Associate Foods Editor

## Spicy Skillet Fish

2  garlic cloves
1  (2-inch) piece fresh ginger, peeled and chopped (about 2 tablespoons chopped)
½  cup chopped fresh cilantro
1  small jalapeño pepper, seeded
1  teaspoon salt
½  teaspoon ground paprika

½  teaspoon ground turmeric
½  teaspoon ground coriander
2  teaspoons vegetable oil
2  pounds catfish, grouper, or flounder fillets (about 6 fillets)
2  tablespoons vegetable oil
Fresh lemon or lime wedges (optional)

• Process first 9 ingredients in a food processor until finely chopped.
• Spread 2 teaspoons spice mixture evenly over both sides of each fillet. Cover and chill 30 minutes.
• Cook fish, in batches, in 2 tablespoons hot oil in a large nonstick skillet over medium-high heat 5 minutes on each side or until fish flakes with a fork. Serve with fresh lemon or lime wedges, if desired. Yield: 6 servings.

*Ranjan Patel*
Roswell, Georgia

*cook's secret*... For a variation, prepare this recipe as directed, and make fish soft tacos with warmed flour or corn tortillas. Drizzle with fresh lime juice, and serve with your favorite rice.

# Red Snapper with Lemon Sauce

*Create a satisfying meal by serving this fish with*
*steamed fresh broccoli and rice pilaf.*

½ cup milk

1 large egg

2 (6- to 7-ounce) red snapper fillets

¼ teaspoon salt

¼ teaspoon freshly ground pepper, divided

¼ cup all-purpose flour

½ cup fine, dry breadcrumbs

3 tablespoons butter or margarine, divided

2 ounces cream cheese

¼ cup shredded fontina cheese*

1 tablespoon lemon rind

2 tablespoons fresh lemon juice

- Whisk together milk and egg.
- Sprinkle fillets with salt and ⅛ teaspoon pepper. Dredge fish in flour; dip in milk mixture, and dredge in breadcrumbs.
- Melt 1 tablespoon butter in a large skillet over medium heat; add fish, and cook 2 to 3 minutes on each side or until fish flakes with a fork. Remove fillets, and drain on paper towels; keep warm.
- Wipe skillet clean, and melt remaining 2 tablespoons butter over medium-low heat. Add remaining ⅛ teaspoon pepper, cream cheese, and remaining ingredients, stirring until smooth. Pour sauce over fillets. Yield: 2 servings.

*Baby Swiss cheese may be substituted for fontina cheese.*

*Elizabeth Langston*
Memphis, Tennessee

*cook's secret*... Use a long, slender fish spatula for turning the delicate fish fillets without breaking them.

iane and Peter Halferty live right on the water in Corpus Christi and love to fish. Peter, a former tugboat captain, says he began cooking because "you can only paint the kitchen so many times!" Peter's recipe was a Runner Up in the Fabulous Entrées category in our 2001 *Southern Living* Holiday Recipe Contest.

*contest winner*

## Coastal Bend Redfish with Shrimp and Crab

½ pound unpeeled, large fresh shrimp
1 cup Beurre Blanc
⅓ cup tomato puree
1 teaspoon sugar
1 teaspoon garlic salt
2 shallots, minced
1 small jalapeño pepper, seeded and minced
¼ cup olive oil, divided
2 plum tomatoes, peeled, seeded, and diced
½ pound fresh jumbo lump crabmeat

4 (6- to 8-ounce) redfish or red snapper fillets, skinned
1 teaspoon salt
1 teaspoon black pepper
12 asparagus spears, cooked
8 small carrots, sliced and cooked
2 zucchini, sliced and cooked
2 large plum tomatoes, seeded and chopped
½ cup grated fontina cheese
Garnish: fresh chopped cilantro

- Peel shrimp, and devein, if desired; chop, and set aside.
- Whisk together Beurre Blanc and next 3 ingredients.
- Sauté shallots and jalapeño in 2 tablespoons hot oil in a large skillet over medium heat 1 minute. Add shrimp, and cook 1 minute or just until shrimp turn pink. Add diced tomato; sauté 30 seconds. Stir in crabmeat and Beurre Blanc mixture; keep warm.
- Brush fillets with remaining 2 tablespoons olive oil; sprinkle with salt and black pepper. Place on a broiling rack in a roasting pan.
- Broil 4 inches from heat 2 minutes on each side or until fish flakes with a fork. Remove to a serving platter. Arrange asparagus and next 3 ingredients around fillets; sprinkle with cheese. Serve with shrimp mixture; garnish, if desired. Yield: 4 servings.

## Beurre Blanc:

| | |
|---|---|
| ¾  cup dry white vermouth | ½  cup butter or margarine, cut into pieces |
| 2  shallots, minced | 1  tablespoon fresh lemon juice |
| 2  tablespoons white wine vinegar | ½  teaspoon salt |
| ¾  cup whipping cream | ⅛  teaspoon ground white pepper |

• Bring first 3 ingredients to a boil in a small saucepan; cook 15 minutes or until liquid is reduced to ¼ cup. Stir in cream, and cook 10 minutes or until liquid is reduced to ⅓ cup. Reduce heat, and whisk in butter, 1 tablespoon at a time; cook, whisking constantly, 5 minutes or until sauce thickens. Stir in lemon juice, salt, and pepper. Yield: 2 cups.

*Peter Halferty*
*Corpus Christi, Texas*

*cook's secret*... Halve the Beurre Blanc recipe if you don't want any left over. The sauce is also great served with steamed fresh veggies.

### Scaling and Filleting a Fish

**To scale a fish,** hold the fish by the tail, and scrape the back of the knife against the scales toward the head. It's a messy job, so work outdoors or cover the area with newspaper.

**To fillet a fish,** hold the knife parallel to the fish and the cutting board; cut lengthwise as close to the backbone as possible. Repeat on the other side.

A quick-and-easy way to cook, poaching is a good way to prepare fragile foods, such as fish. The food is submerged in a cooking liquid, such as court-bouillon, and simmered until it's done. Our Test Kitchens staff created a perfectly seasoned Court-Bouillon to impart taste-tempting, delicate flavor to poached foods.

## Poached Salmon with Yellow Pepper Sauce

| | | | |
|---|---|---|---|
| 2 | large yellow bell peppers | 1 | teaspoon chopped fresh dill |
| 4 | (4-ounce) salmon fillets | ¼ | teaspoon salt |
| 2 | cups Court-Bouillon* | ¼ | teaspoon freshly ground pepper |
| 1 | tablespoon olive oil | | |

• Broil bell peppers on an aluminum foil-lined baking sheet 5 inches from heat about 5 minutes on each side or until peppers look blistered.

• Place peppers in a zip-top plastic bag; seal and let stand 10 minutes to loosen skins. Peel peppers; remove and discard seeds. Set aside.

• Simmer salmon and Court-Bouillon in a large skillet over medium heat 5 minutes or until fish flakes easily with a fork. Remove fish from skillet; keep warm.

• Skim foam from bouillon. Bring bouillon to a boil; reduce heat, and simmer 15 minutes or until reduced to ¼ cup.

• Process roasted peppers, bouillon, oil, and next 3 ingredients in a blender until smooth. Serve with fish. Yield: 4 servings.

*Canned low-sodium fat-free chicken broth may be substituted.

## Court-Bouillon:

*Use Court-Bouillon to poach chicken or fish or as a base for soup.*

| | | | |
|---|---|---|---|
| 12 | whole cloves | 2 | cups dry white wine |
| 1 | onion, peeled | ¼ | cup white wine vinegar |
| 2 | carrots, sliced | 1 | teaspoon dried thyme |
| 2 | celery ribs, sliced | 1 | bay leaf |
| ½ | cup chopped fresh parsley | 1 | teaspoon cracked pepper |
| 2 | quarts water | | |

- Insert cloves evenly into onion.
- Bring onion and remaining ingredients to a boil in a Dutch oven. Reduce heat, and simmer, stirring occasionally, 30 minutes; cool completely.
- Pour mixture through a wire-mesh strainer into a large bowl, discarding solids. Yield: 2 quarts.

*cook's secret...* Sealing the blackened peppers in a zip-top bag steams them and softens the skins so that they're easy to peel away with your fingers.

### Poaching Coaching

- Start with cold water to prevent skin of fish from splitting.
- Use only enough liquid to cover so that the broth will be concentrated.
- Keep the cooking liquid just below the boiling point of 212°.
- Poaching liquid can be reused. Strain it, skim off fat, and chill or freeze it for other poaching or to make soup.
- If the food you are poaching is going to be served chilled, cook it the day before so it can cool in the cooking liquid and absorb more flavor.
- Experiment with flavorings for poaching liquid. For fish or chicken, add herbs, citrus fruit juice or peel, lemon grass, ginger, or soy sauce. For apples or pears, use fruit juice as a poaching liquid and add allspice, cinnamon, cloves, or nutmeg.

Robert Stricklin, Executive Chef at Big Cedar Lodge in Ridgedale, Missouri, showcases the distinctive sweet flavor of trout in the recipes on these two pages.

*chef recipe*

# Sweet Onion–Stuffed Trout

| | |
|---|---|
| 8 medium-size red potatoes, cubed | 2 teaspoons pepper, divided |
| 16 bacon slices, divided | 4 (12-ounce) butterflied trout |
| 4 baby Vidalia onions, sliced | 2 cups all-purpose flour |
| 1 cup whipping cream | ¼ cup olive oil |
| 2 tablespoons butter or margarine | Vidalia Onion Sauce |
| 2 teaspoons salt, divided | |

• Cook potato in boiling water to cover 10 minutes or until tender; drain.
• Chop 8 bacon slices. Cook chopped bacon in a skillet over medium-high heat, stirring often, 10 minutes; add onion, and sauté 10 minutes or until tender. Add potato to skillet, and mash with a fork. Stir in cream, butter, ½ teaspoon salt, and ½ teaspoon pepper; cook, stirring constantly, until thoroughly heated.
• Sprinkle trout with ½ teaspoon salt and ½ teaspoon pepper. Spoon stuffing evenly onto 1 side of each trout; fold other side over stuffing. Wrap 2 bacon slices around each trout, securing with wooden picks.
• Stir together flour, remaining 1 teaspoon salt, and remaining 1 teaspoon pepper in a shallow dish. Dredge fish in flour mixture.
• Fry 2 trout at a time in hot oil in a skillet over medium-high heat 6 minutes on each side or until fish flakes with a fork. Serve with Vidalia Onion Sauce. Yield: 4 servings.

## Vidalia Onion Sauce:

| | |
|---|---|
| 2 baby Vidalia onions, sliced | ¼ teaspoon salt |
| 1 tablespoon olive oil | ¼ teaspoon pepper |
| 2 cups whipping cream | |

• Sauté onion in a large skillet in hot oil over medium-high heat 10 minutes or until tender; stir in whipping cream. Reduce heat, and simmer 15 minutes or until liquid is reduced by half. Stir in salt and pepper. Yield: about 3 cups.

*Chef Robert Stricklin*
Ridgedale, Missouri

*chef recipe*

# Cornmeal-Crusted Trout

| | | | |
|---|---|---|---|
| 2 | bacon slices, chopped | 1 | large egg, lightly beaten |
| 2 | tablespoons olive oil, divided | 1 | teaspoon salt, divided |
| ½ | purple onion, diced | 1 | teaspoon ground black pepper, divided |
| ½ | green bell pepper, diced | 4 | (12-ounce) butterflied trout |
| 3 | garlic cloves, minced | 2 | cups cornmeal |
| ¼ | cup fresh or frozen whole corn kernels | 2 | teaspoons ground red pepper |
| 2 | cups crumbled cornbread | 1 | teaspoon salt |
| 2 | ounces lump crabmeat, drained | 1 | teaspoon garlic powder |
| 2 | tablespoons chopped fresh cilantro | 8 | bacon slices |
| 1 | jalapeño pepper, seeded and chopped | | Picante Aïoli |

• Cook chopped bacon in 1 tablespoon hot oil in a large skillet over medium-high heat 8 to 10 minutes. Stir in onion and next 3 ingredients, and sauté 5 minutes or until tender. Remove from heat; stir in cornbread, next 4 ingredients, ½ teaspoon salt, and ½ teaspoon pepper.

• Sprinkle trout with remaining ½ teaspoon salt and remaining ½ teaspoon pepper. Spoon one-fourth of cornbread mixture on 1 side of each trout. Fold other side over stuffing. Stir together cornmeal and next 3 ingredients; dredge trout in mixture. Wrap 2 bacon slices around each trout, securing with wooden picks.

• Fry 2 trout at a time in remaining 1 tablespoon hot oil 6 minutes on each side or until fish flakes with a fork. Serve immediately with Picante Aïoli. Yield: 4 servings.

## Picante Aïoli:

| | | | |
|---|---|---|---|
| 1 | cup mayonnaise | ¼ | teaspoon salt |
| ⅓ | cup picante sauce | ¼ | teaspoon pepper |
| 3 | garlic cloves, minced | | |

• Stir together all ingredients. Cover and chill at least 30 minutes. Yield: 1⅓ cups.

*Chef Robert Stricklin*
Ridgedale, Missouri

*cook's secret...* Trout is available fresh and frozen, and you can buy fish whole or cut into fillets, or you can have the butcher butterfly it for you. Look for shiny, bright skin; firm flesh; and a clean scent.

Beverly and Tom Burdette vacationed within three blocks of their St. Simons Island beach house for about ten years before making it their own. "It's a family gathering spot with many memories," says Beverly.

Beverly's recipe for crab cakes is made even more special with the addition of her Red Pepper Rémoulade Sauce.

*regional favorite*

# Crab Cakes Our Way

| | |
|---|---|
| 1 pound fresh crabmeat | ½ teaspoon dry mustard |
| 6 to 8 saltine crackers, finely crushed | ½ teaspoon pepper |
| ½ cup mayonnaise | ½ teaspoon Worcestershire sauce |
| 1 large egg, lightly beaten | 2 tablespoons butter or margarine |
| 1 tablespoon minced fresh parsley | Red Pepper Rémoulade Sauce |
| 1½ teaspoons Old Bay seasoning | |

• Drain and flake crabmeat, removing any bits of shell.
• Combine crushed crackers and next 7 ingredients; gently fold crabmeat into mixture. Shape into 6 thin patties.
• Melt butter in a skillet over medium heat. Add crab cakes; cook 4 to 5 minutes on each side or until golden. Drain on paper towels. Serve with Red Pepper Rémoulade Sauce. Yield: 6 cakes.

## Red Pepper Rémoulade Sauce:

| | |
|---|---|
| 1 (7-ounce) jar roasted red bell peppers, drained | 1 tablespoon grated lemon rind |
| 1 cup mayonnaise | 1½ to 2 tablespoons grated or prepared horseradish |
| ¼ cup chopped fresh parsley | 1 tablespoon drained capers |
| ¼ cup dill pickle relish | ¼ teaspoon salt |
| 1 green onion, minced | ¼ teaspoon black pepper |

• Process bell peppers and mayonnaise in a blender or food processor until smooth, stopping to scrape down sides. Add parsley and remaining ingredients; process until almost smooth. Chill 30 minutes. Yield: 2 cups.

*Beverly and Tom Burdette*
Atlanta, Georgia

## Crab Cake Rules

• Start with absolutely fresh crab, preferably jumbo lump. Add an egg or some mayonnaise to moisten the meat; season to taste.

• Use your hands to gently add in just enough breadcrumbs or cracker crumbs to bind the mixture together; form into cakes.

• Place crab cakes on a baking sheet, and chill for at least an hour before sautéing or deep-frying. Cook them until slightly crusty and golden.

## Secrets to Removing Crabmeat

**1.** To get to cooked meat, first twist off the crab legs and claws intact. Crack the claws, and remove meat with a small cocktail fork.

**2.** Invert the crab; pry off the apron (or tail flap), and discard it. Turn the crab right side up again.

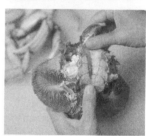

**3.** Insert thumb under the shell by the apron hinge; pry off the top shell and discard it.

**4.** Pull away the inedible gray gills; discard them along with internal organs. Break the body; remove meat from pockets.

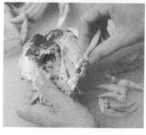

Back in 1948, Charlie Jaeger was one of the first businessmen to bring live crawfish out of the Atchafalaya Basin and into New Orleans on a large scale—some seasons selling more than a million pounds.

If you're familiar with crawfish boils, then you probably understand their importance as a culinary and social rite of spring in Louisiana. If you're not, Andrew Jaeger's House of Seafood in New Orleans reveals the finer points of cooking up these tiny freshwater crustaceans. He also shares his family's Secret Crawfish Boil recipe.

*regional favorite*

## Andrew's Secret Crawfish Boil

| | |
|---|---|
| 1½ gallons water | 1 tablespoon red pepper flakes |
| 10 bay leaves | 1 tablespoon black peppercorns |
| 1 cup salt | 1 teaspoon whole cloves |
| ¾ cup ground red pepper | 4 celery ribs, quartered |
| ¼ cup whole allspice | 3 medium-size onions, halved |
| 2 tablespoons mustard seeds | 3 garlic bulbs, halved crosswise |
| 1 tablespoon coriander seeds | 5 pounds crawfish |
| 1 tablespoon dill seeds | |

- Bring 1½ gallons water to a boil in a 19-quart stockpot over high heat. Add bay leaves and next 12 ingredients to water. Return to a rolling boil.
- Reduce heat to medium, and cook, uncovered, 30 minutes.
- Add crawfish. Bring to a rolling boil over high heat; cook 5 minutes.
- Remove stockpot from heat; let stand 30 minutes. (For spicier crawfish, let stand 45 minutes.)
- Drain crawfish. Serve on large platters or newspaper. Yield: 5 pounds.

*Andrew Jaeger*
New Orleans, Louisiana

*cook's secret...* Each person has his own special way of doing things, but there are two important rules to remember when boiling crawfish. First, you only want to use live ones, so throw out those that don't move. Second, as far as the actual cooking goes, it's really a little boil and a lot of soak. (Overboiling crawfish makes them mushy, which is why the soaking stage is so critical.)

••• Soaking allows the seasonings to gently seep into the shells. The longer you allow them to soak, the more flavorful and spicy they become.

## Crawfish Étouffée

| | | | |
|---|---|---|---|
| ¼ | cup butter or margarine | ½ | to 1 teaspoon ground red pepper |
| 1 | medium onion, chopped | 1 | (14-ounce) can chicken broth |
| 2 | celery ribs, chopped | ¼ | cup chopped fresh parsley |
| 1 | medium-size green bell pepper, chopped | ¼ | cup chopped fresh chives |
| 4 | garlic cloves, minced | 2 | pounds cooked, peeled crawfish tails |
| 1 | large shallot, chopped | | Hot cooked rice |
| ¼ | cup all-purpose flour | | Garnishes: chopped fresh chives, ground red pepper |
| 1 | teaspoon salt | | |

• Melt butter in a large Dutch oven over medium-high heat. Add onion and next 4 ingredients; sauté 5 minutes or until tender. Add flour, salt, and red pepper; cook, stirring constantly, until caramel-colored (about 10 minutes). Add next 3 ingredients; cook, stirring constantly, 5 minutes or until thick and bubbly. Stir in crawfish; cook 5 minutes or until thoroughly heated. Serve with rice. Garnish, if desired. Yield: 4 to 6 servings.

*cook's secret...* 2 pounds frozen cooked crawfish tails, thawed and drained, may be substituted for fresh crawfish. For extra flavor, add the juices from the package of crawfish tails to the étouffée.

As we searched for the recipe for the perfect fried oyster, it quickly became apparent there is no true "regional" style or variation. So our Test Kitchens staff went to work, furiously frying up recipes from all over the South. By the time the deep fryer had cooled, it was Kevin Williamson's recipe that was the clear winner, receiving our highest rating.

"I use buttermilk because that's the way my mom always made them when I was a kid," says Kevin, chef/owner of Ranch 616 in Austin, Texas. "Go straight from the buttermilk into the flour mixture, and then right into the fryer. Serve them immediately so they stay hot and crisp."

*chef recipe*

## Southwest Fried Oysters

| | | | |
|---|---|---|---|
| 2 | pints fresh select oysters, drained | 1½ | teaspoons garlic powder |
| 2 | cups buttermilk | 1½ | teaspoons dried oregano |
| 1 | cup all-purpose flour | ½ | teaspoon dry mustard |
| ½ | cup yellow cornmeal | ½ | teaspoon salt |
| 1 | tablespoon paprika | ½ | teaspoon ground black pepper |
| 1½ | teaspoons chili powder | | Vegetable oil |
| 1½ | teaspoons ground red pepper | | |

• Combine oysters and buttermilk in a large shallow dish or zip-top plastic bag. Cover or seal, and chill at least 2 hours. Drain oysters well.
• Combine flour, cornmeal, and next 8 ingredients. Dredge oysters in flour mixture, shaking off excess.
• Pour oil to a depth of 1 inch into a Dutch oven; heat to 370°. Fry oysters, in batches, 3 minutes or until golden. Drain on paper towels. Serve immediately. Yield: 4 to 6 servings.

*Chef Kevin Williamson*
*Austin, Texas*

*cook's secret...* Heat oil to 370° so that when the oysters are added and the temperature drops, the oil will be right at 350°, the optimum oil temperature for frying oysters. By the time the temperature begins to rise, the oysters are done.

# Oysters Rockefeller

1 cup unsalted butter, divided
½ cup chopped Italian parsley
¼ cup chopped green onions
¼ cup fennel bulb, chopped
1 teaspoon chopped fresh chervil or
  tarragon
2 to 3 chopped celery leaves
2 cups watercress or baby spinach leaves
⅓ cup fine, dry breadcrumbs

2 tablespoons anise-flavored liqueur
¼ teaspoon salt
¼ teaspoon pepper
⅛ to ¼ teaspoon hot sauce
½ (4-pound) box rock salt
2 dozen fresh oysters on the half shell
Rock salt
Garnish: lemon wedges

• Melt 3 tablespoons butter in a skillet over medium-high heat; add parsley and next
4 ingredients. Sauté 2 to 3 minutes. Add watercress, and cook 2 to 3 minutes or until
wilted. Cool.

• Pulse parsley mixture in food processor with the remaining 13 tablespoons butter,
breadcrumbs, and liqueur until smooth, stopping to scrape down sides. Add salt, pepper,
and hot sauce.

• Fill pieplates or a large baking sheet with 2 pounds rock salt. Dampen salt slightly, and
arrange oysters on the beds of salt.

• Top each oyster with a spoonful of the parsley mixture.

• Bake at 450° about 12 to 15 minutes or until lightly browned and bubbly. Serve on a
bed of rock salt, and garnish, if desired. Yield: 4 to 6 servings.

NOTE: *For testing purposes, we used Pernod for anise-flavored liqueur.*

*cook's secret...* Rock salt is traditional but not essential to this dish. It
does stabilize the oyster shells so that they don't topple over.

For cooks who want to learn Chef Giuliano Hazan's approach to cooking—few ingredients, simple directions, quick results, and impressive taste—the cookbook author and his wife, Lael, lead food-filled pilgrimages to the 15th-century Villa Giona, near Verona, Italy. Students explore the flavors of the countryside and then return to the villa. Granted, the ingredients are the very best, but Giuliano, a new Southerner who lives in Sarasota, Florida, thinks you'll do equally well locating what you need for his recipes. "Amazing markets are cropping up in larger cities, and farmers markets are all around," he says.

*chef recipe*

## Risotto with Shrimp and Asparagus

| | | | |
|---|---|---|---|
| ½ | pound unpeeled, medium-size fresh shrimp | 1 | small onion, diced |
| 6½ | cups water | 2 | tablespoons olive oil |
| ½ | teaspoon salt | 1½ | cups Arborio rice |
| ½ | pound fresh asparagus, cut into 1-inch pieces | 1 | teaspoon salt |
| | | ½ | teaspoon pepper |

- Peel shrimp, and devein, if desired. Set aside.
- Bring 6½ cups water and ½ teaspoon salt to a boil in a 3½-quart saucepan. Add asparagus pieces, and cook 4 minutes. Remove asparagus with a slotted spoon, and set aside, reserving broth in pan over low heat to keep warm.
- Sauté diced onion in hot oil in a large Dutch oven over medium heat 6 minutes or until tender and golden.
- Add 1½ cups rice, and cook, stirring constantly, 2 minutes. Reduce heat to medium; add 1 cup reserved hot asparagus broth. Cook, stirring constantly, until liquid is absorbed.
- Repeat procedure with remaining hot broth, ½ cup at a time (cooking time is about 20 minutes). Add shrimp and asparagus pieces, and cook, stirring constantly, 3 minutes or just until shrimp turn pink. Remove from heat; stir in salt and pepper. Serve immediately. Yield: 4 to 6 servings.

*Chef Giuliano Hazan*
*Sarasota, Florida*
Adapted from *Every Night Italian* (Scribner)

Virginia Anthony takes advantage of frozen shrimp for a quick-and-easy pasta dish that takes only 15 minutes to prepare. Frozen shrimp come cooked or raw, unpeeled, tail on, or fully peeled. No matter what brand you prefer, be sure to shop for them at stores with high product turnover.

## Shrimp-and-Spinach Pasta

| | |
|---|---|
| 1 pound frozen, peeled and deveined medium shrimp | 1 (14½-ounce) can diced tomatoes |
| 1 (10-ounce) package frozen chopped spinach, thawed | 1 (14-ounce) can chicken broth |
| ½ medium onion, diced | 1 teaspoon Greek seasoning |
| 1 tablespoon olive oil | 1 (8-ounce) package angel hair pasta, cooked |
| | ½ (4-ounce) package crumbled feta cheese |

• Thaw shrimp according to package directions.

• Drain spinach well, pressing between paper towels, and set aside.

• Sauté onion in hot oil in a large skillet over medium-high heat 5 minutes or until tender. Stir in tomatoes, broth, and Greek seasoning; bring to a boil, and cook, stirring occasionally, 10 minutes.

• Add shrimp; cook 2 minutes. Stir in spinach. Spoon over pasta; sprinkle with cheese, and serve immediately. Yield: 4 servings.

*Virginia Anthony*
Jacksonville, Florida

*cook's secret*... Avoid bags of frozen shrimp with excess ice, particularly in clumps, which is a telltale sign the shrimp has thawed and refrozen.

# salads

# Top 10 Best Kept Salad Secrets

**1.** Dressing clings better to dry leaves of lettuce, offering better flavor. If you're making salad for company, wash and spin your greens in the morning. Then wrap them in paper towels, store in a zip-top plastic bag, and chill until ready to use. They'll keep this way for about 3 days.

**2.** For the freshest flavor and texture from ready-to-eat bagged salad greens, soak the greens in cold water a few minutes; then spin them dry.

**3.** Perk up the flavor of winter tomatoes with a sprinkle of fresh lemon juice, and serve them at room temperature.

**4.** To refresh tired broccoli, cauliflower, or shriveled green beans, drop into a bowl of water with a few ice cubes. Thirty minutes will do the trick for most sliced or chopped produce, but overnight is best for sturdier broccoli and cauliflower cut into large pieces.

**5.** When a recipe calls for chopped celery, try this method: Keeping the stalk intact, start at the top and slice across all the ribs until you've chopped the desired amount. This way you'll chop just enough without having leftover pieces that usually get thrown away.

**6.** Boost commercial salad dressings by stirring in fresh mint, basil, oregano, garlic, or shallots.

**7.** Homemade salad dressings can usually be made ahead and chilled for several days, assuming they don't contain extremely delicate or perishable ingredients. Allow oil-and-vinegar dressings to return to room temperature before serving. Shake them vigorously before serving to blend ingredients.

**8.** If you're out of croutons or want to try something different, sprinkle green salads with toasted almonds, pecans, walnuts, or sunflower kernels. Even small types of cereal seasoned and toasted like croutons add a tasty flavor.

**9.** Chilling the salad plates or serving bowl will keep salad greens crisp longer.

**10.** Don't freeze a gelatin salad that contains fruits and vegetables. The low temperatures can extract liquid from the fruits and vegetables, leaving you with a soupy salad.

ersis Schlosser views cooking as one of her many artistic talents, along with calligraphy and drawing. "I read lots of cookbooks and magazines," she says, "and I come across a variety of ingredients that I'd like to try. For example, I thought about pears and raspberries together and decided to combine them in a salad." Her recipe was the Grand Prize Winner in our 2000 *Southern Living* Holiday Recipe Contest.

*contest winner*

## Pear Salad with Raspberry Cream

| | |
|---|---|
| ¾ cup sour cream | 1 head Bibb lettuce, torn |
| ¼ cup raspberry preserves | 1 small head romaine lettuce, torn |
| 3 tablespoons red wine vinegar | ½ cup freshly shredded Parmesan cheese |
| ⅛ teaspoon Dijon mustard | 6 bacon slices, cooked and crumbled |
| 4 firm, ripe pears | ½ cup fresh raspberries |
| 2 tablespoons lemon juice | |

- Whisk together first 4 ingredients. Set dressing aside.
- Peel pears, if desired; quarter pears. Brush with lemon juice.
- Arrange lettuces on 4 plates. Arrange pear quarters over lettuce. Drizzle with dressing; sprinkle with cheese, bacon, and raspberries. Yield: 4 servings.

*Persis Schlosser*
Denver, Colorado

*cook's secret*... Brush the pear slices with lemon juice as soon as you cut them. The acidity of the lemon juice prevents the pear from darkening.

### Perfect Pears

- Anjou is best eaten fresh or poached. It's not a good candidate for pies or canning.
- Bartlett pears are thin skinned, juicy when very ripe, and highly versatile.
- Bosc is great for poaching or using in pies, muffins, and preserves.
- Comice is excellent for eating out of hand and in salads. It doesn't hold up well when cooked.
- Keep pears at room temperature up to 1 week; store ripe ones in the refrigerator 2 to 3 days.
- Remember to peel very ripe pears before cooking because the skin will become bitter and tough.

After years of encountering certain reader's recipes in our files, we greet these contributors as old friends. Janie Baur, who started cooking at age ten and loves to entertain, is one of those contributors. "Now, I love having friends over for dinner. They love being guinea pigs because they know it's bound to be something good," she says.

# Pear, Jícama, and Snow Pea Salad

| | |
|---|---|
| 1 cup fresh snow pea pods | 1 (2-ounce) package sliced almonds, |
| 1 firm, ripe pear, peeled | toasted |
| 1 small jícama, peeled | Vinaigrette |
| ¾ teaspoon lemon juice | |
| 1 (6-ounce) package fresh baby spinach, sliced | |

• Cook snow peas in boiling salted water to cover 30 seconds or until crisp-tender; drain. Plunge into ice water to stop the cooking process; drain.

• Cut peas, pear, and jícama into thin strips; gently toss pear with lemon juice.

• Layer snow peas, pear, jícama, and spinach in a salad bowl; sprinkle with almonds. Serve with Vinaigrette. Yield: 6 to 8 servings.

## Vinaigrette:

| | |
|---|---|
| ¼ cup balsamic vinegar | ¼ teaspoon coarsely ground pepper |
| 1 teaspoon sugar | ¾ cup olive oil |
| 1 teaspoon Dijon mustard | 2 green onions, chopped |
| 1 garlic clove | 2 tablespoons chopped fresh basil |

• Process first 5 ingredients in a blender or food processor until smooth, stopping to scrape down sides. Gradually add olive oil in a slow, steady stream, and process mixture until well blended.

• Stir in green onions and basil. Serve with salad. Yield: ¾ cup.

*Janie Baur*
*Spring, Texas*

*cook's secret*... To quickly slice spinach, stack several leaves, roll them up, and slice the roll. The spinach will fall into thin shreds.

# Christmas Ribbon Salad

*Our Test Kitchens staff took one of our favorite congealed salads and added cream
cheese to make a lovely pink layer. It's pretty enough for a holiday buffet.*

2 (16-ounce) cans pitted dark sweet
   cherries
2 (3-ounce) packages cherry-flavored
   gelatin
1 envelope unflavored gelatin
2 cups boiling water
1/3 cup sugar

1/2 cup port or sweet red wine
1/4 cup lemon juice
1 (8-ounce) package cream cheese,
   softened
1/2 cup pecans, chopped and toasted
Garnishes: whipped cream, fresh cranberries

- Drain cherries, reserving 1 cup juice. Chop cherries.
- Stir together gelatins and 2 cups boiling water until dissolved. Stir in reserved juice,
sugar, port, and lemon juice. Stir in cherries.
- Pour half of gelatin mixture into a lightly greased 10-cup ring mold or Bundt cake pan.
Cover; chill 2 hours or until almost set. Leave remaining gelatin mixture at room temperature while that in ring mold chills.
- Stir together remaining gelatin mixture, cream cheese, and pecans, blending well. Pour
over slightly set gelatin mixture in mold. Cover and chill 6 hours or until firm. Garnish, if
desired. Yield: 12 servings.

### Secrets for Unmolding Congealed Salads

- Lightly spray the inside of mold with vegetable cooking spray before filling.
- Be sure the salad is firm before unmolding.
- Loosen the edges of mold using a small knife.
- Dip bottom of mold in warm water for 15 seconds before unmolding.
- Moisten serving platter with a little water before inverting mold to help gelatin adhere to
surface. Invert and gently shake to loosen mold.
- If mold sticks, return to warm water for 5 more seconds, and try again.

For years, a group of five friends have managed to meet around the supper table each month—regardless of the circumstances. This began back in 1987 when Phyllis Jones, Stephanie McKee, Jan Tonroy, and Debbie Rubin met through a women's professional organization in Lubbock, Texas. They soon discovered that they had similar professional interests, and they also loved to cook. This prompted the women to meet each month for supper. At the second gathering, Debbie invited her former college roommate, Diane Earl, and "The Fabulous Five" was born. The group was kind enough to share one of their recipes with us.

## Cranberry-Apple Salad

| | |
|---|---|
| 2 tablespoons fresh lime juice | 1 cup walnuts, chopped |
| 2 teaspoons Dijon mustard | ¼ cup sliced green onions |
| ½ cup olive oil | 3 tablespoons sugar |
| 2 large Granny Smith apples, coarsely chopped | 1½ cups dried cranberries |
| | 1 head romaine lettuce, torn |

• Whisk together lime juice and mustard. Gradually whisk in oil.
• Place apple, walnuts, and green onions in a bowl. Pour dressing over apple mixture; toss to coat. Cover and chill 2 hours.
• Sprinkle sugar over cranberries, and toss to coat. Add to apple mixture, and toss. Line a serving platter with lettuce; top with salad. Yield: 4 servings.

*cook's secret...* Regular or diet lemon-lime soft drinks, such as Sprite and 7-Up, can also do double duty as a food preservative. To prevent apples or other fruits from turning brown after slicing, pour over sliced fruit if you're out of lemon. You can add a few ice cubes to help keep the fruit crunchy. The carbonated drink doesn't affect the taste.

*Patricia Haydel*
*Hammond, Louisiana*

"Fresh herbs, chiles, mustards, rich stocks, and wine are key elements in today's Southwestern recipes," says Renie Steves, Fort Worth cooking instructor and culinary consultant.

"The differences in Texas foods twenty years ago and today are vast. Flavors then were generally bland. A typical dinner might have featured fried chicken or chicken-fried steak and a hearty casserole or congealed salad," says Renie. "Now, we turn to a larger family of vegetables and fruits, and count on quicker, easier methods and techniques of cooking to produce big flavor."

Like so many elements of her home state, Renie's spirit and energy as a culinary leader are larger than life. Describing herself as "beyond friendly," Renie views working closely with aspiring young chefs as one of her greatest pleasures. High on her list of career rewards is the stint she served as consultant to the Fort Worth Independent School District, helping transform school lunchroom menus. Renie is the author of *Fort Worth Is Cooking!* and *Dallas Is Cooking!* which spotlight regional chefs and restaurateurs.

*regional favorite*

# Greens with Hot Chile Vinaigrette

| | |
|---|---|
| 8 ounces gourmet salad greens | 3 (¼-inch-thick) red onion slices |
| 1 cup loosely packed fresh cilantro sprigs | ½ jicama, cut into thin strips |
| 2 tablespoons thinly sliced fresh mint leaves | 12 large strawberries, halved |
| 2 tablespoons thinly sliced fresh basil leaves | ½ cup Hot Chile Vinaigrette |
| | 4 ounces roasted pepitas* |

• Combine salad greens and next 6 ingredients; drizzle with Hot Chile Vinaigrette, and toss gently. Sprinkle with pepitas. Yield: 6 servings.

*Pepitas are pumpkin seeds sold in many supermarkets and health-food stores.*

## Hot Chile Vinaigrette:

| | |
|---|---|
| ¼ cup raspberry vinegar | ½ teaspoon pepper |
| 3 tablespoons lemon juice | ½ cup extra-virgin olive oil |
| 1 teaspoon salt | ½ cup hot chile oil |
| 2 teaspoons Dijon mustard | 3 tablespoons minced fresh herbs (basil, |
| 2 teaspoons balsamic vinegar | rosemary, oregano, sage, mint, |
| ½ teaspoon ground cumin | or thyme) |

• Whisk together first 7 ingredients. Gradually whisk in olive and chile oils. Stir in desired fresh herbs. Chill. Yield: 1½ cups.

*Renie Steves*
Fort Worth, Texas

**cook's secret...** If you can't find chile oil for the vinaigrette, steep several split fresh jalapeño or serrano peppers in olive oil for 1 to 2 days.

# Old-Fashioned Layered Salad

*Use a glass bowl or other see-through container*
*to show off the colorful layers of this salad.*

| | |
|---|---|
| 1 cup mayonnaise | 2 cups (8 ounces) shredded Swiss cheese |
| 1 cup salad dressing | 1 (10-ounce) package frozen green peas, |
| 1 tablespoon milk | thawed |
| 1 teaspoon dry mustard | 1 medium-size red onion, diced |
| ½ teaspoon salt | 6 hard-cooked eggs, chopped |
| ½ teaspoon pepper | 1½ cups chopped smoked turkey or bacon |
| 1 head romaine or iceberg lettuce, coarsely | 1 large cucumber, seeded and chopped |
| chopped | (optional) |

• Stir together first 6 ingredients.
• Layer half each of lettuce, next 5 ingredients, and, if desired, cucumber in a bowl. Spread half of dressing over top; repeat layers. Cover and chill 8 hours. Toss salad when ready to serve. Yield: 8 servings.

**NOTE:** *For testing purposes only, we used Miracle Whip Salad Dressing.*

*Amanda Whitsel*
*Hull, Georgia*

*cook's secret...* For layered salads, use fresh, crisp vegetables to handle the weight of the other ingredients as the salad chills. A layered salad is a great make-ahead recipe as chill times for mayonnaise-based dressings can go the distance (up to 8 hours).

# Southern-Style Cobb Salad

*Sugar snap peas are one of spring's most delicious and adaptable vegetables.*
*And like snow peas, you can enjoy the entire pod. Enjoy them in this crisp salad,*
*which is our Test Kitchens' Southern version of the California Cobb Salad.*

| | |
|---|---|
| ½ to 1 pound fresh sugar snap peas | 2 skinned and boned chicken breast |
| 2 heads iceberg lettuce | halves, cooked and sliced |
| 3 hard-cooked eggs | 12 bacon slices, cooked and crumbled |
| 4 plum tomatoes | Blue Cheese–Buttermilk Dressing |
| 1 large avocado | Freshly ground pepper |
| 1 bunch fresh watercress, torn | Garnish: edible flowers |

- Cook peas in boiling water to cover 2 to 3 minutes; drain. Plunge into ice water to stop the cooking process; drain and set aside.
- Cut iceberg lettuce into 6 wedges. Coarsely chop eggs. Remove and discard pulp from tomatoes, and cut into thin strips. Dice avocado.
- Arrange watercress on 6 salad plates. Top with peas, chopped eggs, tomato strips, avocado, and chicken; sprinkle with bacon. Place a lettuce wedge on each plate. Drizzle with Blue Cheese–Buttermilk Dressing; sprinkle with pepper. Garnish with edible flowers, if desired. Yield: 6 servings.

## Blue Cheese–Buttermilk Dressing:

| | |
|---|---|
| 1 (4-ounce) package crumbled blue cheese | ½ to ⅔ cup light mayonnaise |
| | 3 to 4 tablespoons lemon juice |
| 1 cup fat-free buttermilk | 1 garlic clove, minced |

- Stir together all ingredients in a bowl. Serve over salad. Yield: 1¾ cups.

*cook's secret...* If you're a sugar snap purist, simply cook the pods in boiling water for 2 to 3 minutes and then plunge into ice water to stop the cooking process. (Do not overcook.) Toss with a touch of butter, and, if desired, add some grated lemon rind and chopped red bell pepper for a colorful side dish.

*Joy Zacharia*
Associate Foods Editor

### Pea Pointers
- The peak spring harvest for sugar snap peas—a cross between sweet green peas and snow peas—is from April to June.
- Choose bright green, tender pods that are glossy, firm, and plump. Avoid peas with any marks, soft spots, or yellowish color.
- Sugar snap peas have thin strings that can be removed before cooking, if desired. Simply snap off the stem end, pull strings from each side, and rinse.
- Serve soon after purchasing. Store in a zip-top plastic bag in your refrigerator's vegetable bin up to 3 days.
- To freeze, cook in boiling water for 2 minutes. Plunge into ice water, and drain. Pack into airtight containers or zip-top freezer bags. Label and freeze up to 1 year.

This salad is a specialty of the house at Chef Franklin Biggs's Homewood Gourmet restaurant. Test Kitchens Director Lyda Jones says it's one of the recipes her friends request most.

*chef recipe*

# Baby Blue Salad

¾ pound mixed salad greens
Balsamic Vinaigrette
4 ounces blue cheese, crumbled

2 oranges, peeled and thinly sliced
1 pint fresh strawberries, quartered
Sweet-and-Spicy Pecans

• Toss greens with Balsamic Vinaigrette and crumbled blue cheese. Place on 6 individual plates. Arrange orange slices over greens; sprinkle with strawberries, and top with Sweet-and-Spicy Pecans. Yield: 6 servings.

## Balsamic Vinaigrette:

½ cup balsamic vinegar
3 tablespoons Dijon mustard
3 tablespoons honey
2 garlic cloves, minced

2 small shallots, minced
¼ teaspoon salt
¼ teaspoon pepper
1 cup olive oil

• Whisk together first 7 ingredients until blended. Gradually whisk in oil. Yield: 1⅔ cups.

## Sweet-and-Spicy Pecans:

¼ cup sugar
1 cup warm water
1 cup pecan halves

2 tablespoons sugar
1 tablespoon chili powder
⅛ teaspoon ground red pepper

• Stir together ¼ cup sugar and 1 cup warm water until sugar dissolves. Add pecans; soak 10 minutes. Drain, discarding sugar mixture. Combine 2 tablespoons sugar, chili powder, and red pepper. Add pecans, tossing to coat. Place pecans on a lightly greased baking sheet.
• Bake at 350° for 10 minutes or until pecans are golden brown, stirring once. Yield: 1 cup.

*Chef Franklin Biggs*
Homewood, Alabama

*cook's secret...* The spicy nuts double as a great snack in addition to a topping for the salad. Better make two batches if you like to nibble.

# Warm Goat Cheese Salad

*This recipe from our 1997 Recipe Hall of Fame is a hands-down staff favorite.*

| | |
|---|---|
| ½ cup olive oil | 1½ tablespoons sesame seeds |
| ⅓ cup lemon juice | 3 (4-ounce) goat cheese logs |
| 1 tablespoon diced green onions | 1 large egg, lightly beaten |
| 1½ teaspoons Dijon mustard | 3 tablespoons butter or margarine |
| ½ cup Italian-seasoned breadcrumbs | 6 cups torn mixed salad greens |
| 1½ tablespoons grated Parmesan cheese | 12 pitted ripe olives, sliced |

- Combine first 4 ingredients; set aside.
- Combine breadcrumbs, Parmesan cheese, and sesame seeds. Cut each goat cheese log into 4 slices. Dip in egg, and dredge in breadcrumb mixture. Cover and chill for 2 hours.
- Melt butter in a large skillet over medium-high heat. Add goat cheese, and fry 1 to 2 minutes on each side or until browned; drain on paper towels.
- Toss greens with dressing; add olives, and top with warm goat cheese. Yield: 6 servings.

# Spinach-Pecan Salad

*Kathy Moss's family challenged each other to bring some new dishes to Thanksgiving one year, and this salad was her contribution. It was a big hit. As Kathy recalls, "No one in the family had ever thought of spinach for Thanksgiving."*

| | |
|---|---|
| 1 tablespoon butter or margarine | 1 large Granny Smith apple, thinly sliced |
| ½ cup pecan halves | ½ cup crumbled blue cheese |
| 1 tablespoon brown sugar | 2 tablespoons olive oil |
| 1 (6-ounce) package fresh baby spinach | 2 tablespoons white vinegar |

- Melt butter in a small skillet over low heat; add pecans and brown sugar. Cook, stirring constantly, 2 to 3 minutes or until caramelized. Cool on wax paper.
- Place spinach in a large serving bowl. Toss in pecans, apple, and blue cheese. Add oil and vinegar, tossing gently to coat. Yield: 4 servings.

*Kathy Moss*
Siloam Springs, Arkansas

*cook's secret*... To freshen and crisp, rinse bagged spinach, and toss it in a salad spinner just before serving.

Judy and Dave Juergens loved the Virginia location of their weekend getaway so much that they made it their permanent residence. "We built this house as our place to entertain," says Dave. "Nestled in the valley at Wintergreen Resort, it's the perfect spot for our casual approach to dining with a fabulous view."

When they gather on the patio or at a scenic spot, Dave usually prepares the food. "I love to cook for our friends," he says. " We always have great times together." Here are a couple of Dave's easy recipes—just right for casual gatherings.

## Fresh Asparagus Salad

| | |
|---|---|
| 2 pounds fresh asparagus | 1 teaspoon Dijon mustard |
| ¼ cup olive oil | ¼ teaspoon salt |
| 2 tablespoons balsamic vinegar | ¼ teaspoon pepper |
| 1 tablespoon lemon juice | 1 shallot, chopped (optional) |
| 2 teaspoons chopped fresh chives | 1 hard-cooked egg, chopped (optional) |

• Snap off tough ends of asparagus. Cook in boiling salted water to cover 2 to 3 minutes or until crisp-tender; drain. Plunge asparagus into ice water to stop the cooking process; drain and set aside.
• Whisk together oil, next 6 ingredients, and, if desired, shallot.
• Drizzle asparagus with vinaigrette, and sprinkle with chopped egg, if desired. Yield: 6 servings.

*Dave Juergens*
Wintergreen, Virginia

*cook's secret*... It's not size that determines the flavor and texture of asparagus: It's freshness. Select firm, bright green spears with tight tips. Store them in a zip-top plastic bag in the refrigerator. Plan to use asparagus within 2 to 3 days. If the bottoms get dry and tough, bend each spear near the cut end to snap off any tough, fibrous parts. A vegetable peeler also works well to remove tough exteriors.

# Tossed Spinach Salad

| | |
|---|---|
| 1 (10-ounce) package fresh spinach* | 1 cup garlic-seasoned croutons |
| 1 medium-size red onion, thinly sliced | 2 tablespoons grated Parmesan cheese |
| 2 hard-cooked eggs, chopped | Dressing |

• Toss first 5 ingredients in a large bowl; serve with Dressing. Yield: 6 servings.

*1 (10-ounce) package salad greens may be substituted for spinach.*

## Dressing:

| | |
|---|---|
| ¼ cup lemon olive oil | ½ teaspoon salt |
| 3 tablespoons lemon juice | ¼ teaspoon freshly ground pepper |
| 1 tablespoon red wine vinegar | 6 ounces Canadian bacon, cut into |
| 1 teaspoon Dijon mustard | thin strips |

• Whisk together first 6 ingredients. Add Canadian bacon just before serving. Yield: ½ cup.

**NOTE:** *For testing purposes only, we used Stutz Limonato California Extra Virgin Lemon and Olive Oil.*

*Dave Juergens*
*Wintergreen, Virginia*

*cook's secret...* Turn and slice each hard-cooked egg 3 times in an egg slicer to make neat dices that look pretty in this salad.

For almost thirty years, a group of sixteen friends from Midwest City, Oklahoma, has met once a month to share a meal and a good time. The tradition began with a birthday party. "We definitely have similar tastes in food and cooking," says Pat Padgham. "Plus, we're all pretty good in the kitchen, so that makes it fun." According to Pat, one of their favorite recipes over the years is her spinach salad recipe. It's also a favorite in our Test Kitchens.

*special occasion*

## Spinach-and-Strawberry Salad with Tart Poppy Seed Dressing

| | |
|---|---|
| 2 (10-ounce) packages fresh spinach | ⅓ cup sliced almonds, toasted |
| 1 quart fresh strawberries, cut in half | Tart Poppy Seed Dressing |

• Place spinach, strawberries, and toasted almonds in a large bowl, and toss. Drizzle with Tart Poppy Seed Dressing just before serving. Yield: 8 servings.

### Tart Poppy Seed Dressing:

| | |
|---|---|
| ⅓ cup sugar | ¼ teaspoon Worcestershire sauce |
| ¼ cup vinegar | ½ cup vegetable oil |
| 1½ teaspoons chopped onion | 1 tablespoon poppy seeds |
| ¼ teaspoon paprika | |

• Process first 5 ingredients for 30 seconds in a blender. With blender running, pour oil through food chute in a slow, steady stream, and process until smooth. Stir in poppy seeds. Yield: 1 cup.

*Pat Padgham*
*Midwest City, Oklahoma*

*cook's secret*... This dressing keeps up to 1 week in the refrigerator. Leftovers are tasty drizzled over any cut fresh fruit.

Talk with Jane Nackashi, or "Nana," and she'll say, "You're never too old to ask questions." Although she's been cooking for many, many years, Nana says she's still learning about food. Friends new and old often request (and sometimes beg) Nana to make specialties from her homeland of Iraq. Here, Nana shares her cucumber salad recipe which features an herbed yogurt dressing.

*time-saver*

## Creamy Cucumber Salad

| | |
|---|---|
| 1 cup plain yogurt | ¼ teaspoon pepper |
| 2 garlic cloves, minced | 4 cucumbers, peeled, seeded, and thinly |
| 1 tablespoon dried mint | sliced |
| 1 tablespoon dried parsley | Garnish: fresh mint sprig |
| ½ teaspoon salt | |

• Stir together first 6 ingredients. Add cucumbers, and toss. Garnish, if desired. Yield: 6 servings.

*Jane Nackashi*
Jacksonville, Florida

*cook's secret*... Sample this savory yogurt dressing over baked potatoes, in dips, or alongside spicy meat dishes.

Caroline Stuart, a third-generation Floridian now residing in New York, stays true to her Southern roots while putting a salad spin on this regional classic.

*make-ahead*

# Hoppin' John Salad

| | | | |
|---|---|---|---|
| 2 | celery ribs | 1 | teaspoon salt |
| 1 | yellow bell pepper | 1 | teaspoon freshly ground pepper |
| 1 | red bell pepper | ½ | teaspoon ground cumin |
| ½ | medium onion | ½ | cup red wine vinegar |
| 4 | (15-ounce) cans black-eyed peas, rinsed and drained | 2 | tablespoons balsamic vinegar |
| 2 | jalapeño peppers, seeded and diced | ¼ | cup olive oil |
| 2 | tablespoons chopped fresh parsley | 4 | bacon slices, cooked and crumbled |
| 1 | garlic clove, minced | | Garnish: chopped fresh parsley |

• Dice first 4 ingredients. Combine diced vegetables, peas, and next 6 ingredients in a large bowl.

• Combine vinegars in a small bowl, and whisk in oil in a slow, steady stream, blending well. Add to vegetable mixture, tossing gently to coat. Cover and chill 3 to 4 hours. Stir in bacon. Garnish, if desired. Yield: 7 cups.

*Caroline Stuart*
New York, New York

*cook's secret...* Stir the bacon into the salad just before serving to keep the bacon crisp. If you use precooked bacon, crisp it in the microwave according to package directions.

# Carrot-and-Dill Salad

2 (10-ounce) packages French-cut cooking
   carrots*
⅓ cup olive oil
¼ cup red wine vinegar
2 tablespoons lemon juice
2 tablespoons chopped fresh dill or
   2 teaspoons dried dillweed

1 shallot, minced
1 garlic clove, minced
1 teaspoon salt
½ teaspoon pepper
Garnish: fresh dill sprig

• Cook carrot in boiling water to cover in a medium saucepan 10 to 12 minutes or until tender. Plunge carrot into ice water to stop the cooking process; drain.
• Whisk together oil and next 7 ingredients in a medium bowl. Add carrot, and toss gently to coat. Cover and chill 2 hours. Garnish, if desired. Yield: 6 to 8 servings.
*2 pounds carrots, cut into 2- x ¼-inch strips, may be substituted.

Dorothy J. Callaway
Coolidge, Georgia

*cook's secret...* If your fresh-cut carrots from the supermarket look lifeless, revive them in a bowl of ice water.

## Carrot Tips

• Look for firm, smooth carrots with a deep orange color, avoiding those with cracks.
• Carrots are best stored in a plastic bag in the vegetable bin of your refrigerator.
• Keep carrots away from apples, which impart a bitter flavor.

On Sunday afternoons in Helena, Arkansas, three generations of the St. Columbia family share an Italian meal—with a few Southern accents. Joyce and Joe St. Columbia and their children and grandchildren agree that gathering around the table is family time, and nothing is more important. Joyce and Joe are third-generation Arkansans, but their Sicilian ancestry defines them—particularly in Joyce's cooking. Here, she blends Italian herbs with Southern tomatoes in a salad that combines the best of both cultures.

*editor's choice*

## Italian Tomato Salad

| | |
|---|---|
| 3 large tomatoes, chopped* | 3 tablespoons red wine vinegar |
| 1 small red onion, thinly sliced (optional) | ¼ teaspoon salt |
| 1 garlic clove, minced | ⅛ teaspoon pepper |
| 1 tablespoon minced fresh basil | ¼ cup crumbled Gorgonzola cheese |
| 1 tablespoon minced fresh oregano | Garnish: croutons |
| 3 tablespoons olive oil | |

• Combine tomato and, if desired, onion in a large bowl.
• Combine garlic and next 6 ingredients; add to tomato mixture, tossing to coat. Sprinkle with cheese. Chill 8 hours. Garnish, if desired. Yield: 4½ cups.

*6 plum tomatoes may be substituted for 3 large tomatoes.*

*Joyce St. Columbia*
*Helena, Arkansas*

*cook's secret...* "Cooking for family and friends is my way of showing love," Joyce explains. "When you watch them eating something you made and see the satisfaction on their faces, it fulfills everything. Even if you gave me a lot of money, I'd never be any happier than seeing people enjoy my food."

Brenda and Phillip Nunnery and Ann and Bill Dent have been friends for years. The couples, who share a love of great food and fine wines, used to cook together every Sunday. This activity led to them opening a restaurant and wine bar named Cuvée Beach in Destin, Florida. Now, they say it's a rare luxury when they can all relax together at the same time— and when they do get the chance, it's often the men who do the cooking. Here, Phillip and Bill share a recipe for a refreshing tomato salad.

*editor's choice*

## Charred Tomato Salad

| | |
|---|---|
| 8  large tomatoes | 3  tablespoons red wine vinegar |
| 2  tablespoons olive oil | 1  teaspoon kosher salt |
| ⅓  cup sliced fresh basil | ½  teaspoon freshly ground pepper |
| ½  cup olive oil | Garnish: fresh basil leaves |

• Cut tomatoes into quarters; remove and discard seeds. Pat dry, and brush cut sides evenly with 2 tablespoons olive oil.
• Cook tomato quarters, in batches, in a hot cast-iron skillet over high heat 1½ to 2 minutes on each side or until blackened. Remove from skillet, and cool, reserving juice from skillet.
• Toss tomato with reserved juice, basil, and next 4 ingredients in a large bowl. Cover and let stand, stirring occasionally, 1 hour. Garnish, if desired. Yield: 6 to 8 servings.

*Phillip Nunnery and Bill Dent*
Destin, Florida

*cook's secret...* Kosher salt is chunkier than table salt. To substitute table salt, use half the amount you'd use of kosher.

Anoosh Shariat, of Shariat's in Louisville, has cooked Italian, Tex-Mex, and French in his trek from Iran to Germany to Texas, yet the Persian influence of his mother's kitchen lingers with him today in the Bluegrass State. His business partner and wife, Sharron, encourages Anoosh to merge her North Carolina food traditions, the bounty of their home state of Kentucky, and his Persian passion for fresh herbs and spices. "It's kind of magical here. I can implement some of the flavors of my heritage with some of the Southern flavors I've come to love. The flavors of the world combine in our dishes," says Anoosh. "When I moved here, I learned about wonderful regional specialities, such as bourbon, Bibb lettuce, black walnuts, and burgoo. It was like, 'Hey, it's open season; I can experiment.'"

The result is such recipes as this salad. "I wanted to add a dimension to traditional fried green tomatoes," Anoosh explains, "so I used classic Persian flavorings, like cumin and mint—which you don't often find together in Southern food—and paired them with green tomatoes."

*chef recipe*

## Fried Green Tomato Salad

*Served on a tender bed of Bibb lettuce, tart and juicy fried green tomatoes are topped with fragrant Rose Vinaigrette.*

½  cup cornmeal
½  cup buttermilk
1  teaspoon dried mint
1  teaspoon ground cumin
½  teaspoon salt
3  large tomatoes, cut into ¼-inch-thick slices

Vegetable or peanut oil
2  large heads Bibb lettuce, rinsed and torn
½  cup toasted walnuts
Rose Vinaigrette
Garnishes: gourmet edible petite rose petals; chopped green, red, and yellow bell peppers; chopped red onion

• Whisk together first 5 ingredients in a bowl until smooth; dip tomato slices evenly in batter.

- Pour oil to a depth of 2 inches into a large heavy skillet. Fry tomato slices, in batches, in hot oil over medium-high heat 4 minutes on each side or until slices are golden.
- Arrange lettuce on 6 plates; top each with 2 tomato slices. Sprinkle evenly with walnuts; drizzle with Rose Vinaigrette. Garnish, if desired. Yield: 6 servings.

## Rose Vinaigrette:

| | |
|---|---|
| 3 large shallots, finely chopped | 2 teaspoons rose water (optional) |
| ⅓ cup red wine vinegar | ⅓ cup vegetable oil |
| 1 tablespoon honey | 3 tablespoons walnut oil* |
| ¼ teaspoon salt | |

- Stir together first 4 ingredients and, if desired, rose water; whisk in oils. Yield: ¾ cup.

*3 tablespoons vegetable oil may be substituted for walnut oil.*

*Chef Anoosh Shariat*
Louisville, Kentucky

*cook's secret...* For extracrispy fried green tomatoes, dip them in the batter twice.

When *Southern Living* Editor in Chief John Floyd told our Foods staff to get down to potato salad basics, he meant it: "No celery, onion, or pickle," he insisted. We could keep the hard-cooked eggs, however, even though some people consider them heresy.

Because John wanted readers to know that potato salad "is as easy as boiling eggs and potatoes and mixing them with mayonnaise," I found myself on a mission. I asked coworkers, family, and perfect strangers which ingredients they considered essential.

Opinions were strong—and strongly divided. In the 1906 edition of *New Southern Cook Book* (the earliest reference to potato salad I could find), E. P. Ewing added whipped cream to "make [the dressing] light." Other additions, such as pickle and mustard, are more common.

The brand of mayonnaise used is another area of strong personal preference. Duke's, Hellmann's, Blue Plate, and Bama all have passionate advocates. Some are regional favorites: Blue Plate is popular in Louisiana, for example, and Duke's is popular in South Carolina.

With all these considerations, finding a combination that would please many people offered quite a challenge. Then I remembered the wonderfully simple and delicious version my niece Michele Fipps makes. She "married into" the recipe when she joined the Fipps family of Johns Island, South Carolina. "Most of my husband's surviving sisters make this the same way," Michele told me. "The recipe came from their mother who called it 'poor man's salad.' We have it at every family gathering. I always make it right before we leave home because we like it warm or at room temperature."

Associate Foods Editor Mary Allen Perry came up with some variations to satisfy most people's idea of the perfect potato salad.

*Donna Florio*
Senior Writer

# Fipps Family Potato Salad

*Michele Fipps uses Duke's Mayonnaise and grates the*
*eggs on the largest holes of a cheese grater.*

| | | | |
|---|---|---|---|
| 4 | pounds baking potatoes (8 large) | 1 | tablespoon spicy brown mustard |
| 3 | hard-cooked eggs, grated | 1½ | teaspoons salt |
| 1 | cup mayonnaise | ¾ | teaspoon pepper |

• Cook potatoes in boiling water to cover 40 minutes or until tender; drain and cool. Peel potatoes, and cut into 1-inch cubes.
• Stir together potato and egg.
• Stir together mayonnaise and remaining 3 ingredients; gently stir into potato mixture. Serve immediately, or cover and chill, if desired. Yield: 8 to 10 servings.

*Michele Fipps*
Johns Island, South Carolina

**Red Potato Salad:** Substitute 4 pounds red potatoes (8 large red potatoes) for baking potatoes.

**Potato Salad with Sweet Pickle:** Add ⅓ cup sweet salad cube pickles to potato mixture.

**Potato Salad with Onion and Celery:** Add 2 celery ribs, diced, and ½ small sweet onion, diced, to potato mixture.

**Light Potato Salad:** Substitute 1 cup low-fat mayonnaise for regular mayonnaise.

*cook's secret...* Baking potatoes lend a mealy texture to potato salad, and red potatoes give a firmer, waxier texture. Take your pick.

The green beans of my childhood were cooked long and slow with ham or bacon. *Crisp* was not a suitable adjective for these beans, nor was bright green an acceptable color. In fact, if the beans were not cooked to regulation army green, some of the more suspicious among us would avoid them entirely.

As an adult, I had a life-altering experience: I was served crisp, *green* green beans, coated richly with butter and fresh dill. Such a prospect had never occurred to me (nor, it seems, to anyone else in my family).

I've since discovered that green beans actually cook quickly and partner well with a variety of herbs—from basil to tarragon. If the beans you select are tender and stringless, remove only the stem end, leaving the bean whole for visual appeal.

*Donna Florio*
Senior Writer

*make–ahead*

# Green Bean–Potato Salad

*This summery potato salad boasts added crunch from green beans.*

| | | | | |
|---|---|---|---|---|
| 2 | pounds red potatoes | | 2 | tablespoons Dijon mustard |
| 1 | pound fresh green beans | | 2 | tablespoons olive oil |
| ¼ | cup red wine vinegar | | 2 | teaspoons salt |
| 4 | green onions, sliced | | 1 | teaspoon pepper |
| 2 | tablespoons chopped fresh tarragon | | Garnish: fresh tarragon sprig | |

• Combine potatoes and water to cover in a large saucepan; bring to a boil over medium heat, and cook for 13 minutes. Add green beans, and cook 7 minutes or until potatoes are tender. Drain and rinse with cold water. Cut each potato into 8 wedges.

• Whisk together vinegar and next 6 ingredients in a large bowl; add potato wedges and green beans, tossing gently. Cover and chill 2 hours. Garnish, if desired. Yield: 8 servings.

*cook's secret...* We used stringless beans for this recipe. If you purchase beans with strings, be sure to remove them before cooking for best results.

# Green Bean Salad in Tomatoes

1  red bell pepper, sliced
¼  cup chopped fresh cilantro
¼  cup olive oil
3  green onions, sliced
3  tablespoons red wine vinegar
1  garlic clove, pressed
1  teaspoon ground cumin

½  teaspoon salt
¼  teaspoon black pepper
1  (15-ounce) can black beans, rinsed and
   drained
¾  pound small fresh green beans, steamed
6  large firm tomatoes
   Garnish: fresh cilantro sprig

• Combine first 9 ingredients in a shallow dish or a zip-top freezer bag; add black beans and green beans. Cover or seal, and let mixture stand 30 minutes.

• Cut a ¼-inch slice from top of each tomato; scoop out and discard pulp, leaving tomato shells intact. Invert tomato shells, and drain on paper towels.

• Place each shell on a salad plate. Spoon ¼ cup bean mixture into each tomato shell; spoon remaining mixture evenly on plates around shells. Garnish, if desired. Yield: 6 servings.

*cook's secret*... Choose bush beans for their tender, quick-cooking qualities and pole beans for long, slow-cooking dishes.

### Bean Facts

• There are 2 general types of green beans (also known as snap beans): **Bush beans** come in both round and flat varieties, are basically stringless, and are very tender. They grow on bushes, making them easy to harvest commercially. **Pole beans,** resembling runner beans, grow on vines trained on trellises or fences. Pole beans also come in round and flat varieties. Most have strings, but a couple of types are stringless. Because pole beans are labor intensive to grow and must be picked by hand, they often cost more and are not as widely available.

The Pafford family celebrates their heritage with an annual family reunion drawing around two hundred people. For over half of the fifty years that the reunion has been held, the family has gathered at Beverly and Carl Pafford's home in rural Nashville, Georgia. This recipe for Wild Rice Salad is among the Paffords' favorite reunion recipes.

*regional favorite*

## Wild Rice Salad

| | | | |
|---|---|---|---|
| 1 | (6.2-ounce) package fast-cooking long-grain and wild rice mix | ¼ | cup olive oil |
| 2 | cups chopped cooked chicken | ¼ | teaspoon salt |
| ½ | cup dried cranberries | ¼ | teaspoon pepper |
| 1 | Granny Smith apple, peeled and diced | 2 | green onions, chopped |
| 1 | medium carrot, grated | 1 | (2.25-ounce) package sliced almonds, toasted |
| ⅓ | cup white balsamic vinegar* | | |

• Cook rice according to package directions; cool.
• Stir together chicken, next 8 ingredients, and rice in a large bowl. Cover and chill 8 hours. Sprinkle with almonds just before serving. Yield: 6 servings.
*Red wine vinegar may be substituted for white balsamic vinegar.*
**NOTE:** *For testing purposes only, we used Uncle Ben's Long Grain & Wild Rice Fast Cook Recipe.*

*Brenda Pafford*
*Nashville, Georgia*

*cook's secret*... Wild rice isn't actually rice: It's a marsh grass that's expensive and takes longer to cook. Packaged long-grain and wild rice mixes speed up the cooking time and ease the expense while still contributing the firmer texture that characterizes wild rice.

This recipe from Betty Sims, a cooking teacher and former caterer, is for a quick, easy salad that is impressive enough to serve to guests.

*time—saver*

# Artichoke-Rice Salad

| | | | |
|---|---|---|---|
| 1 | (14-ounce) can chicken broth | 8 | pimiento-stuffed olives, sliced |
| 1 | cup uncooked long-grain rice | ½ | cup light mayonnaise |
| 1 | (12-ounce) jar marinated quartered | ½ | teaspoon curry powder |
| | artichoke hearts, drained | 1 | (8-ounce) can sliced water chestnuts, |
| 2 | green onions, chopped | | drained (optional) |

• Bring chicken broth and rice to a boil in a saucepan over medium heat. Cover, reduce heat, and simmer 20 minutes or until tender. Cool slightly.
• Stir together rice, artichoke, next 4 ingredients, and, if desired, water chestnuts; cover and chill at least 2 hours. Yield: 6 to 8 servings.

*Betty Sims*
Decatur, Alabama
Adapted from *Southern Scrumptious:*
*How to Cater Your Own Party* (Betty Sims)

*cook's secret...* Be sure to let the rice cool a little before stirring in the remaining ingredients to lend the best texture to this salad.

As I slipped off my shoes at the back door of Penpit "Penny" Koommoo's home, the aromas of steamed rice, sizzling meat, and chopped fresh herbs greeted me. Luckily for me, Penny, a friend and former colleague, invited me over for a hands-on Thai cooking class in her kitchen. Here, she shares one of her best recipes.

*Joy Zacharia*
Associate Foods Editor

# Spicy Beef Salad

| | | | |
|---|---|---|---|
| 1 | large tomato, cut into thin wedges | 2 | garlic cloves |
| 1 | large sweet onion, cut in half and thinly sliced | 1 | lemon grass stalk, coarsely chopped |
| 1 | cucumber, diced | ¼ | cup fish sauce |
| 2 | green onions, chopped | 2 | tablespoons fresh lemon juice |
| 1 | pound flank steak | 1 | tablespoon chopped fresh ginger |
| 1½ | teaspoons salt, divided | 1 | tablespoon rice wine vinegar |
| 2 | teaspoons ground coriander, divided | 1 | tablespoon vegetable oil |
| 2 | small fresh Thai peppers or serrano peppers | 1 | teaspoon sugar |
| | | | Mixed salad greens |
| | | | Garnish: sliced green onions |

• Combine first 4 ingredients; set aside.
• Rub steak with ½ teaspoon salt and 1 teaspoon coriander.
• Process remaining 1 teaspoon salt, remaining 1 teaspoon coriander, and next 9 ingredients in a food processor or blender until smooth. Chill dressing 1 hour.
• Grill steak, covered with grill lid, over medium-high heat (350° to 400°) 6 minutes on each side or to desired degree of doneness. Let stand 5 minutes. Thinly slice steak.
• Place steak and vegetable mixture in a large bowl, and drizzle with dressing, tossing to coat. Serve over salad greens. Garnish, if desired. Yield: 4 to 6 servings.

*Penpit "Penny" Koommoo*
Hampton, Georgia

*cook's secret...* Lemon grass is an essential herb in Thai cooking. It tastes like fresh citrus, has long leaves that are gray-green, and looks like a stiff green onion. If you can't find it, substitute 2 teaspoons grated lemon rind in this recipe.

Tamy White's main-dish salad can be ready to serve—from start to finish—in under 1 hour. You can serve it right away, or chill it and serve it cold.

## Beef-and-Lime Rice Salad

1 pound lean ground beef
3 cups water
½ teaspoon salt
½ teaspoon ground cumin
1½ cups long-grain rice
1 teaspoon grated lime rind

1 tablespoon fresh lime juice
Toppings: salsa, shredded Cheddar cheese, tortilla chips, sour cream, chopped tomatoes, chopped green onions, avocado slices

• Cook beef in a 3-quart saucepan over medium-high heat, stirring until it crumbles and is no longer pink. Drain and pat dry with paper towels. Wipe pan clean.
• Add 3 cups water, salt, and cumin to pan. Bring to a boil, and add rice; cover, reduce heat, and cook 20 to 25 minutes or until water is absorbed and rice is tender. Stir in beef, lime rind, and lime juice. Serve salad with desired toppings. Yield: 4 servings.

*Tamy White*
Hartwell, Georgia

*cook's secret*... This is a fun make-ahead salad to serve family and friends. Set up a buffet so that everyone can sprinkle on the toppings of their choosing.

Eleanor Gibson puts an Italian spin on traditional Southern cornbread salad in this main-dish salad feast. Leftovers lose texture, so prepare the amount you'll enjoy in a single meal.

## Italian Bread Salad

| | |
|---|---|
| 4 cups cubed French bread | 1 large head romaine lettuce, chopped |
| 6 tablespoons olive oil | 4 or 5 large plum tomatoes, chopped |
| 3 tablespoons red wine vinegar | 2 cups chopped smoked ham |
| 2 garlic cloves, minced | 1 (8-ounce) package fresh mozzarella |
| 1 teaspoon salt | cheese, cubed |
| 1 teaspoon dried oregano | 3 green onions, chopped |
| ¾ teaspoon freshly ground black pepper | |
| ⅛ to ¼ teaspoon dried crushed red pepper | |

• Place bread cubes on a baking sheet. Bake at 325° for 15 minutes or until lightly browned. Set bread cubes aside.

• Whisk together olive oil and next 6 ingredients.

• Reserve 1 cup bread cubes. Scatter remaining cubes on a large serving platter. Top with lettuce and next 3 ingredients. Drizzle with dressing, and toss. Let stand 15 minutes before serving. Sprinkle with reserved bread cubes and green onions. Yield: 4 servings.

*Eleanor M. Gibson*
Latrobe, Pennsylvania

*cook's secret...* For an Italian submarine sandwich flavor, substitute 1 cup thinly sliced salami, such as Genoa, for 2 cups ham in this main-dish salad recipe.

Norie Berndt is never at a loss for what to do with leftover holiday turkey. Here's a recipe that's a family favorite.

## Turkey-Walnut Salad

| | | | |
|---|---|---|---|
| 2 | cups chopped cooked turkey | 2 | celery ribs, sliced |
| ½ | cup dried cranberries | 1 | small red onion, chopped (about ½ cup) |
| ½ | cup light mayonnaise | ¼ | teaspoon salt |
| ¼ | cup chopped walnuts, toasted | ¼ | teaspoon freshly ground pepper |
| 3 | tablespoons chopped fresh parsley | | Mixed salad greens |
| 2 | tablespoons Dijon mustard | | |

- Stir together turkey and next 9 ingredients in a bowl.
- Cover and chill at least 30 minutes. Serve over salad greens. Yield: 6 to 8 servings.

*Norie Berndt*
Pearland, Texas

*cook's secret...* This mixture makes a lower carbohydrate meal when served over salad greens. For a heartier offering, it's great as a sandwich.

There's no mistaking the South's long-standing love of cornbread. It's usually enjoyed hot from the oven and slathered in butter. In those rare instances when you find yourself with leftover cornbread, try Jake Bagley's deliciously unique way to enjoy it as a key ingredient in a main-dish salad.

## Layered Cornbread-and-Turkey Salad

| | |
|---|---|
| 1 (15-ounce) bottle roasted garlic dressing | 1 (12-ounce) jar roasted red bell peppers, drained and chopped |
| ½ cup buttermilk | |
| 1 head romaine lettuce, shredded | 2 cups cornbread, crumbled |
| 1½ cups chopped smoked turkey (about ½ pound) | 8 bacon slices, cooked and crumbled |
| | 5 green onions, chopped |
| 8 ounces crumbled feta cheese | |

• Stir together dressing and buttermilk, blending well.
• Layer a 3-quart glass bowl with half each of lettuce and next 6 ingredients; top with half of dressing. Repeat layers with remaining ingredients and dressing. Cover and chill 2 hours. Toss salad when ready to serve. Yield: 6 to 8 servings.

**NOTE:** *For testing purposes only, we used T. Marzetti's Roasted Garlic Dressing.*

*Jake Bagley*
Orlando, Florida

**M**arion Hall uses only black beans in her version of this salad; we added black-eyed peas for Southern flavor.

## Black Bean and Black-Eyed Pea Salad

1   teaspoon grated lime rind
½   cup fresh lime juice (about 4 limes)
¼   cup olive oil
1   teaspoon brown sugar
1   teaspoon chili powder
½   teaspoon ground cumin
½   to 1 teaspoon salt
1   (15-ounce) can black beans, rinsed
    and drained

1   (15.5-ounce) can black-eyed peas, rinsed
    and drained
1½  cups frozen whole kernel corn, thawed
½   small green bell pepper, chopped
⅓   cup chopped fresh cilantro
    Romaine lettuce
2   large avocados, sliced
    Garnishes: lime wedges, fresh cilantro sprigs

• Whisk together first 7 ingredients in a large bowl. Add black beans and next 4 ingredients, tossing to coat. Cover and chill 30 minutes.

• Serve over lettuce; arrange avocado slices around salad. Garnish, if desired. Yield: 6 servings.

*Marion Hall*
Knoxville, Tennessee

*cook's secret...* Top this salad with grilled or deli rotisserie chicken, leftover steak strips, or canned albacore tuna for a hearty addition to this vegetarian salad.

sandwiches,
soups, and
condiments

# Top 10 Best Kept Sandwich, Soup, and Condiment Secrets

**1.** Consider the texture of breads and fillings when putting the two together. A moist chunky filling, such as chicken salad, will burst out of soft bread, and dry layers of filling will fall out of a hard, crusty roll.

**2.** You can make sturdy sandwiches, such as subs, ahead of time. Wrap them in heavy-duty plastic wrap, zip-top plastic bags, or aluminum foil, and refrigerate up to 4 hours. Don't make sandwiches with moist fillings, such as egg salad, in advance; they'll get soggy.

**3.** If you keep sandwich bread on hand, it stays fresher stored at room temperature 2 or 3 days rather than in the refrigerator. For longer storage, freeze it up to 1 month.

**4.** You can wrap and freeze most sandwiches up to 1 month in moisture-proof wrap. Most sandwiches thaw in the refrigerator in 4 to 6 hours. Avoid freezing sandwiches that contain hard-cooked eggs, sour cream, mayonnaise, lettuce, or tomato. These ingredients don't freeze well; wait to add them just before serving.

**5.** To jazz up canned soup, add a splash of wine or sherry, or sprinkle chopped fresh herbs on top.

**6.** Use a bulb baster to remove fat from the surface of broth or soup. Or wrap an ice cube in damp cheesecloth, and skim it over the surface of a soup; the fat congeals on contact and then is easily removed.

**7.** If you've added too much salt to a soup, simply drop in a peeled, raw potato and cook a few minutes. Then remove the potato before serving the soup.

**8.** To prevent mushy vegetables when making stew, add the quicker cooking foods, such as carrots or canned vegetables, after the meat is tender. Cook the vegetables only until fork-tender, usually about 10 to 20 minutes.

**9.** Don't skimp on sugar in canning recipes. The proper amount of sugar is important for achieving a good gel and for food safety reasons.

**10.** Freeze leftover flour-based and tomato-based sauces in rigid plastic containers, leaving ½-inch headspace. Thaw in the refrigerator or over low heat in a heavy saucepan, stirring often.

Muffulettas remain one of the enduring standards of the New Orleans food scene. Filled with layers of salami, ham, cheese, and olive salad, they are cold-cut competitors of the po'boy. A finely chopped olive salad makes a muffuletta unique.

Who created the first muffuletta is a matter of dispute, but food critic and historian Gene Bourg uncovered a likely scenario. He interviewed elderly Sicilians who had lived in the French Quarter for many years. "They told me vendors used to sell them on the streets, as did Italian groceries," he says. "The name refers to the shape of the bread. *Muffuletta* means 'little muffin.' Italian bakers made muffuletta loaves and sold them to Italian delis. The delis then wrapped the sandwiches in the same paper the bread came in, so the sandwich took on the name."

Central Grocery in New Orleans often gets credit for creating this classic Crescent City sandwich, but you can find delicious variations at other eateries, too, or use this recipe to create your own.

*regional favorite*
## Muffuletta

| | | | |
|---|---|---|---|
| 1 | (10-inch) round Italian bread loaf | ½ | pound sliced cooked ham |
| 2 | cups Olive Salad | 6 | Swiss cheese slices |
| ½ | pound sliced hard salami | 6 | thin provolone cheese slices |

• Cut bread loaf in half horizontally; scoop out soft bread from both halves, leaving a 1-inch-thick shell. Reserve soft bread centers for another use, if desired.

• Spoon 1 cup Olive Salad evenly into bottom bread shell; top with salami, ham, cheeses, and remaining 1 cup Olive Salad. Cover with bread top, and cut crosswise into wedges or quarters. Yield: 4 servings.

## Olive Salad:

- 1 (1-quart) jar mixed pickled vegetables
- 1 red onion, quartered
- 1 (16-ounce) jar pitted green olives, drained
- 1 (6-ounce) can medium pitted ripe olives, drained
- ¼ cup sliced pepperoncini salad peppers
- 2 tablespoons capers
- 1 tablespoon minced garlic
- ½ cup olive oil
- 1½ teaspoons dried parsley flakes
- 1 teaspoon dried oregano
- 1 teaspoon dried basil
- ½ teaspoon black pepper
- 1 (7-ounce) jar roasted red bell peppers, drained and coarsely chopped (optional)

• Drain pickled vegetables, reserving ¼ cup liquid.

• Pulse pickled vegetables 4 times in a food processor or until coarsely chopped; pour into a large bowl. Pulse onion 4 times in food processor or until coarsely chopped; add to pickled vegetables in bowl. Pulse olives and salad peppers in food processor 4 times or until coarsely chopped; add to vegetable mixture. Stir in capers, next 6 ingredients, reserved ¼ cup pickled vegetable liquid, and, if desired, chopped red bell peppers. Cover and chill 8 hours. Chill leftover mixture up to 2 weeks. Yield: 6 cups.

**NOTE:** *We used mixed pickled vegetables that contained cauliflower, onions, carrots, peppers, and celery.*

**Mini Muffulettas:** Substitute 4 (6-inch) French rolls for 1 round loaf. Spoon Olive Salad on the roll bottoms. Layer meats and cheese, and top with additional Olive Salad. Cover with tops of rolls.

*cook's secret...* Store leftover Olive Salad in the refrigerator for up to 2 weeks. Use in sandwiches, or serve with bagel chips.

P o'boy sandwiches are a New Orleans institution. A 1929 New Orleans streetcar strike inspired the owners of Martin Brothers restaurant to start making these sandwiches for the struggling workers, or "poor boys." They stuffed a whole meal into a loaf, wrapped it in butcher paper, and sold it for a nickel. Some say the restaurant made as many as one thousand sandwiches a day.

"I went through college eating these," recalls *Southern Living* photographer Beth Dreiling. Beth's recipe earned acclaim in our Test Kitchens.

# Shrimp Po'boys

| | |
|---|---|
| 2 pounds unpeeled, large fresh shrimp | Peanut oil |
| 1¼ cups all-purpose flour | ⅓ cup butter |
| ½ teaspoon salt | 1 teaspoon minced garlic |
| ½ teaspoon pepper | 4 French bread rolls, split |
| ½ cup milk | Rémoulade Sauce |
| 1 large egg | 1 cup shredded lettuce |

- Peel shrimp, and devein, if desired.
- Combine flour, salt, and pepper. Stir together milk and egg until smooth. Toss shrimp in milk mixture; dredge in flour mixture.
- Pour oil to a depth of 2 inches into a Dutch oven; heat to 375°. Fry shrimp, in batches, 1 to 2 minutes or until golden; drain on wire racks.
- Melt butter; add garlic. Spread cut sides of rolls evenly with butter mixture; place on a large baking sheet.
- Bake at 450° for 8 minutes. Spread cut sides of rolls evenly with Rémoulade Sauce. Place shrimp and lettuce on bottom halves of rolls; cover with roll tops. Yield: 4 sandwiches.

## Rémoulade Sauce:

| | |
|---|---|
| 1 cup mayonnaise | 1 tablespoon chopped fresh parsley |
| 3 green onions, sliced | 1 teaspoon minced garlic |
| 2 tablespoons Creole mustard | 1 teaspoon prepared horseradish |

- Stir together all ingredients; cover and chill until ready to serve. Yield: 1½ cups.

*Beth Dreiling*
Birmingham, Alabama

**K**im Cummins's fresh variation on the classic BLT features a tasty sauce made from avocados and lime juice.

## Southwest BLT Wrap

| | |
|---|---|
| ½ cup salsa | 18 bacon slices, cooked and chopped |
| ⅓ cup frozen corn, thawed | ½ head iceberg lettuce, chopped |
| 6 (8-inch) flour tortillas | Avocado-Lime Sauce |

• Stir together salsa and corn. Set aside.
• Top 1 side of each tortilla evenly with bacon, lettuce, and corn salsa. Drizzle with Avocado-Lime Sauce. Roll up, and, if desired, secure with wooden picks. Yield: 6 servings.

### Avocado-Lime Sauce:

| | |
|---|---|
| 1 avocado, mashed | 1 teaspoon chopped fresh cilantro |
| 4 teaspoons fresh lime juice | Salt to taste |
| ½ cup mayonnaise | Garnish: fresh cilantro |

• Stir together first 5 ingredients in a small bowl. Chill until ready to serve. Garnish, if desired. Yield: 1½ cups.

*Kim Cummins*
Birmingham, Alabama

*cook's secret...* Cook a lot of bacon the easy way—in the oven. Place it on the rack of a roasting pan, and bake at 400° for 20 to 25 minutes or until crisp. This leaves you time to prep the other ingredients.

ention "Hot Brown," and folks either look mystified, or the words
immediately call to mind an open-faced turkey sandwich
smothered in a delicate cheese sauce and topped with crisp bacon strips.
It originated at The Brown Hotel (now The Camberley Brown) in
Louisville in 1923.

The hotel's current executive chef, Joe Castro, comes from a big food
family: He and his brother, John Castro, executive chef at Winston's
Restaurant and a culinary instructor at Louisville's Sullivan University,
often cook together. "A little friendly competition is good," Joe says,
"but when it comes to the Hot Brown, we have varying opinions."
Joe wouldn't change the original recipe, while John believes ripe tomatoes
are key to the flavor of this dish. "The acidity in the tomatoes cuts the
rich cheese sauce," John says.

Here, we offer four versions. One of which is sure to please.

## Kentucky Hot Browns

| | |
|---|---|
| 8 thick white bread slices | 1 cup shredded Parmesan cheese |
| 1 pound roasted turkey slices | 8 bacon slices, cooked |
| Cheese Sauce | 2 large tomatoes, sliced and halved |

• Trim crusts from bread slices, and discard. Place bread on a baking sheet, and broil
3 inches from heat until toasted, turning once.
• Arrange 2 bread slices in each of 4 lightly greased individual baking dishes. Top bread
evenly with turkey. Pour hot Cheese Sauce evenly over turkey, and sprinkle with
Parmesan cheese.
• Broil 6 inches from heat 4 minutes or until bubbly and lightly browned; remove from
oven. Top evenly with bacon and tomato. Serve immediately. Yield: 4 servings.
**NOTE:** *A lightly greased 15- x 10-inch jellyroll pan may be substituted for individual baking
dishes. Arrange bread slices evenly in bottom of pan. Top evenly with turkey and Cheese
Sauce; sprinkle with Parmesan cheese. Proceed with recipe as directed.*

## Cheese Sauce:

½  cup butter or margarine
⅓  cup all-purpose flour
3½ cups milk

½  cup shredded Parmesan cheese
¼  teaspoon salt
¼  teaspoon pepper

• Melt butter in a 3-quart saucepan over medium-high heat. Whisk in flour, and cook, whisking constantly, 1 minute. Gradually whisk in milk. Bring to a boil, and cook, whisking constantly, 1 to 2 minutes or until thickened. Whisk in cheese, salt, and pepper. Remove from heat. Yield: about 4 cups.

**Biscuit Hot Browns:** Bake 4 large frozen biscuits according to package directions. Split biscuits in half, and toast. Substitute biscuits for bread, and proceed with recipe as directed.

**Southwestern Hot Browns:** Substitute 4 large, thick cornbread squares, split and toasted, for bread slices. Sprinkle 1 (4.5-ounce) can chopped green chiles evenly over turkey before adding Cheese Sauce. Sprinkle 1 cup (4 ounces) shredded sharp Cheddar cheese evenly over sauce. Proceed with recipe as directed.

**Hot Browns with Fried Cheese Grits:** Prepare 1 cup regular grits according to package directions. Stir in 1 cup (4 ounces) shredded extra-sharp Cheddar cheese until melted. Pour hot cooked grits into a greased 9-inch square pan. Cover and chill 8 hours or until firm. Invert onto a cutting board, and cut into 4 squares. Cut each square into 4 triangles (see below). Fry grits, in batches, in 2 tablespoons hot vegetable oil in a large nonstick skillet over medium-high heat 2 minutes on each side or until golden brown. Remove from pan, and set aside. Cook 2 large diced sweet onions and 1 tablespoon sugar in 2 tablespoons hot oil in skillet over medium-high heat, stirring constantly, 20 minutes or until deep golden brown. Arrange 4 grits triangles in a single layer in each of 4 lightly greased individual baking dishes; top with turkey, sautéed onion, and Cheese Sauce. Proceed with recipe as directed.

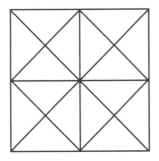

### Cutting Diagram
Cut chilled grits into 4 squares, and cut each square into 4 triangles.

For Lee Guinn and his wife, Jane, of Corpus Christi, Texas, a great day is one spent with friends and family aboard their sailboat, *Carpe Diem*. They stock its galley with tasty food, such as this Turkey Wrap, from their café and juice bar, Somethin' Healthy.

# Turkey Wrap

2   tablespoons ⅓-less-fat cream cheese, softened
1   (9-inch) spinach or tomato-basil wrap
1   tablespoon Dijon mustard
5   smoked turkey breast slices (about 5 ounces)

4   tomato slices
1   cup chopped fresh baby spinach
⅓   cup shredded Monterey Jack cheese
1   to 2 tablespoons chopped fresh basil

• Spread cream cheese over half of 1 side of wrap. Spread mustard over cream cheese and remaining half of wrap. Top with turkey and remaining ingredients; roll up tightly. Cut diagonally in half. Yield: 1 serving.

*Dickson Merkle, Jr.*
Corpus Christi, Texas

*cook's secret*... Use a very sharp serrated-edge knife to cut a sandwich neatly. This will prevent rough edges and squashed layers.

## Wrappin' It Up

The sky's the limit when it comes to creative sandwich wraps. For a variation, try wontons, tortillas, crêpes, several sheets of phyllo, refrigerated bread or pizza dough, or a sushi wrap called a handroll.

Dickson Merkle, Jr., the manager of Somethin' Healthy, brings along delicious offerings when he spends a day sailing with Lee and Jane Guinn. His Mediterranean Wrap and Garden Wrap are favorites.

## Mediterranean Wrap

| | |
|---|---|
| 1 tablespoon ⅓-less-fat cream cheese, softened | ⅓ cup crumbled feta cheese |
| 1 (9-inch) spinach or tomato-basil wrap | ¼ cup chopped tomato |
| ¾ cup chopped fresh baby spinach | 2 tablespoons sliced black olives |
| ½ small avocado, sliced | 1 to 1½ tablespoons chopped fresh basil |
| | 1 tablespoon wine vinaigrette |

• Spread cream cheese over 1 side of wrap. Top with chopped spinach and remaining ingredients. Roll up tightly. Cut diagonally in half. Yield: 1 serving.

**NOTE:** *For testing purposes only, we used Brianna's Blush Wine Vinaigrette.*

*Dickson Merkle, Jr.*
*Corpus Christi, Texas*

*cook's secret*... When tomatoes are out of season, consider using Roma, or plum, tomatoes. They offer quality flavor and texture even during the winter months.

## Garden Wrap

| | |
|---|---|
| 2 to 3 tablespoons hummus | ¼ cucumber, peeled and chopped |
| 1 (9-inch) whole wheat-and-honey wrap | 2 tablespoons chopped red bell pepper |
| ¼ cup shredded carrot | 1 tablespoon lemon juice |
| ⅓ cup shredded Monterey Jack cheese | ¼ teaspoon salt |
| ¼ cup shredded red cabbage | ¼ teaspoon black pepper |

• Spread hummus evenly over 1 side of wrap.
• Stir together carrot and remaining 7 ingredients. Sprinkle over hummus. Roll up tightly. Cut diagonally in half. Yield: 1 serving.

**NOTE:** *Hummus may be found in the refrigerated deli section of the supermarket, near the gourmet cheeses. We used preshredded carrots found in the produce section of the supermarket.*

*Dickson Merkle, Jr.*
*Corpus Christi, Texas*

Cooking teacher and former caterer Betty Sims is a master of entertaining. Her recipe for Portobello Mushroom Burgers puts a meatless spin on the classic burger.

*editor's choice*

# Portobello Mushroom Burgers

| | |
|---|---|
| 1½ cups mesquite wood chips | ⅓ cup chopped fresh basil |
| ⅓ cup olive oil | 2 tablespoons Dijon mustard |
| 1 tablespoon minced garlic | 1 teaspoon lemon juice |
| 1 medium-size red onion, cut into 6 slices | ½ teaspoon salt |
| 6 large portobello mushroom caps | ½ teaspoon pepper |
| 6 hamburger buns, split | 6 romaine lettuce leaves |
| 1 cup light mayonnaise | 2 tomatoes, cut into 6 slices each |

• Soak wood chips in water at least 30 minutes; drain.
• Prepare a charcoal fire on grill; scatter wood chips over hot coals.
• Whisk together oil and garlic; brush on both sides of onion and mushrooms.
• Grill onion and mushrooms, covered with grill lid, over medium-high heat (350° to 400°) 4 minutes on each side or until tender. Grill bun halves, cut sides down, 2 minutes or until lightly browned.
• Stir together mayonnaise and next 5 ingredients. Layer 6 bottom bun halves evenly with lettuce, onion, mushroom, mayonnaise mixture, and 2 tomato slices; top with remaining bun halves. Yield: 6 servings.

*Betty Sims*
Decatur, Alabama
Adapted from *Southern Scrumptious: How to Cater Your Own Party* (Betty Sims)

*cook's secret...* Refrigerate fresh mushrooms, unwashed, for no more than 3 days. They're best kept in a paper or cloth bag that allows them to breathe. Don't store mushrooms in plastic because this material causes them to deteriorate more quickly.

# Avocado Deluxe Sandwich

8  thin avocado slices

¼  cup Italian dressing

1  tablespoon mayonnaise

4  oatmeal or whole wheat bread slices,
    toasted

4  (1-ounce) process American cheese slices

8  thin tomato slices

1  cup alfalfa sprouts

- Toss avocado slices gently with Italian dressing; drain well, reserving dressing.
- Spread mayonnaise evenly over 1 side of each bread slice. Top bread slices evenly with avocado, American cheese slices, tomato, and alfalfa sprouts.
- Drizzle sandwiches evenly with reserved Italian dressing, and serve immediately. Yield: 4 servings

*cook's secret...* The easiest way to "pit" an avocado is to slice all the way around the pit and through both ends of the fruit with a chef's knife. Then twist the halves in opposite directions, and pull them apart. Tap the pit sharply with the knife, and twist the blade to lift the pit.

*Vanessa McNeil*
Test Kitchens Specialist

The popularity of pimiento cheese seems to remain largely confined to states below the Mason-Dixon, where it assumes its place as a Southern delicacy. "I've seldom met a non-Southerner who knew what it was," says novelist and North Carolina native Reynolds Price. But once the unfamiliar have a chance to sample this concoction, Reynolds adds, "they take to it on contact."

So what is pimiento cheese? To the uninitiated, it's little more than grated cheese, chopped pimiento peppers, and a little mayonnaise. However, to those fans who rank pimiento cheese right next to cold fried chicken and deviled eggs as essentials at any proper country picnic, it's so much more. To devotees, pimiento cheese becomes a must-have.

Admirers agree that sharp Cheddar cheese is the mixture's backbone. High-quality mayonnaise, such as Hellmann's or Duke's, is also a given. But the opinions begin to veer on the issue of texture. Southern cookbook author James Villas shares common questions regarding whether the cheese should be grated or mashed. If grated, should it be coarse or fine? If mashed, is the fork or the modern food processor the best tool?

Associate Foods Editor Mary Allen Perry happily agreed to share her secret recipe, but admitted, "My recipe was originally that of my great grandmother Kersh, who lived until she was 98 years old—slim, trim, and fearless of fat content."

# Pimiento Cheese

1½ cups mayonnaise
1 (4-ounce) jar diced pimiento, drained
1 teaspoon Worcestershire sauce
1 teaspoon finely grated onion
¼ teaspoon ground red pepper

1 (8-ounce) block extra-sharp Cheddar cheese, finely shredded
1 (8-ounce) block sharp Cheddar cheese, shredded

• Stir together first 5 ingredients in a large bowl; stir in cheeses. Store in refrigerator up to 1 week. Yield: 4 cups.

**Jalapeño Pimiento Cheese:** Add 2 seeded and minced jalapeño peppers.

**Cream Cheese-and-Olive Pimiento Cheese:** Reduce mayonnaise to ¾ cup. Stir together first 5 ingredients, 1 (8-ounce) package softened cream cheese, and 1 (5¾-ounce) jar drained sliced salad olives. Proceed with recipe as directed.

**Pecan Pimiento Cheese:** Stir in ¾ cup toasted chopped pecans.

*cook's secret...* The secret to perfect pimiento cheese is in the combination of textures that comes from a box grater. Each side grates a different size, so you really taste the flavor of the individual cheeses.

*Mary Allen Perry*
Associate Foods Editor

For over a dozen years, Doe Cote has served delicious, nutritious fare at one of Charleston's, downtown fixtures, Doe's Pita Plus. A transplant from Massachusetts with a love of Middle Eastern food, Doe says she opened the restaurant to fill a "big void" in her adopted hometown.

Her Avocado Salad–Hummus Pita pleases vegetarians and meat-lovers alike. Fresh Fruit Salad Pita is topped with tangy yogurt and brown sugar.

# Avocado Salad–Hummus Pita

Hummus
4 pita rounds, halved
Avocado Salad
Romaine lettuce leaves

Tomato slices
Alfalfa sprouts (optional)

• Spread ¼ cup of Hummus inside each pita half. Spoon Avocado Salad evenly into each half. Add lettuce, tomato, and, if desired, sprouts. Serve immediately. Yield: 8 servings.

## Hummus:

1 (15½-ounce) can chickpeas, rinsed and drained
3 garlic cloves, minced
⅓ cup tahini*

¼ cup fresh lemon juice
¼ cup water
¾ teaspoon salt

• Process chickpeas in a food processor until smooth, stopping to scrape down sides. Add garlic and remaining ingredients; pulse until blended. Yield: 2 cups.

*Tahini is sesame seed paste, found in the import sections of large supermarkets or in health food stores.

## Avocado Salad:

| | | | |
|---|---|---|---|
| 2 | large ripe avocados, coarsely chopped | 2 | tablespoons fresh lemon juice |
| 4 | large radishes, chopped | 2 | tablespoons olive oil |
| 2 | celery ribs, chopped | ½ | teaspoon salt |
| 2 | green onions, chopped | ¼ | to ½ teaspoon freshly ground pepper |

• Combine all ingredients. Cover and chill 1 hour. Yield: 2½ cups.

*Doe Cote*
Charleston, South Carolina

*cook's secret...* You can also use the Hummus recipe as a dip for lightly steamed or blanched veggies, such as sugar snap peas, asparagus, and carrots.
••• Cut avocados quickly turn brown. There's no foolproof way to prevent this, but brushing with lemon juice or an ascorbic acid solution helps.

# Fresh Fruit Salad Pita

| | | | |
|---|---|---|---|
| ⅓ | cup fresh orange juice (about 1 orange) | 1 | pint fresh strawberries, sliced |
| 2 | large oranges, peeled, sectioned, and coarsely chopped | 1 | pint fresh blueberries |
| | | 12 | pita rounds, halved |
| 2 | large apples, coarsely chopped | 1 | (8-ounce) container fat-free vanilla yogurt |
| 2 | cups green grapes | | |
| 1 | cantaloupe, cut into 1-inch cubes | 3 | tablespoons brown sugar |

• Combine first 7 ingredients in a bowl.
• Spoon ½ cup of fruit mixture into each pita half with a slotted spoon. Top each evenly with yogurt; sprinkle with brown sugar. Serve immediately. Yield: 24 servings.

*Doe Cote*
Charleston, South Carolina

*cook's secret...* The easiest way to section an orange is to slice off the top and bottom of the orange, and then stand it upright. Following the contour of the fruit, slice off the peel, pith, and membrane in thick strips. Holding the fruit over a bowl, cut along each side of the membrane between the sections, letting each segment drop into the bowl as it's sliced.

W̶e added fresh lime juice for tang and honey for extra sweetness to Dickson Merkle's recipe for chilled soup. For a pretty presentation, garnish the soup with watermelon balls and fresh mint sprigs.

*special occasion*

## Chilled Watermelon Soup

*If your watermelon is good and sweet, omit the honey.*

| | |
|---|---|
| 4 cups seeded watermelon cubes | ¼ to ½ teaspoon ground ginger |
| ⅓ cup apple juice | 1 tablespoon honey (optional) |
| 2 tablespoons fresh lime juice | ⅓ cup plain fat-free yogurt |
| 1 teaspoon chopped fresh mint | |

• Process first 5 ingredients and honey, if desired, in a blender or food processor until smooth, stopping to scrape down sides. Cover and chill 1 hour. Serve in individual bowls with a dollop of yogurt. Yield: 4 cups.

*Dickson Merkle, Jr.*
Corpus Christi, Texas

*cook's secret...* When spooning up a slightly sweet fruit soup, consider serving the soup in a variety of glass compotes or balloon wine glasses.

Sheryl Davidson's Creamy Avocado Soup can be prepared in only 15 minutes, and it requires no cooking. Chill the soup for 3 hours to bring out the best flavor.

*make-ahead*

# Creamy Avocado Soup

| | | | |
|---|---|---|---|
| 3 | avocados, quartered | 1 | teaspoon salt |
| ½ | cup coarsely chopped fresh cilantro | ¼ | teaspoon pepper |
| ¼ | cup coarsely chopped onion | ¼ | teaspoon ground cumin |
| ¼ | cup coarsely chopped green onions | ¼ | to ½ teaspoon hot sauce |
| ¼ | cup coarsely chopped fresh parsley | 1 | (32-ounce) container chicken broth |
| 1 | to 3 tablespoons lime juice | 1 | (16-ounce) container sour cream |
| 1 | teaspoon chili powder | | |

• Process avocado in a blender or food processor until mixture is smooth, stopping to scrape down sides. Add chopped cilantro and next 9 ingredients, and process until mixture is smooth, stopping to scrape down sides. Pour into a large bowl; stir in chicken broth and sour cream. Cover and chill 3 hours. Yield: 8 cups.

*Sheryl Davidson*
*Atlanta, Georgia*

*cook's secret...* For a lighter soup, substitute 1 (16-ounce) container of light sour cream.

ancy Petitt and her husband, Gary, are part of a handful of commercial chestnut growers in the South. "In the South, we tend to grow a Chinese variety, which is a little sweeter and easier to peel than European types," says Nancy. Chestnut trees are spread sixty-seven to the row on Delmarvelous Farms, a thirty-acre farm in the Delaware peninsula. The farm boasts over sixteen hundred chestnut trees, each hand-planted and nurtured by the Petitts.

There are a number of ways to prepare chestnuts, but roasting, which makes for a rich and creamy texture, is perhaps the best-known method. Chestnuts can also be prepared on the cooktop or in the microwave, Nancy points out. Her recipe for Chestnut Soup shows the nut's versatility.

## Chestnut Soup

| | |
|---|---|
| 1   leek | ⅛   teaspoon ground nutmeg |
| 3   tablespoons butter or margarine, divided | 2   (32-ounce) containers chicken broth |
| 2   McIntosh apples, peeled and chopped | ¾   pound whole chestnuts, shelled |
| 2   celery ribs, chopped | (about 2 cups nut meat) |
| 1   small onion, thinly sliced | 1   cup whipping cream or half-and-half |
| 1   bay leaf | 2   tablespoons all-purpose flour |
| 1   thyme sprig | Toppings: sour cream, grated fresh nutmeg |
| 1   teaspoon salt | (optional) |

• Remove root, tough outer leaves, and tops from leek, leaving 2 inches of dark leaves. Cut into quarters lengthwise. Thinly slice leek; rinse well, and drain.

• Melt 1 tablespoon butter in a medium saucepan over medium heat. Add leek, apple, celery, and onion; sauté 5 minutes. Add bay leaf and next 3 ingredients; sauté 8 to 12 minutes or until apple and vegetables are tender.

• Stir in chicken broth and chestnuts. Bring to a boil; reduce heat, and simmer 1 hour or until chestnuts are tender. Stir in cream. Discard bay leaf.

• Process leek mixture, in batches, in a food processor or blender until smooth. Return mixture to saucepan.

• Melt remaining 2 tablespoons butter in a small skillet. Stir in flour until smooth; cook, stirring constantly, 2 to 3 minutes.

• Add flour mixture to pureed mixture. Bring to a boil; reduce heat, and simmer 3 to 5 minutes or until thickened. Serve warm. Top with sour cream and grated fresh nutmeg, if desired. Yield: 10 cups.

*Nancy and Gary Petitt*
Townsend, Delaware

*cook's secret...* To peel a chestnut, cut an X on the flat side of the nut using a serrated knife, making sure you cut all the way through the shell. This keeps the shell from bursting.

### Cooking with Chestnuts
• One pound of fresh, unpeeled chestnuts yields about 3 cups of nut meat.
• One pound of dried chestnuts (which are always peeled) equals about 3 pounds of fresh, unpeeled nuts.
• Store fresh chestnuts in a zip-top freezer bag in the freezer or in the crisper of the refrigerator.

aroline Stuart's work as a full-time assistant to James Beard, considered by many to be the father of American cooking, led her to establish the James Beard Foundation, which promotes the culinary profession and offers more than $400,000 a year in culinary scholarships. Her Southern culinary traditions are evident in her recipes, such as this squash-and-shrimp bisque.

## Curried Butternut-Shrimp Bisque

| | |
|---|---|
| 1 pound unpeeled, medium-size fresh shrimp | 2 teaspoons curry powder |
| 3 tablespoons unsalted butter | 1 teaspoon dried thyme |
| 1 large yellow onion, chopped | 1 cup whipping cream |
| 1 (3-pound) butternut squash, peeled, seeded, and cut into ½-inch cubes | ¼ teaspoon salt |
| | ¼ teaspoon ground red pepper |
| 3 (14-ounce) cans chicken broth, divided | Garnishes: whipping cream, paprika |

- Peel shrimp, and devein, if desired. Set aside.
- Melt butter in a 4-quart heavy saucepan over medium-high heat; add onion, and sauté 7 to 8 minutes or until tender. Reduce heat to medium; add squash, and cook, stirring occasionally, 15 minutes or until tender.
- Add 1 can broth, shrimp, curry, and thyme, and cook 2 to 3 minutes or just until shrimp turn pink. Let cool slightly.
- Process mixture in a blender or food processor until smooth, stopping to scrape down sides.
- Return mixture to saucepan; add remaining broth, and bring to a boil. Stir in 1 cup whipping cream, salt, and pepper; reduce heat to low, and simmer 5 minutes. Garnish, if desired. Yield: 9½ cups.

*Caroline Stuart*
New York, New York

*cook's secret...* To peel shrimp, pull off the head, if it's still attached. Then pull off the legs on the inside curve of the shrimp, and peel off the shell, beginning at the top, by running your thumb under the section of the shell located between the legs. Using a small knife or shrimp deveiner, make a slit down the back of the shrimp, and remove the sand vein.

Tom Noelke, chef/owner of Gulf Coast Grill in Macon, Georgia, simmers corncobs with chicken broth for wonderful depth of flavor.

*chef recipe*

# Sweet Corn Soup with Crab

| | | | |
|---|---|---|---|
| ⅓ | cup diced salt pork | 4¾ | cups chicken broth |
| 2 | tablespoons butter or margarine | 2 | corncobs |
| ¼ | cup white cornmeal | 1 | pound fresh lump crabmeat, drained |
| 2 | celery ribs, diced | 1 | cup whipping cream |
| 1 | medium onion, diced | ¼ | cup chopped fresh cilantro |
| 1 | red bell pepper, diced | ½ | teaspoon salt |
| 1 | jalapeño pepper, diced | ¼ | teaspoon ground white pepper |
| 3 | cups fresh sweet corn kernels (about 6 ears) | | Garnish: fresh cilantro sprigs |

• Brown salt pork in a Dutch oven over medium heat; remove pork, and reserve for another use.

• Add butter to pork drippings in Dutch oven over medium heat; whisk in cornmeal, and cook, whisking constantly, 1 minute. Add celery and next 4 ingredients; sauté 2 minutes.

• Add broth and corncobs. Bring to a boil; reduce heat, and simmer 30 minutes. Remove and discard corncobs. Stir in crabmeat and next 4 ingredients; cook until thoroughly heated. Garnish, if desired. Yield: 10½ cups.

*Chef Tom Noelke*
Macon, Georgia

*cook's secret...* If you have just a few ears of corn, keep them in their husks in the refrigerator until you're ready to cook them. To store, dip unshucked ears in cold water, seal them in a zip-top plastic bag, and refrigerate up to 5 days.

Toppings that include avocado slices and boiled shrimp add tasty texture to Bill Dent and Phillip Nunnery's Gazpacho. Both men are great "grill cooks" and wine aficionados who actually help select the labels sold at Cuvée Beach, a restaurant and wine bar in Destin, Florida, co-owned by their wives, Ann Dent and Brenda Nunnery.

# Gazpacho

| | |
|---|---|
| 8 large tomatoes | ¼ cup fresh lemon juice |
| 2 cucumbers | 2 teaspoons salt |
| 1 large green bell pepper | 1 teaspoon paprika |
| 1 large yellow bell pepper | 2 to 3 teaspoons hot sauce |
| 1 small red onion | Toppings: sour cream, avocado slices, |
| 1 jalapeño pepper, seeded | croutons, boiled shrimp, chopped |
| 1 large garlic clove | fresh cilantro, chopped fresh mint |
| 1 (32-ounce) bottle vegetable juice | Garnishes: green and yellow baby |
| ⅓ cup red wine vinegar | tomatoes, fresh basil sprigs |
| 1 tablespoon grated lemon rind | |

• Peel tomatoes and cucumbers. Cut tomatoes, cucumbers, bell peppers, and onion into quarters. Remove and discard cucumber and bell pepper seeds.

• Process vegetables, jalapeño pepper, and garlic in a blender or food processor until almost smooth, stopping to scrape down sides. Transfer mixture to a large bowl, and stir in vegetable juice and next 6 ingredients. Cover and chill, stirring often, 8 hours. Serve with toppings, if desired. Garnish, if desired. Yield: 12½ cups.

*Bill Dent and Phillip Nunnery*
Destin, Florida

*cook's secret...* To peel a large number of tomatoes, cut a small X at the base of each, and drop into a pot of boiling water just until the skins begin to loosen (about 10 to 15 seconds). Remove the tomatoes with a sieve, tongs, or long fork, and hold under cold running water. The peels practically slip off.

# Butternut Squash–Lime Soup

| | | | |
|---|---|---|---|
| 8 | cups vegetable broth | ½ | cup canned diced tomatoes |
| 1 | butternut squash, peeled and cut into ¾-inch pieces | 4 | (6-inch) corn tortillas, cut into ½-inch strips |
| ½ | cup fresh lime juice | ½ | cup fresh cilantro leaves |
| 1 | teaspoon dried sage leaves | ½ | teaspoon black pepper |
| 3 | to 6 whole cloves | ¼ | teaspoon salt |
| 1 | garlic bulb, chopped and divided | 1 | teaspoon Dragon Salt |
| 1 | large onion, chopped | 1 | lime, thinly sliced (optional) |
| 1 | to 2 serrano or jalapeño peppers, seeded and minced | | |

- Bring first 5 ingredients and half of garlic to a boil in a Dutch oven; reduce heat, and simmer 20 minutes. Remove and discard cloves.
- Sauté onion in a large skillet coated with vegetable cooking spray over medium-high heat 5 minutes or until tender. Add peppers and remaining garlic; sauté 1 to 2 minutes. Add ½ cup broth mixture, stirring to loosen browned bits from bottom of skillet. Stir onion mixture and diced tomatoes into soup.
- Place tortilla strips on a baking sheet. Bake at 350° for 5 minutes or until crisp. Add cilantro, black pepper, salt, and 1 teaspoon Dragon Salt to soup. Ladle into bowls; top with toasted tortilla strips and, if desired, lime slices. Yield: 6 servings.

## Dragon Salt:

| | | | |
|---|---|---|---|
| ⅓ | cup coarse-grain sea salt | 2 | tablespoons paprika |
| ⅓ | cup coarsely ground black pepper | 1 | tablespoon dried basil |
| ¼ | cup ground red pepper | 1 | tablespoon celery seeds |
| ¼ | cup dried dillweed | | |

- Combine all ingredients. Store in an airtight container. Yield: about 1½ cups.

*Crescent Dragonwagon*
Eureka Springs, Arkansas
Adapted from Crescent's Lime Soup Yucatan from *Passionate Vegetarian*
(Workman Publishing Company, Inc.)

*cook's secret*... Dragon Salt is terrific as a dry rub for steaks, chicken, and pork chops. Try it sprinkled on hot popcorn, too. Or mix it in olive oil as a dip for crusty bread.

I learned to love soups because of my mother," says Mary Treviño, founder of El Mirador, a landmark San Antonio restaurant. "She was from Guanajuato, Mexico, and didn't have much money, so she had to be creative. Soups were a great way to make dinner out of whatever you had on hand." Mary particularly enjoys *caldo xochitl,* a spicy, broth-based chicken-and-vegetable soup, because it's a complete meal that isn't heavy.

## Spicy Chicken-Vegetable Soup

2½  quarts water
1  (2½- to 3-pound) whole chicken
3  bay leaves
1  tablespoon salt
1  tablespoon ground cumin
1  teaspoon black pepper
1  fresh basil sprig
4  whole cloves
4  garlic cloves
1  tablespoon dried oregano
2  zucchini, chopped

2  carrots, sliced
1  large green bell pepper, chopped
1  medium onion, chopped
1  (15½-ounce) can chickpeas, rinsed and drained
Tomato Rice
Toppings: chopped fresh cilantro, chopped green onions, minced jalapeño pepper, coarsely chopped tomato, chopped avocado

• Combine first 7 ingredients in a large stockpot; bring to a boil, skimming surface to remove excess foam.
• Process cloves, garlic, and oregano in a food processor until finely chopped.
• Add garlic mixture to broth, and cook, stirring occasionally, 35 minutes or until chicken is done. Remove chicken from broth, and cool. Skim fat from broth, and set broth aside.
• Skin and bone chicken; shred chicken, and set aside.
• Add zucchini and next 4 ingredients to broth; bring to a boil, and cook 5 minutes. Add chicken. Serve with Tomato Rice and desired toppings. Yield: 3 quarts.

## Tomato Rice:

| | | | |
|---|---|---|---|
| ¾ | cup long-grain rice | 1 | large garlic clove, minced |
| 1 | teaspoon lemon juice | 1 | tablespoon chicken base |
| 1 | cup hot water | 1 | cup hot water |
| 2 | tablespoons olive oil | 1 | teaspoon ground cumin |
| 2 | tomatoes, chopped | ½ | teaspoon salt |
| 1 | medium-size green bell pepper, chopped | ½ | teaspoon black pepper |

• Soak rice in lemon juice and 1 cup hot water 5 minutes; drain.

• Sauté rice in hot oil in a large saucepan over medium-high heat 10 minutes or until golden. Stir in tomato, bell pepper, and garlic.

• Stir together chicken base and remaining 4 ingredients; stir into rice mixture. Cover, reduce heat, and simmer 15 minutes or until liquid evaporates. (Do not uncover while rice is cooking.) Yield: 1½ cups.

**NOTE:** *Chicken base, a highly concentrated paste made from chicken stock, may be found with broth and bouillon in supermarkets.*

*Mary Treviño*
San Antonio, Texas

*cook's secret...* Chilling the broth for Spicy Chicken-Vegetable Soup overnight allows the fat to solidify and come to the surface, making it easier to skim.

# Lime Soup

*Cinnamon may seem like an unlikely partner to lime juice,*
*but the combination creates a perfect flavor match.*

| | | | |
|---|---|---|---|
| 3 | whole cloves | ½ | teaspoon salt |
| 1 | teaspoon to 2 teaspoons dried oregano | | Toppings: diced cooked chicken, diced |
| 1 | (3-inch) cinnamon stick | | avocado, lime slices, fried tortilla |
| 4 | (32-ounce) containers chicken broth | | strips, shredded Monterey Jack |
| ½ | to ⅔ cup fresh lime juice | | cheese |

• Cook first 3 ingredients in a large stockpot over medium-high heat 2 to 3 minutes, stirring constantly. Add broth, lime juice, and salt. Bring to a boil; reduce heat, and simmer 1 to 2 minutes. Remove and discard cloves and cinnamon stick. Serve soup with desired toppings. Yield: 4 quarts.

*Mary Treviño*
San Antonio, Texas

A culinary icon of Charleston, South Carolina, she-crab soup was traditionally a rich combination of cream, crabmeat, roe (eggs), and a splash of sherry. The meat from a female crab is said to be sweeter, but it was the addition of her red-orange roe that created the dish's depth of flavor and beautiful pale color—and resulted in the name she-crab soup.

These days, roe is not harvested because of an ecological effort to preserve the supply of crabs. So is it still she-crab soup if there's no roe? Yes . . . and no. The heart of the recipe remains the same. But if you find it made with roe, savor every precious spoonful.

You'll find some variations, but purists know to stick to the basics. Fresh crabmeat is essential. For all of you lucky enough to catch your own crabs, you'll need about a dozen. If you remove the shell of the female crab and discover what looks like a mass of tiny red-orange beads inside, you've struck gold—that is, roe. Remove it carefully, and stir it into the soup with the crabmeat. (Female crabs with roe on the outside must be returned to the water.)

## She-Crab Soup

| | |
|---|---|
| 1 quart whipping cream | ⅓ cup all-purpose flour |
| ⅛ teaspoon salt | 2 tablespoons lemon juice |
| ⅛ teaspoon pepper | ¼ teaspoon ground nutmeg |
| 2 fish bouillon cubes | 1 pound fresh crabmeat, drained |
| 2 cups boiling water | Garnish: chopped parsley |
| ¼ cup unsalted butter | ⅓ cup sherry (optional) |

• Combine first 3 ingredients in a heavy saucepan; bring to a boil over medium heat. Reduce heat, and simmer 1 hour. Set aside.
• Stir together fish bouillon cubes and 2 cups boiling water until the bouillon dissolves.
• Melt butter in a large heavy saucepan over low heat; add flour, stirring until smooth. Cook 1 minute, stirring constantly. Gradually add hot fish broth; cook over medium heat until thickened. Stir in cream mixture, and cook until thoroughly heated. Add lemon

juice, nutmeg, and crabmeat. Ladle into individual serving bowls. Garnish, if desired. Add a spoonful of sherry to each serving, if desired. Yield: about 6 cups.

**NOTE:** *For testing purposes only, we used Knorr Fish Bouillon. It's important to use good-quality sherry, not cooking sherry, for this soup.*

## cook's secret... Use live crabs on the day they're purchased or caught; refrigerate until just before cooking.

**...** To make canned crabmeat taste fresher, soak it in ice water 10 minutes, drain, and pat dry to help remove some of the metallic taste.

### Blue Crabs 101

Blue crabs are the star of this soup. If you're lucky enough to get the meat from fresh crabs, keep these tips in mind.

- Choose live crabs that are active and heavy for their size.
- For steamed crabs, combine 6 tablespoons coarse sea salt, 6 tablespoons Old Bay seasoning, 3 tablespoons pickling spice, 2 tablespoons celery seeds, and 1 tablespoon crushed red pepper flakes (optional). Bring 1 cup water and 1 cup vinegar to a boil in a stockpot. Place a rack in the stockpot. Add 1 dozen live crabs; sprinkle with the seasoning mixture. Cover and cook for 20 to 25 minutes or until crabs turn bright red. Rinse with cold water; drain well.
- To get the cooked meat, twist off crab legs and claws. Crack claws; remove meat with a small fork. Next, remove the apron, or tail flap, from the underside; discard. Insert thumb under shell by apron hinge; remove top shell. Pull away the gray gills; discard them along with internal organs. Break the body; remove meat from pockets. Pick through the meat to remove all shell fragments.

Former NFL star Dan Pastorini fights fires and tackles hearty appetites with the Chappell Hill Volunteer Fire Department these days. Fellow fireman John Gunn cooks up a gumbo that's a firehouse favorite.

# Gumbo

| | |
|---|---|
| 2 pounds unpeeled, large fresh shrimp | 1 teaspoon salt |
| ¼ cup vegetable oil | 1 teaspoon black pepper |
| ¼ cup all-purpose flour | ½ teaspoon ground red pepper |
| 1 medium onion, chopped | 4 green onions, chopped |
| 1 medium-size green bell pepper, chopped | 1 to 2 teaspoons filé powder |
| 1 (32-ounce) container chicken broth | Hot cooked rice |
| 3 garlic cloves, diced | French bread |

• Peel shrimp, and devein, if desired; set aside.
• Cook oil and flour in a Dutch oven over medium heat, whisking roux constantly, until it is dark caramel–colored (about 12 minutes).
• Reduce heat to low; add onion and bell pepper, and sauté 5 minutes or until tender.
• Add broth gradually, stirring until blended. Stir in garlic and next 3 ingredients; cover and simmer, stirring occasionally, 30 minutes.
• Add shrimp and green onions; cook, covered, 10 minutes or just until shrimp turn pink.
• Remove from heat, and stir in filé powder. Let stand 10 minutes before serving; serve over rice with French bread. Yield: 8 cups.

*John Gunn*
Chappell Hill, Texas

*cook's secret...* When a roux is cooked to the dark stage, as is done in most gumbo recipes, it loses some of its thickening power. That's why you'll often see filé powder added after the gumbo has cooked: It adds a little extra thickening.

*Vanessa McNeil*
Test Kitchens Specialist

# Shrimp-Crab Gumbo

Roux
9 (14½-ounce) cans chicken broth
2½ cups chopped onions
1 cup chopped green onions
½ cup chopped celery
2 garlic cloves, chopped
1 (10-ounce) can diced tomatoes with green chiles
1 (8-ounce) can tomato sauce

1 (16-ounce) package frozen sliced okra (optional)
3 pounds unpeeled, medium-sized fresh shrimp
1 (16-ounce) container lump crabmeat
½ cup chopped fresh parsley
1 tablespoon filé powder (optional)
Hot cooked rice

- Stir together first 8 ingredients and, if desired, okra; bring to a boil. Reduce heat, and simmer, stirring occasionally, 3 hours.
- Peel shrimp and devein, if desired. Add shrimp to broth mixture; cook, stirring often, 15 minutes or just until shrimp turn pink. Stir in crabmeat and parsley. Remove from heat; stir in filé powder, if desired. Serve over hot cooked rice. Yield: 1¼ gallons.

## Roux:

1½ cups vegetable oil

2 cups all-purpose flour

- Heat oil in a large cast iron skillet over medium heat; gradually whisk in flour, and cook, whisking constantly, until flour is dark mahogany–colored (about 30 minutes). Proceed with gumbo recipe, or cool completely; store in an airtight container up to 2 weeks. Yield: 3½ cups.

### Secrets to a Perfect Roux

**1.** Stir together the oil and flour, and start whisking.

**2.** When caramel colored, the roux is almost ready. Let it get a little darker, and don't leave it for a second.

**3.** When dark and mahogany colored, it's ready. Remove it from the heat immediately so that it won't burn.

The origin of Brunswick Stew is the cause of much heated discussion. Depending on which version of the story you accept, the dish was created either in Brunswick County, Virginia, in 1828, or on St. Simons Island, Georgia, in 1898.

In Virginia, skilled "stewmasters" do most of the cooking, and they do it in large quantities. The flavors differ from one stewmaster to the next, says John Drew Clary of Lawrenceville, but the basic ingredients are the same: boiled chicken, potatoes, onions, butterbeans, corn, and tomatoes. The mixture is cooked and stirred for hours, resulting in a thick stew that can be—and is—eaten with a fork. Virginians serve their Brunswick Stew as a main dish with bread on the side.

John Drew has been cooking up stews since 1973, but he says business picked up considerably in 1988, when the Virginia General Assembly issued a decree naming Brunswick County, Virginia, the home of Brunswick Stew. Now, he says, "We generally cook one Saturday a month between September and May. We cook five hundred quarts at once, and we sell it all ahead of time. The money we make goes for community causes."

Georgians tend to cook in smaller batches, and unless you have the good fortune to know someone who cooks stew at home, cafés are the place to taste this delicacy. "Our stew is more tomato-barbecue based," says Brad Brown, mayor of Brunswick, Georgia. "We use barbecued pork and chicken, but a few people even add some ground beef. And ours has a different consistency; you can see what's in there. The Virginia version is sort of mushy."

It's true that some Virginia stewmasters gauge doneness by whether a stirring paddle will stand up in the middle of the pot; however, *mushy* is not an adjective these strong-willed stewers would accept. With due respect to Mayor Brown, our friends in Virginia likely would say their stew just has more body.

As to the ownership of the original Brunswick Stew recipe, we'd rather not muddy the broth. We'll leave the deciding to the folks of Virginia and Georgia.

*regional favorite*

# Brunswick Stew

*Brunswick Stew has endless variations, though this pork and chicken version seems to be typical. While a bowl of Brunswick Stew can easily stand alone, it's not uncommon to serve it with barbecue.*

| | |
|---|---|
| 1 (4½-pound) pork roast | ¼ cup sugar |
| 1 (4½-pound) hen | ¼ cup all-purpose flour |
| 3 (16-ounce) cans whole tomatoes, undrained and chopped | 1 cup water |
| 1 (8-ounce) can tomato sauce | 1 teaspoon salt |
| 3 large onions, diced | ½ teaspoon black pepper |
| 2 small green peppers, diced | ½ teaspoon ground turmeric |
| ¾ cup vinegar | 2 tablespoons hot sauce |
| | 1 (16-ounce) package frozen shoepeg corn |

• Place roast, fat side up, on a rack of a roasting pan. Insert meat thermometer, being careful not to touch bone or fat. Bake at 325° about 30 to 35 minutes per pound or until thermometer registers 160°. Cool. Trim and discard fat; cut pork into 2-inch pieces.

• Place hen in a Dutch oven, and cover with water. Bring to a boil; cover, reduce heat, and simmer 2 hours or until tender. Remove hen from broth, and cool. (Reserve broth for another use.) Bone hen, and cut meat into 2-inch pieces.

• Coarsely grind pork and chicken in a food processor or with meat grinder. Combine ground meat, tomatoes, and next 5 ingredients in a large Dutch oven.

• Combine flour and water, stirring until smooth; stir into meat mixture. Stir in salt and next 3 ingredients. Cook over medium heat 30 minutes, stirring occasionally. Add water, if needed, to reach desired consistency. Stir in corn, and cook 10 more minutes. Yield: 22 cups.

**NOTE:** *Brunswick Stew freezes well. To serve, thaw and cook until thoroughly heated.*

*Lorene Carlisle*
*Columbus, Georgia*

*cook's secret...* To make the stew thicker, cook it longer, being sure to stir it often.

When Frogmore Stew was first cooked in the 1960s, Frogmore was a little hamlet on St. Helena Island, near Beaufort, South Carolina. In the 1980s, however, the postal service abolished the name Frogmore. That changed the name of the popular dish to Lowcountry Boil or Beaufort Stew—except, of course, among the proud (and peeved) residents of Frogmore.

Richard Gay, whose family owns Gay Fish Company on St. Helena, created the dish in the early sixties. "I was on weekend duty in the National Guard," he says, "and I'd sometimes get a lot of shrimp, put it in a pot with sausage and corn, and boil it up. Within an hour, we could have a complete meal for a hundred people. The boys teased me that since I was from Frogmore, we'd name it Frogmore Stew. We put out copies of the recipe at the seafood market at the dock and began selling the other ingredients as well.

"Every time I see someone else serve it, there are a couple of ingredients that I don't use," he says. He adds a half-pound of butter for every six people, and he prefers crab boil seasoning that comes in a bag so that loose spices don't get all over the corn. (We used a loose, finely ground seasoning blend in our stew, however, and the results were delicious.)

"People on vacation like it because you cook everything in one pot," Richard says. Beachgoers often serve it on heavy brown paper or even newspaper for ease of cleanup.

Richard is justifiably proud of his creation and its popularity. Ten years ago, he petitioned the South Carolina senate to have Frogmore Stew named the state seafood dish. "There was a state dog, flag, and flower," he says, "but no seafood dish." He let the matter drop when he moved to Tulsa, but he still dreams of the day when his boil will be the state's official seafood dish, proudly bearing the name Frogmore Stew.

# Frogmore Stew

*We found that the sausage adds plenty of richness to*
*this dish, so we omitted the butter.*

| | |
|---|---|
| 5 quarts water | 6 ears fresh corn, halved |
| ¼ cup Old Bay seasoning | 4 pounds unpeeled, large fresh shrimp |
| 4 pounds small red potatoes | Old Bay seasoning |
| 2 pounds kielbasa or hot smoked link | Cocktail sauce |
| sausage, cut into 1½-inch pieces | |

• Bring 5 quarts water and ¼ cup Old Bay seasoning to a rolling boil in a large covered stockpot.

• Add potatoes; return to a boil, and cook, uncovered, for 10 minutes.

• Add sausage and corn, and return to a boil. Cook 10 minutes or until potatoes are tender.

• Add shrimp to stockpot; cook 3 to 4 minutes or until shrimp turn pink. Drain. Serve with Old Bay seasoning and cocktail sauce. Yield: 12 servings.

**NOTE:** *For testing purposes only, we used Hillshire Farms Kielbasa.*

*cook's secret...* Richard Gay cooks his stew in a large pot with a removable drain basket. He fills the pot with enough water to cover all the ingredients once they're added and brings it to a boil with a lot of butter. Then Richard says to add the seasoning and let it cook for a while. The shrimp is the last thing that goes in; then stir. All the shrimp come to the top when they're done. Turn off the heat, and let it sit for a few minutes, stirring a couple of times. Then just drain, and serve.

Teresa Stokes knows the value of providing her family with a good home-cooked meal. And with three boys to chauffeur to soccer, basketball, art, and Boy Scouts, she appreciates hearty recipes that can be prepared quickly. Her recipe for chicken stew pleases her family every time she serves it.

*time—saver*

## Speedy Chicken Stew

| | | | |
|---|---|---|---|
| 2 | (14-ounce) cans chicken broth | ½ | large sweet onion, diced |
| 2 | chicken bouillon cubes | ⅛ | teaspoon ground red pepper |
| 1 | (20-ounce) package frozen creamed corn | ¼ | teaspoon dried thyme |
| 1 | (10-ounce) package frozen baby lima beans | 3 | cups chopped cooked chicken |
| 1 | large baking potato, peeled and diced | 1 | (14½-ounce) can seasoned diced tomatoes with garlic, basil, and |
| 1 | small jalapeño pepper, seeded and minced (optional) | | oregano |
| | | 1 | (6-ounce) can tomato paste |

• Combine first 9 ingredients in a Dutch oven. Bring to a boil over medium-high heat, stirring often. Reduce heat, and simmer 15 to 20 minutes or until potatoes and lima beans are tender. Stir in chicken, diced tomatoes, and tomato paste; simmer 10 more minutes. Yield: 6 servings.

*Teresa Stokes*
*Birmingham, Alabama*

*cook's secret...* There's one important guideline to remember about stews: Don't cheat on the simmering time—the simmer helps extract maximum flavor and ensure fork-tender results.

$A$ssociate Foods Editor Mary Allen Perry whipped up this Southern favorite using convenience products. It's every bit as good as its labor-intensive counterpart and takes less than 10 minutes to prepare.

*time–saver*

# Turnip Greens Stew

*Frozen seasoning blend is a mixture of diced onion, red and green bell peppers, and celery.*

| | |
|---|---|
| 2 cups chopped cooked ham | 1 (16-ounce) package frozen seasoning blend |
| 1 tablespoon vegetable oil | |
| 3 cups chicken broth | 1 teaspoon sugar |
| 2 (16-ounce) packages frozen chopped turnip greens | 1 teaspoon seasoned pepper |

• Sauté chopped ham in hot oil in a Dutch oven over medium-high heat 5 minutes or until lightly browned. Add chicken broth and remaining ingredients; bring greens mixture to a boil. Cover, reduce heat to low, and simmer, stirring occasionally, 25 minutes. Yield: 6 to 8 servings.

**NOTE:** *For testing purposes only, we used McKenzie's Seasoning Blend.*

*Mary Allen Perry*
Associate Foods Editor

*cook's secret...* To transform this recipe into **Collard Stew,** substitute 1 (16-ounce) package frozen chopped collard greens and 1 (16-ounce) can black-eyed peas, drained, for 2 packages turnip greens. Prepare recipe as directed, cooking collard greens 15 minutes; add black-eyed peas, and cook 10 more minutes.

For Ella and Dottie Brennan, owners of New Orleans's Commander's Palace, the restaurant's courtyard is an ideal spot for brunch. The garden becomes their personal space when the restaurant is closed.

Ella worked with her family at Brennan's restaurant in New Orleans for twenty-eight years before moving over to Commander's Palace three decades ago. Dottie joined her big sister after the Korean War, and the two have worked together ever since. Now their niece, Lally, and Ella's daughter, Ti Martin, oversee the day-to-day operations of the restaurant.

"It's like having a party every day," Ella says. She always takes time to visit with friends who come into the restaurant. "You have to mix the fun in with the work," she says, "or you won't get either."

## Rémoulade Sauce

| | |
|---|---|
| 6 garlic cloves, peeled | 2 tablespoons mild paprika |
| 3 celery ribs, chopped | 2 tablespoons Worcestershire sauce |
| 1/3 cup white vinegar | 1 tablespoon hot sauce (or to taste) |
| 1/2 cup egg substitute | 1 teaspoon ground red pepper |
| 1/4 cup ketchup | 1 1/2 cups vegetable oil |
| 1/4 cup prepared horseradish | 6 green onions, sliced |
| 1/4 cup Creole mustard | Kosher salt and black pepper to taste |
| 1/4 cup yellow mustard | |

• Process first 12 ingredients in a blender or food processor until smooth. With blender running, add oil in a slow, steady stream until thickened. Stir in green onions and salt and black pepper to taste; cover and chill until ready to serve. Yield: 5 cups.

*Ti Adelaide Martin and Jamie Shannon*
New Orleans, Louisiana
Adapted from *Commander's Kitchen* (Broadway Books)

*cook's secret*... You can make this sauce up to several days ahead to serve with peeled, boiled shrimp. Leftover sauce will keep in the refrigerator for 2 weeks and is delicious on sandwiches, chicken or crab cakes, or salad.

# Giblet Gravy

Giblets and neck from 1 turkey
4 cups water
½ cup butter or margarine
1 small onion, chopped
1 celery rib, chopped
1 carrot, chopped

¼ cup all-purpose flour
2 egg yolks
½ cup half-and-half
½ teaspoon salt
½ teaspoon pepper
½ teaspoon poultry seasoning

- Bring giblets, neck, and 4 cups water to a boil in a medium saucepan over medium heat. Cover, reduce heat, and simmer 45 minutes or until tender. Drain, reserving broth. Chop giblets and neck meat, and set aside.
- Melt butter in a large skillet over medium heat; add chopped vegetables, and sauté 5 minutes. Add flour, stirring until smooth (photo 1). Add reserved broth; cook, stirring constantly, 10 minutes or until thickened (photo 2). Reduce heat to low. Remove vegetables using a handheld, wire-mesh strainer, and discard, leaving gravy in skillet (photo 3).
- Whisk together egg yolks and half-and-half. Gradually stir about one-fourth of hot gravy into yolk mixture; add to remaining hot gravy. Add giblets and neck meat; cook, stirring constantly, 4 to 5 minutes or until a thermometer registers 160°. Stir in salt, pepper, and seasoning. Serve immediately. Yield: 4 cups.

## Secrets to a Perfect Giblet Gravy

**1.** Melt butter in skillet; add vegetables, and sauté. Add flour, stirring until smooth.

**2.** Add the reserved broth; cook, whisking constantly, until thickened.

**3.** Remove vegetables using a wire-mesh strainer, and discard, leaving gravy in skillet. Proceed with recipe as directed.

*cook's secret...* Stir the flour into the buttery sautéed vegetables until the flour dissolves to prevent lumps from forming.

Altruism is a way of life at the Upper Sand Mountain Parish in Sylvania, Alabama. For over twenty-eight years, Reverend Dorsey Walker has set the example by directing the parish's effort to offer food, clothing, shelter, and emergency care to low-income families. "The parish is a co-op of eleven small-membership United Methodist churches providing assistance to folks all over the state," he says.

None of this would be possible without the tremendous dedication of volunteers who serve on the Mission Service Teams. Gathering from around the country for one-week trips, team members—many of them students—tend the community gardens, work in the parish's Better Way Cannery, and participate in other activities.

Inside an old renovated church, now home to the Better Way Cannery, team members outfitted in red aprons busily shuck corn and chop carrots for vegetable soup that is distributed in the parish's food pantry. Others ladle freshly cooked Green Tomato–Blueberry Jam (page 356) into jars to be sold at the Better Way Clothing Shoppe.

Dorsey hopes that this unique and delicious jam, along with several other green tomato–based products, will help pave the way to the cannery's—and ultimately the parish's—financial independence. The long-term goal is simple: Self-sufficiency so that even more funds can be channeled to families in need.

With the help of a federal grant and hardworking volunteers, the line of specialty products (including pickles, marmalade, and relish) was finally launched under the label Sand Mountain's Finest. The parish kindly shared these wonderful recipes with us.

# Green Tomato Pickles

| | |
|---|---|
| 5 pounds green tomatoes, chopped | 2 teaspoons mustard seeds |
| 1 large onion, chopped | 2 teaspoons whole allspice |
| 2 tablespoons pickling salt | 2 teaspoons celery seeds |
| 1½ cups firmly packed brown sugar | 1½ teaspoons whole cloves |
| 2 cups cider vinegar (5% acidity) | 3 cups water |

• Sprinkle tomato and onion with pickling salt; let stand 4 to 6 hours. Drain and pat dry with paper towels; set aside.

• Combine brown sugar and vinegar in a Dutch oven; cook over medium heat, stirring constantly, until sugar dissolves.

• Place mustard seeds and next 3 ingredients on 6-inch square of cheesecloth; tie with string. Add spice bag, tomato-and-onion mixture, and 3 cups water to vinegar mixture.

• Bring to a boil, stirring constantly; reduce heat, and simmer, stirring occasionally, 25 minutes or until tomato and onion are tender. Remove and discard spice bag.

• Pour hot mixture into hot jars, filling to ½ inch from top. Remove air bubbles; wipe jar rims. Cover at once with metal lids, and screw on bands.

• Process in boiling-water bath 10 minutes. Yield: 7 pints.

# Green Tomato Marmalade

| | |
|---|---|
| 1 cup water | 6 large green tomatoes, chopped |
| 2 oranges, thinly sliced | (about 4 pounds) |
| 1 lemon, thinly sliced | ½ teaspoon salt |
| 4 cups sugar | |

• Cook first 3 ingredients in a Dutch oven over medium heat 17 to 20 minutes or until fruit is tender. Add sugar and remaining ingredients, stirring until sugar dissolves.

• Bring to a boil, stirring constantly; reduce heat, and simmer, stirring occasionally, 3½ hours or until mixture thickens.

• Pour hot mixture into hot jars, filling to ¼ inch from top. Remove air bubbles; wipe jar rims. Cover at once with metal lids, and screw on bands.

• Process in boiling-water bath 10 minutes. Yield: 3 pints.

*cook's secret...* Check that your home-canned products have sealed correctly after they cool by pressing down on the center of each lid; it should not spring back when released. If it does, the mixture is safe to eat but should be stored in the refrigerator.

# Green Tomato–Blueberry Jam

5 cups fresh blueberries, stemmed*

4 large green tomatoes, coarsely chopped
    (about 4 pounds)

1½ cups water

5 cups sugar

3 (1.75-ounce) packages fruit pectin

¼ cup lemon juice

2 teaspoons ground cinnamon

½ teaspoon ground nutmeg

• Pulse blueberries and chopped tomato in a blender or food processor 3 or 4 times or until mixture is almost smooth.

• Cook blueberry mixture, 1½ cups water, and sugar in a Dutch oven over medium heat, stirring constantly, until sugar dissolves.

• Stir in fruit pectin and remaining ingredients. Bring to a boil; cook, stirring constantly, 5 minutes or until mixture thickens.

• Pour hot mixture into hot jars, filling to ¼ inch from top. Remove air bubbles; wipe jar rims. Cover at once with metal lids, and screw on bands.

• Process in boiling-water bath 10 minutes. Yield: 5 pints.

*5 cups frozen blueberries, thawed, may be substituted for fresh blueberries.

**NOTE:** *For testing purposes only, we used Sure-Jell Fruit Pectin.*

*cook's secret*... Jam is generally less firm than jelly and is made with crushed or finely chopped fruit rather than juice. Commercial pectin is sometimes added to home-made jams to create the desired consistency.

# Green Tomato Pie Filling

*This delicious recipe also makes a great condiment served with roasted meat.*

| | |
|---|---|
| 17 medium-size green tomatoes, chopped (about 6¾ pounds) | 2 cups water |
| 10 medium Granny Smith apples, peeled and chopped (about 4¾ pounds) | ½ cup cider vinegar (5% acidity) |
| | 2 tablespoons grated orange rind |
| 1 (15-ounce) package raisins | 2 tablespoons grated lemon rind |
| 1 (15-ounce) package golden raisins | 1 cup fresh lemon juice |
| 2½ cups sugar | 1 tablespoon ground cinnamon |
| 2½ cups firmly packed brown sugar | 1 teaspoon ground nutmeg |
| | 1 teaspoon ground cloves |

- Combine all ingredients in a Dutch oven; simmer over medium-low heat, stirring often, 2½ hours or until tomato and apple are tender and liquid thickens.
- Pour hot mixture into hot jars, filling to ½ inch from top. Remove air bubbles; wipe jar rims. Cover at once with metal lids, and screw on bands.
- Process in boiling-water bath 15 minutes. Yield: 6 quarts.

**Green Tomato Pie:** Roll each crust from 1 (15-ounce) refrigerated piecrusts package into ⅛-inch thickness. Press 1 piecrust into a 9-inch pieplate; fold edges under, and crimp. Spoon 4½ cups Green Tomato Pie Filling into piecrust; dot with 2 tablespoons butter. Cut remaining piecrust into ½-inch strips; arrange in a lattice design over filling. Sprinkle evenly with 2 tablespoons sugar. Bake pie at 425° for 10 minutes; reduce oven temperature to 350°, and bake 30 minutes or until golden.

*cook's secret...* When canning, the degree of acidity of the vinegar is critical to ensuring food safety. Make sure the vinegar you use is labeled as 5% acidity.

# Sunny Orange Marmalade

*This marmalade is pictured on the cover. It's the perfect*
*complement to Quick Whipping Cream Biscuits (page 71).*

| | |
|---|---|
| 12 oranges (about 6 pounds) | 4 cups water |
| 2 lemons | 9 cups sugar |

• Peel oranges, and cut rind into thin strips. Chop pulp, discarding seeds. Cut lemons into thin slices, discarding seeds.

• Combine orange rind, chopped pulp, lemon slices, and 4 cups water in a large Dutch oven; bring to a boil. Reduce heat, and simmer 15 minutes. Remove from heat; cover and chill 8 hours or overnight.

• Combine fruit mixture and sugar in a Dutch oven; bring to a boil. Reduce heat, and simmer, stirring occasionally, 1½ hours or until a candy thermometer registers 215°.

• Pack hot marmalade into hot, sterilized jars, filling to ¼ inch from top. Remove air bubbles; wipe jar rims. Cover at once with metal lids, and screw on bands.

• Process in boiling-water bath 5 minutes. Yield: 5 pints.

*cook's secret...* For a quicker marmalade, cut unpeeled oranges into quarters, and then remove and discard the seeds. Pulse the oranges in a food processor until they are coarsely chopped, and proceed with the recipe.

*Jan Moon*
Former Test Kitchens Professional

There's something rewarding about making homemade spreads. But most of us—like, um, me—don't want to sweat over the stove all day, no matter how much we like our family and friends. Fret not. These recipes from Rita Gibbon, Lynn Young, and Nancy Smith are made in small batches, and most can be ready in less than 40 minutes. The recipe below and those on the following two pages are perfect for first-time "jammies" as well as seasoned preservers.

*Joy Zacharia*
Associate Foods Editor

# Peach-Rosemary Jam

| | |
|---|---|
| 4 cups peeled and chopped fresh peaches or nectarines | 2 rosemary sprigs |
| 1 teaspoon grated lime rind | 1 (1.75-ounce) package powdered fruit pectin |
| ¼ cup fresh lime juice | 5 cups sugar |

• Bring first 5 ingredients to a full rolling boil in a Dutch oven. Boil 1 minute, stirring constantly. Add sugar to peach mixture, and bring to a full rolling boil; boil 1 minute, stirring constantly. Remove from heat. Remove and discard rosemary sprigs; skim off any foam.
• Pour hot mixture into hot jars, filling to ¼ inch from top. Remove air bubbles; wipe jar rims. Cover at once with metal lids, and screw on bands.
• Process in boiling-water bath 10 minutes. Yield: 7 (½-pint) jars.

*Rita Gibbon*
Birmingham, Alabama

*cook's secret...* Select good-quality fruit that's fully ripe for making jams and jellies. Contrary to popular belief, less-than-perfect fruit is not good for preserving because the quality of the canned product depends on the quality you begin with.

# Strawberry-Port Jam

2 (10-ounce) packages frozen unsweetened
   strawberries, thawed
1½ cups ruby port
1 teaspoon grated lemon rind

½ teaspoon ground nutmeg
1 (1.75-ounce) package powdered fruit
   pectin
4 cups sugar

• Chop or crush thawed strawberries in a 4-cup measuring cup. Add water to strawberries to measure 2½ cups.

• Stir together strawberry mixture, ruby port, grated lemon rind, and ground nutmeg in a large saucepan. Stir in fruit pectin.

• Bring mixture to a full rolling boil, and boil, stirring constantly, 1 minute. Add sugar, stirring constantly, and bring to a full rolling boil. Boil 1 minute. Remove from heat, and skim off any foam.

• Pour hot jam into hot jars, filling to ¼ inch from top. Remove air bubbles; wipe jar rims. Cover at once with metal lids, and screw on bands.

• Process in boiling-water bath 10 minutes. Yield: 7 (½-pint) jars.

**NOTE:** *Ruby port is a deep red–colored sweet wine typically enjoyed as an after-dinner drink. It's usually sold in liquor stores because of a higher alcohol content than other wines.*

*Lynn Young*
Knoxville, Tennessee

*cook's secret*... Use frozen strawberries in this recipe instead of fresh ones. Frozen strawberries hold their shape better than fresh.

# Easiest Pepper Jelly

½ cup apple jelly
½ cup orange marmalade
1 tablespoon seeded and chopped
   jalapeño pepper

1 tablespoon chopped green onion
1 teaspoon apple cider vinegar

• Stir together all ingredients in a large saucepan over low heat until jelly and marmalade are melted and mixture is blended. Cool. Cover and chill 8 hours. Yield: 1 cup.

*Nancy Smith*
Blue Ridge, Georgia

# Tart Basil Jelly

6¼ cups sugar
2 cups water
1 cup white vinegar

1 cup loosely packed fresh basil leaves
6 drops green liquid food coloring
2 (3-ounce) packages liquid fruit pectin

• Bring first 5 ingredients to a boil in a large saucepan. Add pectin, and bring to a full rolling boil. Boil 1 minute. Remove from heat. Remove and discard basil leaves; skim off any foam.

• Pour hot mixture into hot, sterilized jars, filling to ¼ inch from top. Remove air bubbles; wipe jar rims. Cover at once with metal lids, and screw on bands.

• Process in boiling-water bath 5 minutes. Yield: 7 (½-pint) jars.

**Southwest Jelly:** Add 1 seeded and thinly sliced jalapeño pepper, and substitute 1 cup cilantro leaves for 1 cup basil leaves. Substitute 20 drops red liquid food coloring for 6 drops green food coloring.

**Mint Jelly:** Substitute 1 cup mint leaves for 1 cup basil leaves.

**NOTE:** *Jellies usually require only 5 minutes of processing because of their high acid content.*

*Lynn Young*
Knoxville, Tennessee

*cook's secret...* Serve this jelly atop goat cheese or cream cheese with crispy crackers for a last-minute appetizer.

There's nothing like the taste of fresh basil, so our Test Kitchens staff came up with these top-rated recipes that preserve the flavor all season long.

Although dried basil bears little resemblance to fresh, frozen basil purees retain much of their summer flavor if properly prepared and stored in airtight containers. Like pesto, basil puree is traditionally made with olive oil, but we also tried substituting tomato sauce for a fat-free version and were pleased with the results. Basil leaves are tender and damage easily, so use a food processor to rapidly incorporate the ingredients with quick, clean cuts that minimize bruising and exposure to air.

Each of these recipes using fresh basil takes less than 10 minutes to prepare and can be used in dozens of different ways—and each stores well in the freezer.

## Basil Puree

Process 4 cups loosely packed basil leaves and 1 cup olive oil *or* 1 (8-ounce) can tomato sauce in a food processor until basil is finely chopped. Spoon mixture into ice-cube trays, and freeze. Store frozen cubes in zip-top freezer bags up to 6 months. Yield: about 1 cup or 8 (2-tablespoon) cubes.

*cook's secret*... Use Basil Puree anytime you need a burst of fresh basil flavor: in soups, sauces, or salad dressings. Thaw and add to marinades; or drizzle over grilled meats and vegetables.

# Basil Pesto

Process 4 cups loosely packed basil leaves, 6 garlic cloves, ¼ teaspoon salt, and 1 cup each of shredded Parmesan cheese, toasted pine nuts, and olive oil in a food processor until smooth, stopping to scrape down sides. Spoon mixture into ice-cube trays, and freeze. Store cubes in zip-top freezer bags up to 6 months. Yield: 2 cups or 16 (2-tablespoon) cubes.

*cook's secret...* Pesto is great to have on hand for last-minute hors d'oeuvres. It stands alone as a dip and also works as a spread for pizzas and sandwiches.

# Basil-Garlic Butter

Process 1 cup softened butter and 2 garlic cloves in a food processor until smooth. Add ½ cup firmly packed basil leaves, and pulse 3 to 4 times or until basil is finely chopped. Store in the refrigerator up to 1 week, or freeze in airtight containers up to 4 months. Yield: 1 cup.

*cook's secret...* If desired, shape butter into a log; wrap in wax paper, and chill. When firm, slice into small rounds, and freeze. Serve with hot crusty French bread or baked potatoes. Toss with hot, cooked pasta and Parmesan cheese or steamed vegetables.

# Pesto–Goat Cheese Spread

Process 1 (11-ounce) log goat cheese, 1 (8-ounce) package softened cream cheese, 2 cups loosely packed basil leaves, ½ cup toasted pine nuts, 3 garlic cloves, and 2 tablespoons balsamic vinegar in a food processor until smooth. Chill 2 hours before serving. Store in refrigerator up to 1 week, or freeze in airtight containers up to 4 months. Serve with toasted pita chips or baguettes. Yield: 3 cups.

*cook's secret...* To turn this spread into "croutons" for a salad, shape cheese mixture into logs, and wrap in wax paper; slice chilled logs into ½-inch rounds. Dip rounds in lightly beaten egg; dredge in Italian breadcrumbs. Pan-fry over medium-high heat in butter 1 minute on each side or until golden. Serve warm over a crisp, green salad.

sides

# Top 10 Best Kept Sides Secrets

**1.** Many vegetable casseroles can be assembled ahead and chilled overnight. Wait to add any toppings or breadings until ready to bake so that the toppings don't become soggy. Let the casseroles stand at room temperature about 20 minutes before baking.

**2.** When buying frozen vegetables, look for well-frozen packages. Damp packages or packages that are a solid block have probably defrosted once. When vegetables thaw and refreeze, quality declines.

**3.** Measure seasonings into a bowl; then add them to the pot. Don't sprinkle spices and herbs directly from the bottles over a steaming pot. Steam gets into the bottle and speeds the loss of flavor and aroma of the spices.

**4.** Whenever you chop peppers, onions, or celery, chop more than you need and freeze the extras separately in zip-top freezer bags or other small containers. They will be ready to cook in any recipe.

**5.** When you need only a small amount of grated onion for a recipe, squeeze a piece of onion through your garlic press.

**6.** Cook most vegetables as briefly as possible in as little liquid as possible to retain nutrients, color, and texture. The microwave is perfect for cooking fresh vegetables because you need only a scant amount of water. In turn, the vegetables cook quickly, retaining good color and nutrients.

**7.** Potatoes that are cooked with their peels on and then cut hold their shape better and retain more nutrients than those that are peeled and cut before cooking.

**8.** Stir a little cream, your favorite herb, or roasted garlic into instant mashed potatoes to make them come alive with real potato taste and texture. We particularly like frozen mashed potatoes.

**9.** For a tasty variation, cook rice in a flavorful liquid, such as chicken broth, beef broth, or fruit juice.

**10.** One of our favorite ways to cook vegetables is to roast them. Cut large vegetables into chunks, toss with olive oil, and sprinkle with seasonings. Roast on a jellyroll pan at 450° for 5 to 15 minutes or just until browned on the edges, tossing once during roasting.

*L*ike many of you, I grew up on canned asparagus—even today I still make my mother's canned asparagus casserole. But once I tasted it fresh, I was even more enthralled, and I eagerly await the arrival of spring's first spears.

Although asparagus is available year-round (canned, frozen, and through hothouse sources), the optimum season runs from February through June. The most tender stalks are apple green and pencil thin with purple-tinged tips; older, more mature plants have thicker spears.

*Patty Vann*
Former Associate Foods Editor

*time–saver*

# Almond Asparagus

*You'll love the contrast of tender goodness and crispy crunch in Almond Asparagus.*

| | |
|---|---|
| 2 **pounds fresh asparagus** | ¾ **cup slivered almonds, toasted** |
| 2 **tablespoons butter or margarine** | ½ **teaspoon salt** |
| 1 **tablespoon lemon juice** | ¼ **teaspoon pepper** |

• Snap off tough ends of asparagus. Cook asparagus in boiling water to cover 3 minutes or until crisp-tender; drain. Plunge asparagus into ice water to stop the cooking process; drain.
• Melt butter in a large skillet over medium heat; add asparagus, and sauté 3 to 5 minutes. Toss asparagus with lemon juice and remaining ingredients. Yield: 4 servings.

*Ethel C. Jernigan*
Savannah, Georgia

*cook's secret*... Use fresh asparagus as soon as possible. Store stalk side down in a glass of water; cover with plastic wrap, and refrigerate up to 4 days.

# Sesame Asparagus

| | |
|---|---|
| 1 pound fresh asparagus | ⅛ teaspoon freshly ground pepper |
| 2 tablespoons peanut oil, divided | 2 teaspoons soy sauce |
| 2 large shallots, minced | ½ teaspoon dark sesame oil |
| 1 tablespoon sesame seeds | |

• Snap off tough ends of asparagus. Cook half of asparagus in 1 tablespoon hot peanut oil in a large skillet over medium-high heat 3 to 4 minutes on each side.

• Stir together shallot and remaining 4 ingredients. Sprinkle half of shallot mixture over asparagus in skillet; cook 1 to 2 minutes or until shallot is tender. Remove asparagus from skillet, and keep warm. Repeat procedure with remaining asparagus, peanut oil, and shallot mixture. Yield: 4 servings.

*Hannah Youngblood*
Smithfield, North Carolina

*cook's secret*... It's best to remove and discard the tough ends of asparagus spears before cooking. The easiest way to do this is to bend each end until it snaps. It will snap where the most tender part begins.

Green beans may have undergone more of a cooking transformation than any other popular Southern vegetable in the last couple of generations. Our grandmothers simmered them for hours, usually flavored with a ham hock, proclaiming them done only after they showed no resistance to the fork whatsoever. Today's cooks forgo the ham bone in favor of flavor alternatives that are lower in fat, such as broth, and they get them in and out of the pot as quickly as possible to maximize color, texture, and nutrients. Green beans partner well with such herbs as rosemary. Try the combo in this recipe that blends chewy ravioli with the crunch of quickly cooked beans.

## Green Bean Alfredo with Cheese Ravioli

| | | | |
|---|---|---|---|
| 1 | (1-pound) package frozen cheese-filled ravioli | 1½ | cups whipping cream |
| 3 | tablespoons butter or margarine | ¾ | cup dry white wine or chicken broth |
| 1 | pound fresh green beans | ¾ | teaspoon freshly ground pepper |
| 2 | garlic cloves, pressed | ¼ | cup shredded Parmesan cheese |
| ½ | teaspoon chopped fresh rosemary | | Garnish: fresh rosemary sprigs |

• Cook ravioli according to package directions; keep warm.
• Melt butter in a large nonstick skillet over medium-high heat; add green beans, garlic, and rosemary, and sauté 6 minutes or until beans are crisp-tender. Remove mixture, and set aside.
• Add whipping cream to skillet, and bring to a boil, stirring constantly. Cook, stirring constantly, 10 minutes.
• Return green bean mixture to skillet; add wine and pepper, and cook 5 minutes. Stir in 2 tablespoons cheese. Serve over ravioli, and sprinkle evenly with remaining 2 tablespoons cheese. Garnish, if desired. Yield: 6 servings.

*cook's secret*... The general rule for substituting fresh herbs for dried herbs, which have more concentrated flavor, is to use 3 times the amount of fresh as dried. Rosemary is the exception to this rule: Use equal amounts of fresh versus dried.

K itty Pettus's green bean recipe is one of our all-time favorites. It's full of old Southern flavor and boasts a crisp-tender crunch to match today's taste preferences.

*regional favorite*

## Tangy Green Beans with Pimiento

| | | | |
|---|---|---|---|
| 1½ | pounds fresh green beans, trimmed | ¼ | cup red wine vinegar |
| 3 | bacon slices | 1 | teaspoon sugar |
| 1 | large onion, chopped | ½ | teaspoon salt |
| 3 | garlic cloves, minced | ½ | teaspoon pepper |
| 1 | (2-ounce) jar diced pimiento, drained | ½ | teaspoon cumin seeds |

• Cook green beans in boiling water to cover 4 to 5 minutes. Drain and plunge beans into ice water to stop the cooking process; drain and set aside.

• Cook bacon in a large skillet until crisp; remove bacon from skillet, and drain on paper towels, reserving 2 tablespoons drippings in skillet. Crumble bacon, and set aside.

• Sauté onion and garlic in hot bacon drippings over medium-high heat until tender. Stir in pimiento and remaining 5 ingredients. Stir in beans; reduce heat, cover, and simmer 5 minutes. Sprinkle with bacon. Yield: 6 servings.

*Kitty Pettus*
*Huntsville, Alabama*

*cook's secret...* We use stringless beans in our recipes. If you purchase beans with strings, be sure to remove them before cooking for best results.

This no-fuss recipe is a holiday favorite of Test Kitchens Director Lyda Jones, who recommends using any leftover sauce with turkey to make a delicious open-faced sandwich.

# Broccoli with Pimiento Cheese Sauce

2 pounds fresh broccoli, cut into spears
Pimiento Cheese Sauce
1 cup soft white breadcrumbs

2 tablespoons butter, melted
⅓ cup shredded Parmesan cheese

- Arrange broccoli in a steamer basket over boiling water. Cover and steam 5 minutes or until crisp-tender.
- Arrange broccoli in a lightly greased 11- x 7-inch baking dish. Pour Pimiento Cheese Sauce evenly over broccoli.
- Combine breadcrumbs, melted butter, and Parmesan cheese; sprinkle evenly over cheese sauce.
- Bake at 375° for 20 minutes or until thoroughly heated. Yield: 6 to 8 servings.

## Pimiento Cheese Sauce:

¼ cup butter
¼ cup all-purpose flour
2 cups milk
¼ teaspoon salt

1 teaspoon Worcestershire sauce
2 cups (8 ounces) shredded sharp Cheddar cheese
1 (4-ounce) jar diced pimiento, drained

- Melt butter in a heavy saucepan over medium heat; add flour, stirring until smooth. Cook, stirring constantly, 1 minute.
- Add milk gradually; cook, stirring constantly, until mixture is thickened and bubbly. Stir in salt and remaining ingredients. Yield: 3½ cups.

*cook's secret...* For smooth, lump-free sauce, warm the milk in the microwave before adding it to the roux.

*Lyda Jones*
Test Kitchens Director

Monique Wells, a Houston native now living in Paris, sustains her Southern heritage through the food she remembers from her childhood. This recipe shows the influence of her Texas and Creole Louisiana roots.

# Fried Cabbage

| | | | |
|---|---|---|---|
| 4 | bacon slices | 1 | teaspoon salt |
| 1 | large head fresh cabbage, coarsely chopped | 1 | teaspoon pepper |

• Cook bacon in a large skillet 10 minutes or until crisp. Remove bacon, and drain on paper towels, reserving 1 tablespoon drippings in skillet. Crumble bacon.

• Add cabbage to hot drippings in skillet; sprinkle with salt and pepper. Sauté cabbage over medium-high heat 10 to 12 minutes or until tender. Sprinkle with bacon. Yield: 4 to 6 servings.

*Monique Wells*
Paris, France

*cook's secret...* To quickly chop the cabbage, quarter it, cut away the core, and thinly slice the cabbage into shreds. Then coarsely chop the shreds.

I love carrots," says Trish Conroy. "They're great as a side dish." This old-fashioned bake, she says, has become a family favorite. It was a favorite, too, with our 2001 *Southern Living* Holiday Recipe Contest judges. It was a Runner Up in the 8-Ingredient-or-Less Vegetable Sides category.

*contest winner*

# Carrot Soufflé

| | | | |
|---|---|---|---|
| 1 | pound carrots, peeled and chopped | 3 | tablespoons all-purpose flour |
| 3 | large eggs, lightly beaten | 1 | teaspoon baking powder |
| ½ | cup sugar | 1 | teaspoon vanilla extract |
| ½ | cup butter or margarine, melted | | |

- Bring carrots and water to cover to a boil in a medium saucepan; cook 45 minutes or until very tender. Drain.
- Process carrots in a food processor until smooth.
- Stir together carrot puree, eggs, and remaining ingredients. Spoon into a lightly greased 1-quart baking dish.
- Bake at 350° for 45 minutes or until set. Yield: 8 servings.

*Trish Conroy*
*Lynchburg, Virginia*

*cook's secret...* Baked soufflés are delicate and need to be tested carefully for doneness. Try to prevent moving the dish or exposing it to sudden drafts of cold air. Soufflés are done when a knife inserted halfway between the center and edge comes out clean. If you remove a soufflé from the oven too early, it will sink in the center.

"In Texas, everyone has some type of pepper jelly on hand," says Test Kitchens Specialist Vanessa McNeil, a Texas native. "It's a great way to add an extra boost of flavor to vegetables and sauces." Red pepper jelly adds a kick to carrots in this recipe.

*editor's choice*

## Pepper Jelly–Glazed Carrots

| | |
|---|---|
| 1 (2-pound) package baby carrots | 2 tablespoons butter or margarine |
| 1 (10½-ounce) can condensed chicken broth, undiluted | 1 (10½-ounce) jar red pepper jelly |

• Combine carrots and chicken broth in a skillet over medium-high heat. Bring to a boil, and cook, stirring often, 6 to 8 minutes or until carrots are crisp-tender and broth is reduced to ¼ cup.
• Stir in butter and red pepper jelly, and cook, stirring constantly, 5 minutes or until mixture is thickened and glazes carrots. Yield: 6 servings.

*cook's secret...* To give this recipe a little bite, use hot pepper jelly rather than mild sweet bell pepper jelly.

**B**ok choy stalks and fresh ginger strips add a distinctive, personal touch to Iris Spira's recipe for turnip greens.

# Super-Charged Greens

| | |
|---|---|
| 2 (1-pound) packages prewashed fresh turnip greens | 2 garlic cloves, thinly sliced |
| 3 bok choy stalks, halved lengthwise and cut into ¾-inch pieces | 8 thinly sliced fresh ginger strips (about 1½ inches long) (optional) |
| 1 medium onion, diced | 2 to 3 tablespoons vegetable oil |
| 1 red bell pepper, chopped | 1½ teaspoons seasoned salt |
| | ½ teaspoon black pepper |

• Remove and discard stems and discolored spots from greens. Wash greens thoroughly; drain and tear greens into 1- to 2-inch pieces.

• Sauté bok choy, next 3 ingredients, and, if desired, ginger in hot oil in a Dutch oven over medium heat 3 minutes or until onion is tender. Add greens, salt, and black pepper; cook, stirring often, 5 minutes or until greens wilt. Cover and simmer 30 minutes. Yield: 6 to 8 servings.

*Iris Spira*
Plano, Texas

*cook's secret...* Bok choy is an elongated Chinese cabbage with long, white, celery-like stalks and larger deep green leaves. If you can't find it, substitute regular cabbage.

At the Charleston Grill, Chef Esau Graham takes almost two days to make the stock and cook these greens. He adapted this recipe for busy home cooks.

*chef recipe*

## Esau's Collard Greens

| | | | |
|---|---|---|---|
| 1 | pound hickory-smoked bacon, finely chopped | ½ | cup red wine vinegar |
| 3 | medium-size sweet onions, finely chopped | 1 | tablespoon Old Bay seasoning |
| 8 | garlic cloves, finely chopped | 4 | teaspoons sugar |
| 4 | (32-ounce) containers chicken broth | 2 | teaspoons celery seeds |
| 5 | pounds fresh collard greens, washed, trimmed, and cut into strips | 1 | teaspoon pepper |
| 1 | pound smoked ham, chopped, or 1 ham bone with meat | ½ | teaspoon salt |
| | | | Garnish: duck cracklings or pork rinds |

- Cook bacon in a 9-quart stockpot 10 to 12 minutes or until semicrisp. Add onions, and sauté 5 minutes; add garlic, and sauté 1 minute.
- Stir in broth, greens, and next 7 ingredients. Cook, uncovered, over medium heat 2 hours or until greens are tender. Garnish, if desired. Yield: 10 to 12 servings.

**NOTE:** *Esau occasionally adds beer or dark ale to the recipe near the end of cooking and simmers until the extra liquid is reduced.*

*Chef Esau Graham*
Charleston, South Carolina

*cook's secret...* To clean collard greens, break the bunch apart. Remove any tough stalks from the center of the leaves, and stack the leaves one on top of the other. Roll them up cigar-style. Cut the roll into 1-inch slices, yielding a chiffonade, or strips, of greens. Then wash the strips under cold water. "This way, sand can't hide in nooks and crannies of the greens," Esau explains. Now the grit-free greens are ready for cooking.

Jan Birnbaum, Baton Rouge–bred and New Orleans–trained, didn't set out to open Napa Valley's token Southern restaurant. However, when he turned his imagination free in his own kitchen at Catahoula Restaurant & Saloon in Calistoga, California (after successful stints at Paul Prudhomme's K-Paul's Louisiana Kitchen and Campton Place in San Francisco), the South danced its way onto the menu—never to stray.

"I must answer the question 'Are you really from New Orleans?' about fourteen times a night," says the former engineering major. "Once they hear that, everything's okay. Now I'm bringing Southern favorites like catfish and grits to Napa. And with the grits, all I do is add a little extra love (translation: cream and butter) and some redeye gravy."

Jan shares his recipe for Collard Green Risotto and Pot Liquor, a blending of his Southern experience and the cross-country cooking that followed. "Pot liquor is one of those things that 80% of the world doesn't know about, but it sounds like greatness and like something your mama made and was the best thing you ever had," he says.

*chef recipe*

## Collard Green Risotto and Pot Liquor

| | |
|---|---|
| 1 tablespoon olive oil | ¼ teaspoon salt |
| 3 bacon slices, cut into ½-inch pieces | ¼ teaspoon pepper |
| 1 large onion, chopped | 3 cups chicken broth |
| 2 garlic cloves, chopped | ¼ cup molasses |
| 1 pound fresh collard greens, cut into | 2 tablespoons butter or margarine |
|     2-inch pieces | Risotto |

• Heat oil in a Dutch oven; add bacon, and cook until crisp. Add onion, and sauté 5 to 7 minutes or until tender. Add garlic; sauté 1 minute.

• Stir in collard greens, salt, and pepper; sauté over medium heat 5 minutes or until greens wilt. Stir in chicken broth. Reduce heat to medium-low; cover and cook mixture 45 minutes or until greens are tender.

- Pour greens mixture through a wire-mesh strainer into a container, reserving greens and pot liquor. Whisk molasses and butter into pot liquor.
- Stir greens into Risotto.
- Place 1 cup Collard Green Risotto in each of 6 bowls. Ladle pot liquor mixture evenly on top. Serve immediately. Yield: 6 servings.

## Risotto:

| | | | |
|---|---|---|---|
| ½ | cup butter or margarine | 2 | bay leaves |
| 1 | medium onion, chopped | 5½ | cups hot chicken broth, divided |
| 2¼ | cups uncooked Arborio rice | ¼ | teaspoon salt |
| 2 | garlic cloves, chopped | ¼ | teaspoon pepper |
| 2 | cups dry white wine | ⅛ | teaspoon hot sauce |

- Melt butter in a Dutch oven over medium-high heat; add onion, and sauté 5 to 7 minutes or until tender.
- Stir in rice and garlic; sauté 2 minutes. Reduce heat to medium; add wine and bay leaves. Cook 5 minutes or until liquid is reduced by half.
- Add 1 cup chicken broth, salt, pepper, and hot sauce; cook, stirring often, until liquid is absorbed.
- Repeat procedure with remaining broth, ½ cup at a time. (Cooking time is about 45 minutes.) Remove and discard bay leaves. Yield: 6 servings.

*Chef Jan Birnbaum*
Calistoga, California

*cook's secret...* Young collards with small leaves are more tender and less bitter than mature collards.

*M*aque choux (or mock cabbage) is a dish Georgette Dugas grew up making and eating in South Louisiana. She added her touches, including andouille sausage. "It's not exactly the way my mother made it," she says, "but I thank her for the basics." Georgette's recipe was the Grand Prize Winner in the 8-Ingredient-or-Less Vegetable Sides category of the 2001 *Southern Living* Holiday Recipe Contest.

*contest winner*

# Cajun Corn Maque Choux

| | | | |
|---|---|---|---|
| 1 | small onion, chopped | ¼ | pound andouille sausage, cooked and diced |
| ¼ | cup chopped green bell pepper | | |
| 1 | to 2 tablespoons olive oil | ¼ | cup chopped green onion tops |
| 3 | cups frozen shoepeg corn, thawed | ¼ | teaspoon salt |
| 2 | plum tomatoes, diced | ¼ | teaspoon black pepper |

• Sauté onion and bell pepper in hot oil in a large skillet over medium heat 8 minutes or until tender. Add corn, tomato, and sausage; cook, stirring often, 15 minutes. Stir in green onions, salt, and black pepper; cook 5 minutes. Yield: 6 servings.

*Georgette Dugas*
Crowley, Louisiana

*cook's secret*... This dish is the Cajun version of succotash, which was gleaned from the native Americans who populated Louisiana. Andouille sausage spices up this version; other Cajuns have been known to add spicy crawfish tails.

Bill Dent and Phillip Nunnery man the kitchen while their wives, Ann Dent and Brenda Nunnery, see to their restaurant, Cuvée Beach, in Destin, Florida. This recipe is frequently on their grill.

# Grilled Corn with Jalapeño-Lime Butter

| | |
|---|---|
| ½ cup butter, softened | 6 ears fresh corn |
| 2 jalapeño peppers, seeded and minced | 1 tablespoon olive oil |
| 2 tablespoons grated lime rind | 2 teaspoons kosher salt |
| 1 teaspoon fresh lime juice | 1 teaspoon freshly ground pepper |

• Combine first 4 ingredients, and shape into a 6-inch log; wrap in wax paper, and chill 1 hour.

• Rub corn with olive oil; sprinkle evenly with salt and ground pepper.

• Grill corn, covered with grill lid, over high heat (400° to 500°), turning often, 15 to 20 minutes or until tender. Serve with flavored butter. Yield: 6 servings.

*Bill Dent and Phillip Nunnery*
Destin, Florida

*cook's secret...* Wear rubber gloves when seeding a jalapeño because the seeds and veins are hot and can burn your hands. Jalapeños can be purchased fresh or canned.

Thanks to hard work, an unbeatable personality, and the popularity of his nationally televised cooking shows, Curtis Aikens has become a celebrity. In his hometown of Conyers, Georgia, however, Curtis is just one of the family as he cooks up Southern favorites with his mom for a homecoming meal.

*chef recipe*

## Barbecue Eggplant

| | | | |
|---|---|---|---|
| 1 | large eggplant, peeled and cut into ¼-inch slices | ¼ | teaspoon pepper |
| 2¼ | teaspoons salt | 2 | tablespoons olive oil |
| | | ⅓ | cup barbecue sauce |

• Sprinkle eggplant slices with 2 teaspoons salt; let stand 1 hour. Rinse eggplant well, and pat dry. Sprinkle eggplant with remaining ¼ teaspoon salt and pepper; drizzle with oil. Let stand 15 minutes.

• Place eggplant on a rack in a broiling pan. Broil 5 inches from heat 10 minutes on each side, basting with barbecue sauce the last 3 minutes. Yield: 6 servings.

**NOTE:** *For testing purposes only, we used K.C. Masterpiece for barbecue sauce.*

*Chef Curtis Aikens*
Conyers, Georgia

*cook's secret*... Refrigerate fresh, uncut eggplants for up to 2 days.
••• Sprinkling eggplant slices with salt and letting them stand removes the bitterness they sometimes contain. Rinse and pat the slices dry before proceeding.

Harry Adams's quick-and-easy secret to crunchy fried okra is a crisp coating of saltine cracker crumbs.

*regional favorite*

# Crunchy Fried Okra

| | |
|---|---|
| 1½ cups buttermilk | 1 teaspoon salt |
| 1 large egg | 1 pound fresh okra, cut in half lengthwise |
| 2 cups saltine cracker crumbs (2 sleeves) | Peanut oil |
| 1½ cups all-purpose flour | |

- Stir together buttermilk and egg.
- Combine cracker crumbs, flour, and salt.
- Dip okra pieces in buttermilk mixture; dredge in cracker crumb mixture.
- Pour oil to a depth of 2 inches into a Dutch oven or cast-iron skillet; heat to 375°.

Fry okra, in 3 batches, 2 minutes or until golden, turning once. Drain on paper towels. Yield: 4 to 6 servings.

*Harry Adams*
Augusta, Georgia

*cook's secret*... Look for okra with firm green pods no more than 4 inches long. To test for tenderness, touch tops of each pod with the tip of a knife, which should easily pierce the skin. If not, discard the pod. Store okra no more than 3 days in the refrigerator.

Nutty Okra features two Southern all-stars—peanuts and okra—in one grand-slam recipe. Jina Breazeale uses a food processor to effortlessly chop the peanuts for her recipe.

## Nutty Okra

| | |
|---|---|
| 1 cup all-purpose baking mix | ½ teaspoon pepper |
| ½ cup finely chopped dry-roasted, salted peanuts | 1 pound fresh okra, cut into ¼-inch pieces |
| 1 teaspoon salt | Peanut oil |

• Stir together baking mix, chopped peanuts, salt, and pepper in a large bowl. Add okra, tossing to coat; gently press peanut mixture into okra.
• Pour oil to a depth of 2 inches into a Dutch oven or cast-iron skillet; heat to 375°. Fry okra, in batches, 4 minutes or until golden; drain on paper towels. Yield: 4 servings.

*Jina Breazeale*
Guyton, Georgia

*cook's secret*... Frozen okra can easily be substituted for fresh in this recipe. Use 1 (16-ounce) package frozen cut okra, thawed, in place of fresh.

Familiar ingredients and Indian recipes create a vibrant fusion of tastes and culture, as this recipe from Ranjan Patel illustrates.

## Simple Stir-Fried Okra

*We prepared this recipe with frozen whole okra. The results were consistently tender, fragrant, and fresh-tasting.*

| | | | |
|---|---|---|---|
| 1 | medium-size sweet onion, chopped | 2 | tablespoons vegetable oil |
| 1 | teaspoon mustard seeds* | 1 | (16-ounce) package frozen okra, |
| ½ | teaspoon ground cumin | | thawed, or 1 pound fresh okra |
| ¼ | teaspoon dried crushed red pepper | ¾ | teaspoon salt |

• Sauté first 4 ingredients in hot oil in a large skillet over medium-high heat 5 minutes or until onion is tender.

• Add okra; sauté 15 minutes or until okra is lightly browned. Stir in salt. Yield: 4 to 6 servings.

*½ teaspoon dry mustard may be substituted for 1 teaspoon mustard seeds.*

*Ranjan Patel*
*Roswell, Georgia*

*cook's secret*... Unless you want to use okra for its thickening effect, don't cut the pods; just remove the tip of the stem.

B everly and Tom Burdette enjoy summer dinners at their forties-era beach house on St. Simons Island, Georgia, with their neighbors, who are like family. This recipe is one of the Burdette's specialties.

## Cheesy Baked Vidalia Onions

| | | | | |
|---|---|---|---|---|
| 4 | small Vidalia onions | | 1 | tablespoon seasoning blend |
| 2 | tablespoons chicken broth | | ½ | teaspoon garlic salt |
| 2 | tablespoons dry white wine | | ½ | teaspoon lemon pepper |
| 2 | tablespoons Worcestershire sauce | | 4 | tablespoons butter or margarine |
| ½ | teaspoon hot sauce | | 4 | ounces Jarlsberg cheese, cut into pieces* |

• Peel onions; cut a thin slice from bottom of each one, forming a base for onions to stand on. Scoop out a shallow hole in top of each onion.

• Place each onion on a 12-inch square of heavy-duty aluminum foil; fold up sides of each foil square, forming a basin for liquid. Allow some overhang of foil, leaving tops of onions exposed.

• Stir together broth and next 3 ingredients; drizzle evenly over onions. Stir together seasoning blend, garlic salt, and lemon pepper. Sprinkle onions evenly with seasoning mixture. Top each with 1 tablespoon butter.

• Press foil edges together; gently twist to seal. Place on a baking sheet.

• Bake at 400° for 1 hour and 15 minutes. Gently unseal foil edges, leaving onions and liquid in foil cups. Top onions evenly with cheese.

• Broil 5½ inches from heat 1 to 2 minutes or until cheese melts. Serve immediately. Yield: 4 servings.

*Swiss cheese, Monterey Jack cheese with peppers, or fontina cheese may be substituted for Jarlsberg cheese.

**NOTE:** For testing purposes only, we used Morton Nature's Seasons Seasoning Blend for seasoning blend.

*Beverly and Tom Burdette*
*Atlanta, Georgia*

*cook's secret...* Dry onions can be stored in a cool, dry, well-ventilated place 2 to 3 months. Because they are so sweet, Vidalias have a shorter shelf life than other dry onions. To extend the life of Vidalias, store them so that they aren't touching each other; some cooks hang them in old panty hose with knots tied in between each onion.

*M*ichelle Weaver, who was raised in North Alabama, is a sous-chef at the Charleston Grill in the Charleston Place Hotel. She kicks up the flavor in her black-eyed peas by adding a jalapeño pepper.

*chef recipe*

## Michelle's Black-Eyed Peas

*Michelle makes her peas separately and serves them*
*on a bed of rice or simply on the side.*

| | |
|---|---|
| 1 (16-ounce) package dried black-eyed peas | 1 celery rib, chopped |
| 3 cups low-sodium chicken broth | 2 medium carrots, diced |
| 2 cups water | 1 small jalapeño pepper, seeded and diced |
| 2 (8-ounce) smoked ham hocks | 1 teaspoon salt |
| 1 large onion, chopped | 1 teaspoon black pepper |

• Place peas in a Dutch oven; add water to cover 2 inches above peas. Bring to a boil; boil 1 minute. Cover, remove from heat, and let stand 1 hour. Drain peas, and set aside.
• Bring broth, 2 cups water, and ham hocks to a boil in Dutch oven over medium-high heat. Cover, reduce heat, and cook 1 hour.
• Add peas, onion, and remaining ingredients; cook, covered, 45 minutes to 1 hour or until peas are tender, stirring occasionally. Yield: 6 to 8 servings.

*Chef Michelle Weaver*
Charleston, South Carolina

*cook's secret...* The jalapeño ranks near the middle of the hotness scale for peppers. If you want to push your limits, try the habanero pepper. It's considered one of the hottest chiles.

Hoppin' John, a mixture of rice and peas cooked in a flavorful broth, is traditionally served in the South on New Year's Day to bring good luck the rest of the year. Esau Graham, chef at the Charleston Grill in the Charleston Place Hotel, uses field peas, also called cow peas, in the Hoppin' John he prepares for his family. "I don't know who came up with using black-eyed peas," Esau says fervently. "Black-eyed peas are not the real McCoy."

*chef recipe*

## Esau's Hoppin' John

*When Esau makes this dish, he stirs in a dark, thick stock right after the rice goes in. Because it takes hours to make that stock, we used chicken broth (a lighter color) and still got great results.*

| | |
|---|---|
| 1 (16-ounce) package dried field peas or black-eyed peas | 1 cup medium-size sweet onion, finely chopped |
| 3 garlic cloves, peeled | 2 garlic cloves, minced |
| 3 bay leaves | 10 cups water, divided |
| 2 sprigs fresh rosemary | 2 cups uncooked short-grain rice |
| 2 to 3 sprigs fresh thyme | 3 teaspoons kosher salt, divided |
| 6 ounces fatback* | 1 teaspoon pepper |
| 2 (8-ounce) smoked ham hocks | Chicken broth |

• Place field peas in a Dutch oven; add water to cover 2 inches above peas. Bring to a boil, and boil 1 minute. Cover, remove from heat, and let stand 1 hour. Drain peas, and set aside.

• Place peeled garlic cloves and next 3 ingredients in the center of a large coffee filter; bring sides up, and tie with kitchen twine. Set garlic-and-herb bag aside.

• Sauté fatback in Dutch oven over medium-low heat 10 minutes or until crisp. Remove fatback, reserving drippings in Dutch oven, and discard fatback.

• Add ham hocks to Dutch oven, and cook 5 minutes or until skin becomes crispy and lean portion of each ham hock is tender. (Use the tines of a fork to test tenderness.)

• Add onion and minced garlic; sauté 2 minutes. Add 6 cups water. Bring to a boil, reduce heat to medium, and cook, uncovered, 1½ hours.

• Bring remaining 4 cups water to a boil in a saucepan; stir in rice and 2 teaspoons salt. Cover, reduce heat, and simmer 20 minutes or until liquid is absorbed. Set rice aside.

- Add field peas, garlic-and-herb bag, remaining 1 teaspoon salt, and pepper to ham hock mixture in Dutch oven. Bring to a boil over medium-high heat. Reduce heat, and simmer, stirring occasionally, 45 minutes. Remove and discard garlic-and-herb bag.
- Stir cooked rice into field pea mixture; simmer 5 minutes or until heated through, adding broth, if necessary. Yield: 6 to 8 servings.

*Salt pork may be substituted.*

**NOTE:** *Esau uses short-grain rice. He says you can substitute long-grain rice, prepared according to package directions, but it will have a drier texture.*

*Chef Esau Graham*
Charleston, South Carolina

*cook's secret*... Use a coffee filter, rather than cheesecloth, to bundle herbs and garlic for a simple bouquet garni. Gather the edges of the coffee filter, and tie them with a string. Drop the bundle into the cooking liquid to infuse it with flavor. The garlic-and-herb bag is easy to remove; just pull it out by the string.

### Quick Soak for Dried Beans

While the traditional method of cooking dried beans or field peas requires an 8-hour or overnight soak in water at room temperature, you can also get great results with Esau's shortcut that he uses in his Hoppin' John recipe (it takes just over 1 hour).

- Place the beans in a large pot; add water 2 inches above the beans, and bring to a boil.
- Cover, remove from heat, and let stand 1 hour.
- Drain the beans, and continue cooking according to the recipe or package directions.

Test Kitchens Director Lyda Jones suggests this beautiful finishing touch to Edwina Gadsby's mashed potato recipe: Pipe dollops of potatoes on top of the recipe using a large star-shaped tip.

*special occasion*

# Caramelized Onion-and-Gorgonzola Mashed Potatoes

| | |
|---|---|
| 3 pounds Yukon gold potatoes, peeled and quartered | 2 teaspoons chopped rosemary |
| 1¾ teaspoons salt, divided | ½ cup butter or margarine |
| 2 tablespoons butter or margarine | ¾ cup half-and-half |
| 1 tablespoon olive oil | ¾ cup crumbled Gorgonzola or blue cheese |
| 2 medium onions, diced | ¾ teaspoon pepper |
| 4 garlic cloves, minced | Garnish: fresh rosemary sprigs |

• Bring potato, 1 teaspoon salt, and water to cover to a boil in a Dutch oven; cook 20 to 25 minutes or until tender. Drain and keep warm.

• Melt 2 tablespoons butter with oil in a skillet over medium heat; add onion, and cook, stirring often, 12 to 17 minutes or until tender. Add garlic, and cook 3 minutes. Stir in rosemary; remove from heat.

• Mash potato with a potato masher; stir in ½ cup butter, half-and-half, and cheese until blended. Stir in onion mixture, remaining ¾ teaspoon salt, and pepper. Spoon enough mixture into a decorative, ovenproof dish or 13- x 9-inch baking dish to fill bottom; pipe or dollop remaining mixture over top.

• Broil 3 inches from heat 5 minutes or until top is lightly browned. Garnish, if desired. Yield: 6 servings.

*Edwina Gadsby*
*Great Falls, Montana*

*cook's secret...* If you don't have a decorating tip for piping the potatoes, spoon mixture into a zip-top freezer bag; cut off the tip from 1 corner of the bag, and squeeze dollops on top. Or just dollop the potatoes from a spoon.

Frank Stitt, owner of Highlands Bar and Grill, Bottega, and Chez Fonfon in Birmingham, Alabama, enjoys cooking simple meals for friends. His recipe for new potato gratin is one of those comfort foods you'll turn to time and again.

*chef recipe*

## New Potato Gratin with Lima Beans and Egg

|   |   |   |   |
|---|---|---|---|
| 6 | small new potatoes, thinly sliced | 3 | hard-cooked eggs, quartered |
| ½ | cup frozen large lima beans, thawed | ½ | teaspoon salt |
| 3 | stale French bread slices | ½ | teaspoon pepper |
| ¼ | cup (1 ounce) shredded Gruyère cheese | ½ | cup whipping cream |
| ¼ | cup shredded Parmesan cheese |   |   |

• Cook potato slices in boiling, salted water to cover 13 minutes. Add beans, and cook 2 more minutes. Remove from heat; drain well.

• Pulse bread slices in a blender or food processor 8 or 10 times or until bread is crumbly.

• Place potato slices and lima beans in a greased 10-inch deep-dish pieplate; sprinkle with half of Gruyère and half of Parmesan. Top evenly with egg; sprinkle with remaining cheeses, salt, and pepper. Pour cream around inside edge of pieplate; sprinkle evenly with breadcrumbs.

• Bake at 475° for 10 minutes or until lightly browned. Yield: 6 to 8 servings.

*Chef Frank Stitt*
Birmingham, Alabama

*cook's secret*... New potatoes are young red potatoes that haven't had time to become starchy and therefore have a waxy texture that's good for boiling. New potatoes should be used within 2 or 3 days of purchase. There's no need to peel them unless you want to; just scrub them well before slicing.

Mount Moriah Fellowship Baptist Church has no pastor, members, or regular services. The doors closed about forty years ago when the last members moved away. But this Alabama church comes to life once a year to warm the hearts of the people who once considered it home.

Homecoming brings about three hundred people back to Mount Moriah to share stories, celebrate family connections, and enjoy a home-cooked dinner on the grounds.

This once-a-year congregation established an endowment that funds scholarships, maintains the building and grounds, and contributes to the various needs of the community.

Here's a sample of the bounty that covers the tables for dinner on the grounds of the little church that lives on.

## Creamy Vegetable Casserole

1 (10¾-ounce) can cream of broccoli soup, undiluted

1 (10¾-ounce) can cream of chicken soup, undiluted

1 (8-ounce) container sour cream

1 (16-ounce) package frozen cauliflower, carrots, and snow pea pods, thawed

2 (10-ounce) packages frozen white and wild rice with French-style green beans, thawed

½ teaspoon pepper

1 cup (4 ounces) shredded Swiss cheese

¼ cup sliced almonds

• Combine first 7 ingredients; spoon into a lightly greased 13- x 9-inch baking dish. Bake at 350° for 20 minutes; sprinkle with sliced almonds, and bake 20 more minutes or until top is bubbly. Yield: 8 servings.

**NOTE:** *For testing purposes only, we used Birds Eye Farm Fresh Mixtures for frozen mixed vegetables; we used Green Giant for frozen rice and green beans.*

*Bill Jackson*
Alpine, Alabama

*cook's secret*... Two (10-ounce) cans of chunk white chicken, drained, may be added to make this recipe a main dish.

# Praline-Topped Sweet Potatoes

⅔ cup butter or margarine, softened and divided

2 (14½-ounce) cans mashed sweet potatoes

¾ cup sugar

2 large eggs, lightly beaten

1 teaspoon vanilla extract

1 cup firmly packed light brown sugar

½ cup all-purpose flour

1 cup chopped pecans

• Combine ⅓ cup butter and next 4 ingredients, stirring well; pour into a buttered 11- x 7-inch baking dish.

• Combine remaining ⅓ cup butter, brown sugar, flour, and chopped pecans, stirring until crumbly. Sprinkle over potato mixture.

• Bake at 350° for 30 minutes. Yield: 8 servings.

*Linda Owens*
Mount Vernon, Texas

*cook's secret...* Though casseroles are among the easiest recipes to double and freeze, they take up lots of space. To save space in the freezer, line the casserole with heavy-duty aluminum foil or plastic wrap, leaving a generous overhang on all 4 sides. Add the casserole mixture, and freeze until solid. Remove the foil liner, and wrap the food, using the overhangs, or seal it in a zip-top freezer bag. Label the food package, and return it to the freezer. When ready to serve, remove wrapping and return food to the dish to thaw and to reheat.

Chef Marvin Woods of Hollywood Prime in Hollywood, Florida, specializes in Caribbean cooking, but this recipe respects his Carolina roots. Rutabagas look similar to turnips, but they're actually in the cabbage family.

*chef recipe*

## Rutabaga-Carrot Mash

| | | | |
|---|---|---|---|
| 2 | medium rutabagas, peeled and chopped | ½ | cup butter or margarine |
| 4 | carrots, peeled and chopped (about 2 cups) | 1 | (10-ounce) can chicken broth |
| | | 1 | teaspoon salt |
| 1 | sweet onion, peeled and quartered | ½ | teaspoon pepper |

• Cook rutabagas in boiling water to cover in a Dutch oven over medium heat 20 minutes. Add carrots and onion; continue boiling 20 minutes or until vegetables are tender. Drain and place into food processor fitted with metal blade. Add ½ cup butter and remaining ingredients; process until smooth. Serve immediately. Yield: 8 to 10 servings.

*Chef Marvin Woods*
Hollywood, Florida

*cook's secret*... Choose rutabagas that are heavy for their size and firm to the touch. They typically have a waxy coating on the outside to help hold in moisture. It's harmless and comes off when you peel the rutabaga.

Associate Foods Editor Mary Allen Perry adds a twist to a regional classic recipe that delivers authentic Southern flavor in a flash. Her recipe for Succotash is ready to eat—start to finish—in 30 minutes.

*time–saver*

# Succotash

1 (10-ounce) package frozen petite
   lima beans
1 (16-ounce) package frozen shoepeg
   white corn
2 tablespoons butter or margarine
2 tablespoons all-purpose flour

1 teaspoon sugar
½ teaspoon salt
½ teaspoon seasoned pepper
1¼ cups milk
   Garnish: cooked and crumbled bacon

• Cook lima beans according to package directions; drain.

• Pulse corn in a food processor 8 to 10 times or until coarsely chopped.

• Melt butter in large saucepan over medium heat; add flour, stirring until smooth. Cook, stirring constantly, 1 minute; stir in sugar, salt, and seasoned pepper. Gradually add milk, stirring until smooth.

• Stir in corn, and cook, stirring often, 12 to 15 minutes or until corn is tender and mixture is thickened. Stir in drained lima beans. Garnish, if desired, and serve immediately. Yield: 6 to 8 servings.

*Mary Allen Perry*
Associate Foods Editor

*cook's secret...* Turn this recipe for Succotash into one for creamed corn by simply omitting the lima beans.

When Pat Mowry throws a party, you can bet that no matter how lovely the decor and food are inside her Pass Christian, Mississippi, home, guests will always end up outside. The attraction is understandable: The view of the Gulf of Mexico is exceptional, and the spacious porch is furnished with cushiony seating. This recipe is one of Pat's favorites to include in a warm-weather menu.

## Spinach-Stuffed Squash

*Stuff the squash the day before.*

| | | | |
|---|---|---|---|
| 4 | large yellow squash | 2 | (10-ounce) packages frozen chopped spinach, cooked and well drained |
| 1½ | teaspoons salt, divided | | |
| ¼ | cup butter or margarine, melted and divided | 1 | (8-ounce) container sour cream |
| ½ | cup grated Parmesan cheese, divided | 2 | teaspoons red wine vinegar |
| | | ¼ | cup fine, dry breadcrumbs |
| ¼ | teaspoon pepper | 1 | tablespoon cold butter or margarine, cut into pieces |
| 1 | small onion, chopped | | |

• Combine squash, ½ teaspoon salt, and water to cover in a Dutch oven. Bring to a boil, and cook 10 minutes or until tender. Cool.

• Cut squash in half lengthwise, and remove seeds. Drizzle cut sides of squash evenly with 2 tablespoons melted butter; sprinkle evenly with 2 tablespoons cheese, ½ teaspoon salt, and pepper.

• Pour remaining 2 tablespoons melted butter in a large skillet over medium-high heat, and add onion; sauté 4 minutes or until tender. Stir in cooked spinach, sour cream, red wine vinegar, and remaining ½ teaspoon salt. Spoon spinach mixture evenly into squash halves. Place squash in a 13- x 9-inch baking dish. Sprinkle with breadcrumbs and remaining 6 tablespoons cheese, and dot with cold butter.

• Bake at 350° for 15 minutes or until thoroughly heated. Yield: 6 to 8 servings.

*Pat Mowry*
Pass Christian, Mississippi

*cook's secret...* To save prep time before the meal, prepare and stuff the squash the day before. Cover and chill it overnight. Let it stand at room temperature 20 minutes before baking.

Ken Burnette is a volunteer fireman for the Chappell Hill Volunteer Fire Department in Texas. There, he has the opportunity to hone his cooking skills along with the other volunteers who enjoy cooking both for recreation and to raise money for the fire department.

## Squash Dressing

| | | | |
|---|---|---|---|
| 5 | medium-size yellow squash, sliced (1¾ pounds) | 1 | (8¾-ounce) can cream-style corn |
| 1 | medium onion, chopped | ½ | cup chunky picante sauce |
| 1 | large egg, lightly beaten | 2 | tablespoons butter, softened |
| 1 | (6-ounce) package Mexican-style cornbread mix | ¼ | teaspoon salt |
| | | ⅛ | teaspoon pepper |

• Boil sliced squash and chopped onion in water to cover in a Dutch oven 30 minutes or until squash is tender; drain and lightly mash squash with a fork. Add beaten egg and remaining ingredients; stir until mixture is blended.
• Spoon dressing into a lightly greased 1½-quart baking dish.
• Bake at 350° for 50 minutes or until set. Yield: 4 to 6 servings.

*Ken Burnette*
Chappell Hill, Texas

*cook's secret...* When selecting yellow squash, be sure to look at the stem; it can indicate the quality of the squash. If the stem is hard, dry, shriveled, or dark, the squash isn't fresh.

I'm embarrassed to admit this, but before I came to work at *Southern Living,* I had never tasted a fried green tomato. Call me deprived, even ignorant, but for some reason I had never found the gumption to sample this traditional Southern favorite. To my narrow way of thinking, tomatoes ought to be red and fresh, not green and fried.

That all changed one day at taste-testing. Test Kitchens Specialist Vanessa McNeil was frying a mess of tomatoes, pulling them out of the skillet in batches just as the Foods staff arrived to sample the day's recipes. "Y'all please eat these right away," she said. "I want you to taste them while they're still hot." They were golden and crisp, with a pleasingly rugged exterior. Unlike the evenly applied coatings found in prebreaded frozen products, this crust had character. Some of us started munching on the inviting medaillons before we made it to the table and even turned back for seconds before we sat down. The combination of fried cornmeal and flour encasing hot, tart, juicy tomatoes was exquisite.

I was hooked. I vowed to learn what it takes to make a great fried green tomato. So I obtained the recipe printed here and then asked Vanessa for some pointers. It seems she has frying down to an art.

"I use a cast-iron skillet at home but have found that any good heavy skillet works fine," she says. "Actually, an electric skillet is great. It keeps an even heat, so the tomatoes all cook nicely."

Vanessa also recommends using firm tomatoes and frying them in fairly shallow oil, about ¼- to ½-inch deep. "You don't want to cover the tomatoes with grease," she says. "And keep the temperature at 360° to 375°. If you like, you can add about 3 tablespoons bacon grease for more flavor." Salt the fried tomatoes as they drain, and serve them hot.

*Donna Florio*
Senior Writer

# Fried Green Tomatoes

*If your family has a large appetite, you may want to double this recipe.*

| | |
|---|---|
| 1 large egg, lightly beaten | ½ teaspoon pepper |
| ½ cup buttermilk | 3 medium-size green tomatoes, cut into |
| ½ cup all-purpose flour, divided | ⅓-inch slices |
| ½ cup cornmeal | Vegetable oil |
| 1 teaspoon salt | Salt to taste |

- Combine egg and buttermilk; set aside.
- Combine ¼ cup all-purpose flour, cornmeal, 1 teaspoon salt, and pepper in a shallow bowl or pan.
- Dredge tomato slices in remaining ¼ cup flour; dip in egg mixture, and dredge in cornmeal mixture.
- Pour oil to a depth of ¼ to ½ inch into a large cast-iron skillet; heat to 375°. Drop tomatoes, in batches, into hot oil, and cook 2 minutes on each side or until golden. Drain on paper towels or on a wire rack. Sprinkle hot tomatoes with salt to taste. Yield: 4 to 6 servings.

*cook's secret...* Fried green tomatoes will retain their heat for a little while after cooking, so let them cool just a touch before you eat them so that you won't burn your mouth! After that, all you need is a fork.

*Vanessa McNeil*
Test Kitchens Specialist

Two Southern cousins, tangy tomatoes and tomatillos, are at the heart of this zesty recipe. Because Southerners' romance with green tomatoes is an enduring one, our Test Kitchens staff paired them with tomatillos, their equally flavorful Southwestern relatives, for an innovative dish.

## Fried Green Tomato Stacks

*For bacon drippings, fry 3 or 4 bacon slices in a skillet until crisp.*
*Remove bacon from skillet, and reserve bacon for another use.*

| | |
|---|---|
| 3 tomatillos, husked | 1 cup buttermilk |
| 2 tablespoons bacon drippings | Peanut oil |
| 1 garlic clove, pressed | 1 (8-ounce) package cream cheese, |
| 1½ teaspoons salt, divided | softened |
| 1 teaspoon pepper, divided | 1 (4-ounce) package goat cheese, |
| ½ teaspoon paprika | softened |
| ¼ cup thinly sliced fresh basil | ⅓ cup milk |
| 1½ cups self-rising yellow cornmeal | 1 teaspoon sugar |
| 4 large green tomatoes, cut into | Garnish: fresh basil leaf |
| 18 (¼-inch) slices | |

• Bring tomatillos and water to cover to a boil in a small saucepan; reduce heat, and simmer 10 minutes. Drain tomatillos, and cool.

• Process tomatillos, bacon drippings, garlic, ½ teaspoon salt, ½ teaspoon pepper, and paprika in a food processor or blender until smooth; stir in basil. Cover and chill until ready to serve.

• Stir together cornmeal, ¾ teaspoon salt, and remaining ½ teaspoon pepper. Dip tomato slices in buttermilk; dredge in cornmeal mixture.

• Pour oil to a depth of ½ inch into a skillet; heat to 375°. Fry tomato slices, in batches, in hot oil 1 to 2 minutes on each side; drain on a wire rack over paper towels. Keep warm.

• Combine cream cheese, next 3 ingredients, and remaining ¼ teaspoon salt. Place 1 fried tomato slice on each of 6 salad plates; top each evenly with half of cream cheese mixture. Top each with 1 fried tomato slice and remaining cream cheese mixture. Top with remaining 6 fried tomato slices; drizzle with tomatillo dressing. Garnish, if desired. Yield: 6 servings.

*cook's secret...* Purchase tomatillos with dry, tight-fitting husks for longest shelf life. Keep them in a plastic bag in the refrigerator up to 2 weeks.

Editor in Chief John Floyd's mother's version of mac and cheese was a huge hit in our Test Kitchens and received our highest rating. We loved her easy method for making the thickener for the cheese sauce: The ingredients are simply shaken in a quart jar.

## Golden Macaroni and Cheese

1 (8-ounce) package elbow macaroni (about 2 cups uncooked macaroni)
2 cups milk
¼ cup all-purpose flour
1 teaspoon onion salt
2 (10-ounce) blocks sharp Cheddar cheese, shredded (about 4½ cups) and divided*

1 cup soft breadcrumbs (4 slices, crusts removed)
¼ cup butter or margarine, melted

• Cook macaroni according to package directions; drain well. Set aside.
• Place milk, flour, and onion salt in a quart jar; cover tightly, and shake vigorously 1 minute.
• Stir together flour mixture, 3½ cups cheese, and macaroni.
• Pour macaroni mixture into a lightly greased 13- x 9-inch baking dish or 2 (11-inch) oval baking dishes. Sprinkle evenly with breadcrumbs and remaining 1 cup cheese; drizzle evenly with melted butter.
• Bake at 350° for 45 minutes or until golden brown. Yield: 8 servings.
*20 ounces loaf pasteurized prepared cheese product, shredded or cut into small cubes, may be substituted. Omit breadcrumbs if using prepared cheese product.
**NOTE:** *For testing purposes only, we used Kraft Cracker Barrel Sharp Cheddar Cheese.*

*Louise Floyd*
Potters Station, Alabama

*cook's secret...* For a divine main dish, stir in chopped cooked ham before baking and then sprinkle the top with chopped cooked bacon before serving.

When out-of-town friends ask Jim Peyton where to find the best food in San Antonio, he simply replies, "my house." For over twenty years, Jim has devoted himself to the study of Mexican cooking. As a result, he enjoys nothing more than preparing authentic south-of-the-border food—in his trademark casual style—for family and friends. His recipe received high marks from our Test Kitchens staff.

## Orphan's Rice

*The name of this dish comes from the Spanish name,*
*which loosely translated means "feast for orphans."*

| | | | |
|---|---|---|---|
| 1 | tablespoon butter | 2 | tablespoons vegetable oil |
| ¾ | cup pecan halves | 1 | (10-ounce) package yellow rice |
| ½ | cup slivered almonds | 3 | cups low-sodium chicken broth |
| ⅓ | cup pine nuts | 2 | bacon slices, cooked and crumbled |
| ½ | small onion, minced | ¼ | cup finely chopped ham |
| 1 | garlic clove, minced | 1 | tablespoon minced fresh parsley |

• Melt butter in a skillet over medium heat. Add pecan halves, almonds, and pine nuts, and sauté, stirring often, 3 minutes or until almonds are light golden brown.
• Sauté onion and garlic in hot oil in a saucepan over medium-high heat 5 minutes or until tender. Add rice, and sauté, stirring constantly, 1 minute. Add broth, and cook rice 18 minutes. Remove from heat.
• Stir in nuts, bacon, ham, and parsley. Cover and let stand 10 minutes. Yield: 6 to 8 servings.

**NOTE:** *Jim likes to use 3 different nuts for this recipe; however, feel free to use all the same variety.*

*Jim Peyton*
San Antonio, Texas

*cook's secret*... Orphan's Rice may have roots in Moorish Spain and Mexico, but with ham, bacon, and pecans, this hearty recipe is sure to be a hit on any Southern table. The original recipe used white rice and saffron; we used packaged yellow rice to streamline. It contains salt, so no additional salt is needed in this recipe.

Living is easy on Lynn and George O'Connor's houseboat—and so are the menus. Their recipe for Greek Rice Pilaf is frequently in demand when entertaining guests on the boat or at home.

# Greek Rice Pilaf

| | | | |
|---|---|---|---|
| ¼ | cup butter or margarine | ¼ | cup chopped fresh parsley |
| 3 | cups uncooked quick rice | ½ | teaspoon salt |
| 1 | bunch celery, chopped | ½ | teaspoon pepper |
| 1 | medium onion, chopped | 4 | bay leaves |
| 2 | (10½-ounce) cans beef consommé | | Garnish: sliced green onions |

• Melt butter in a large skillet over medium-high heat; add rice, celery, and onion, and sauté 5 minutes or until vegetables are tender.
• Stir in consommé and next 4 ingredients. Pour mixture into a lightly greased 13- x 9-inch baking dish.
• Bake, covered, at 350° for 45 minutes or until rice is done. Remove bay leaves. Garnish, if desired. Yield: 6 to 8 servings.

**NOTE:** *For testing purposes only, we used Minute Rice.*

*Lynn and George O'Connor*
Little Rock, Arkansas

*cook's secret*... To round out the menu, there's enough time to grill chicken breasts and sliced zucchini while this rice bakes.

Making your first cornbread dressing is a rite of passage, something you just want to be able to do so your mama can feel good about your upbringing.

The ingredients you use say something about you. Cooks from coastal areas are likely to stir in seafood. Sausage is added in many locales. And you can argue over whether cornbread, biscuits, or store-bought stuffing mix works best as a base. I guess that's what I found intimidating. All those special twists made it seem impossible for a rookie like me to pull it off.

Eventually, however, I decided to find a classic recipe, put aside my fear of excessive sage, and give it a try. I picked one with a cornbread base. It was actually relatively easy to make. Most of the required ingredients were already in my cupboard, and none of them were expensive.

To boost the flavor of this dish, boil inexpensive cuts of turkey, such as wings, and substitute the drippings for part of the chicken broth. And if you, like my mother, are "anti-sage" (she prefers poultry seasoning), you can reduce or omit it. However, if you've based your judgment on the dried variety, try fresh sage before omitting. It gives the dressing a more delicate flavor.

What I love most about making dressing is that it makes my kitchen smell like my mother's. Whenever there was dressing on the table, I was surrounded by people I loved. I can't think of a better reason to make it.

*Valerie Fraser*
Creative Development Director

# Cornbread Dressing

1 cup butter or margarine, divided
3 cups white cornmeal
1 cup all-purpose flour
2 tablespoons sugar
2 teaspoons baking powder
1½ teaspoons salt
1 teaspoon baking soda
7 large eggs

3 cups buttermilk
3 cups soft breadcrumbs
2 medium onions, diced (2 cups)
1 large bunch celery, diced (3 cups)
½ cup finely chopped fresh sage*
6 (10½-ounce) cans condensed chicken broth, undiluted
1 tablespoon pepper

- Place ½ cup butter in a 13- x 9-inch pan; heat in oven at 425° for 4 minutes.
- Combine cornmeal and next 5 ingredients; whisk in 3 eggs and buttermilk.
- Pour hot butter into batter, stirring until blended. Pour batter into pan.
- Bake at 425° for 30 minutes or until golden brown. Cool.
- Crumble cornbread into a large bowl; stir in breadcrumbs, and set aside.
- Melt remaining ½ cup butter in a large skillet over medium heat; add onions and celery, and sauté until tender. Stir in sage, and sauté 1 more minute.
- Stir vegetables, remaining 4 eggs, chicken broth, and pepper into cornbread mixture; pour evenly into 1 lightly greased 13- x 9-inch baking dish and 1 lightly greased 8-inch square baking dish. Cover and chill 8 hours.
- Bake, uncovered, at 375° for 35 to 40 minutes or until golden brown. Yield: 16 to 18 servings.

*1 tablespoon dried rubbed sage may be substituted for fresh sage.*

**Andouille Sausage, Apple, and Pecan Dressing:** Brown ¾ pound diced andouille sausage in a skillet over medium heat; drain. Add sausage; 2 Granny Smith apples, chopped; and 2 cups chopped toasted pecans to dressing. Proceed as directed, baking 40 to 45 minutes or until done.

*cook's secret...* The recipe looks a little soupy when you mix it, but the end result is wonderfully moist. If you like yours a little drier, cut down on the chicken broth.

**P**auline Lanciotti adds pork sausage and chopped pecans to her cornbread dressing for a delicious twist on the traditional.

## Cornbread, Sausage, and Pecan Dressing

| | |
|---|---|
| 1 (16-ounce) package ground pork sausage | ¼ cup dry sherry or chicken broth |
| 1 large onion, chopped | ¼ cup milk |
| 2 large celery ribs, chopped | ½ teaspoon salt |
| Basic Cornbread, crumbled | ½ teaspoon dried thyme |
| 1½ cups coarsely chopped pecans | ¼ to ½ teaspoon pepper |
| 1½ cups chicken broth | ¼ teaspoon ground nutmeg |
| ¼ cup chopped fresh parsley | |

• Cook sausage in a large skillet over medium heat, stirring until it crumbles and is no longer pink. Remove sausage, reserving 1 tablespoon drippings in skillet. Drain sausage on paper towels.

• Sauté onion and celery in hot drippings over medium-high heat until tender. Remove vegetables with a slotted spoon.

• Combine sausage, vegetables, cornbread, and remaining ingredients in a large bowl, stirring gently until moistened. Spoon into a lightly greased 13- x 9-inch baking dish.

• Bake, covered, at 350° for 30 minutes or until thoroughly heated. Yield: 12 servings.

### Basic Cornbread:

| | |
|---|---|
| 2 cups buttermilk self-rising white cornmeal mix | ¼ cup butter or margarine, melted |
| | 1 large egg, lightly beaten |
| ½ cup all-purpose flour | 2 cups buttermilk |

• Heat a well-greased 9-inch oven-proof skillet at 450° for 5 minutes.

• Stir together all ingredients in a bowl. Pour batter into hot skillet.

• Bake at 450° for 20 minutes or until golden brown. Yield: 1 (9-inch) cornbread (about 5 cups crumbled).

*Pauline Lanciotti*
Morgantown, West Virginia

*cook's secret...* You know you've added enough broth to the dressing mixture when you can shake the dressing and it shimmies or jiggles. Adding any more broth will make it soupy.

Jill Conner Browne, author of *The Sweet Potato Queens' Book of Love,* is so well known for her love of deviled eggs that fans often bring them to her book signings. "It's the combination of taste and textures," she says, that inspires her devotion. "I like to put the whole thing in my mouth—I don't like to bite it. I guess that's just a personal thing, kind of like how you eat your Oreos."

The Jackson native prefers her deviled eggs basic, with only sweet pickles added to the yolk-mayo-mustard combo. Being the Sweet Potato Queen, boss of all the other Queens, Jill naturally possesses an egg plate. And not just any pressed-glass discount store version. "I own a Gail Pittman egg plate," she says regally. She offers these last words on the importance of deviled eggs in Southern society: "If they invented a special plate for it, that says it all right there."

*regional favorite*

## Basic Deviled Eggs

*If you're feeding more than three people (or Jill Conner Browne),
you'll likely need to double this recipe.*

| | |
|---|---|
| 6 **large eggs** | ⅛ **teaspoon salt** |
| 2 **tablespoons mayonnaise** | **Dash of pepper** |
| 1½ **tablespoons sweet pickle relish** | **Garnish: paprika** |
| 1 **teaspoon prepared mustard** | |

• Place eggs in a single layer in a saucepan; add water to depth of 3 inches. Bring to a boil; cover, remove from heat, and let stand 15 minutes.

• Drain immediately and fill the saucepan with cold water and ice. Tap each egg firmly on the counter until cracks form all over the shell. Peel under cold running water.

• Slice eggs in half lengthwise, and carefully remove yolks. Mash yolks with mayonnaise. Add relish, mustard, salt, and pepper; stir well. Spoon yolk mixture into egg whites. Garnish, if desired. Yield: 6 servings.

Although Edie Bullard's Mexican Deviled Eggs are not too spicy, you can prepare a milder version by reducing the amount of minced jalapeños.

## Mexican Deviled Eggs

| | |
|---|---|
| 6 hard-cooked eggs | ¼ teaspoon ground cumin |
| ¼ cup mayonnaise | ⅛ teaspoon salt |
| 2 tablespoons pickled jalapeño slices, minced | Garnishes: chile powder and fresh parsley sprigs |
| 1 tablespoon prepared mustard | |

• Cut eggs in half lengthwise, and carefully remove yolks.
• Mash egg yolks in a small bowl. Stir in mayonnaise and next 4 ingredients, and blend well.
• Spoon or pipe yolk mixture evenly into egg-white halves. Garnish, if desired. Yield: 6 servings.

*Edie Bullard*
Detroit, Michigan

*cook's secret...* The secret to preventing a greenish ring around the yolk of hard-cooked eggs is to avoid overcooking them. The best way to cook them is to place the eggs in a single layer in a saucepan and add enough water to cover 1 inch above the eggs. Bring them to a boil; immediately cover, and remove from the heat. Let the eggs sit, covered, for 15 minutes; then pour off the water.

Alana Chandler uses either fresh parsley sprigs and sliced pimientos or chopped pecans to top her Pecan-Stuffed Deviled Eggs for a festive presentation. You might be tempted to use chopped onion, but we found that grating the onion gives the filling a better texture.

# Pecan-Stuffed Deviled Eggs

| | | | |
|---|---|---|---|
| 6 | hard-cooked eggs | ½ | teaspoon chopped fresh parsley |
| ¼ | cup mayonnaise | ½ | teaspoon dry mustard |
| 1 | teaspoon grated onion | ⅛ | teaspoon salt |
| 1 | teaspoon white vinegar | ⅓ | cup coarsely chopped pecans |

• Cut eggs in half lengthwise, and carefully remove yolks.
• Mash yolks in a small bowl. Stir in mayonnaise and next 5 ingredients, and blend well. Stir in pecans.
• Spoon or pipe yolk mixture evenly into egg-white halves. Yield: 6 servings.

*Alana Chandler*
*Richardson, Texas*

*cook's secret*... My favorite trick for transporting deviled eggs is to store the filling and eggs in separate zip-top freezer bags. When you're ready to serve, simply snip one of the bottom corners of the bag containing the filling and squeeze it into the egg halves.

••• The easiest way to peel eggs is to remove cooked eggs from heat and pour off the water. Add about 1 inch of cold water and several ice cubes to the saucepan. (It's okay if the inside of the eggs are still warm.) Cover the pot, and shake vigorously so that the eggs crack all over. Peel under cold running water, starting at the large end—the air pocket there will give you something to grip.

*Kate Nicholson*
*Associate Foods Editor*

# menus

## "New" Southern Supper
Serves 6
Black-Eyed Pea Cakes (page 47)
Classic Mint Julep (page 65)
Chicken with White Barbecue Sauce (page 244)
New Potato Gratin with Lima Beans and Egg (page 389)
Warm Goat Cheese Salad (page 293)

## Southern Sunday Dinner
Serves 4 to 6
Mama's Fried Chicken (page 241)
Esau's Collard Greens (page 375)
Michelle's Black-Eyed Peas (page 385)
Hot-Water Cornbread (page 78)
Mystery Pecan Pie (page 143)

## Supper Club Soiree
Serves 6 to 8
Molasses Pork Tenderloin with Red Wine Sauce (page 223)
Broccoli with Pimiento Cheese Sauce (page 370)
Rutabaga-Carrot Mash (page 392)
Homemade Butter Rolls (page 90)
Chocolate Pound Cake (page 123)

## Creole Creation
Serves 6
Down-Home Chicken and Onions (page 248)
Spinach-Stuffed Squash (page 394)
Cajun Corn Maque Choux (page 378)
Praline-Pumpkin Torte (page 134)

## Southwestern Thanksgiving
Serves 6 to 8
Garden Sangría (page 67)
Basil-Cheese Torta (page 18)
Smoky Barbecue Brisket (page 202)
Orphan's Rice (page 400)
Pepper Jelly-Glazed Carrots (page 373)
Texas toast
Luscious Lemon Pie (page 153)

## Down-Home Gathering
Serves 6
Sweet 'n' Saucy Meat Loaf (page 214)
Caramelized Onion-and-Gorgonzola Mashed Potatoes (page 388)
Tangy Green Beans with Pimiento (page 369)
Graham Banana Pudding (page 170)

## Make-Ahead Brunch
Serves 8
Bloody Marys (page 60)
Cheesy Bacon-and-Ham Casserole (page 238)
Cut fresh fruit
Quick Whipping Cream Biscuits (page 71)
Peach-Rosemary Jam (page 359)

## Casual Company Dinner
Serves 6
Tapenade (page 12)
Baked Fish with Parmesan-Sour Cream Sauce (page 265)
Fresh Asparagus Salad (page 294)
Sour Cream Dinner Rolls (page 91)
Watermelon Sorbet (page 172)

## Comfort Food Lunch
Serves 6
Golden Macaroni and Cheese (page 399)
Michelle's Black-Eyed Peas (page 385)
Crunchy Fried Okra (page 381)
Sliced tomatoes
Old Southern Biscuits (page 72)

## New Year's Feast
Serves 8
Texas Caviar (page 14)
Champagne Punch (page 59)
Fig-Balsamic Roasted Pork Loin (page 220)
Super-Charged Greens (page 374)
Sweet Potato Biscuits (page 74)

# metric equivalents

Recipes in this cookbook use the standard United States method for measuring liquid and dry or solid ingredients (teaspoons, tablespoons, and cups). The following charts are provided to help cooks outside the U.S. successfully use these recipes. All equivalents are approximate.

## metric equivalents for different types of ingredients

A standard cup measure of a dry or solid ingredient will vary in weight depending on the type of ingredient. A standard cup of liquid is the same volume for any type of liquid. Use the following chart when converting standard cup measures to grams (weight) or milliliters (volume).

| standard cup | fine powder (ex. flour) | grain (ex. rice) | granular (ex. sugar) | liquid solids (ex. butter) | liquid (ex. milk) |
|---|---|---|---|---|---|
| 1 | 140 g | 150 g | 190 g | 200 g | 240 ml |
| ¾ | 105 g | 113 g | 143 g | 150 g | 180 ml |
| ⅔ | 93 g | 100 g | 125 g | 133 g | 160 ml |
| ½ | 70 g | 75 g | 95 g | 100 g | 120 ml |
| ⅓ | 47 g | 50 g | 63 g | 67 g | 80 ml |
| ¼ | 35 g | 38 g | 48 g | 50 g | 60 ml |
| ⅛ | 18 g | 19 g | 24 g | 25 g | 30 ml |

## useful equivalents for dry ingredients by weight

(To convert ounces to grams, multiply the number of ounces by 30.)

| | | | | |
|---|---|---|---|---|
| 1 oz | = | 1/16 lb | = | 30 g |
| 4 oz | = | ¼ lb | = | 120 g |
| 8 oz | = | ½ lb | = | 240 g |
| 12 oz | = | ¾ lb | = | 360 g |
| 16 oz | = | 1 lb | = | 480 g |

## useful equivalents for length

(To convert inches to centimeters, multiply the number of inches by 2.5.)

| | | | | | | | |
|---|---|---|---|---|---|---|---|
| 1 in | | | | = | 2.5 cm | | |
| 6 in | = | ½ ft | | = | 15 cm | | |
| 12 in | = | 1 ft | | = | 30 cm | | |
| 36 in | = | 3 ft | = | 1 yd | = | 90 cm | |
| 40 in | | | | = | 100 cm | = | 1 m |

## useful equivalents for cooking/oven temperatures

| | fahrenheit | celsius | gas mark |
|---|---|---|---|
| freeze water | 32° F | 0° C | |
| room temperature | 68° F | 20° C | |
| boil water | 212° F | 100° C | |
| bake | 325° F | 160° C | 3 |
| | 350° F | 180° C | 4 |
| | 375° F | 190° C | 5 |
| | 400° F | 200° C | 6 |
| | 425° F | 220° C | 7 |
| | 450° F | 230° C | 8 |
| broil | | | grill |

## useful equivalents for liquid ingredients by volume

| | | | | | | | |
|---|---|---|---|---|---|---|---|
| ¼ tsp | | | | | = | | 1ml |
| ½ tsp | | | | | = | | 2 ml |
| 1 tsp | | | | | = | | 5 ml |
| 3 tsp | = | 1 tbls | | = | ½ fl oz | = | 15 ml |
| | | 2 tbls | = | ⅛ cup | = | 1 fl oz = | 30 ml |
| | | 4 tbls | = | ¼ cup | = | 2 fl oz = | 60 ml |
| | | 5⅓ tbls | = | ⅓ cup | = | 3 fl oz = | 80 ml |
| | | 8 tbls | = | ½ cup | = | 4 fl oz = | 120 ml |
| | | 10⅔ tbls | = | ⅔ cup | = | 5 fl oz = | 160 ml |
| | | 12 tbls | = | ¾ cup | = | 6 fl oz = | 180 ml |
| | | 16 tbls | = | 1 cup | = | 8 fl oz = | 240 ml |
| 1 pt | = | 2 cups | = | 16 fl oz | = | 480 ml |
| 1 qt | = | 4 cups | = | 32 fl oz | = | 960 ml |
| | | | | 33 fl oz | = | 1000 ml |
| | | | | | = | 1 liter |

# contributors

# index